Institutions and Economic Change

Institutions and Economic Change
ERRATA SLIP

Please replace Table 9.1 on page 203 with the following:

Table 9.1   *Banker–entrepreneur interaction as a Stag Hunt game*

		Entrepreneur	
		1 (Reliable)	2 (Unreliable)
Banker	1 (Informed)	u, v	0, 1
	2 (Arm's length)	1, 0	1, 1

Please replace Table 9.3 on page 208 with the following:

Table 9.3   *Banker–entrepreneur interaction as a symmetric fully privileged Stag Hunt game*

		Entrepreneur	
		1 (Reliable)	2 (Unreliable)
Banker	1 (Informed)	2, 2	0, 1
	2 (Arm's length)	1, 0	-1, -1

Please label the Y axis q on Figures 9.1, 9.2 and 9.3 on pages 205, 206 and 209 respectively.

Thomas Marmefelt is Lecturer and Doctoral Candidate at Jönköping International Business School, Sweden.

Institutions and Economic Change

New Perspectives on Markets, Firms and Technology

Edited by

Klaus Nielsen

Professor of Social Sciences, Roskilde University, Denmark

and

Björn Johnson

Associate Professor of Economics, Aalborg University, Denmark

EUROPEAN ASSOCIATION FOR EVOLUTIONARY POLITICAL ECONOMY

Edward Elgar

Cheltenham, UK • Northampton, MA, USA

Published by
Edward Elgar Publishing Limited
8 Lansdown Place
Cheltenham
Glos GL50 2HU
UK

Edward Elgar Publishing, Inc.
6 Market Street
Northampton
Massachusetts 01060
USA

A catalogue record for this book is available from the British Library

Library of Congress Cataloguing in Publication Data
Institutions and economic change: new perspectives on markets, firms
    and technology/edited by Bjorn Johnson, Klaus Nielsen.
        "Originates from the Sixth Annual Conference of EAEPE ... held in
    Copenhagen in October 1994"—Preface.
        Includes bibliographical references and index.
        1. Institutional economics—Congresses. 2. Evolutionary
    economics—Congresses. 3. Technological innovations—Economic
    aspects—Congresses. I. Johnson, Bjorn, 1943–   . II. Nielsen,
    Klaus, 1948–   . III. European Association of Evolutionary
    Political Economy. IV. Conference of EAEPE (6th: 1994:
    Copenhagen, Denmark)
    HB99.5.I585   1998
    338.9—dc21

                                                        97–30629
                                                            CIP

Printed and bound in Great Britain by Bookcraft (Bath) Ltd.

ISBN 1 85898 322 3

Contents

List of figures   vii
List of tables   viii
Notes on contributors   ix
Preface   xi

Introduction: Institutions and economic change   xiii
Björn Johnson and Klaus Nielsen

PART I   PROSPECTS FOR EVOLUTIONARY AND
          INSTITUTIONAL THEORY

1 The institutional embeddedness of economic change: an appraisal
   of the 'evolutionary' and 'regulationist' research programmes   3
   Benjamin Coriat and Giovanni Dosi
2 The learning economy: challenges to economic theory and policy   33
   Bengt-Åke Lundvall

PART II   INNOVATION AND TECHNOLOGICAL DEVELOPMENT

3 The evolutionary approach to technological change: a framework
   for microeconomic analysis   57
   Luis E. Arjona Béjar
4 The glocalization of technology   84
   Marc Humbert
5 Technological performance and variety: the case of the German
   electronics industry   109
   Uwe Cantner, Horst Hanusch and Georg Westermann
6 High R&D intensity without high tech products: a Swedish
   paradox?   131
   Charles Edquist and Maureen McKelvey

PART III THE THEORY OF THE FIRM AND RELATIONS
          BETWEEN FIRMS

7 Black boxes, grey boxes: the scope of contracts in the theory
   of the firm   153
   Margherita Turvani

8   Governance of transactions: a strategic process model   172
    Bart Nooteboom
9   Schumpeterian banker–entrepreneur interaction and the
    spontaneous evolution of bank–industry networks: why
    institutional endowments matter   200
    Thomas Marmefelt

PART IV   MARKETS, ECONOMIC SYSTEMS AND THE ROLE
           OF MORAL NORMS

10 Varieties of capitalism and varieties of economic theory   215
    Geoffrey M. Hodgson
11 Financial markets and economic development: myth and
    institutional reality   243
    Jan A. Kregel
12 Moral standards and transaction costs: long-term effects   258
    Michael Yaffey

Index   291

Figures

3.1	Output of IEP equipment in Japan and in the US	67
3.2	Share of Japanese manufacturers in total placements of photocopiers in Western Europe	71
3.3	Polyethylene trade balance/production ratios	74
4.1	A segment of a cross-border network in the IT industry	100
5.1	Average efficiency series electronics sector	118
6.1	Share of export and of production of manufacturing products in R&D-intensive industries (Sweden), 1970–90	143
6.2	Share of ISIC 3522 (Drugs and Medicine) of manufacturing production in five countries, 1970–90	144
6.3	Share of ISIC 3825 (Office Machinery and Computers) of manufacturing production in five countries, 1970–90	144
6.4	Share of ISIC 383 (Electrical Machinery and Components) of manufacturing production in five countries, 1970–90	145
6.5	Share of ISIC 3845 (Aerospace) of manufacturing production in five countries, 1970–90	145
6.6	Share of ISIC 385 (Technological Goods) of manufacturing production in five countries, 1970–90	146
8.1	Inclination towards opportunism	176
8.2	Interaction between X and Y	179
8.3	Situation A: $VYX > 0$; $VXY > 0$	185
8.4	Situation B: $VYX < 0$; $VXY < 0$; $CAPX > 0$	186
8.5	Situation C: $VYX < 0$; $CAPX > 0$; $VXY > 0$	187
8.6	Value of Y to X	192
8.7	Switching costs	194
8.8	Room for opportunism	195
8.9	Relation management	196
9.1	Institutional dynamics of banker–entrepreneur interaction when $u = v = 2$	205
9.2	Institutional dynamics of banker–entrepreneur interaction when $u = v = 4$	206
9.3	Institutional dynamics of banker–entrepreneur interaction when the bank convention is fully privileged	209

Tables

1.1 Weak and strong varieties of institutionalism 8
1.2 Levels of analysis 22
3.1 Share of major exporters of photo- and thermo-copying apparatus in total market economy exports 68
3.2 Main photoconductor and development systems introduced in the early 1970s 69
3.3 Trade balances in polyethylene, 1988 73
3.4 Average logarithmic rates of growth of polyethylene production, 1965–89 74
3.5 New polyethylene plants in developing countries that started to operate from 1979 onwards 75
4.1 Globalization of technology 87
4.2 Four definitions of a national system of innovation 92
5.1 Number of firms in each technology field 120
5.2 Average ι for each technology 120
5.3 Movements between technology fields during the period 1985–91 121
5.4 Average ι change of moving firms 122
5.5 Regression results for the electronics sector 124
5.6 Efficiency of patenting and non-patenting firms in 1991 126
5.7 Patenting of technology fields in electronics 126
8.1 Sources of cooperation 174
8.2 Instruments 183
8.3 Typology of strategy 184
9.1 Banker–entrepreneur interaction as a Stag Hunt game 203
9.2 Results of the local stability analysis 204
9.3 Banker–entrepreneur interaction as a symmetric fully privileged Stag Hunt game 208
9.4 Results of the local stability analysis 208
10.1 Varieties of analysis and varieties of capitalism 237
12.1 Kohlberg's six stages of moral development 285

Contributors

Luis E. Arjona Béjar is Lecturer and Researcher at CIDE, Mexico, and at the Escuela de Negocios Caixavigo, Vigo, Spain.

Uwe Cantner is Associate Professor at the Department of Economics of the University of Augsburg, Germany.

Benjamin Coriat is Professor at the University of Paris XIII, Villetaneuse, France.

Giovanni Dosi is Professor at the Department of Economics, University of Rome 'La Sapienza', Italy, and Research Director at the International Institute for Applied Systems Analysis, Laxenburg, Austria.

Charles Edquist is Professor at the Department of Technology and Social Change of the University of Linköping, Sweden.

Horst Hanusch is Professor at the Department of Economics of the University of Augsburg, Germany.

Geoffrey M. Hodgson is Lecturer at the Judge Institute of Management Studies, University of Cambridge, United Kingdom.

Marc Humbert is Professor at University of Rennes 1, CERETIM, Rennes, France.

Jan. A. Kregel is Professor at the University of Bologna, Italy.

Björn Johnson is Associate Professor at the Department of Business Studies of Aalborg University, Denmark.

Bengt-Åke Lundvall is Professor at the Department of Business Studies of Aalborg University, Denmark.

Thomas Marmefelt is Lecturer and Doctoral Candidate at the International Business School, Jönköping, Sweden.

Maureen McKelvey is Assistant Professor at the Department of Technology and Social Change of the University of Linköping, Sweden.

Klaus Nielsen is Professor at the Department of Social Sciences of Roskilde University, Denmark.

Bart Nooteboom is Professor at the Faculty of Management and Organization of the University of Groningen, The Netherlands.

Margherita Turvani is Researcher at the University of Venice, Italy.

Georg Westermann is Professor at Fachhochschule Harz, Wernigerode, Germany.

Michael Yaffey is Lecturer at the Development and Project Planning Centre of the University of Bradford, United Kingdom.

Preface

This book studies the relationship between institutions and economic change. The concept of institution has become more and more important in the analysis of both societal cohesion and economic change. Institutions are most often associated with social stability and cohesion if not inertia and blockage of change. However, institutions also enable and shape economic change; they reduce uncertainty and form patterns of interaction as well as the way we look upon and interpret society. The present volume presents theories of the relationship between institutions and economic change as well as their application in fields such as innovation, the firm, markets and economic systems.

The book originates from the Sixth Annual Conference of EAEPE (European Association for Evolutionary Political Economy) held in Copenhagen in October 1994. EAEPE is a rapidly growing association with well over 600 members in late 1996. It is a major goal of EAEPE to develop institutional and evolutionary theory so that it can meet the challenges of the modern world. The theme of the conference in Copenhagen was 'Challenges to evolutionary and institutional theory: growth, uncertainty and change'. This book comprises a selection of contributions which provide important and innovative responses to these challenges. It includes sections on the economics of technological change, the theory of the firm and relations between firms, and the analysis of markets and economic systems. In addition, the book outlines prospects for future theoretical development.

As editors we are indebted to several institutions which have sponsored the preparation of this book. The Danish Social Science Research Council and the National Bank of Denmark sponsored the EAEPE conference in Copenhagen; and the Department of Social Sciences at the University of Roskilde, Denmark, has also contributed in cash and in kind. We also want to express our gratitude to Andrew Thejls-Crabtree and Jennifer Thorlaksen from the University of Roskilde for their assistence in the editorial process.

Introduction: institutions and economic change

Björn Johnson and Klaus Nielsen

NOVELTY, UNCERTAINTY AND INTERACTION

The rediscovery in economic theory of the importance of institutions is accompanied by a shift in perspective and a new focus: from the allocation of given and scarce resources to the creation, distribution and use of new resources, especially knowledge. There are good reasons for this. The creation of new resources and the emergence of novelty in the economy, for example in the form of organizational and technical innovations, is deeply affected by uncertainty and is formed by many kinds of interaction, cooperation and confrontation between individuals, groups and classes. In the practical affairs of everyday life institutions reduce uncertainty; they form the patterns of interaction, and the ways in which we view and interpret society. They make economic life including its change understandable and manageable. On the theoretical level the concept of institution is of growing importance for the analysis of both cohesion and change in the economy.

It is evident that institutions shape economic change, and, therefore, contemporary institutional economics focuses on processes of economic change. In order to understand phenomena like economic growth and development (or the lack of them), and structural, technical and organizational change, it is necessary to specify and analyse the institutional set-up of the economy. This has been reinforced by an increasing awareness of the enormous complexity of the modern economy and the large differences between countries as far as institutional set-up is concerned. Furthermore, it has become clear that institutions of different kinds hang together in more or less coherent systems characterized by the roles and the interactions of the various institutions.

Generally, institutional theory is still relatively underdeveloped. The concept of institution is used in many different ways. It lacks the clarity one might expect from a core concept in social theory. Such crucial elements as a comprehensive taxonomy of institutions and institutional change are missing, which means that descriptions of and comparisons between institutional set-ups lack precision and, are at best, tentative. However, in spite of this 'performance gap' in institutional theory, it is clear that if you unpack the 'given' tastes, resources and technologies from their black boxes in mainstream economics in order to analyse long-run economic change, institutions have to accompany them.

STABILITY, CHANGE AND LEARNING

In a way it is paradoxical that a growing interest in institutions should lead to, or at least go hand in hand with, a focus on economic change. After all, institutions are often understood as phenomena which restrict and pattern behaviour and are responsible for stability rather than change in the economy. They are, for example, sometimes referred to as 'rigidities' and 'ceremonies' or 'innovation brakes', which through their immanent inertia retard the dynamics of technical change. Stubborn institutions are often supposed to create mismatch problems, which prevent the realization of the productive potentials of new technologies. Obviously, terms like 'institutional set-up' and 'institutional framework' are more easily associated with the stable and lasting aspects of society than with its transformation and change. Institutional economists used to ask how institutions kept society together in spite of the conflicting interests between its members. Now they ask how institutions and institutional changes create the stability and the resources necessary for change and how they make ubiquitous and continuous innovation possible.

The connection between institutions and change becomes rather obvious once the importance of knowledge and learning for the structure and change of the modern economy has been realized. This is reflected in the increasing importance of concepts like the 'knowledge based economy' and the 'learning economy'. From such a perspective neoclassical economic theory appears both myopic and misdirected. Profit-maximizing behaviour is not instrumental in either production of knowledge or its optimal allocation. A totally different perspective is needed. Knowledge is created, distributed, utilized and forgotten through what might broadly be called learning processes. These cannot be understood in terms of equilibrium theory; by definition, in a position of general equilibrium nothing occurs which can make the agents change their decisions, no new policies are formed and all learning processes have stopped. Instead, learning must be understood as an on-going, uncertain and open-ended process, which depends on interactions between a variety of people and organizations with different knowledge endowments.

Almost all learning processes are social and interactive rather than individual, and new knowledge is created through an institutionally embedded process in which the institutions themselves change as the result of the interactions leading to new knowledge. The institutional context forms the interactions between people within as well as between organizations, and this feeds the processes of technical, organizational and institutional learning. Institutionally shaped interactive learning inevitably brings new resources into the economy as well as destroying parts of its existing resources.

Institutions are often associated with some basic functions in relation to the economy (Edquist and Johnson, 1997). They provide information, reduce uncertainty, manage conflicts and cooperation, and create incentives and trust. These functions not only give stability and structure to the economy, they are also crucially important for innovation. All innovative activities are riddled with uncertainty and in the modern economy there are many institutions to assist in coping with the technical and the financial uncertainties of innovation. There are technical universities, science parks and technological service systems. There are patent laws and other intellectual property rights. There are selective and durable relationships between banks and firms and established ways to finance entrepreneurial activities and uncertain investments in new products and processes. In a similar way innovative activities more often than not lead to changes in income distribution and in the patterns of power and responsibility thereby provoking different kinds of conflicts. Institutions in the forms of negotiation procedures, reeducation and training arrangements, social security rights, etc., are needed to distribute the costs of change and to handle the conflicts which accompany the processes of innovation. Furthermore, institutional support and special incentives may be needed to create shared values and mutual trust between people and organizations to induce them to engage in uncertain and often conflict-ridden innovative activities. Intellectual property rights and tax allowances, as well as non-monetary incentives and collective incentives like publication possibilities, intellectual prestige, status norms, access to communication between departments within firms and between different firms in networks, and so forth, may be seen in this light.

For these reasons, then, an institutional perspective is one of innovation and change and the institutional set-up of an economy becomes crucial for growth and development. The concept of institution is a core concept for the understanding of both societal cohesion and change. These phenomena are deeply interrelated.

KNOWLEDGE AND INSTITUTIONS

Traditionally, institutional economics has not focused on learning and knowledge creation. Institutional economists have, for example, not had very much to say about the character and mechanisms of technical innovation. Innovation theorists, on the other hand, have often carefully underlined the importance of institutions, but at the same time they have tended to use a narrow and mechanistic concept of institutions, which has effectively prevented a deeper understanding of the innovation process. Lately, however, there have been signs of a cross-fertilization between institutional theories and theories about innovation. Innovation theory now takes institutions more seriously and tends to use the concept in a broader and more sophisticated way than before. Furthermore, innovation is recognized as a deeply rooted and widely spread phenomenon dependent on a multitude of interconnections between institutions, on one hand, and the creation and distribution of knowledge, on the other.

There are at least two ways, one narrow and one broad, of analysing knowledge creation in the economy. According to the narrow perspective knowledge is produced in and distributed from a specific sector of the economy (schools, universities, research and development organizations, technological service systems, etc.) and is supported by specific institutions (intellectual property rights, disclosure norms, etc.). The broader view takes these factors into account but also sees knowledge creation as being connected with, and a by-product of, ordinary economic activities such as procurement, production and marketing in all sectors of the economy. Furthermore, from this point of view there are important interactions between the production, the distribution and the utilization of new knowledge. Terms like learning by doing, learning by selling, learning by using, and learning by interacting are associated with the combined phenomena of creation, distribution and use of knowledge in this broader sense.

In a similar way there seems to be at least two ways, a narrow and a broad one, of understanding institutions. On the one hand, the term refers to concrete phenomena (usually organizations) such as banks, universities, patent offices, etc., which have some permanence and are easy to recognize. On the other hand, the concept of institution refers more broadly to social phenomena which restrict and pattern interactions in society like laws, regulations, rules, norms, established practices and routines. In this broader perspective institutions are not only humanly designed constraints on rational decision-making, but they also play the basic role of shaping people's cognitions, views, visions and actions.

What we have seen lately, as reflected in the contributions of the present volume, is a tendency towards using both the broader concept of institutions and the broader view of knowledge creation and distribution. This has reduced the distance between institutional theory and innovation theory and led to interactive inspiration.

THEORIES OF EVOLUTION AND INSTITUTIONS

The connection between institutions, on the one hand, and learning and economic change, on the other, is reflected in the current rapid development of evolutionary theories of economic change. It may be fruitful to think of knowledge as 'evolving'. Boulding (1978) has even suggested that 'something very much like knowledge' is the answer to the question of 'what evolves?' The idea that science and technology are evolving is not a new one. Many writers have noticed the similarity between mutations in biological evolution and new ideas, hypotheses and theories in science. Evolutionary economic theories have noted the presence of various selection mechanisms in relation to these. Furthermore, the development of scientific knowledge is (thus) seen as an uncertain and open-ended process which is impossible to foresee in any detail (see Nelson, 1995) for an overview of recent evolutionary theorization of economic change).

There are signs of a mutual attraction and new connections between institutional and evolutionary economics (Hodgson, 1993). For example, institutions are seen as being equivalents to genes in biological evolution. But economic evolution is very different from biological evolution and such metaphors have to be used with care. On a more general level institutions have been regarded as basic elements in social evolution; they form selection environments for innovations, and they store and transmit knowledge from one period to another. In particular, routines are often regarded as basic elements in both institutional and evolutionary economics. Furthermore, in evolutionary economic theory it is generally assumed that evolutionary processes are embedded in institutions (see the chapter by Coriat and Dosi in the present volume).

In an evolutionary perspective organizational and technological learning are looked upon as diversity-creating processes which are cumulative in the sense that new knowledge builds on already existing knowledge. These processes are affected by selective forces so that some avenues of knowledge creation are promoted at the expense of others, and some parts of the existing stock of knowledge are destroyed or forgotten. In such a perspective the importance of institutions and the connections between institutions and economic change become more obvious. Institutions affect the creation, storing, distribution, use and destruction of knowledge since they shape the visions, the interactions, the decisions and the routines of economic agents at all levels within and outside organizations and markets; they form the processes of technical and organizational change.

COMPETENCE AND INSTITUTIONS AT THE FIRM LEVEL

It was underlined above that learning is connected to ordinary economic activities in all parts of the economy. In capitalist economies some of the most important learning processes take place within firms and in various kinds of interaction between firms or between firms and other organizations. The intra-firm learning processes are conceptualized in evolutionary theory of the firm

(Nelson and Winter, 1982). Instead of an optimizing procedure such as profit maximization, Nelson and Winter developed an evolutionary model in which selection operates on the firms' internal routines. Habits and routines act as relatively durable repositories of knowledge and skills. Routines are maintained if firms are sufficiently profitable. If profitability falls below the level aspired to, a search for new routines is initiated.

Evolutionary approaches of the Nelson–Winter type constitute an important subset of the so-called 'competence-based', 'resource-based', or 'capabilities' theories of the firm (see Hodgson, 1997, for an overview). These theories contrast with the contractual theories, emanating largely from the work of Coase (see Foss, 1993, and Teece and Pisano, 1994, for overviews). According to Coase, not only the existence of the firm, but also the efficient boundaries of the firm and the internal organization of the firm can be explained if the concept of transaction cost is added to the price-theoretical apparatus. Williamson's transaction cost economics, the 'nexus of contracts' theories, agency theory, and the incomplete contract approach all belong to this class of theories of the firm. Relations between economic agents within or outside of the firm are governed by 'contracts' which optimize on transaction costs including costs of internal governance.

The contractual theories have been criticized for focusing on static efficiencies and neglecting dynamic efficiencies. Another critique points at the reduction of the role of management to the creation of incentives and, accordingly, the neglect of other aspects of management including strategic management. Furthermore, they have been criticized for an inadequate approach to the issue of knowledge. Contractual theories specify whether information is symmetrical or asymmetrical, and whether the future is uncertain or not. However, the tacit or social components of knowledge as embodied in firms' capabilities are not included in these theories.

Competence-based theories differ from the contractual theories in relation to all these critical points. They assume that tacit and social knowledge are crucial in matters of economic organization. Accordingly, there is an important role for strategic management in cultivating firms' endowment of capabilities. This perspective also implies a concern for dynamic efficiencies rather than static efficiencies.

The relevant capabilities and competences of the firm are firm-specific rather than agent-specific. The knowledge of the firm is something more than the sum of the knowledge of the individuals constituting the firm. The firm-specific knowledge is what Nelson and Winter call 'routines', that is, the 'organizational memory' of the firm. A broader concept of such routines encompasses 'the forms, rules, procedures, conventions, strategies, and technologies around which organizations are constructed and through which they operate. It also includes the structure of beliefs, frameworks, paradigms, codes, cultures, and knowledge that buttress, elaborate and contradict the formal routines' (Levitt and March, 1988, p. 320). The competence perspective on the firm stresses the social nature and the tacitness of such routines.

THE IMPORTANCE OF TRUST AND NORMS

The interaction between institutional and evolutionary approaches implies new perspectives on phenomena such as trust between economic agents and the role of social and moral norms in economic life. These phenomena are normally left in the darkness by mainstream economic theory, but are, nevertheless, crucial for an understanding of economic change.

Relations between firms often take the form of relatively stable cooperation, that is, user-producer networks, or, more generally, inter-firm networks. Such networks do not merely minimize transaction costs. They also generate 'learning by interacting'. In addition, cooperation between firms does not merely originate from individual self-interest but might also have non-egoistic sources such as values and norms of proper conduct or be based on friendship, kinship or empathy (Gambetta, 1988). Furthermore, the prevalence and generation of trust in inter-firm relations limits opportunistic firm behaviour. Opportunism then becomes an endogeneous variable dependent on interaction and trust rather than a fact of life to be counteracted through contracts and enforcement mechanisms.

Most often, economists either ignore the role of norms or attempt to reduce norm-oriented action to some type of optimizing behaviour. However, some recent contributions have provided strong arguments for the non-reducability of norms and the importance of focusing on the independent role of norms in economic processes. Elster has argued theoretically (Elster, 1989a) and based on empirical evidence (Elster, 1989b) that at least some social norms cannot be explained by self-interest. In a major contribution to development studies, Platteau (1994) argues that market mechanisms require that most actors observe norms of veracity, which has its psychological origins in culture and socialization processes. Trust is an important part of what the sociologist James Coleman has called 'social capital': the ability of people to work together for common purposes in groups and organizations. This can be expressed in terms better known among economists: human capital embodies not only the knowledge and skills of individual human beings; an important part of human capital has to do with people's abilities to associate with others, and this ability depends on the degree to which communities of people share norms and values.

Ironically, capitalist society with its anonymous forces of self-interest needs trust the most for two reasons. First, formal contractual relationships are more important in capitalist societies than in societies where monitoring is conducted by kinship relations. Second, the modern juridicial system cannot practically monitor the extensive growth of contractual agreements (Khalil, 1994, p. 340). We already find with Adam Smith an awareness of the fact that a market economy cannot function properly without certain moral norms and cultural habits. Law, contract and rational economic behaviour are not enough to ensure a properly functioning market economy. At least a minimum reservoir of habitual reciprocity, moral obligation and trust must prevail. The well-being of nations depends on the size of this reservoir: 'one of the most important lessons we can learn from an examination of economic life is that a nation´s well-being, as well as its ability to compete, is conditioned by a single pervasive cultural characteristic: the level of trust inherent in society' (Fukuyama, 1995, p. 7).

Trust is an important explanatory variable in contemporary economic studies. The actual behaviour of economic agents cannot be explained without taking account of the prevalence or lack of trust in the specific context. Unfortunately, trust is an intangible asset, easier to destroy than to build up.

THE PLAN OF THE BOOK

The contributions of this volume focus on the phenomena mentioned above: learning, knowledge, trust and norms. They do so from evolutionary and institutional prespectives. The volume reflects the general shift of perspective to resource creation rather than resource allocation. The overall theme of the book is the relations between institutions and change in the economy. Obviously, only a few aspects of such a vast theme can be treated. After an introductory section on prospects for future theoretical development the book focusses on new perspectives within three fields: (a) the study of innovation and technological change, (b) the theory of the firm and inter-firm relations, and (c) the analysis of markets, economic systems and the role of moral norms. These are among those fields wherein the neoclassical approach is most obviously insufficient whereas evolutionary and institutional economics have much to offer.

Part I: Prospects for Evolutionary and Institutional Theory

The first section of the book focuses on theories of institutions and economic change in general. Both contributions outline prospects for future theoretical development. Whereas Coriat and Dosi discuss the relations between evolutionary and institutionalist theories and the prospects for their future interaction, Lundvall focuses on the concept of learning, the current and future role of learning processes, and its implications for economic theory and policy.

Recent years have seen the emergence of several economic theories which share the common preoccupation of developing an alternative to neoclassical theory based on an understanding of economic change as a historical, institutionally embedded process. Two alternative research programmes can be distinguished: on the one side, an emerging evolutionary theory of economic dynamics, and, on the other side, various strands of institutionalist theories. Currently, the alternative research programmes coexist in mutually benificial interactionist manners, for instance, within the framework of EAEPE. However, there are also profound differences between the programmes as far as scientific ambitions, theoretical foci and research methods are concerned, and it is possible that the future will be characterized by distinct, path-dependent differentiation more than mutual interbreeding.

The contribution of Benjamin Coriat and Giovanni Dosi explores the prospects of future interaction and integration of evolutionary theory and various strands of institutionalist theories, with particular emphasis on the regulation approach. They summarize the characteristics and different styles of explanation of the two research programmes and discuss the links, overlaps, tensions and possible interbreedings between them. Coriat and Dosi identify differences in levels of observation which hide potentially fruitful complementarities. They suggest that a theory-informed dialogue between microfounded evolutionary approach and the more aggregate, albeit institutionally richer, regulation approach is a formidable but analytically promising challenge. Coriat and Dosi point to some unresolved questions and areas of possible conflict but they also outline the building blocks of an ideal evolutionary-institutionalist research programme.

The starting point in the contribution by Bengt-Åke Lundvall is the assumption that the current economy is one where knowledge is the most strategic resource and learning the most important process. This has important theoretical implications. It challenges the fundamental focus on scarcity in economic theory and it implies that the economic process can only be understood as socially embedded. Strategic skills and competences are developed in interactive processes and shared within subgroups and networks. Some elements of tacit knowledge may become even more important for economic performance than hitherto. The learning economy implies challenges not only to economic theory but also to economic policy. Policies promoting information infrastructures and accelerating innovation risk reinforcing inequality and threatening social cohesion unless the exclusion of a big and growing proportion of the labour force from normal waged work as a result of the accelerated change is counteracted by other measures. A 'New New Deal' is called for. Lundvall discusses what kinds of economic policies and social compromises are needed.

Part II: Innovation and Technological Development

The emphasis of knowledge and learning process originates, in particular, from studies of innovation and technological development. Evolutionary and institutional theories have gained prominence within this field of economics which has always been one of the weakest in neoclassical theory. The second section of the book contains four contributions with theoretical and empirical studies of technological change. They include reviews of the literature within the various fields of study (see particularly the contributions by Arjona Béjar and Humbert). The phenomena of globalization and localization of technology are reconceptualized by Humbert. The other chapters also include contributions to theoretical development. Furthermore, three of them present results from in-depth empirical studies of two technologies (Arjona Béjar), an industrial sector (Cantner, Hanusch and Westermann) or a country (Edquist and McKelvey).

Luis E. Arjona Béjar presents an outline of the main tenets of the evolutionary approach in economics and a selective review of the literature on technological change. Furthermore, he uses the evolutionary approach to technological change to develop a framework for microeconomic analysis which he then adapts in a study of the development of two technologies from the polyethylene and photocopying equipment industries. He focuses on the relationship between new technology and international trade. He studies how change in the patterns of trade relates to the introduction of innovations and their international diffusion. These phenomena have traditionally been studied from an equilibrium perspective, as the market-coordinated outcome of demand and supply forces. The perspective adopted in this article rather focuses on three key elements of the evolutionary process: the technology itself, the population of firms, and the selective environment. This approach unveils the crucial importance of the mechanisms of variety creation and selection which are absent in a market equilibrium perspective.

In studies of the development of technology different economists from within the evolutionary and institutionalist tradition have characterized current trends in apparently contradictory ways. Some have stressed the importance of 'national systems of innovation' for the production, diffusion and application of new technology. Others have stressed the homogenizing effects of the process of globalization which in the field of technology encompasses not only its exploitation but also its generation through transnational forms of technological collaboration.

Marc Humbert argues in his contribution that although there is a genuine trend towards the globalization of the process of technology creation this is not leading to a 'de-socialization' of the innovation process. The persistence of strong international differences is seen as confirmation of the fact that innovation processes are still localized societal processes and will remain so although in different forms than in the past. The article briefly reviews the literature on the globalization of technology and assesses by means of empirical evidence its present state. In addition, it reviews and discusses the argument of embeddedness of innovation processes within national systems. The conclusion outlines the challenges and opportunities of what is termed the 'glocalization' of technology.

Humbert argues that the increasing generation of innovation in trans-border networks, the easy import of foreign technologies, and the increasing harmonization of standards challenge and transform national systems. However, local competitiveness is still seen to depend on the domestic capabilities to exploit foreign sources of technology. Globalization provides not only challenges but also opportunities for localized processes of innovation as it may give birth to glocalization, that is, new localized processes of innovation and new localized networks.

Variety and diversity are central concepts in the evolutionary approach to economics. The emphasis is on the on-going creation of variety, which is the fuel of evolutionary processes, ensuring that evolution has no final consummation. On the contrary, neoclassical economics conceptualized these phenomena as temporary exceptions. Equilibrium states wipe out anything but single best-practices. For instance, neoclassicists explain the existence of different technologies and performances of firms within the same industrial sector as an effect of technical and allocative inefficiencies and as such as temporary phenomena.

This explanation is challenged by Uwe Cantner, Horst Hanusch and Georg Westermann. Following recent advances in evolutionary theories of technological change it is assumed that the heterogeneous performance of firms may be the result of the coexistence and competition of several different technologies. Moreover, this diversity is also seen as a potential major force pushing forward technological progress. The article contributes to this literature with an empirical analysis of technological performance and diversity within the electronics sector in Germany in the period from 1985 to 1991. Traditional econometric methods are seen as unsuitable for this purpose. The authors therefore apply a non-parametric, linear programming procedure. The study detects several best-practice technologies ('technology fields') in the sector. Technology leaders can be assigned to each specific technology field. It is shown that the perceived intra-industry heterogeneity can be explained by the technological performance of the firms, measured either by the firm-specific R&D-capital stocks (technology input) or the patenting activities of the firms (technology output).

Charles Edquist and Maureen McKelvey argue in their contribution that a paradox is visible in the Swedish economy. On the one hand, the expenditure on R&D is considerably higher than the OECD average; on the other hand, the proportion of high-tech products in total manufacturing is below the OECD average. Swedish industry does use advanced production technologies but there seem to be problems in translating R&D results into R&D-intensive products, and they have apparently been aggravated in the last twenty years. The problems are analysed by means of evolutionary and institutional theory. The situation is considered serious because countries specializing in high tech are seen to have better longer-term economic prospects than countries specializing in less innovative sectors. Edquist and McKelvey argue that the paradox is connected to specific Swedish factors at the firm and national levels. The Swedish production structure and industrial R&D are heavily dominated by large firms which tend to stay close to existing products when innovating. This partly explains the persistence of traditional patterns of export specialization based on 'refined' natural resources. In addition, political and institutional factors, such as state support to ailing industries and the devaluations of the Swedish crown, have played a key role in reducing firms' incentives to innovate.

Part III: The Theory of the Firm and Relations between Firms

The theory of the firm is another field where evolutionary and institutional economics is at the forefront of theoretical development offering a research programme which leads to new empirical insight. As mentioned above, the competence-based theories of the firm view the firm as a repository of (tacit and social) knowledge and capabilities. Other evolutionary and institutional approaches stress elements such as trust and moral norms which have traditionally been discussed in sociology rather than economics.

The third section of the book presents and discusses these new perspectives on the firm and the relations between firms. Turvani reappraises three classical contributions to the theory of the firm, which leads to a confrontation of the competence perspective with the transaction cost approach. This contribution focuses on the relations inside the firm, in particular the employer–employee relation. The other two chapters concern relations between firms. Nooteboom presents an elaborate framework for the analysis and design of such relations in general. Marmefelt analyses the evolution of relations between bankers and entrepreneurs and how collective action is necessary to achieve the optimal result. The contributions of this section are characterized by common or overlapping themes, such as decision-making under uncertainty, cognition and learning, tacit or idiosyncratic knowledge, trust, and networks.

Margherita Turvani discusses the origin of the controversy between the contractarian and the competence perspectives by means of critical reflections on the notion of contract and its scope in organizing human activity. The point of departure is the seminal contributions of Knight, Coase and Simon. Knight's concept of judgment is seen, together with Simon's concept of liquidity of resources, to offer a perspective different from the Coasean one. In this perspective the firms' reason for existence is found not in transaction costs but in the way human beings deal with cognitive and decision processes. From this follows two different perspectives on incomplete contracting. According to a Coasean perspective, incomplete contracts originate from the fact that markets do not provide the information required, which leads to various problems of design and enforcement. On the other hand, if we assume an evolutionary perspective derived from the contributions of Knight and Simon, the vacuum in contracts is seen to allow the exercise of judgment, i.e. the production of firms' tacit or idiosyncratic knowledge. This is seen as more appropriate because the division of labour is necessarily accompanied by the divison of knowledge, because human cognitive activities are far more complex than choosing among known alternatives, and because new knowledge is created as a result of problem-solving activities.

Bart Nooteboom develops in his contribution a framework for the analysis and design of relations between firms. The interaction studied deals with the tension that arises in relations between the advantages due to cooperation and the risks due to mutual dependence. The framework incorporates elements from transaction cost economics: 'relation-specific investments' yield switching costs; 'bounded rationality' opens up for opportunism; and 'legal governance and private ordering' constrain such opportunities. It also includes elements that derive from sociology rather than economics: ethical norms and other institutions also constrain possibilities for opportunism; trust, bonding and habituation constrain the inclination towards opportunism; and learning forms a crucial dimension of the value of interaction. Like Turvani, Nooteboom is critical of the implicit theory of knowledge in transaction cost economics: it is blind to the role of transactional relations in shifting perceptions, knowledge and preference, or more generally, development of competence. Nooteboom adopts a different perspective wherein transactions are viewed as embedded in relations that develop in time, where learning requires networks between firms, and trust forms an important dimension in such relations. On the other hand, transaction cost economics is seen to offer important insight in the nature and extent of risk in transactions. Both trust and opportunism are likely to arise in transaction relations, and neither should be ignored. Therefore, in spite of the differences between the two outlooks, Nooteboom seeks to integrate them.

Thomas Marmefelt focuses on a specific type of relationship between firms: banker–entrepreneur interaction. Inspired by Schumpeter, the institutional forms of interaction between bankers and entrepreneurs are seen as crucial for the innovation process. Cooperation in bank–industry networks based on mutual trust and network commitment is beneficial for innovativeness because bankers' learning-by-financing would provide more credit at low costs. The evolution of banker–entrepreneur interaction is analyzed as an evolutionary game. There are two stable strategies: bank–industry networks and market-oriented banker–entrepreneur relations. Marmefelt shows how bank–industry networks evolve spontaneously only when the institutional endowments, such as developed banking and network commitment, are sufficient. It follows that some collective action might be necessary to make the spontaneous evolution of bank–industry networks feasible.

Part IV: Markets, Economic Systems and the Role of Moral Norms

Whereas the second and the third part of the book focus on more delimited issues such as innovation and firms, the fourth and final section includes contributions on some grand and wide-ranging issues. Hodgson discusses how different theoretical approaches explain the actual variety of capitalist economic systems. Kregel challenges the fundamental idea in neoclassical economics of optimal allocation of resources in market equilibrium under perfect competition, an idea or ideal which originates from Walras's theory. The conclusion constitutes a radical and wide-ranging challenge to neoclassical economics. Another issue with wide-ranging consequences is the economic role of moral norms. In the final chapter, Yaffey discusses and reformulates the role of norms in economic interaction, using psychology to open up the black box of 'trust'.

Geoffrey M. Hodgson examines the type of economic analysis of capitalism presented in neoclassical, Austrian, Marxian and institutionalist schools of economic thought. He argues that all except the institutionalist school are insensitive to the variety of capitalisms; they are blind to the cultures and institutions which characterize different kinds of capitalism. The following issues are addressed in relation to each of the different schools of economic thought: the problem of universal versus specific assumptions in economic analysis; the question of 'necessary impurities' in all economic systems; and the relationship between actor and structure. Hodgson argues that there is no unique or optimal version of capitalism that will necessarily triumph over other versions. The advantages of one type of capitalism over another are typically dependent on their historical path and context and thereby nothing can be said about its eventual superiority to other models. Institutionalist concepts and theories such as the concept of habits and the theory of cumulative causation are considered the best tools and the best framework in an understanding of the variety of capitalist economic systems.

If variety and diversity prevail, then it is obvious that each institution is particular and each institutional set-up is a special case. If capitalist economic systems vary, then their institutions and institutional contexts function in their own particular ways, and develop path-dependently in their own particular directions. It follows that theories based on a particular institutional context are 'institution-bounded'. Their applicability is bounded to this context.

According to Jan Kregel, this is exactly what characterizes the mainstream interpretation of Walras's original theory. Kregel discusses the foundation of Walras's theory. He challenges the view of post-Keynesians and institutionalists that the theory is devoid of any real-world content. He also challenges the claims of proponents of general equilibrium theory that it can be applied independently of any real institutions. He shows that Walras's theory is a rather accurate representation of the functioning of a particular institution, the Paris Bourse. He argues that the theory has little applicability outside its specific historical and institutional context. This observation has radical consequences. It follows that the fundamental idea of optimal allocation of resources is merely a description of the distribution of shares after the determination of equilibrium prices at the Paris Bourse, and its applicability is restricted to similar institutional contexts. Accordingly, the idea of the stock exchange as the perfect market is based on a very weak foundation. This is also so with the widespread idea that the creation of a stock market is a necessary precondition for economic development. Markets cannot provide a basis for the evaluation of alternative allocations of resources. Bank–industry networks are seen as better means to direct resources to the most advantageous uses.

Michael Yaffey discusses a phenomenon which is of course highly dependent on the specific institutional and cultural context: the economic importance of moral norms or shared values. He focuses on the role of moral norms in reducing opportunism in market transactions. His contribution takes as its starting point a critical dialogue with recent contributions to the new institutional economics (North and Platteau). It is suggested that the existence of counter-opportunistic moral standards and norms is a vital though intangible social asset. It is impossible to measure it except through proxy indicators and the asset can decay imperceptibly. Yaffey discusses the genesis of such counter-opportunistic moral norms and the role of institutions in this respect. He integrates psychological research results in his attempt to do so. They show that the behaviour of adults is the outcome of a process of moral development carried out by a matrix of institutions, linked and interlocked by widely accepted moral standards, values and norms. Market operations benefit from this, but do not themselves undertake it, and indeed competitive self-interest might counteract this outcome. The whole constitutes an intangible social asset which requires maintenance expenditure.

This conclusion bears a resemblance to those made in the contributions by Nooteboom and Marmefelt. The preservation and increase of the social assets of moral norms, trust and (network) commitment from a major economic objective which cannot be confidently left to market forces.

REFERENCES

Boulding, K.J. (1978), *Ecodynamics: A New Theory of Societal Evolution*, Beverley Hills: Sage.

Edquist, C. and Johnson, B. (1977), 'Institutions and Organisations in Systems of Innovation', in Edquist, C. (ed.) *Systems of Innovation, Technologies, Institutions and Organisations*, London and Washington: Pinter.

Elster, J. (1989a), 'Social Norms and Economic Theory', *Journal of Economic Perspectives*, 4, 99–117.

Elster, J. (1989b) *The Cement of Society*, Cambridge: Cambridge University Press.

Foss, N.J. (1993), 'Theories of the firm: contractual and competence perspectives', *Journal of Evolutionary Economics*, 3, 127–44.

Fukuyama, F. (1995), *Trust: The Social Virtues and the Creation of Prosperity*, New York: The Free Press.

Gambetta, D. (ed.) (1988), *Trust: Making and Breaking Cooperative Relations*, Oxford: Basil Blackwell.

Hodgson, G.M. (1993), *Economics and Evolution: Bringing Life Back into Economics*, Cambridge: Polity Press.

Hodgson, G.M. (1997), 'Evolutionary and competence-based theories of the firm', in C. Pitelis (ed.), *The Economics of Industrial and Business Strategies*, Cheltenham, UK and Lyme, US: Edward Elgar.

Khalil, E. (1994), 'Trust', in Hodgson, G.M., Samuels, W.J. and Tool, M. (eds) *The Elgar Companion to Institutional and Evolutionary Economics*, Aldershot: Edward Elgar.

Levitt, B. and J.G. March (1988), 'Organizational capabilities and interfirm relations', *Metroeconomica*, 45, 248–65.

Nelson, R.R. (1995), 'Recent evolutionary theorizing about economic change', *Journal of Economic Literature*, XXXIII (March), 48–90.

Nelson, R.R. and S.G. Winter (1982), *An Evolutionary Theory of Economic Change*, Cambridge, MA: Harvard University Press.

Platteau, J.-P. (1994), 'Behind the market stage where real societies exist', *Journal of Development Studies*, Vol. 30, no. 3 and no. 4.

Teece, D.J. and G. Pisano (1994), 'The dynamic capabilities of firms: an introduction', *Industrial and Corporate Change*, 3, 537–56.

PART I

Prospects for Evolutionary and
Institutional Theory

1. The institutional embeddedness of economic change: an appraisal of the 'evolutionary' and 'regulationist' research programmes

Benjamin Coriat and Giovanni Dosi

1. INTRODUCTION

There are at least two complementary ways to present the ideas which follow. One is with reference to some 'grand' questions that have faced social sciences since their inceptions, namely, how do institutions shape the behaviour of individual agents, within and outside the economic arena? And what are institutions in the first place? How do they come about and how do they change? What are the relationships between 'agency' and structure? And also, nearer economic concerns, what is the role of institutions in economic coordination and change?

Another, more modest, way of tackling some of these grand issues is to see how this is done in practice by different research programmes which nonetheless share a common preoccupation with understanding economic change as a historical, institutionally embedded process.

This is what we shall attempt to do in this work, by discussing the links, overlapps, tensions and possible interbreedings between an emerging evolutionary theory of economic dynamics and various strands of institutionalist theories, with particular attention to the regulation approach.

Some definitions of what we mean by those terms and of where we put the boundaries of different theories are in order. We shall introduce these, in a rather telegraphic fashion, in Sections 2–4. In Section 5 we sketch, as an illustration, interpretations of the growth process in general, and, in particular, the case – very familiar to institutionalist macroeconomists – of the so-called 'Fordist' phase of development experienced by Western countries after World War II, and we assess the different 'styles' of explanation of evolutionary and regulation theories, respectively. In turn, these differences in 'style' partly hide different levels of observation – hence, probably, entailing fruitful complementarities – and partly also reveal genuine differences in the choice of explanatory variables and causal relationships. We shall discuss some of these issues with respect to the nature of institutions and behavioural microfoundations in Section 6. Finally, in Section 7 we propose a sort of taxonomy of potentially complementary levels of descriptions and analytical methodologies and, together, we suggest some items that in our view are high on both evolutionist and institutionalist research agendas.

2.   EVOLUTIONARY THEORIES: SOME DEFINITIONS

For the purposes of this work we will restrict our discussion to evolutionary theories of *economic* change. In brief, a sort of 'archetypical' evolutionary model possesses, in our view, the following characteristics (much more detailed discussions of the state-of-the-art are in Hodgson (1993), Dosi and Nelson (1994), Nelson (1995), and Silverberg and Verspagen (1995a))

1. As Sidney Winter used to summarize it, the methodological imperative is dynamics first! That is, the explanation of why something exists rests intimately on how it became what it is. Or putting it in terms of negative prescriptions: never take as a good 'explanation' either an existence theorem or a purely functionalist claim (entity x exists because it performs function y . . .).
2. Theories are explicitly microfounded, in the sense that they must involve or at least be consistent with a story of what agents do and why they do it.[1]
3. Agents have at best an imperfect understanding of the environment they live in, and, even more so, of what the future will deliver. Hence, 'bounded rationality' in a very broad sense is generally assumed.
4. Imperfect understanding and imperfect, path-dependent learning entails persistent heterogeneity among agents, even when facing identical information and identical notional opportunities.
5. Agents are always capable of discovering new technologies, new behavioural patterns, and new organizational set-ups. Hence, also, the continuous appearance of various forms of novelty in the system.
6. Related to the last point, while (imperfect) adaptation and discovery generate variety (possibly in seemingly random fashion), collective interactions within and outside markets perform as selection mechanisms, yielding also differential growth (and possibly also disappearance) of different entities which are, so to speak, 'carriers' of diverse technologies, routines, strategies, etc.
7. As a result of all this, aggregate phenomena (e.g. regularities in the growth process or in industrial structures, etc.) are 'explained' as emergent properties. They are the collective outcome of far-from-equilibrium

interactions and heterogeneous learning. Finally, they often have a metastable nature, in the sense that while persistent on a time-scale longer than the processes generating them, tend to disappear with probability one.[2]

This is not the place to review the growing number of contributions which share some or all of these seven broad methodological building blocks[3].

Suffice it to mention, first, the flourishing number of formal models and historical interpretations of economic growth as an evolutionary process propelled by technical change which have followed the seminal work of Nelson and Winter (1982): see among others Dosi *et al.* (1988), Day and Eliasson (1986), Silverberg and Verspagen (1994), Conlisk (1989), Chiaromonte and Dosi (1993), Silverberg and Soete (1993) and the discussion in Nelson (1995) and Silverberg and Verspagen (1995a).

Second, the diffusion of innovations has been fruitfully analysed, from different angles, as an evolutionary path-dependent process (cf. among others David (1985 and 1992), Silverberg *et al.* (1988), Arthur *et al.* (1987), Nakicenovic and Grübler (1992), and Metcalfe (1992)).

Third, the very development of an evolutionary perspective has been deeply intertwined with the historical analysis of the processes by which technical change is generated, ranging from the microeconomic level all the way to 'national systems of innovation' (within an enormous literature, see Freeman (1982), David (1975), Rosenberg (1976 and 1982), Basalla (1988), Mokyr (1990), Granstrand (1994), Vincenti (1990), Nelson (1992), and the reviews in Dosi (1988) and Freeman (1994)).

Fourth, a growing number of industrial case studies and models of industrial change fits quite well the evolutionary conjectures outlined above (again, just as examples, see Pavitt (1984), Utterback and Suarez (1992), Klepper (1993), Malerba and Orsenigo (1994), Winter (1984), and Dosi *et al.* (1995)).

Fifth, one is starting to explore learning itself as an evolutionary process at the levels of both individuals and organizations (limiting ourselves to economic applications, see Marengo (1992), Marengo and Tordjman (1996), Lindgren (1992), Dosi *et al.* (1995b), Levinthal (1990), Warglien (1995), and Palmer *et al.* (1994)). This links also with a wide tradition of studies in the fields of organizational economics which is impossible to review here (but see the remarks in Winter 1986 and 1995).

Finally, there is a good overlap between the evolutionary perspective as we have defined it and various types of 'self-organization' models (see Lesourne (1991)), and also with the expanding field of evolutionary games (see for example Young (1993), Kandori *et al.* (1993), and Kaniovski and Young (1994)). Short of any detailed discussion of analogies and differences (which will be briefly mentioned below), let us just mention that certainly they have in common the emphasis on dynamics (point 1 above) and bounded rationality assumptions (point 3), but much less so the role of novelty (point 5) and the focus on non-equilibrium, finite time, properties (point 7)[.4]

So, yes: indeed, we do have a rich and growing body of economic literature which at last tackles change and evolution, whereby increasing returns are the norm rather than the exception (and, with that, also the possibility of 'lock-ins'), history counts, and agents are presumed to be less than perfectly rational and knowledgeable. But where do institutions fit in this picture?

Let us now turn to this issue.

3.   INSTITUTIONS AND EVOLUTION

Again, for the sake of clarity, starting with some definitions helps.

Here we use the term 'institution' with a broad meaning to include

(a)   formal organizations (ranging from firms to technical societies, trade unions, universities, all the way to state agencies);
(b)   patterns of behaviours that are collectively shared (from routines to social conventions to ethical codes);
(c)   negative norms and constraints (from moral prescriptions to formal laws).

Distinctions between the three subcategories will be made in the following when necessary.

The proposition that in a sense 'institutions count' in shaping economic coordination and change is certainly shared by all breeds of 'evolutionists' mentioned earlier with various strands of 'neo-institutionalists' (see for example Williamson (1985 and 1995), and North (1990 and 1991)), and also, of course, with 'old' institutionalism (drawing back to Veblen, Commons, and so on). But, clearly, the tricky issue is *in which sense* they count.

Simplifying to the extreme, two archetypical, opposing views can be found in all this literature. At one end of the spectrum, the role of institutions can be seen as that of (i) parameterizing the environmental state variables (say the comparative costs of markets, hybrids and hierarchies in Williamson or, nearer to evolutionary concerns, technological opportunities and appropriability conditions); and (ii) constraining the menus of actions available to the agents (which in some game-theoretic versions reduces to 'the rules of the game'). Conversely, at the opposite end, let us put under the heading of embeddedness view all those theories which claim, in different fashions, that institutions not only 'parameterize' and 'constrain', but, given any one environment, also shape the 'visions of the world', the interaction networks, the behavioural patterns, and, ultimately, the very identity of the agents. (In the contemporary literature, under this heading come, for example, Granovetter (1985), and also

March and Olsen (1989) and DiMaggio and Powell (1991), just to name a few, and has a close relative in 'cultural theory': cf. Schwartz and Thompson (1990) and Grendstad and Jelle (1995)). Note that where a theory is placed along this spectrum has significant implications in terms of the predictions that it makes with respect to the collective outcomes of interactions and to the directions of change. On the grounds of the former view, the knowledge (by the analyst) of the (institutionally shaped) system parameters is sufficient to determine the collective outcomes (precisely, under 'perfect' rationality with the caveat of multiple equilibria; and approximately, under 'bounded' rationality). Conversely, the embeddedness view implies that in order to understand 'what happens' and the directions of change over time much richer institutional details are needed. (First of all, one is likely to require to know much more about the multiple institutions of which the agents are part, and also much more of their histories.)

As discussed at greater length in Dosi (1995), three other dichotomies are relevant here. The first concerns the origin of the institutions. Briefly put, are institutions themselves a *primitive* of the theory or is *self-seeking rationality* the primitive and institutions are a derived concept? Under the latter view, whatever institution one observes, one has to justify it, asking the question how self-seeking agents have come to build it (with an answer that could be either via forward-looking rationality or myopic adaptation). Conversely, under the former view, the existence of an institution is 'explained' relying much more heavily on the institutions that preceded it and the mechanisms which led to the transition. One is also entitled to ask why people embedded in certain institutions behave the way they do (that is, how institutions shape their specific 'rationality' and equally specific perceptions of their interests).

The second dichotomy regards the degrees of intentionality of institutional constructions, that is, whether they are purposefully built according to some sort of collective *constitutional* activity or, conversely, are mainly the outcome of an unintentional *self-organization* process.

The third dichotomy concerns the efficiency properties (and the equilibrium nature) of institutions themselves. Do they exist *because* they 'perform a function' and, thus, are the equilibrium outcome of some process that selected in favour of that function? Or conversely, paraphrasing Paul David (1994), are they mainly 'carriers of history', in the sense that they tend to path-dependently reproduce themselves well beyond the time of their usefulness (if they ever had one)?

The four dichotomies together define the distance between any one institutionalist view and the standard 'neoclassical' paradigm (institution-free, with perfectly rational agents, well formed and invariant preferences, etc.). As shown in Table 1.1, one may identify different *gradations* of institutionalism, ranging from *weak* forms retaining a lot of the canonic microfoundations to *strong* forms wherein institutions have much more life of their own and also much more influence on what microentities think and do.

Table 1.1   Weak and strong varieties of institutionalism

	'Weak' Institutionalism	'Strong' Institutionalism
(1) Role of institutions	Parameterize system variables; contain menu of strategies	Also 'embed' cognitive and behavioural patterns; shape identities of actors
(2) 'Primitives' of the theory	(Perfectly or boundedly) rational self-seeking agents; institutions as derived entities	Institutions as 'primitives'; forms of 'rationality' and perceptions of self-interest as derived entities
(3) Mechanisms of institution-formulation	Mainly intentional, 'constitutional', processes	Mainly unintentional self-organization processes
(4) Efficiency properties	Institutions perform useful coordinating and governance functions; may be considered equilibria in some selection space	Institutions as 'carriers of history'; reproduce path-dependently, often irrespectively of this functional efficiency

How does the evolutionary research programme (as we have defined it) relate to the various strands of institutionalism, if it does at all? It is our view that the links are indeed profound (the famous plea for an evolutionary approach to economic analysis by one of the founding figures of institutionalism, T. Veblen (1898), is a historical symbol of this intuitive relationship). However, it seems to us also true that the linkages so far still are to a large extent implicit.

Certainly there are a lot of institutional assumptions in evolutionary reasoning. So, for example, it is quite natural to assume that the particular behavioural rules, interaction mechanisms and learning patterns that one finds in evolutionary models are embedded into particular institutions. In fact, markets themselves are viewed as specific, history-contingent, institutions.

Moreover, it is plain that *routines* – which play a prominent role in evolutionary theorizing of economic behaviours – are shaped by the history of the organizations in which they have developed and also by a broader institutional history. (For example, one is quite at ease with the idea that the routines and strategies of a firm from Victorian Manchester are likely to be quite different from those of American multidivisional corporations analysed by Alfred Chandler; that differences in the institutional contexts contribute to explaining the behavioural differences between contemporary Japanese, American, and European firms, etc.).

Finally, a lot of effort has gone into the understanding of the specificities of the institutions supporting technological change (see, for example, Nelson (1993), Lundvall (1992) and the chapters by Nelson and Freeman in Dosi *et al.* (1988)).

However, it is fair to say that the institutional embeddedness of technological opportunities, routines, forms of market interactions and selection mechanisms, etc., while abundantly acknowledged, has received little attention on its own (with the exception of those institutions more directly linked with innovative activities and notwithstanding the suggestions in Lundvall (1992) aiming to provide a broader institutional meaning for the notion of 'national systems of innovation'). So, for example, one is still lacking any systematic mapping between classes of institutional arrangements of the economy and classes of interaction mechanisms/adjustment rules that one finds in evolutionary theories. As a consequence, one is equally still unable to map institutional arrangements into particular dynamic properties of aggregate variables such as income and productivity growth, employment, etc. (See, however, Chiaromonte *et al.* (1992) for an initial, still quite preliminary attempt.) Conversely, these types of mapping are precisely the *starting point* of 'strong' institutionalist approaches as defined above. As a term of comparison, let us consider in particular the 'regulation' school.

4.   AN INSTITUTIONALIST VIEW OF THE ECONOMIC SYSTEM: THE 'REGULATION' APPROACH

For those who are not familiar with this tradition of studies, which originally developed in France (see Aglietta (1982), Boyer and Mistral (1978), Boyer (1987, 1988a, 1988b and 1990), Coriat (1991), Jessop (1990), and Boyer and Saillard (1995)). First note that by 'regulation', in French, one does not mean the legal regulatory apparatus as understood by the same term in English. Rather, its meaning is nearer the notion from system theory of different parts or processes that under certain conditions reciprocally adjust yielding some orderly dynamics. Hence *regulation* stands for the relatively coherent socio-economic tuning of any one economic system, and different *regimes of regulation* capture the specificities in the 'mechanisms and principles of adjustment associated with a configuration of wage relations, competition, State interventions and hierarchisation of the international economy' (Boyer 1987, p. 127).

In this perspective, and unlike evolutionary models, the description of the system is immediately institutional and taxonomic, attempting to identify some sort of archetypical structural forms which distinguish alternative socio-economic regimes.[5]

For our purposes here, let us define different regimes of accumulation in terms of the institutional arrangements concerning six domains, namely:

1. *The wage-labour nexus.* Under this heading come the nature of the social division of labour; the type of employment and the mechanism of governance of industrial conflict; the existence and nature of union representation; the systems of wage formation; and so on.
2. The forms of *competition* in the product markets (whether nearly-competitive or oligopolist: the related mechanism of price formation; and so on).
3. The institutions governing *financial markets* and monetary management (including the relationships between banks and industry, the role of stock exchanges in industrial financing, the mechanisms of liquidity creation in the system, etc.).
4. The norms of *consumption* (that is, the composition and changes in the baskets of consumption and their differences across social groups).
5. The forms of *state intervention* in the economy (for example, monetary and fiscal policies; 'state as arbiter' versus state as an active player with respect to social conflict, income distribution, welfare and so on).
6. The organization of the *international system* of exchanges (for example, the rules of international trade; the presence/absence of a single hegemonic power; the patterns of specialization; and so on).

The identification of discrete regimes implies, then, a sort of combinatorial exercise among these six domains; the historically informed identification of dominant ones in particular periods; the assessment of the conditions of their viability and eventual crises; the specific realizations of a dominant regime in different countries. So a lot of work has been done in order to identify the nature of the 'classical' (or 'competitive') regime which ran through most of the nineteenth century, as opposed to a 'Fordist' (or 'monopolistic') regime coming to maturity in the developed West after World War II (cf. Aglietta (1982), Boyer and Mistral (1978) and the works reviewed in Boyer and Saillard (1995)). The focus of the analysis is to a great extent the *long term*, influenced by Marxism and the French historical tradition of the *Annales*, and the emphasis is macroinstitutional: it is centred, for example, on the institutions governing 'social compromises' among major social groups (Delorme and André (1983),

Coriat (1982 and 1990)), educational institutions (Caroli (1995)), financial institutions, and so on.

One could say that the regulation approach is an ambitious attempt – paraphrasing John Hicks – to develop a 'theory of contemporary history'. It has proved indeed to be a very rich source of heuristics and categories for historical analyses and comparative studies (a thorough survey of the state of the art is in Boyer and Saillard (1995)). But there are also a few exercises of formalization of types of reduced forms of the theory whereby the (institutionally-shaped) regularities in the above six domains are summarized by some functional relations linking aggregate variables (for example, wages with prices, productivity and employment; productivity growth with the growth of output, investments and R&D; output growth with investment and exports: see in particular Boyer (1988b) and the contributions by Billandot, Juillard and Amable in Boyer and Saillard (1995)). The models have a strong Keynesian/Kaldorian ascendency, but certainly expand upon the ancestors, and, more important, attempt to capture the differences across regimes in terms of different parametrizations and functional specifications of those aggregate relationships (for example, do wages depend mainly on unemployment, as in the 'competitive' regime, or are they basically linked to consumer prices and productivity, as in the 'Fordist' regime? Does some sort of 'Verdoorn–Kaldor law' apply to productivity growth? How sensitive are investments to profits as opposed to 'accelerator' effects? and so on). In these reduced forms, the stability of 'regimes' is investigated in terms of the existence of stable steady states engendered by particular ranges of parameters. Moreover, by specifying dynamic couplings across these same aggregate variables one is able to identify quite rich long-term patterns including bifurcations (Lordon (1993)) and phase transitions.

At this point, readers not too familiar with both the evolutionary and the regulation approaches might reasonably wonder what they have in common. *Prima facie,* they do indeed share some methodological commitment to the understanding of dynamic patterns which do not simply involve 'more of the same'. They both also depart from the canonic view of the economy as a 'naturally' self-regulating system. Moreover, their microfoundations (explicit in most 'evolutionary' contributions, implicit in most of the 'regulationist' ones) imply much less than perfect rationality and foresight. And, finally they share a deep commitment to the idea that 'institutions matter'. But what else beyond that? Are they talking about the same objects of analysis? And, when they do, how do their interpretations overlap or diverge? In order to clarify these issues for the discussion, let us briefly check the two perspectives against an object of inquiry that both have abundantly addressed, namely growth, and in particular the observed patterns during the period after World War II.

5. SOME DIFFERENT THEORETICAL STORIES ON GROWTH, IN GENERAL, AND THE POST-WAR PERIOD, IN PARTICULAR

It is revealing to compare the bare bones of the interpretative stories that 'evolutionists' and 'regulationists' would be inclined to put forward about the basics of the growth process, were they forced to summarize them in a few sentences.

Most likely, the story provided within an evolutionary perspective would start with a multitude of firms searching for more efficient techniques of production and better-performing products, and competing in the markets for products and finance. Differential success in search, together with different behavioural rules and strategies (concerning, for example, pricing, investment, and so on) would then determine their differential revealed performances (in terms, for example, of their profitability, market shares, or survival probabilities) and hence their ability to grow in the next 'period'. Aggregate growth, in this view, is essentially driven by technological advances. Similarly, the eye of the analyst is naturally led to look for the origins, nature and accessability of technological opportunities; the ease with which firms can imitate each other (that is, appropriability conditions); the ways firms are able to store and augment their knowledge (that is, the relationships between organizational routines and competences); and finally the mechanisms and speed of market selection.

As already emphasized, such an evolutionary story is comfortable with complementary institutional factors. Most straightforwardly, for example, it is consistent with (and indeed demands) an institutionally grounded explanation of the mechanisms of generation of 'opportunities' to be tapped by private agents; of the legal framework contributing to shape appropriability conditions; of the origins of particular sets of corporate routines; of the nature of market interactions; of the ways wages react to the changes in the demand for labour induced by technical change and growth; and so on.

However, compare this story with the much more directly institution-based story within a regulation perspective. In the latter, plausibly, the starting point would be an analysis of the factors which render a particular regime of accumulation viable (note incidentally that while it was possible to tell a caricature of an evolutionary story of capitalist growth in general, here one needs history-contingent specifications from the start). One part of the story would concern the institutions governing wage formation, the labour process and income distribution – determining labour productivity and the surplus available for investment. Another part of the story would focus on the mechanisms of generation of aggregate demand (including the ways income distribution and social institutions affect the composition and dynamics of consumption baskets).

Yes another part would address the ways the state intervenes into the economy (is it a 'Keynesian'/welfare state or is it a laisser-faire one?, and so on) Moreover, one would look at the ways products and financial markets are organized. In a nutshell, the answer to the question of 'what drives growth' is found in the consistency conditions among those major pieces of institutional organization of the socio-economic fabric. Hence, consistent matching fosters sustained growth, while mismatching engenders instability, crises and macroeconomic depression.

Having focused, *in primis,* on the institutional features of the system, the approach in manners somewhat symmetrically opposite to the 'evolutionary' interpretation is complementary to detailed specifications of the patterns of technological change. For example, it is easily acknowledged that technological innovation is a major determinant of the division of labour and work organization; of the importance of economics of scale (and thus of the aggregate relationships between productivity growth and income growth); of demand patterns; of international competitiveness; and so on. However, it is fair to say that what appears as the major driver of growth in the evolutionary account, here (in the regulation approach) tends to feature more in the background among the necessary or constraining conditions for growth, while the opposite applies to the thread of country-specific and period-specific institutions.

A similar difference (which might be just a matter of emphasis or might be much more; see below) emerges when handling the interpretation of specific historical circumstances. Compare, as an illustration, Nelson and Wright (1992) and Aglietta (1982) on American performance in this century (notwithstanding the only partial overlap between the two, with the former focused on technological performance and the latter, more broadly, on growth patterns). In brief, the Nelson–Wright story reconstructs the origins of American leadership after World War II, tracing it back to

> two conceptually distinct components. There was, first of all, the longstanding strength in mass production industries that grew out of unique conditions of resource abundance and large market size. There was, second, a lead in 'high technology' industries that was new and stemmed from investment in higher education and in research and development, far surpassing the levels of other countries at the time. (Nelson and Wright, 1992, p. 1960)

The erosion of that leadership is then analysed in terms of the factors which allowed a more or less complete technological catching-up by other OECD countries over the last four decades (subject to the qualifications put forward by Patel and Pavitt (1994) on the long-term specificities in the patterns of technological accumulation by individual countries).

Nelson and Wright do not explicitly talk about the impact of technology on growth, but a strong evolutionary conjecture is that innovation and imitation have a major importance in explaining both trade patterns and growth patterns (for some empirical tests see Dosi *et al.* (1990), Verspagen (1993), Amendola *et al.* (1993), and Fagerberg (1994)). Conversely, the Aglietta story, directly concerning American (and international) *growth* patterns, is an archetypical application of the regulation framework sketched above. The conditions for a sustained regime of growth are identified into the 'virtuous' complementarity (i) mechanization/automation/standardization of production (entailing also ample opportunities for the exploitation of economics of scale); (ii) the development of 'Fordist' patterns of management of industrial relations; (iii) mechanisms of governance of the labour market on the grounds of implicit or explicit conventions indexing wages on productivity and consumer prices (with the effect, among others, of smoothing business cycles and sustaining effective demand); (iv) symmetrically, relatively stable forms of oligopolistic organization of product markets (which, combined with the wage dynamics described above, sustained rather stable patterns of income distribution and easy 'accelerator-driven' investment planning); (v) the diffusion in consumption of mass-produced durables; (vi) 'welfare' and 'Keynesian' fiscal policies; (vii) the development of an international monetary regime conducive to international exchanges (the Bretton Woods set-up) under the hegemony of one economic and technological leader (the USA).

Correspondingly, the end of the 'Golden Age' following World War II is seen as the outcome of 'mismatched dynamics', for institutional and technological reasons, at all the foregoing seven levels: the exhaustion of the potential for economies of scale; inflationary pressures amplified by wage formation mechanism; the entry of new competitors destabilizing cosy oligopolistic arrangements; increasing social conflict favoured by near-full-employment conditions; the collapse of the Bretton Woods regime; and so on.

Are these two basic stories essentially two complementary ways of looking at a broadly similar object? But in this case where does the complementarity precisely rest? Or do they entail competing explanations of the same phenomena? As we shall see, it is our conjecture that there is a bit of both – and sorting out what is what would be already a significant step ahead.

6.   DIFFERENT LEVELS OF ANALYSIS OR COMPETING INTERPRETATIONS?

Certainly, part of the difference in the 'building blocks' of the basic stories outlined above relates to different levels of observation and different primary phenomena to be explained (and this, of course, militates for a would-be complementarity). In many respects, a much greater parsimoniousness on institutional assumptions that one finds in evolutionary models is due to the higher level of 'historical abstraction' in which they are set. Metaphorically speaking, this is the level at which one investigates the properties of an (imperfect) Invisible (or oligopolistically visible) Hand operating in presence of the Unbound Prometheus – as David Landes puts it – of technological change. In other words, evolutionary models – at least the first generation of them – start by addressing, in a first approximation, some stylized properties of capitalist dynamics in general, such as the possibility of self-sustained growth driven by the mistake-ridden search by self-seeking agents. Relatedly, the primary objects of interpretation are broad statistical regularities (or 'stylized facts') at aggregate level, such as exponential growth, the rough constancy of distributive shares, the secular increase in capital/labour ratios, the degrees of persistency in macro fluctuations and more generally the spectral density of time series; the broad patterns of divergence/convergence of per capita income in the world economy; etc. (see Nelson and Winter (1982), Dosi *et al.* (1994a), Silverberg and Verspagen (1994) and the (far too modest!) overview in Silverberg and Verspagen (1995a)). Similarly, at 'meso' level – that is, that of single industries – evolutionary models have proved to be quite capable of interpreting statistical phenomena such as skewed distributions of firms by size, 'life cycle' patterns of evolution, inter-sectoral differences in industrial structures grounded in different 'technological regimes', and so on (cf. Dosi *et al.* (1995)).

With respect to this level of observation, in many ways, the degree of abstraction of regulation theories *is* much lower and the interpretative ambition is higher, in the sense that the aim goes well beyond the account of broad statistical invariances but points at the understanding of discrete forms of development and the transitions across them. Similarly, the degree of institutional specification is bound to be much higher and, as it happens, the 'microfoundations' much more implicit (when they are there at all).

So we have here a potentially fruitful complementarity concerning two different levels of description (see also below). As we see it, the aggregate functional and institutional regularities which are the starting point of most regulation models[6] could possibly be shown to be emergent properties of underlying, explicitly microfounded, evolutionary models, appropriately enriched in their institutional specifications.

Take for example the Verdoorn–Kaldor functional form relating productivity growth and income growth which is postulated in regulation models. Evolutionary models are in principle suited to establishing the microeconomic conditions under which it emerges in the aggregate as a stable relation: for example what are the micro-learning processes that sustain it? What happens to its form and parametrizations if one varies the underlying mechanisms of search and sources of technological opportunities? Under what circumstances can one identify phenomena of 'symmetry breaking' engendered by microfluctuations and yielding the transition to different structural forms?

Similarly, with respect to wage formation mechanisms, the 'structural forms' in the regulation account tend to postulate aggregate invariances, say in the elasticities of wages to unemployment, prices and productivity. Conversely, evolution-inspired models of the labour market and labour processes (still to be built!) might well account for the conditions of their emergence, stability and crises. And the same could be said for most other primary building blocks of regulation models.

Of course we do not want to push the 'emergence philosophy' too far. It would be naive to think that straightforward links between levels of description can be made without resorting to a lot of further 'phenomenological', history-based, specifications. Jokingly, we illustrate all this with the parallel of the cow. If anyone is asked to describe what a cow is, it would be silly to start from a quantum mechanics account of the atoms composing it, and then move on to the levels of atoms, molecules, cells ... all the way to the morphological description of the cow. However the example is handy because it illustrates, first, the consistency in principle between the different levels of description; second, the fact that a good deal of higher-level properties (for example, concerning cells' self-maintenance) can be understood as emerging properties from lower-level dynamics; and, third, that without a lot of additional 'phenomenological' information, generic emergent properties are not enough to determine why that animal is a cow and not an elephant or a bird.

Admittedly, in economics we are very far from such a consistency across levels of descriptions (and certainly the compression to one single ahistorical level that the neoclassical tradition has taught us did not help). However, we want to suggest that a theory-informed dialogue between bottom-up (microfounded, and so on) evolutionary approaches and more top-down (aggregate, albeit institutionally richer) regulation ones is likely to be a formidable but analytically promising challenge.[7] Not only would it help to rigorously define the bridges between micro behaviours and entities at different levels of aggregation, but it would also highlight potential conflicts of interpretation which are currently often confused by level-of-description issues. Having said that, a few unresolved questions and areas of possible conflict come to mind.

The Descriptive Counterparts of Socio-Economic Regimes

We have already mentioned earlier that, in a sense, the regulation approach sets itself the ambitious task of dissecting the anatomy of discrete regimes of growth. But then, it seems to us, a unavoidable task is the empirical *and statistical* identification of these regimes. Some work has been done in this direction, concerning especially long-term wage dynamics, but also labour productivity and demand formation (for surveys, see Chapter 10 by C. Leroy, Chapter 22 by M. Juillard and Chapter 23 by B. Amable in Boyer and Saillard

(1995), and also Boyer (1988b)). However, a lot remains to be done – difficult as it is. For example, if phases of development and crises are traced back to the properties of underlying regimes, how are they revealed by the dynamics of statistical aggregates? And which ones? And at which level of aggregation? (for example, are GDP series too noisy and unprecise so that one should look at sectoral data?) Or is one forced to the conclusion that current econometric methods are ill-suited to detect changes which appear very important when inspecting qualitatively 'how the economy works', but are blurred by statistical noise in the reported series?

An answer to these questions will help a lot in pinning down the common objects of interpretation (and also in revealing the comparative merits of an institutionalist approach to macroeconomics as compared to more traditional ones). Moreover, a crucial part of the regulationist exercise involves the mapping of socio-economic regimes into dynamic properties of the system. But then a lot more work is required to find statistical proxies for those regimes themselves (this mirrors the effort that scholars in the evolutionary tradition have started putting into the statistical identification of 'technological regimes'; cf. Malerba and Orsenigo (1994)).

The Institutional Specifications of the Evolutionary Model

In a sort of complementary way, in order to start talking about (roughly) the same things, it is urgent that a new generation of evolutionary models begins experimenting systematically with variations in the institutional contexts in which evolutionary processes are embedded. One can think of different ways of doing it (corresponding also to different degrees of difficulty). First, holding constant the system parameters concerning, for example, notional technological opportunities, one may ask what happens to aggregate dynamics if one changes behavioural routines (an early example is in Chiaromonte *et al.* (1992)), and the constraints on those routines themselves (well expanding upon the exercise of Nelson and Winter (1982) regarding different financial constraints on borrowed funds). Second, even holding routines constant, one should experiment with different interaction environments (for example, centralized versus pairwise forms of interaction; price-based competition versus selection based on multidimensional product attributes; bank-based versus market-based access to finance; and so on). In fact a major claim of both evolutionary and regulation theories is that markets are themselves institutional constructions whose organizational details deeply affect collective outcomes. However one knows very little of how markets actually work[8] and even less does one have taxonomies of sort of 'archetypes' of markets which can thereafter be stylized and formally explored. Third, one might allow for routines themselves to be learnt in different institutional environments.[9] That would imply, in turn, the identification of distinct learning procedures in different environments. Fourth (and harder), it might be time to explore in an evolutionary perspective other domains of economic activity (for example, the labour market, financial markets, the endogenous dynamics of consumer preferences, and so on).

Some Possible Misunderstandings: Microfoundations, Representative Agents and Methodological Individualism

In the argument so far, an implicit assumption has been that the degrees of 'bottom-up-ness' or 'top-down-ness' (including the presence and details of interactions among lower-level entities with emergence of higher-level properties) is essentially conditional on the levels and modes of description themselves.

So, for example, we do not have any problem in acknowledging the descriptive power of the now-discredited Keynesian 'income multipliers', as a concise way of accounting – under historical conditions to be specified – for a specific relationship between modal behaviours of 'firms' and 'consumers'. In turn, such an aggregate description implies, of course, that functional roles in society count. (Here there should be little disagreement between the evolutionary and regulation approaches). The underlying idea is that an economic agent, Mr Jones – even when he is at the same time a worker at factory X, a shareholder of company Y which owns that factory, and a consumer of the products of that factory and of many other ones will behave according to modal patterns deriving from an institution-shaped logic of appropriateness, as James March puts it (how should Jones, as a consumer or as a worker, behave?). Most likely what Mr Jones does as a worker ought to be interpreted on the grounds of the collective history of many Mr Joneses, their experiences at the workplace, their successes and failures in industrial bargaining, etc. Analogously, the same should apply to his behaviour as a consumer or a shareholder. The basic point here is that a reduction of Mr Jones' behaviour to a coherent exercise of utility-maximization in a largely institution-free environment misses the point and is interpretatively misleading or, at best, void of any descriptive content. Mr Jones might, for example, feel safe to buy shares of very conservative companies in order to ensure a rosy retirement age, fight in the meantime at the workplace against the very practices that these same companies try to implement, and buy Japanese products even when that endangers the wealth possibly stemming from the companies whose shares he bought.

Having said that, however, it seems to us that the hypothesis of institutional embeddedness of social behaviours – largely shared by the evolutionary and regulationist approaches – cannot be pushed to the dangerous borders of some renewed functionalism. There is some echo of all that when one finds a too cavalier use of sorts of 'functional representative agents' in regulationist interpretations ('the behaviour of the Fordist firm', 'the unionized worker', and so on). If anything, those stylized behavioural archetypes ought to be considered as rough first approximations, demanding further investigations into their microfoundations and the conditions of their sustainability over time. For example, under what context conditions will the behaviours of many Mr Joneses (or, for that matter, of many firms 'Jones Inc.') remain relatively invariant over time? What are the conditions on interactions and statistical aggregation which sustain relatively invariant mean behaviours? And, conversely, under what circumstances do non-average behaviours induce symmetry-breaking and, possibly, phase transitions? (Note that this last issue is particularly relevant when accounting for the dynamics across different regimes). Certainly, we share Boyer and Saillard's general conjecture that

> a mode of *regulation* elicits a set of procedures and individual and collective behaviours which ought at the same time to reproduce [particular] social relations . . . and sustain the prevailing regime of accumulation. Moreover, a mode of regulation must assure the compatibility among a collection of decentralized decisions, without necessarily requiring the acknowledgment by the agents of the principles which govern the dynamics of the system as a whole. (Boyer and Saillard (1995), p. 64, our translation)

Work to support this claim (at both levels of empirical investigations and formal modelling) is urgently needed, and in our view is also another area of fruitful complementarity between 'evolutionists' and 'regulationists'.

In this respect, a possible misunderstanding has to be dispelled. The requirement of microfoundations of aggregate statements (that is, foundations in what a multitude of agents actually do and, possibly, think), which we have emphasized throughout this work, must not at all be considered equivalent to any advocacy for foundations into any 'methodological individualism'. The latter, in its canonic form, requires, first, that any collective state of the system ought to be explained on the grounds of what people contributing with their actions to determine that state think and do; and, second, that these micro 'thoughts', strategies and actions are the primitives of the theory. Our claim is much weaker. We share, in principle, the first requirement,[10] but we strongly deny the second. So for example, we are perfectly happy with 'microfoundations' which are themselves macrofounded, that is, where what 'people think and do' is *deeply but imperfectly* shaped by the organization and states of the system itself.

As an illustration consider the following toy model. Take a competitive world (as similar as possible to a Temporary General Equilibrium, of pure exchange – in order to make things simple). Suppose the state of the system, $s(0)$ at time $t(0)$ is defined by a price vector $p(0)$ and allocations $\omega_i(0)$ to each agent $i,(\omega_i \varepsilon \Omega(0))$. As usual, given prices and allocations, preference relations will determine the demand functions. If we specify a mechanism of exchange (which indeed the theory seldom does) this yields well-defined transition laws to the price sequence p(1), p(2) . . . and Ω(1), Ω(2) . . . (the subsequent allocations). This is obviously a microfounded story. However, add to the story that the *preference relations themselves* depend, imperfectly, on the lagged p( ) and Ω( ), for example, because of phenomena of reduction of cognitive dissonance ('. . . don't desire what you were not able to get . . . '), social imitation, learning-how-to-like-what-you-have, and so on. In this case, we still have a microfounded story, but of course (a) individual preferences stop being a 'primitive' of the explanation, and (b) we have here a sort of 'macrofoundation of the micro', in the sense that what micro entities do is to a good extent determined by the collective history of the system itself.[11] This metaphor, we suggest, is of wide applicability, well-beyond the foregoing caricatural example.

A Crossroad for Dialogue (or Conflict): The Nature of Economic Routines

We have mentioned earlier that both evolutionary and regulation approaches share the idea that a good deal of individual and collective behaviours are 'boundedly rational', context-dependent and relatively inertial over time, shaped as they are by equally inertial institutions in which they are embedded. In a word, both approaches share the view that a good deal of the reproduction of the socio-economic fabric rests on the development and implementation of organizational routines. However, as we discuss at much greater length in Coriat and Dosi (1995), most organizational routines entail a double nature: on the one hand, they store and reproduce problem-solving competences, while, at the same time, they are also mechanisms of governance of potentially conflictual relations.

As it happens, the evolutionary approach has focused almost exclusively on the 'cognitive' aspects of routines (and by doing that has begun to open interesting avenues of dialogue with disciplines like cognitive psychology and artificial intelligence), but it has largely neglected the dimensions of power and control intertwined into the routines themselves.[12]

Almost the opposite applies to the regulation approach, which has tended to emphasize the requirements of social coherence implied by routines, but has not paid much attention to their knowledge content.

All this might be all right again as a first approximation but it is clearly unsatisfactory as an end result in either approach. Pushing it to the extreme, in the former perspective, an answer to the question of 'how Renault (or GM or United Biscuits ...) behaves' is inclined to account for operating procedures, mechanisms of knowledge accumulation, learning strategies, and so on leaving in the background phenomena like the conflict between different social groups, the links that particular organizational rules bear with income distribution and the exercise of power (well beyond their knowledge content), and so on. Conversely, the regulationist answer, by putting most of the emphasis on the latter phenomena, tends to convey the idea that governance is the paramount role of routines, quite irrespectively of the fact that Renault or GM have to know how to produce cars and United Biscuits cakes, and they have got to do it well, and better over time. The risks of one-sided accounts are particularly great when accounting for the *origins* of routines themselves, with an evolutionary inclination to trace them back to cognitive dynamics only, and the regulationists feeling a bit too comfortable with a reduction of the problem to a selection dynamics among well-specified menus of actions/strategies/conventions.[13]

We argue in Coriat and Dosi (1995) that the double nature of routines, and related to this the double marks on their origins, are challenging points of encounter between the evolutionist and institutionalist research programmes. Or, conversely, it could be the crossroad where the former take some sort of 'hypercognitive' route, whereby microeconomics and cognitive psychology tend to simply merge, and regulationists could well discover that 'methodological individualism' and weaker forms of 'neo-institutionalism' (cf. Table 1.1) are not so bad after all.

7. SOME CONCLUSIONS: TOWARDS A DEMANDING AND EXCITING INTERBREEDING?

Notwithstanding a series of important analytical issues – which might indeed be a source of serious interpretative conflict, and of which we have provided some illustrations – we do see an ideal sequence of modes of interpretation and levels of description in which both the evolutionist and regulationist programmes could ambitiously fit. As sketched in Table 1.2, they run from a sort of 'nano-economics', wherein the abandonment of any magic of a perfect and invariant rationality forces a dialogue with cognitive and social psychology, organization theory, and sociology, all the way to grand historical conjectures on the long-term destinies of contemporary forms of socio-economic organization. Even a quick look at the table highlights the enormous gaps between what we know and what such an ideal evolutionary-institutionalist research programme would demand. These gaps are high at all levels but in our view four issues are particularly urgent on the agenda.

A first one concerns co-evolutionary processes. The essence of the co-evolutionary point is that what happens in each partly autonomous domain of the system (for example, technology or institutional structures) shapes and constrains what is going to happen in the other ones. Hence, the overall dynamics is determined by the ways each domain evolves but also by the ways the various domains are coupled with each other.[14] We have listed 'co-evolution' under a separate level or description in order to demarcate that broad area

Table 1.2 *Levels of analysis*

	Objects of analysis (some still to be explored)	Examples of 'analytical styles'
Level 0 – From nanoeconomics to microeconomics	(i) Nature and origins of routines and, generally, behavioural norms (ii) Learning processes (iii) Mechanisms of expectation formation (iv) Nature and evolution of microorganizations (e.g. business firms) (v) Embedding mechanisms of individual behaviours into the institutional context (vi) The evolution of criteria of actions and 'visions of the world'	From H. Simon to Holland *et al.* (1986); microanalytic part of Nelson and Winter (1982); Cohen and Bacdayan (1994); Egidi (1994); organizational economic 'competences', and so on; Coriat (1994b); Dosi *et al.* (1994b); Marengo (1992); Warglien (1995); Marengo and Tordjman (1996); Possible economic applications of Fontana and Buss (1994a and b); and a lot to be done
Level 1 – From microeconomics to aggregate properties	(i) Generic properties of growth fuelled by technical changes (ii) Industrial evolution (iii) Self-organizing properties of labour markets (iv) The dynamics of consumption patterns	Explicit microfounded models with aggregate emergent statistical properties, for example, Nelson and Winter (1982); Silverberg and Verspagen (1994); Lesourne (1991); Dosi *et al.* (1995)
Level 2 – Aggregate dynamics	(i) Functional relations among aggregate variables (ii) Socio-economic regimes: consistency conditions among processes of economic adjustment and institutions	More 'stylized' but (hopefully) institutionally richer macro models (necessarily microfounded): from Keynesian/Kaldorian models to Boyer (1988a/b) and Silverberg (1987)
Level 3 – 'Co-evolution'	(i) Co-evolutionary patterns between technologies, corporate organizations and broader institutions (ii) Coupled institutional dynamics (iii) 'Political discretionality' and institutional inertias	A lot of appreciative theorizing from historians but relatively little modelling (but see the suggestion in Nelson (1994) on industrial dynamics); a vast regulation-inspired empirical literature (cf. Boyer and Saillard (1995))
Level 4 – 'Grand history'	General interpretative conjectures on long-term historical patterns	From Karl Marx ... Schumpeter ... to Freeman and Perez (1988) ... to Aglietta (1982) and Boyer and Mistral (1978) (just to name the perspectives discussed in the work)

22

covering, for example, the interactions between the forms of economic organization, social and political institutions and technical change. However, co-evolutionary issues appear at all levels of description. For example, the emergence and development of each industry ought to be seen as a co-evolutionary process between technologies, corporate organizations and supporting institutions (Nelson (1994)). Analogously, the origins of organizational routines (cf. above) is intimately a co-evolutionary process, shaped by diverse and probably conflicting selection criteria (that is, problem-solving versus governance requirements).

A second (and related) item which is high on the research agenda considers the transition across different socio-economic regimes of growth: for example, at which level can such transitions be detected? (This will probably be conditional on the type of transition one is talking about.) What are the effects of 'higher-level' changes (for example, in the institutional set-ups or in the policy environment) upon microeconomic behaviour? And, conversely, under what circumstances do non-average microbehaviours become 'autocatalytic' and eventually induce higher-level phase transitions? What kind of co-evolutionary processes do particular classes of transitions entail?

A third priority item, in our view, concerns what could be called, in shorthand, the relationships between emergence and embeddedness, or, putting it another way, the role of 'bottom-up' processes shaping/generating higher-level entities (or at least aggregate statistical patterns) versus 'top-down' processes by which higher-level entities (for example, institutions, established mechanisms of interaction, etc.) shape/generate 'lower level' behaviours. One of the claims underlying this whole chapter is that the links work both ways and that one ought to account for 'macrofoundation of the micro' as well as 'microfoundations of the macro'. But how does one get beyond suggestive metaphors and elaborate more rigorous, albeit highly simplified, models which nonetheless capture the intuition? (Note that what we mean is something more than a feedback between a system-level state variable (say, a price or a market share) and the argument of an individual decision algorithm (say, pricing or investment rules): somewhat deeper, we think it is not beyond reach to develop models whereby micro decision algorithms themselves are shaped by macro states and, conversely, possibly non-linear interactions among the former change collective interaction rules/constraints/perceived payoffs/perceived opportunities.) But in turn, all this involves difficult issues concerning, again, coordination; relative time-scales of change; relative invariances of 'structures' and conditions of their stability.

Fourth, we suggest that the nature of learning processes, too, ought to deserve priority attention. As Lundvall (in this volume) emphasizes the *objects of learning* ('know what', 'know why', 'know how', 'know who' . . .) are likely to discriminate among classes of learning processes. And, certainly, the competence gap between the intrinsic complexity of any one cognition/decision problem at hand and the pre-existing abilities of (individual or collective) agents fundamentally shapes learning processes (for a discussion, cf. Dosi and Egidi (1991)). But, in turn, it is only a weird twist of contemporary economic thought that gives credibility to the idea that incrementalist procedures, either based on sophisticated hypothesis testing (such as in Bayesian models) or stimulus–response reinforcements, are the general paradigm of learning (note that this applies to 'evolutionary games', but also to most evolutionary models in general) that one has developed so far.[15]

As a way forward, we suggest, possibly building upon preliminary (and still very rudimentary) attempts by, among others, Marengo (1992), Egidi (1994), Cohen and Bacdayan (1994), Marengo and Tordjman (1996) and also Dosi *et al.* (1994c), a priority task is to account for the formation and collective establishment of cognitive categories, problem-solving procedures (routines?) and expectations about the identities and behaviours of other social actors.[16]

Yes, all this is an enormous task. Very fascinating and extremely difficult. The way we see it pursued, it involves tight and troublesome interchanges between empirical investigations, 'appreciative theorizing' and formal modelling efforts. It is likely also to involve major adjustments in the building blocks of institutionalist/evolutionary theories themselves.

We are probably now witnessing a rare window of opportunity for fulfilling the promise of making economics an 'evolutionary/institutionalist discipline'. The blame for failing to do so will fall mainly on ourselves, rather than the sectarian attitudes of chair committees or international journal editors.

NOTES

Support for this research from the Italian Ministry of Universities and Research (MURST, 'Progetti 40%') and from the International Institute for Applied Systems Analysis (IIASA), Laxenburg, Austria, is gratefully acknowledged. An earlier version of this chapter has appeared in French in Boyer and Saillard (1995).

1. Note, however, that there are a few 'aggregate' (that is, non-microfounded) models which are nonetheless 'evolutionary' in spirit (for a survey, see Silverberg and Verspagen (1995)).
2. On the notions of 'emergence' and 'metastability' cf. the discussion in Lane (1993).
3. Note that, given the above quite broad definition of the evolutionary research programme, it may well describe also the contributions of authors who would not call themselves 'evolutionist' in any strict sense.
4. To repeat, this is not meant to be a thorough review but just an approximate roadmap. Moreover, at least a partial overlap with the evolutionary archetype can be found in quite diverse fields of economic theory: see for example Aoki (1995) and Stiglitz (1994).
5. A related perspective, which it is not possible to discuss here, pursued especially by 'radical' American economists, is known as the theory of 'Social Structures of Accumulation'. See for example Bowles and Gintis (1993) and the references therein.
6. Note that we do not mean only formal, mathematically expressed, 'models', but also rigorous, albeit verbally expressed, theory-based propositions about whatever phenomena.

7. Broad historical interpretations building upon a *lato sensu* evolutionary microeconomics, such as Freeman and Perez (1988), might be considered as another point of departure of this dialogue.

8. A noticeable exception is Kirman and Vignes (1992) on the fish market in Marseille (!).

9. A simple adaptive learning mechanism nested in a macro model is presented in Silverberg and Verspagen (1995b). Much more constructive models of behavioural learning are in Marengo (1992), Marengo and Tordjman (1996) and Dosi *et al.* (1994c), but they are far from any macro model. Moreover, they, too, lack experiments on different institutional specifications.

   Note that, here, by routines we specifically mean those rules of thumb concerning such things as pricing, R&D, investments, and so on. It is a fundamental point of evolutionary theories that different techniques are intimately associated also with different production routines. And, indeed, the models provide a representation of the dynamics of the latter via a low-dimensional representation of search outcomes in the technology space. However, a major step forward would be an explicit account of the dynamics of the underlying problem-solving routines (see also below).

10. We also want to emphasize the fact that we share the requirement *in principle*, even if it might turn out that in many circumstances the micro–macro link turns out to be practically impossible. It is a circumstance familiar also to natural sciences where it is often the case that one can write the aggregate statistical properties (say, in a thermodynamic problem) without being able to derive them from an underlying micro description (say, detailed balance equations).

11. We have repeatedly stressed the *imperfect* adaptation of agents to the macro configurations of the system. A perfect adaptation would indeed imply a strong functionalist conjecture ('people do and think what they are supposed to do, given the functional requirements of the system itself'). In our view, on the contrary, it is precisely imperfect adaptation which is an important source of dynamics.

12. This notwithstanding the acknowledgment of their importance: cf. for example, Nelson and Winter's definition of routines as truces among conflicting interests (Nelson and Winter (1982)).

13. In turn, as known, once the problem is posed in these terms it can be formally handled by means, for example, of 'evolutionary games' (cf. Boyer and Orlean (1992) for such an attempt). Far from denying the usefulness of such exercises as sorts of gedankenexperiment on collective adaptation under potential conflict of interests (or conflicts between individual incentives and collective good), they still deliver a quite partial picture of the object of inquiry. For example, in the current state of the art we do not know of any model allowing for adaptation on preferences themselves (i.e. in game terms, endogenously evolving payoff matrices). Neither there is the discovery of new 'strategies' (with the exception of Lindgren (1992)). And finally, 'learning' tends to neglect any cognitive/problem-solving aspect and be reduced to a stimulus–response mechanism of reinforcement (possibly mitigated by stochastic search or mistakes).

14. A co-evolutionary view runs against, for example, 'technological determinism' (that is, technology proceeds exclusively according to its inner logics, and institutions ought simply to adjust, with varying lags) but also 'social determinism' (for example, technology is purely a 'social construction'). On the contrary, the co-evolutionary view does accept that technological change and social change have their own inner logics (possibly conflicting with each other) and does attempt to explain, for example, the emerging trajectories of technical change as the outcome of such a coupling.

15. Incidentally, 'Bayesian' and 'Pavlovian' learning have most characteristics in common since both claim (i) what Savage would have called a 'small world' hypothesis (the notional set of events and response strategies is given from the start); and (ii) there is a striking transparence of the links between actions and consequences. Hence, ultimately, the difference between the two just rests on what the theorist assumes the agent to consciously know, without much influence on the ultimate outcomes. So, for example, it is easy for biologists overwhelmed by economists' fascination to build models of rats who behave in equilibrium 'as if' understanding strategies involving first-order conditions and Lagrange multipliers, or conversely, respectable economists claiming 'Pavlovian' convergence to sophisticated Rational Expectation equilibria.

16. By way of a comparison, recall that even in the most sophisticated state-of-the-art accounts, in economics, of behaviours and interactions (even under conditions of imperfect information) agents are assumed to *obviously* have the correct 'transparent' understanding of the causal links of the environment, and to *obviously* know how to solve the technical problems at hand.

REFERENCES

Abramovitz, M. (1989), *Thinking about Growth*, Cambridge/New York: Cambridge University Press.

Aglietta, M. (1974), *Accumulation et regulation du capitalisme en longue période. L'exemple des Etats-Unis (1870–1970)*, thesis, Paris, October.

Aglietta, M. (1982), *Regulation and Crisis of Capitalism*, New York, Monthly Review Press.

Aglietta, M. (1993), 'La finance au Japon, Changements de structures·et adaptations des comportements'. Communication au colloque, 'Mode de regulation au Japon et Relations Internationales: de l'histoire longue aux transformations recentes', *Japon in Extenso, Revue*, No. 33, 1994.

Amendola, G., G. Dosi and E. Papagni (1993), 'The dynamics of international competitiveness', *Weltwirtschaftliches Archiv*.

Aoki, M. (1995), 'Unintended Fit: Organisational Evolution and Government Design of Institutions in Japan', Working Paper, Department of Economics, Stanford University.

Arthur, B., Y. Ermoliev and Y. Kaniovski (1987), 'Path-dependent processes and the emergence of macrostructures', *European Journal of Operations Research*, 30, 294–303.

Basalla, G. (1988), *The Evolution of Technology*, Cambridge, Cambridge University Press.

Basle, M., J. Mazier and J.F. Vidal (1984), 'Quand les crise durent ... ', *Economica*, Paris.

Bowles, S. and H. Gintis (1993), 'The revenge of homo economicus: contested exchange and the revival of political economy', *Journal of Economic Perspectives*, 7, 83–102.

Boyer. R. (1978), 'La crise: une mise en perspective historique', *Critique de l'Economie Politique, Revue*, Paris.

Boyer, R. (1986a), *La Théorie de la Regulation, une analyse critique*, Paris: La Découverte.

Boyer, R. (1986b), *La Théorie du travail en Europe*, Paris: La Découverte.

Boyer, R. (1987), 'Regulation', in *The New Palgrave*, London: Macmillan.

Boyer, R. (1988a), 'Technical change and the theory of "Regulation"', in Dosi *et al.* (1988).

Boyer, R. (1988b), 'Formalizing growth regimes', in Dosi *et al.* (1988).

Boyer, R. (1990), *The Regulation School: A Critical Introduction*, New York, Columbia University Press.

Boyer, R. and J. Mistral (1978), *Accumulation, inflation et crise*, Paris: Puf.

Boyer, R. and A. Orlean (1991), 'Les transformations des conventions salariales entre Théorie et histoire. D'Henry Ford au fordisme', *Revue Economique*, 42(2) (Mars), 233–72.

Boyer, R. and A. Orlean (1992), 'How Do Conventions Evolve?', *Journal of Evolutionary Economics*.

Boyer, R. and Y. Saillard (eds) (1995), *Théorie de la Regulation. L'état des savoir*, Paris: La Découvert.

Caroli, E. (1995), *Formation, Institutions et Croissance Economique*, These IEP, Paris.

CEPREMAP (1977), *Approches de l'inflation: l'exemple francais*, Convention de recherches no. 22, mimeo, December.

Chiaromonte, F. and G. Dosi (1993), 'Heterogeneity, Competition and Macroeconomic Dynamics', *Structural Change and Economic Dynamics*, 4, 39–6.

Chiaromonte, F., G. Dosi and L. Orsenigo (1992), 'Innovative learning and institutions in the process of development: on the microfoundations of growth regimes', in R. Thomson (ed.), *Learning and Technological Change*, London, Macmillan.

Cohen, M. and P. Bacdayan (1994), 'Organizational routines as stored procedural memory: evidence from a laboratory study', *Organization Sciences*, 5, 554–68.

Commons, J.R. (1934), *Institutional Economics*, University of Wisconsin Press, Madison.

Conlisk, J. (1989), 'An aggregate model of technical change', *Quarterly Journal of Economics*, 104, 787–821.

Coriat, B. (1982), *L'atelier et le Chronomètre*, Paris: Bourgeois.

Coriat, B. (1990), *L'atelier et le Robot*, Paris: Bourgeois.

Coriat, B. (1991–94), *Penser à l'Envers – Travail et Organisation dans la firme Japonaise,* C. Bourgois; 2nd revised edition Bourgois/Choix 1994.

Coriat, B. (1993), 'L'hypothèse du Compagnie-isme', *Mondes en Developpement Revue*, no. 4, Paris.

Coriat, B. (1994a), 'La Théorie de la Régulation. Origines, Specificites, Enjeux', in *Future Antérieur,* Paris, L'Harmattan; special issue of *Théorie de la Regulation et critique de la Raison Economique.*

Coriat, B. (1994b), 'Variety, routines and networks: the metamorphosis of the Fordist firms', *Industrial and Corporate Change*, 4(1), Oxford University Press.

Coriat, B. and G. Dosi (1995), 'Learning How to Govern and Learning How to Solve Problems. On the Coevolution of Competences, Conflicts and Organisational Routines', IIASA Working Paper, WP-95-06, Laxenburg, Austria; forthcoming in A. Chandler, P. Hagström and Ö. Sölvell (eds), *The Dynamic Firm*, Oxford, Oxford University Press.

Coriat, B. and O. Weinstein (1995), *Les nouvelles Theories de l'Entreprise*, Paris: Hachette.

David, P. (1975), *Technical Choice, Innovation and Economic Growth*, Cambridge: Cambridge University Press.

David, P.A. (1985), 'Clio and the Economics of QWERTY', *American Economic Review. Papers and Proceedings*, (75), 332–7.

David, P.A. (1992), 'Heroes, herds and hysteresis in technological change: Thomas Edison and the battle of the systems', *Industrial and Corporate Change*, 1, 139–80.

David, P.A. (1994), 'Why are institutions the carriers of history?', *Structural Change and Economic Dynamics.*

Day, R. and G. Eliasson (eds) (1986), *The Dynamics of Market Economics*, Amsterdam: North Holland.

Delorme, R. and C. André (1983), *L'Etat et l'Economie*, Paris: Seuil.

DiMaggio, P.J. and W.W. Powell (1991), 'The iron cage revisited: institutional isomorphism and collective rationality in organisational fields', in W.W. Powell and P.J. DiMaggio (eds), *The New Institutionalism in Organisational Analysis*, Chicago: University of Chicago Press.

Dosi, G. (1982), 'Technical paradigms and technical trajectories. A suggested interpretation of the Determinants and Directions of technical change and the transformation of the economy', *Research Policy,* March.

Dosi, G. (1984), Technical Change and Industrial Transformation, London: Macmillan.

Dosi, G. (1988), 'Sources, procedures and microeconomic effects of innovation', *Journal of Economic Literature*, 26, 126–73.

Dosi, G. (1991), 'Perspectives on evolutionary theory', *Science and Public Policy*.

Dosi, G. (1995), 'Hierarchies, markets and power: some foundational issues on the nature of contemporary economic organisations', *Industrial and Corporate Change*, (4), 1–19.

Dosi, G. and M. Egidi (1991), 'Substantive and procedural uncertainty. An exploration of economic behaviours in changing environments', *Journal of Evolutionary Economics*.

Dosi. G. and L. Marengo (1994), 'Some elements of an evolutionary theory of organisational competences', in R.W. England (ed.), *Evolutionary Concepts in Contemporary Economics*, Ann Arber: University of Michigan Press.

Dosi, G. and R.R. Nelson (1994), 'An introduction to evolutionary theories in economics', *Journal of Evolutionary Economics*, 4, 153–72.

Dosi, G., K. Pavitt and L. Soete (1990), *The Economics of Technological Change and International Trade*, Brighton: Wheatsheaf; New York: New York University Press.

Dosi, G., S. Fabiani, R. Aversi and M. Meacci (1994a), 'The dynamics of international differentiation: a multi-country evolutionary model', *Industrial and Corporate Change*, 3, 225–42.

Dosi, G., C. Freeman and S. Fabiani (1994b), 'The process of economic development: introducing some stylized facts and theories on technologies, firms and institutions', *Industrial and Corporate Change*, 3, 1–46.

Dosi, G., L. Marengo, A. Bassanini and M. Valente (1994c), 'Norms as Emergent Properties of Adaptive Learning. The Case of Economic Routines', Working Paper, WP-94 -73, Laxenburg, Austria.

Dosi, G., O. Marsili, L. Orsenigo and R. Salvatore (1995), 'Learning, market selection and the evolution of industrial structures', *Small Business Economics*.

Dosi, G., C. Freeman, R.R.Nelson, G. Silverberg and L. Soete (eds) (1988), *Technical Change and Economic Theory*, London: Francis Pinter; New York: Columbia University Press.

Dupuy, J.P. (1980), 'Convention et Common Knowledge', *Revue économique*, 40(2), 381–400.

Dupuy, J.P., F. Emard-Duvernay, O. Favereau, A. Orlean, R. Salais and L. Thevenot (1989), 'L'économie des conventions', *Revue economique*, 40(2).

Eggertsson, T. (1990), *Economic Behaviour and Institutions*, Cambridge: Cambridge University Press.

Egidi, M. (1994), 'Routines, Hierarchies of Problems, Procedural Behaviour: Some Evidence from Experiments', IIASA Working Paper WP-94-58, Laxenburg, Austria.

Eliasson, G. (1986), 'Micro-heterogeneity of firms and stability of industrial growth', in R. Day and G. Eliasson (eds), *The Dynamics of Market Economics*, Amsterdam: North Holland.

England, R.W. (ed.) (1994), *Evolutionary Concepts in Contemporary Economics*, Ann Arbor: University of Michigan Press.

Fagerberg, J. (1994), 'Technology and international differences in growth rates', *Journal of Economic Literature*, 32, 1147–75.

Favereau, O. (1986), 'La formalisation du role des conventions dans l'allocation des ressources', in R. Salais (ed.), *Le travail. Marches, règles, conventions*, Paris: INSEE-Economica.

Fontana, W. and L. Buss (1994a), '"The arrival of the fittest": toward a theory of biological organisation', *Bulletin of Mathematical Biology*, 1–64.

Fontana, W. and L. Buss (1994b), 'What would be conserved if the "Tape Were Run Twice!"', *Proc, Nat. Acad. Sci.*, USA.

Freeman, C. (1982), *The Economics of Industrial Innovation*, 2nd edn, London: Francis Pinter.

Freeman, C. (1994), 'The economics of technical change', *Cambridge Journal of Economics*, 18, 463–514.

Freeman. C. and C. Perez (1988), 'Structural crises of adjustment', in Dosi *et al.* (1988).

Granovetter, M. (1985), 'Economic action and social structure: the problem of embeddedness', *American Journal of Sociology*, 91, 481–510.

Granstrand, O. (ed.) (1994), *The Economics of Technology*, Amsterdam, Elsevier/North Holland.

Grendstad, G. and P. Selle (1995), 'Cultural theory and the new institutionalism', *Journal of Theoretical Politics*, (7), 5–27.

Hamilton, G.G. and R.C. Feenstra (1995), 'Variety of hierarchies and markets: an introduction', *Industrial and Corporate Change*, 4, 51–91.

Hanusch, H. (ed.) (1988), *Evolutionary Economics*, Cambridge: Cambridge University Press.

Hayek, F. (1937), 'Economics and Knowledge', *Economica*, 4.

Hodgson, G. (1988). *Economics and Institutions*, Cambridge: Polity Press; Philadelphia: University of Pennsylvania Press.

Hodgson, G. (1993), *Economics and Evolution*, Cambridge: Polity Press; Ann Arbor: Michigan University Press.

Holland, J.H., K.J. Holyoak, R.E. Nisbett and P.R. Thagaro (1986), *Induction*, Cambridge, Mass.: MIT Press.

Jessop, B. (1990), 'Regulation theories in retrospect and prospect', *Economy and Society*, 19(2), 153–216.

Kandori, M., G.J. Mailath and R. Rob (1993), 'Learning, mutation and long run equilibria in games', *Econometrica*, 61, 29–56.

Kaniovski, Y. and P. Young (1995), 'Learning Dynamics in Games with Stochastic Perturbations', *Games and Economic Behaviour*.

Kirman, A.P. and A. Vignes (1992), 'Price dispersion: theoretical considerations and empirical evidence from the Marseille fish market', in K. Arrow (ed.), *Issues in Contemporary Economics*, vol.I, London: Mcmillan.

Klepper, S. (1993), 'Entry, Exit, Growth and Innovation over the Product Cycle', Carnegie-Mellon University, Working Paper.

Kuran, T. (1991), 'Cognitive limitations and preference evolution', *Journal of Institutional and Theoretical Economics.*

Lane, D. (1993), 'Artificial worlds and economics', Parts I and II, *Journal of Evolutionary Economics*, 3, 89–107 and 177–97.

Langlois, R.N. (ed.) (1986), *Economics as a Process: Essays in the New Institutional Economics*, Cambridge/New York: Cambridge University Press.

Lesourne, J. (1991), *Ordre et Désordre*, Paris: Economica.

Levinthal, D. (1990), 'Organisational adaptation and environmental selection: interrelated processes of change', *Organisation Science*, 2, 140–5.

Lewis, D.K. (1969), *Convention: A Philosophical Study*, Cambridge, Mass.: Harvard University Press.

Lindgren, R. (1992), 'Evolutionary phenomena in simple dynamics', in C.G. Langton (ed.), *Artificial Life II.*, Redwood City: Addison-Wesley.

Lordon, F. (1993), 'Endogenous Structural Change and Crisis in a Multiple Time-Scales Growth Model', CEPREMAP Working Paper 9324, Paris.

Lundvall, B.-Å. (ed.) (1992), *National Systems of Innovation*, London: Francis Pinter.

Malerba, F. and L. Orsenigo (1994), 'The Dynamics and Evolution of Industries', Laxenburg, Austria, IIASA, Working Paper, WP-94-120.

March, J.G. and J.P. Olsen (1989), *Rediscovering Institutions: The Organizational Basis of Policies*, New York: Free Press.

Marengo, L. (1992), 'Coordination and organisational learning in the firm', *Journal of Evolutionary Economics*, 2, 313–26.

Marengo, L. and H. Tordjman (1996), 'Speculation, Heterogeneity and Learning: A Model of Exchange Rate Dynamics', Kyklos.

Metcalfe, S. (1992), 'Variety, structure and change: an evolutionary perspective on the competitive process', *Revue d'Economie Industrielle*, 65, 46–61.

Mokyr, J. (1990), *The Lever of Riches*, Oxford: Oxford University Press.

Nakicenovic, N. and A. Grübler (eds) (1992), *Diffusion of Technologies and Social Behaviour,* Berlin/Heidelberg/New York: Springer Verlag.

Nelson, R.R. (1987), *Understanding Technical Change As An Evolutionary Process*, Amsterdam: North Holland.

Nelson, R.R. (ed.) (1993), *National Innovation Systems: A Comparative Study*, Oxford/New York: Oxford University Press.

Nelson, R.R. (1994),' The co-evolution of technology, industrial structure, and supporting institutions', *Industrial and Corporate Change*, 3, 47–63.

Nelson, R. (1995), 'Recent evolutionary theorizing about economic change', *Journal of Economic Literature*, 33, 48–90.

Nelson, R. and S. Winter (1982), *An Evolutionary Theory of Economic Change*, Cambridge, Mass.: Bellkap Press of Harvard University Press.

Nelson, R.R. and G. Wright (1992), 'The rise and fall of American technological leadership: the post-war era in historical perspective', *Journal of Economic Literature*, 30, 1931–64.

North, D. (1990), *Institutions, Institutional Change and Economic Performance*, Cambridge: Cambridge University Press.

North, D. (1991), 'Institutions', *Journal of Economic Perspectives*, 75, 264–74.

Orlean, A. (ed.) (1994), *L'économie des conventions*, Paris: PUF.

Palmer, R.G., W.B. Arthur, J.H. Holland, B. LeBaron and P. Taylor (1994), 'Artificial economic life: a simple model of a stockmarket', *Physica D*, 75, 264–74.

Patel, P. and K. Pavitt (1994), 'Uneven (and divergent) technological accumulation among advanced countries: evidence and a framework of explanation', *Industrial and Corporate Change*, 3, 759.

Pavitt, I. (1984), 'Sectoral patterns of innovation: toward a taxonomy and a theory', *Research Policy*, 13, 343–75.

Reynaud, B. (1992), *Le Salaire, La règle et Le Marché*, C. Bourgois: Paris.

Reynaud, B. (1992c), *Les nouvelles Théories du Salaire*, Paris: La Découverte, Collection Repères.

Rosenberg, N. (1976), *Perspectives on Technology*, Cambridge: Cambridge University Press.

Rosenberg, N. (1982), *Inside the Black Box*, Cambridge: Cambridge University Press.

Saviotti, P. and S. Metcalfe (eds) (1991), *Evolutionary Economies*, London/Chur: Harwood Academic Press.

Schwartz, M. and M. Thompson (1990), *Divided We Stand: Redefining Polities, Technology and Social Choice*, Brighton: Harvester Wheatsheaf.

Silverberg, G. (1987), 'Technical progress, capital accumulation and effective demand: a self-organization model', in D. Batten, J. Casti and B. Johansson (eds), *Economic Evolution and Structural Adjustment*, Berlin/New York: Springer Verlag.

Silverberg, G. and L. Soete (eds) (1993), *The Economics of Growth and Technical Change: Technologies, Nations, Agents*, Aldershot: Edward Elgar.

Silverberg, G. and B. Verspagen (1994), 'Learning, innovation and economic growth: a long-run model of industrial dynamics', *Industrial and Corporate Change*, 3, 199–223.

Silverberg, G. and B. Verspagen (1995a), 'Evolutionary Theorizing on Economic Growth', IIASA Working Paper WP-95-78j; forthcoming in K. Dopfer (ed.), *The Evolutionary Principles of Economics*, Kluwer.

Silverberg, G. and B. Verspagen (1995b), 'From the Artificial to the Endogenous: Modelling Evolutionary Adaptation and Economic Growth', IIASA, Working Paper, WP-95-, Laxenburg, Austria.

Silverberg, G., G. Dosi and L. Orsenigo (1988), 'Innovation, diversity and diffusion: a self-organisation model', *Economic Journal*, 98, 1032–54.

Solow, J.A. (1990), *The Labour Market as a Social Institution*, Basil Blackwell.

Stiglitz, J.E. (1994), 'Economic growth revisited', *Industrial and Corporate Change*, 3, 65–110.

Tordjman, H. (1993), *Dynamiques spéculations, hétérogénéité des agents et apprentissage: le cas des taux de change*, Thèse CEFI, Universite d'Aix-Marseille II, Janvier 1994.

Utterback, J. and F. Suarez (1992), 'Innovation, Competition and Market Structure', *Research Policy*, 21, 1–21.

Veblen, T. (1898), 'Why is economics not an evolutionary science?', *Quarterly Journal of Economics*, 12.

Verspagen, B. (1993), *Uneven Growth Between Independent Economics: The Evolutionary Dynamics of Growth and Technology*, Aldershot: Avebury.

Vincenti, W. (1990), *What Do Engineers Do and How Do They Know It?*, Baltimore: Johns Hopkins University Press.

Warglien, M. (1995), 'Hierarchical selection and organisational adaptation', *Industrial and Corporate Change*, 4, 161–86.

Williamson, O.E. (1975), *Market and Hierarchies*, New York: Free Press.

Williamson, O.E. (1985). *The Economic Institutions of Capitalism*, New York: Free Press.

Williamson, O.E. (1990). 'The firm as a nexus of treaties: an introduction', in M. Aoki, B. Gustafsson and O.E. Williamson (eds), *The Firm as a Nexus of Treaties*, London: Sage.

Williamson, O.E. and W.G. Ouchi (1981), 'The markets and hierarchies and visible hand perspectives', in A.H. van de Ven and W.F. Joice (eds), *Perspectives on Organisational Design and Behaviour*, New York: Wiley.

Williamson, O.E. (1995), 'Hierarchies, market and power in the economy: an economic perspective', *Industrial and Corporate Change*, 4, 21–50.

Williamson, O.W. and S.G. Winter (1991), *The Nature of the Firm: Origins, Evolution, and Development*, Oxford University Press.

Winter, S.G. (1964), 'Economical natural selection and the theory of the firm', *Yale Economic Essays*.

Winter, S.G. (1982), 'An essay on the theory of production', in S.H. Hymans (ed.), *Economics and the World around It*, Ann Arbor: University of Michigan Press.

Winter, S.G. (1984). 'Schumpeterian competition under alternative technological regimes', *Journal of Economic Behaviour and Organisation*, 5, 287–320.

Winter, S.G. (1986), 'The research program of the behavioural theory of the firm: orthodox critiques and evolutionary perspectives', in B. Gilad and S. Kaish (eds), *Handbook of Behavioural Economics*, Greenwich, Conn.: JAI Press.

Winter, S.G. (1987a), 'Natural selection and evolution', *New Palgrave*, 3, Macmillan.

Winter, S.G. (1987b), 'Competition and selection', *New Palgrave*, 2, Macmillan.

Winter, S.G. (1995), 'Four R's of Profitability: Rents, Resources, Routines and Replication', IIASA Working Paper, WP-95-07, Laxenburg, Austria.

Witt, U. (ed.) (1991), *Explaining Process and Change: Approaches to Evolutionary Economics*, Ann Arbor: University of Michigan Press.

Young, P. (1993), 'The evolution of conventions', *Econometrica*, 61, 59–84.

2. The learning economy: challenges to economic theory and policy

Bengt-Åke Lundvall

INTRODUCTION

In this chapter the focus is on new features in our societies which have to do with the changing roles of learning and knowledge in the economic process. Some of the new characteristics are reasonably well-established in theoretical and empirical terms. Others are less so, and some of the propositions should be regarded as conjectures based upon a personal interpretation of empirically based trends, especially new trends in the demand for labour.

The starting point is the assumption that the current economy is one where knowledge is the most strategic resource and learning the most important process. This observation has important implications for economic theory. It challenges the fundamental focus on scarcity in economic theory and it implies that the economic process can only be understood as being socially embedded.[1] It becomes important to distinguish new trends in the knowledge-base and their impact on the economy. In what follows we propose the following interpretations.

While the information technology revolution makes more kinds of knowledge codifiable, some elements of tacit knowledge become even more important for economic performance and success than before. The traditional dichotomy between collective and private knowledge is becoming less relevant. As indicated in a recent contribution by Kenneth Arrow (1994), hybrid forms of knowledge which are neither completely private nor completely public become increasingly important. More and more strategic know-how and competence is developed interactively and shared within subgroups and networks. Access to and membership of such subgroups is far from free. This change in the character of knowledge may be regarded as the other side of the more generally recognized organizational developments where the dichotomy between market and hierarchy is challenged by hybrid forms which have been called *industrial networks* (Freeman, 1991).

These changes are part of an even more far-reaching process of socio-economic change – we are moving towards a network society where the opportunity and capability to get access to and join knowledge- and learning-intensive networks is determining the relative socio-economic position of individuals and firms. The economy is becoming a hierarchy of networks with some global networks at the top and an increasing proportion of social exclusion at the bottom of the pyramid. The acceleration in the rate of change and the rate of learning is at the roots both of the creation of new organizational forms such as industrial networks and the polarization in OECD labour markets.

This is why policies promoting information infrastructures and accelerating innovation risk reinforcing inequality and threatening the social cohesion of the economy, if the social and distributional dimensions are neglected. Computer literacy and access to network facilities tend to become even more important in determining the future of citizens than literacy in the traditional sense has been. Promoting broad access to skills and competencies, and especially the capability to learn, is the key element in any strategy aiming at limiting the degree of social exclusion. There is a growing risk that IT becomes an acronym for Intellectual Tribalism. A 'New New Deal' focusing on the uneven distribution of knowledge and information is called for.

THE LEARNING ECONOMY – REMARKS ON TERMINOLOGY

The term 'the learning economy' signifies a society where the capability to learn is critical to economic success. It is akin to 'the information society' which indicates that a big and increasing proportion of the workforce is involved in the production, storing, handling and distribution of information. But the two concepts differ because the outcome of learning, i.e. knowledge, is a much wider concept than information. Information is the part of knowledge which can be transformed into 'bits' and easily transmitted through a computer network, while learning gives rise to know-how, skills and competencies which are often tacit rather than explicit and which cannot easily be transmitted through telecommunication networks.

This distinction is important also in relation to economic analysis because it makes it clear that learning is something different from and more complex than a transfer of information and that learning cannot be reduced to acts of transaction. The economics of information is relevant to the analysis of the learning economy and so is transaction cost analysis but none of them covers more than a part of the analytical needs. The formation of individual skills and competencies in interactive processes, and the establishment of economic competence at the level of an organization and in networks of organizations, have characteristics akin to transactions. They may involve the exchange of information but, fundamentally, a different analytical perspective is called for.

Sometimes, the term 'knowledge-based economy' has been used as a substitute for 'the learning economy' and obviously there is a strong link between the two concepts. Learning (and forgetting!) may be regarded as the flow concept(s) corresponding to the stock of knowledge.[2]

There are two reasons to prefer the concept of *the learning economy*. First, it helps us to avoid an analysis where the focus is only on the institutions aiming directly at producing and distributing knowledge (schools, universities, R&D-laboratories etc.) to the exclusion of routine-based learning. In the tradition of economic theory, the concept of learning has connotations of learning-by-doing (Arrow, 1962) and learning-by-using (Rosenberg, 1982) which emphasize knowledge-creation as a by-product of routine activities.

Second, currently, there is a special need to focus on how economic structures and the institutional set-up affect the process of learning. To focus on the *stock of knowledge* is useful for understanding the long-term pattern of economic growth but it may imply a focus on allocation of existing resources (the stock of knowledge) rather than the formation of new resources (innovation). The general message in this chapter is that there is an urgent need to reassess structures and institutions in relation to how they affect learning and innovation rather than to evaluate them only in terms of static efficiency.

Different Kinds of Knowledge and Learning

In order to understand the role of learning it is necessary to make distinctions between different kinds of knowledge. In an earlier paper we (Lundvall and Johnson, 1994) proposed distinctions between four different kinds:

- Know-what;
- Know-why;
- Know-how;
- Know-who.

Know-what refers to knowledge about 'facts'. How many people live in New York, what are the ingredients in pancakes and the date of the battle of Waterloo are examples of this kind of knowledge. Here, knowledge is close to what is normally called information – it can be broken down into bits. There are complex areas, where experts must have a lot of this kind of knowledge in order to fulfil their jobs – practitioners of law and medicine belong to this category. It is interesting to note that many of these experts will, typically, work in independent, specialized, consulting firms.

Know-why refers to scientific knowledge of principles and laws of motion in nature, in the human mind and in society. This kind of knowledge has been extremely important for technological development in certain areas as for example chemical and electric/electronic industries. To have access to this kind of knowledge will often make advances in technology more rapid and reduce the frequency of errors in procedures of trial and error. Again, the production and reproduction of know-why is often organized in specialized organizations, such as universities. To get access to this kind of knowledge, firms have to interact with these organizations either through recruiting scientifically trained labour or directly through contacts with university laboratories.

Know-how refers to skills – the capability to do something. It might relate to production but also to many other activities in the economic sphere. The businessmen judging the market prospects for a new product or the personnel manager selecting and training the staff have to use their know-how and the same is true for the skilled worker operating complicated machine-tools. It is important to realize that it is not only 'practical people' who need skills, however. One of the most interesting and profound analyses of the role and formation of know-how is actually about the need for skills among scientists (Polanyi, 1958/1978). Know-how is typically a kind of knowledge developed and kept within the border of the individual firm. But as the complexity of the knowledge-base is increasing, a mix of a division of labour and cooperation between organizations tends to develop in this field. One of the most important rationales for the formation of long-term inter-organizational relationships and of industrial networks is the need for firms to be able to share and combine elements of know-how.

This is why know-who becomes increasingly important. It refers to a mix of different kinds of skills including what might be characterized as social skills. Know-who involves information about who knows what and who knows how to do what. But it especially involves the formation of special social relationships to the expertise involved which makes it possible to get access to and use their knowledge efficiently. This kind of knowledge is important in the modern economy where there is a need to have access to many different kinds of knowledge and skills which are widely dispersed because of a highly developed division of labour among organizations and experts. For the modern manager and organization it is especially important to utilize this kind of knowledge as a response to the acceleration in the rate of change. The know-who kind of knowledge is internal to the organization to a higher degree than any of the three other kinds of knowledge. In principle it is possible to establish markets for this kind of knowledge – for instance in a corrupt economy where bribery gives privileged access to important people – but normally introducing markets would change and radically depreciate the usefulness and value of the relationships.

LEARNING DIFFERENT KINDS OF KNOWLEDGE

Learning to master the four kinds of knowledge takes place through different channels. While know-what and know-why can be obtained through reading books, attending lectures and accessing databases, the other two categories are rooted primarily in practical experience. Written manuals may help but in order to use them some basic skills in the field of application may be needed.

Know-how will typically be learnt in apprenticeship-relations where the apprentice follows his master and relies upon him as his trustworthy authority (Polanyi, 1958/1978, p. 53 *et passim*). Know-how and the capability to act skilfully is what makes a good skilled worker and artisan. But, it is also what distinguishes the excellent from the average manager and scientist. Most natural sciences involve field work or work in laboratories to make it possible for students to learn some of the necessary skills. In management science, the strong emphasis on case-oriented training reflects an attempt to simulate learning based on practical experience.

This kind of basically tacit knowledge is not easily transferred. It will typically develop into a mature form only through years of experience in everyday practice – through learning-by-doing. This is true for lawyers, doctors and businessmen as well as for connoisseurs and artists. 'Wunderkinder' who seem to be born with a fully developed skill in a specific area do exist but they are exceptional.

Know-who is learnt in social practice and some of it is learnt in specialized education environments. Communities of engineers and experts are kept together by reunions of alumni and by professional societies giving the participant access to information bartering with professional colleagues (Carter, 1989). It also develops in day-to-day dealings with customers, subcontractors and independent institutes. One important reason why big firms engage in basic research is that it gives them access to networks of academic experts crucial for their innovative capability (Pavitt, 1991). Again, know-who is socially embedded knowledge which cannot easily be transferred through formal channels of information.

LEARNING AND THE RATE OF CHANGE

Is it really correct to say that the current society is a learning economy as compared to earlier stages of development? In a sense knowledge has always been a crucial resource in the economy. The natural resources and the pure, physical, human effort put very strict limits on how much and what can be produced and consumed. Even so-called primitive economies have relied upon the know-how of producers. Knowledge was layered in traditions and routines passed on from generation to generation, and some learning took place and led to increased know-how and made population growth possible.

The most important consequence of the advent of industrialization was not that it involved the use of knowledge, but rather that it made learning a much more fundamental and strategic process than before. In traditional societies people lived their whole life on the basis of a rather narrow and constant set of skills. This is no longer the case in the industrial economy.

Early industrialization had an ambiguous effect on skills. On the one hand, it increased the demand for skill-intensive mechanical engineering for constructing machinery. On the other hand, the labour process for those using the machinery was often characterized by a low and narrowly defined demand for skills. But the main effect of entering the industrial era was that technical and organizational change became the order of the day both for engineers and workers. And there is a strong relationship between the rate of change and the rate of learning.

Change provokes learning. Without change little learning is needed. In a recent article by von Hippel (1994) 'learning-by-doing' is identified with problem-solving in connection with the introduction of new machinery. In this case learning in terms of problem-solving is forced upon workers and engineers by the R&D-department responsible for developing and introducing the new machinery. But the change agent might as well have been external to the organization: for instance, a customer defining new needs, a supplier promoting new process equipment, or a competitor introducing new products.[3]

But learning also lies behind change. Experiences of the everyday activities of the firm form an agenda for change and they also help to direct the process of change and to speed it up. It has been increasingly recognized that change in the form of technical and organizational innovations is rooted in a process of interactive learning (OECD, 1992, p. 26 *et passim*). In the interaction between individuals and organizations new combinations of different pieces of knowledge take the form of product and process innovations. There is thus a dual relationship between learning and change.[4]

THREE STYLIZED FACTS

Recent empirical studies focusing on the composition of the demand for labour support the general perspective presented so far. This is true for long-term economic growth analysis as well as for studies of more recent trends.

1. Analytical work on long-term economic growth has demonstrated that in the twentieth century the factor of production which has been growing most

rapidly has been human capital. And there are no signs that the growing intensity in the use of human capital has reduced the rate of return on investment in education and training. On this basis economists and economic historians have argued that technical progress has favoured the productivity of skilled rather than unskilled labour (Abramowitz, 1989, pp. 27f.).

2. Recently, the Canadian government pursued a number of studies of the degree of knowledge-intensity in job creation and job destruction in the 1980s. Using two different definitions (R&D-intensity and proportion of staff with a university degree) it was found that net job creation was predominantly taking place in the knowledge-intensive parts of the economy. This tendency was significant across regions, across firm sizes and in services as well as in manufacturing (Industry Canada, 1993 and 1994).

3. One of the most striking and worrying results coming out of OECD's Jobs Study is the strong tendency in the 1980s towards a polarization in labour markets. In the US relative wages for less skilled workers dropped dramatically leaving a substantial proportion (almost 20 per cent) of the workforce at a level of earnings below the poverty line. In Italy, Germany and France there was no polarization in terms of wages but the employment situation worsened dramatically for the unskilled leaving an increasing proportion excluded from the labour market. United Kingdom combined these two negative characteristics. It is interesting to note that among the major OECD economies only Japan avoided an increase in polarization in both the pay and the job opportunity dimension in the 1980s (OECD, 1994a).

INTERPRETATION AND EXPLANATION

These three sets of observations illustrate the fact that knowledge and learning has become extremely important in determining the economic fate of individuals, firms and national economies. They have in common that they indicate increasing rather than decreasing returns to the investment in knowledge: the growing proportion of human capital has not reduced its rate of return, the movement of resources into more knowledge-intensive activities seems to be accelerating rather than decelerating and the relative scarcity of skilled workers has increased in spite of a rapidly growing supply of skilled workers and a decrease in the proportion of unskilled labour. Finally, they indicate that the different forms of investments in knowledge are complementary rather than each other's substitutes: for instance, the introduction of new technology reinforces the demand for skilled labour.

Why did this polarization of the labour market take place and why did the process accelerate in the 1980s? At least three different hypotheses have been put forward in this context. Globalization, biased technological change and changes in firm behaviour are the major factors evoked in the debate.

Especially in connection with the establishment of NAFTA (the North American Free Trade Agreement) there was an intense debate about the impact of intensified international competition on the demand for less skilled workers in the US. The main result coming out of the empirical work pursued in this context was that increasing imports from low-wage countries does contribute to the polarization but that the scale of the import increase is so limited that it could not possibly by itself explain more than a small part of the phenomenon (Katz and Murphy, 1992).

An alternative explanation, arguing in accordance with the Abramowitz analysis, is that technological change recently has become even more strongly biased in favour of skilled workers. The evidence is still scattered and weak but studies of the use of information technology indicate such a tendency. Both US and Danish data show that the polarization of wages and employment opportunities is most dramatic in firms which have introduced computers and other forms of information technology in the workplace (Krueger, 1993; Lauritzen, 1994).

Finally, some scholars are sceptical both about the globalization and the technology-bias theses and point to institutional change in the labour market and changes in firm behaviour as the main explanations of falling real wages for the low-skilled workers in the US. According to these scholars, the weakening of trade unions has had a negative impact on the relative position of the least skilled workers because it has incited US employers to implement a low-wage strategy in which delocalization and out-sourcing are important elements (Howell, 1994).

One general problem with these proposed explanations is that most of the analysis is based on data from the US and it is not always clear to what degree it applies to Europe. Another weakness which reflects the present state of economic methodology is that the three hypotheses have normally been tested separately and regarded as alternatives to each other. It is more plausible that they interact in their impact on jobs. In what follows we propose an interpretation which regards the three elements as factors which work together in promoting an acceleration in the rate of change and learning.

According to standard economics, the major policy response to the polarization of job opportunities should be to make sure that wages were flexible downwards. But in the US this kind of flexibility has resulted in a growing proportion of 'working poor', while in the UK the increased wage differences imposed by Thatcherite policies have gone hand in hand with an even stronger polarization than before in terms of job opportunities. The kind of flexibility characterizing the Japanese economy which avoided polarization has little to do with textbook labour market flexibility. This is one area where a new understanding of the economy as a learning economy is fundamental in order to avoid misinterpretations and outdated and misdirected solutions.

ACCELERATION OF LEARNING AND CHANGE?

I propose that there is some truth in all the three explanations but that their major impact is that together they have speeded up the rate of change and that the demand for rapid learning has become intensified. Changes in technology, especially information technology, and changes in international competition have had an impact on the way firms organize themselves and the three factors combine in accelerating learning at all levels of the economy.

There is little doubt that over a longer time span there has been an acceleration in the rate of learning and change. We have only to go back a few generations to find ancestors who were doing the same things in the same ways as their grandparents and normally they did it in the same locality. Change has accelerated enormously since the beginning of the industrial revolution and people have been forced to engage in learning to do things differently and to operate in new environments.

But what about the rate of change in the medium term? It is not easy to find reliable and valid indicators for the rate of change and learning. The number of scientific articles is growing exponentially but this might have more to do with the institutional context than with an increase in the rate of learning. The rate of growth of the economy is actually lower than in the 1950s and the 1960s. Indicators of structural change in terms of changes in the sectoral composition of production and employment do not give clear indications in this respect. While changes in the structure of employment seem to slow down in the 1980s, a slight acceleration seems to have occurred when sectors are measured in terms of output (OECD, 1994b, p. 15 and 1994c, p. 143).

Some anecdotal evidence indicates an acceleration of change. In 1993 the theme of the annual conference of European R&D-managers – EIRMA – was 'Accelerating Innovation' and among the experts present there was little doubt that there had been an acceleration of the rate of technical innovation in the 1980s (EIRMA, 1993).[5]

Another phenomenon which involves a much broader set of actors than the R&D-intensive firms is the movement towards flexible specialization where producers increasingly compete by responding rapidly to volatile markets. Organizational change in terms of 'just in time' and lean production strategies may be regarded as responses to the need to speed up change. Again rapid change will imply a strong demand for a capability to learn and respond to new needs and market opportunities.[6]

A third phenomenon has to do with the introduction of more intense competition in sectors which have been living a more protected life. Competition may come from the opening of national markets for services for imports or from deregulation and privatization of activities. In this process the rate of change will accelerate even more rapidly than in the ones which have been used to competition.

Another way of indicating the growing importance of change and learning has been proposed by Carter (1994). She shows that there is a close connection between the proportion of non-production workers and the rate of change in a sector and actually she argues that the major function of non-production workers is to create or to react to change. On the basis of data on employment patterns in manufacturing in the US, it is demonstrated that a growing proportion of costs are costs of change rather than costs of production.

CHANGES IN THE RELATIONSHIPS BETWEEN TACIT AND CODIFIED KNOWLEDGE

One of the important trends in our economies is the increasing importance of codified knowledge (David, 1994). In the wake of World War II, science became a major factor in economic development. Specialized R&D-laboratories were established, first in firms belonging to the chemical and electrical industries, and later in a wider set of sectors. The Manhattan project resulting in the first nuclear bomb and the cold war period including the space race between the Soviet Union and the United States contributed to the general idea that a strong science base is important for international competitiveness. The massive investments in education and training following the Sputnik-chock also gave a major impetus to the codification of knowledge.

The development of information technology may be regarded as a response to the need for handling codified knowledge more effectively. Conversely, the very existence of information technology and communications infrastructures gives a strong impetus to the process of codification of knowledge. All knowledge which can be codified and reduced to information can now be transmitted over long distances with very limited costs. The area of potential applications of codified knowledge is extended and it makes it more attractive to allocate resources to the process of codification.

Codification may be understood as a process of generalizing what is specific and translating messages into a common and shared language. It involves the establishment of technical standards and of basing technical development on general scientific principles. A special aspect relates to the design of the innovation process itself where information technology makes it possible to pursue developmental work on computers through virtual experiments rather than through real tests in real laboratories. Increasingly this takes place in the testing of new drugs and in the design of big and complex systems such as aeroplanes and ships.

This new step in the degree of codification of knowledge is important because it moves the border between tacit and codified knowledge. However, it does not necessarily reduce the relative importance of skills, competencies and other elements of tacit knowledge. The easier and less expensive access to information makes skills and competencies relating to the selection and efficient use of information even more crucial than before. In general, skills related to handling codified knowledge become more important in the labour markets. This shift in the demand for skills may be a further element reinforcing the polarization in labour markets. The case studies showing that the polarization is most strongly developed in firms using computers point in this direction.

The most fundamental aspect of learning is perhaps the transformation of tacit into codified knowledge and the movement back to practice where new kinds of tacit knowledge are developed. Such a spiral movement is, according to Nonaka (1991), at the very core of individual as well as organizational learning. Also, in the real world the distinction between the two is not always as clear-cut as is normally assumed. At any point of time a certain amount of knowledge is in the pipeline, in the process of codification. While some engineers and scientists are involved in producing innovations and inventions a much larger proportion is engaged in standardization and in codifying and generalizing knowledge.

THE NEED FOR A NEW DEAL

One basic hypothesis of this paper is that the speed-up of the rate of change imposed by growing international competition, deregulation and new technological opportunities gives an incentive to firms to hire personnel with a high learning capability. The information technology and the codification of new kinds of technology reinforce the acceleration and lead to a preference for workers with general competencies in handling codified knowledge. These tendencies increase the proportion of workers promoting change and lead to a further acceleration in the rate of change. The process is thus characterized by cumulative causation excluding a large and growing proportion of the labour force from normal waged work. If this hypothesis is correct there is a need to develop a new perspective on policy-making and to look for a new kind of social compromise.

One alternative is, paradoxically, to further speed up the rate of learning in the sectors facing international competition in order to obtain a bigger share in the most rapidly growing markets. Another is to create a sheltered sector where learning takes place at a slower rate. A third, and perhaps the most important, is to redistribute the access to information networks and the capabilities to learn in favour of the potentially excluded. Finally, to slow down some kinds of change by installing rigidities in the system may be a way of channelling processes of learning in directions less disruptive to social cohesion. Some major private agents have already moved in this direction when confronted with situations where costs of change have become too high as compared to benefits.

Speeding Up Change

In the OECD Jobs Study the basic message is that countries should try to remain at 'the head of the pack' in terms of innovation and change (OECD, 1994a, p. 3 *et passim*). It is true that national innovation systems where firms are able to move rapidly into new growth areas in world markets and into areas of new promising technologies are better off than systems where the firms get stuck in stagnating activities. They will increase their share of world markets and value added at the global level. The number of jobs and real wages can be increased simultaneously.

This model has certain characteristics in common with the Japanese post-war economy. In the highly productive export-oriented part of the economy learning has been extremely effective in promoting income generation through moving rapidly into the most promising markets and technologies.

The very success of the model now seems to undermine it, however. One general problem of this strategy is of course that not every country can lead the pack and it may be argued that the other side of the Japanese success is the crisis in the labour markets in the rest of the OECD countries (Lundvall, 1995). In the US and Europe, the very strength of the Japanese capability in the high growth areas has forced the firms to speed up learning and change in activities characterized by slower growth and in technologies where the cost/benefit ratio of accelerating change is less favourable. Attempts to correct for the uneven development of competitiveness through currency rate corrections and manipulations have proved quite ineffective and the resulting financial instability has further undermined growth and job creation.

In spite of what is said in the OECD Jobs Study speeding up change in Europe and the US might not be the most promising response, however, and especially if it is not combined with a change in the pattern of specialization. An important explanation of the unemployment problem is the uneven development within the triad and the polarization in the labour markets in the US and the major European economies reflects an acceleration of learning in low growth areas.

Creating a Sheltered Sector

Even if the US and Europe were more successful in entering areas where learning curves are steep and markets are growing fast this might not by itself solve the problem of social exclusion. A rapid growth in the tradeables sectors would give rise to a high and rapidly growing income level but only for a shrinking part of the potential labour force. To keep the living standard of the growing proportion of excluded workers at what has been established as a minimum to avoid poverty would include a dramatic increase in income transfers.

One way to reduce the burden of redistribution for governments and at the same time to reduce the proportion of workers excluded from the labour market would be to stimulate the creation or conservation of *a private sheltered sector*, where change took place more slowly and the rate of learning and productivity were lower.

Again this corresponds to the Japanese development where the rate of change and learning in the tradeables sector has been very high while agriculture and parts of the services sector have remained sheltered from competition. The rate of change has been slowed down in the sheltered sectors not primarily through open protectionism but rather through complex informal institutional mechanisms. It should be pointed out that it might be misleading to call this a Japanese *strategy* since it is far from clear to what degree conscious choices were made to establish and reproduce such a dual system.

Today the international pressure to break up the sheltering institutions is mounting, however. From the point of view of the rest of the OECD countries they appear to be trade barriers efficiently blocking the entrance of foreign competition. There are also domestic forces working in the same direction emanating from the tradeable sector which experiences an increasing pressure on its profits when confronted with high currency rates and protectionist responses abroad.

Network Access and Skill Formation as Social Policy

A third kind of policy response which is supplementary to the other two is one where the focus is on the development of human resources in a broad sense. Primary and secondary education of a high quality reaching all citizens and giving special attention to those having the greatest difficulties in learning would be an important part of such a strategy. But even more important and more difficult would be to establish incentives for firms and individuals to engage in upgrading the learning capability of the adult population and, again, with special attention to those who run the biggest risk of being excluded.

The further development of information infrastructures may, if it is not consciously managed, reinforce exclusion. To give workers and the unemployed a chance to learn and develop their cognitive skills and to give them skills specifically related to the use of computers would be another important part of this strategy. On the other hand, the very advent of information infrastructures and the growing political attention it attracts could be used to focus on these kinds of problems. Information infrastructures can be regarded both as something which threatens to aggravate the polarization in labour markets and as one element of the solution. Giving the weaker persons and groups privileged access to networks and using the networks to develop on-line learning would be a solution that increased the capability to cope with rapid learning without exclusion.

The traditional approach to social exclusion has been, *ex post*, and through governments, to organize income transfers from the employed to the unemployed and unemployable. There are signs that this way of attacking the problem does not work any more for a number of reasons. The very scale of the problem and the limited willingness to pay taxes is one problem. The fact that exclusion tends to become chronic rather than temporary in this kind of regime is another. In the new context strategies which attack the problem *ex ante* and which limit the creation of polarization and exclusion through a different distribution of access to learning and networking become correspondingly more adequate. This implies among other things the need for a new division of labour and new forms of cooperation within governments. Policies focusing on industrial development, technology, and especially information technology, have to be coordinated more strongly with economic and social policies.

Slowing Down Change

An alternative to increasing the capability to cope with rapid change and accelerating the rate of learning would be to slow down change. Is it possible to do so? It is a difficult question since we have got so used to connecting change with economic growth and growth with increasing welfare. But it is possible that rates of change have become too high – that hyper-acceleration of change and learning may take place. 'Hyper-acceleration' refers to a situation where all parties would gain from slowing down the rate of learning but where the rules of the game are such that they give incentives to continuously accelerate the rate.

In order to illustrate that this is not completely far-fetched two examples may be evoked. The first refers to the Japanese automobile industry where some years ago the leading producers realized that the product life cycle of car models was becoming too short. The amount of resources which had to be allocated to product development, the coordination problems with subcontractors and the sales and services organizations and the quality control were becoming such a heavy burden that it gave an incentive for the major firms to enter into an agreement to avoid a further shortening of the product life cycle.

The second example refers to the sector producing information technology and computers where experts and management tend to agree that the acceleration of technology and supply-driven change was a major factor in undermining the market. The rate of learning imposed on final users became too high and the resulting disappointments when applying the technologies backfired taking the form of a stagnation in demand.[7]

These two examples do not tell us how to slow down change and learning in the economy as a whole. They indicate, however, that hyper-acceleration of learning may develop but also that there might be major players in the economy who would be willing to support a certain slow-down in the rate of change.

The Ethical Dimension in the Learning Economy

The production and distribution of all kinds of knowledge is strongly rooted in the social system. It is generally accepted that information is not easily transacted in the market. One of Arrow's paradoxical statements is that you cannot know the full value of information if you do not have full access to it. And if you have full access to it there is no reason to pay for it. Property rights are not easily defined. On the one hand it is true that the one who sells information will not lose access to it while the one who buys it can reproduce it and distribute it to all potential customers (Arrow, 1973).

It is also obvious that trade in information by definition involves information impactedness and an asymmetrical distribution of information. Accordingly, transaction costs will be high when opportunistic behaviour is part of the game. These statements are, I believe, generally accepted.

What is perhaps less obvious is how these circumstances force the social context into the centre of economic analysis. Arrow has stated another paradox in this connection. He says that 'you cannot buy trust – and if you could buy it, it would be of no value whatsoever' (Arrow, 1971). This simple statement is radical in its implications. First, given that trust is necessary in order to make the economy work – and this is true for any trade in information and it is even more true in connection with processes of interactive learning – it becomes clear that there must be something outside the pure instrumental rationality of individual agents to keep the economy together.

Some social scientists have tried to overcome this kind of problem by introducing social exchange as an instrumental process (Blau, 1964). The basic idea is that if you are nice and honest to me, I will be nice and honest to you and as time goes by both parties will be willing to invest more and more trust in the relationship. There is some truth in these models but there is something lacking. If there were nothing but instrumental calculations behind cooperation it is difficult to see how any kind of stable and trust-based relationships could develop. If you knew that your partner was continuously calculating the utility of being honest to you, you would not give away too much sensitive information.

Another implication is that the level of transaction costs involved in connection with selling and buying information will reflect the degree of trust and the relative frequency of opportunistic behaviour in the local context. The learning capability would be even more dependent on the presence of trust. Tacit knowledge and know-how will typically be transferred and shared not through market operations but through a process of interactive learning. Such processes are extremely vulnerable to opportunistic behaviour and cheating.

This implies that the more an economy becomes dependent on the formation and efficient use of knowledge the more important its ethical foundations become. This points to a fundamental contradiction in the modern economy.

There are strong tendencies towards generalizing the market and letting it penetrate more and more deeply into all kinds of relationships. Today this is reinforced especially by the globalization and deregulation of financial markets which tend to undermine all kinds of non-market regulations and relationships at the national level.

But economies where the market loses its roots in the social system and where all agents act exclusively on the basis of strategic and instrumental rationality will find that their capacity to learn and innovate will become undermined. Russia and some of the Eastern European countries illustrate what happens when the market is given free play and where trust is absent in the relationships between economic agents. Building formal institutions and introducing new laws will not help much if the social foundations are absent.

There are serious warning signals indicating that we are now in the midst of a process threatening the very social foundations which made rapid economic growth possible over a long period. The social exclusion of growing segments of the population is one factor pointing in this direction. A society which does not care for its weaker citizens will have difficulties in maintaining and fostering a social climate of trust and acceptance. This problem is aggravated by the fact that the financial sector increasingly offers rapid profits to young brainy people who get their living from financial speculation. A third factor is the growing number of scandals involving the economic and political elite in economic criminality.

On the other hand, it may be argued that the increasing importance of learning for economic performance in itself forms a countervailing power against these tendencies. The more advanced layers of management realize that it would be impossible to keep up with the rapid rate of change in the economy were the personnel to act exclusively on the basis of individual economic incentives and threats of losing their jobs. Without a minimum of loyalty to the organization, employees have all the opportunities to slow down processes of organizational learning. The same is true for inter-firm relationships and networks of firms. Without a minimum of social trust, transaction costs become too high and interactive learning too difficult.

One of the dramas which we will be witnessing during the coming decades is the struggle between a financial and individualistic logic and a logic more compatible with the increasing importance of interactive learning.

INTERNATIONALIZATION AND THE CHANGING ROLE OF NATION STATES

These general tendencies reflecting changes in the role of knowledge are further reinforced by the internationalization of certain economic activities. Historically, the nation state has been the most important institutional framework for learning and innovation. This is obviously true for the legal system and for social policies compensating losers in the overall game of creative destruction. But it has also been true for informal and formal institutions (such as reputation mechanisms, professionals sharing, and self-imposed codes of conduct) reducing the scope for opportunistic behaviour.

Today, these elements of the national system are challenged by internationalization of economic activities and most forcefully by the internationalization of financial markets. National systems which have been extremely successful in building trust and promoting learning – such as Japan – have come under increasing pressure to move towards 'pure' market relationships and to weaken some of the social institutions which have been the pillars of the innovation system.

Since the new institutional frameworks at the global level are not built at the same rate as the national ones are undermined, more and more economic activities take place in a social void and without the support of institutions of trust. What seems to happen in this situation is that regional, transnational or local networks establish their own specific rules of the game which are valid inside but not necessarily outside the network. We are witnessing a movement towards what one might call intellectual tribalism.

Networks or tribes engage in interactive learning in competition with other networks or tribes. Inside the network they share knowledge and build trust relationships. But in their interaction with individuals and organizations belonging to other tribes they remain opportunistic and when it is to their advantage they break the rules of decency.

NATIONAL SYSTEMS OF INNOVATION

In spite of a far-reaching process of internationalization national systems still play a major role in determining how common global trends affect economic performance. Japan is the only major OECD economy characterized neither by high rates of unemployment nor by polarization in labour markets. Some of the most rapidly growing Asian economies have in common with Japan a strong emphasis on education and training as well as an egalitarian income distribution. These countries have handled the acceleration in the rate of change differently from most of the OECD countries. The smaller OECD countries and especially the Nordic ones have also been more successful in avoiding social exclusion than the major OECD countries.

This reflects systemic features which distribute the social pressure emanating from an acceleration of change and innovation differently across nations. In the US model learning is done the hard way – individuals carry most of the burden of change in a kind of lottery where both the losses and the potential gains are high. Learning takes place through job changes and through moving between firms.

The Japanese model is one where learning to a higher degree takes place internally as organizational learning. The degree of flexibility within firms is high and the firms – at least the big and advanced ones – share the risk of negative change with the individual.

Some of the European systems such as the UK and France have old and established elitist education and training systems based on a mix of plutocracy, aristocracy and elitocracy. The education system fosters rigidities in the workplace both vertically as barriers to upward mobility and horizontally between job functions (especially in France) and the flexibility will mainly be inter-firm. Rigidities give less incentives for learning new skills than both the US and the Japanese system. Following Thatcherite prescriptions and imposing more of the US kind of flexibility in these systems results in dramatic increases in social inequality – it weakens the losers while keeping their chances for upward mobility low.

The Nordic countries are also characterized by a high rate of mobility between firms and jobs but they combine it with a welfare state system aimed at sharing the costs of change between winners and losers.

Each of these systems has its own comparative advantages and disadvantages when it comes to coping with the acceleration in the rate of change. In the US most of the increasing pressure is put on the weakest segments of the population, in the Nordic countries it is the welfare state and its institutions which come under pressure and in Japan it is the institutions providing a shelter for certain labour-intensive activities. None of the systems can cope with the acceleration of change without running into problems reflecting the fact that the predominant institutional set-up is not fully adapted to the context of the globalized learning economy. In the longer term we believe that systems providing solutions based on solidarity will come out as the strongest but in the short term free-riding and playing on people's egoistic motives seem to flourish.

CONCLUSION

In standard economics it is generally recognized that information cannot be easily transacted in markets and that market failure is present in connection with both the production of and the trade in knowledge. From this recognition to understanding the full implications of the learning economy is, however, still a long way. This is illustrated most clearly by the present overstatement of what market forces can do in connection with solving the problems of unemployment and social exclusion. The assumption that more competition and wage flexibility is the key to solving the problem of unemployment neglects the fact that learning is a social process which can prosper only if society remains cohesive. The impact on the social and moral foundations of society must be taken into account by any policy aiming for long-term economic efficiency.

The alternative to the flexibilization strategy recommended by mainstream economists is not necessarily just to speed up the rate of innovation and learning, however. There are indications that currently the rate of change tends to outgrow the capacity to learn. The idea of slowing things down may seem alien to most of us but we still need to consider it seriously. The Japanese example shows that it might be quite efficient to introduce some specific rigidities which work as brakes on those processes of change which are the most socially disruptive. The alternative is a polarized society with little cohesion and such a society is not viable in the long run. Under all circumstances there is a need to redefine policies relating to technical change, industrial development, education and training as well as information infrastructures so that they take into account the distributional impact of policy alternatives. Traditional policies trying to correct income distributions *ex post* have reached their limits and an *ex ante* approach is called for.

NOTES

1. These are points I have made before in papers produced together with colleagues from Aalborg. They are at the core of the argument in Lundvall (1992). They have been further developed in Lundvall and Johnson (1994).
2. The concept of 'the knowledge-based information economy' has played a major role in several of the contributions by Eliasson, who emphasizes the role of micro-based economic competence

in the process of economic growth (Eliasson, 1990). An early and interesting contribution to the role of learning in the process of innovation is Cantley and Sahal (1980).

3. Some learning may take place also in a technically stable environment, however. See for instance Lundberg (1961) regarding the so-called Horndahl effect where productivity was increased continuously through several decades in spite of very limited investments and very little change in the production technology.

4. This perspective should be confronted with von Hippel's analysis (von Hippel, 1994) of 'sticky data'. According to von Hippel, the normal outcome of a situation where it is difficult to codify and transfer information is not cooperation and interactive learning but rather that the different parties establish a division of labour in a sequential mode. The process of innovation is regarded as one where the locus of innovation shifts back and forth between agents according to their special competencies. A similar perspective is immanent when applying theories of industrial organization emphasizing specialized assets to the process of innovation (Christensen, 1995). An interesting research agenda would be to test empirically the perspective of interactive learning with this division-of-labour approach.

5. It is interesting to note the introductory remarks to the conference by the EIRMA President, Dr E. Spitz:

> In a time of intensive global competition, speeding up the innovation process is one of the most important ingredients which enable the company to bring to the market the right product for right prices at the right time....
>
> *We know that it is not only the R&D process which is important; we have to put emphasis on integration of technology in the complete business environment, production, marketing, regulations and many other activities essential to commercial success. These are the areas where the innovation process is being retarded.*
>
> *This subject is a very deep seated one which sometimes leads to important, fundamental rethinking and radical redesign of the whole business process. In this respect, especially during the difficult period in which we live today, where pressure is much higher, our organisations may, in fact, need to be changed.* (EIRMA, 1993, p. 7; emphasis added)

6. For an interesting collection of case studies illustrating the change in organizations responding to the need for flexible specialization see Andreasen *et al.* (1995).

7. This was one of the main conclusions from the OECD High Level Seminar on Information Technology held in Paris in 1993.

REFERENCES

Abramowitz, M. (1989), *Thinking about Growth*, Cambridge: Cambridge University Press.

Andreasen, L.E. *et al.* (eds) (1995), *Europe's Next Step: Organisational Innovation, Competition and Employment*, Frank Cass.

Arrow, K.J. (1962), 'The Economic Implications of Learning by Doing', *Review of Economic Studies*, vol. XXIX, no. 80.

Arrow, K.J. (1971), 'Political and Economic Evaluation of Social Effects and Externalities', in M. Intrilligator (ed.), *Frontiers of Quantitative Economics*, North Holland.

Arrow, K.J. (1973), *Information and Economic Behaviour*, Stockholm: Federation of Swedish Industries.

Arrow, K.J. (1994), 'Methodological individualism and social knowledge', Richard T. Ely Lecture, *AEA Papers and Proceedings*, vol. 84, no. 2, May 1994.

Blau, P.M. (1964), *Exchange and Power in Social Life*, New York: John Wiley.

Cantley, M. and D. Sahal (1980), *Who Learns What? A Conceptual Description of Capability and Learning in Technological Systems*, Laxenburg: IIASA.

Carter, A.P. (1989), 'Know-how trading as economic exchange', *Research Policy* , vol. 18, no. 3.

Carter, A.P. (1994), 'Production workers, metainvestment and the pace of change', paper prepared for the meetings of the International J.A. Schumpeter Society, Munster, August 1994.

Christensen, J.F. (1995), 'The innovative assets and inter-asset linkages of the firm', revised version of paper presented at the EUNETIC Conference on Evolutionary Economics of Technological Change, Strasbourg, 1994.

David, P. (1994), 'Technological change, intangible investments and growth in the knowledge-based economy: the US historical experience', paper presented at the OECD conference on Employment and Growth in the Knowledge-Based Economy, Copenhagen, November 1994.

EIRMA (1993), *Speeding Up Innovation*, conference papers for the EIRMA Helsinki conference, May 1993.

Eliasson, G. (1990), 'Innovation, industrial competence and the micro-foundations of economic expansion', in E. Deiaco, E. Hornell and G. Vickery (eds), *Technology and Investments: Crucial Issues for the 1990s*, Pinter Publishers.

Freeman, C. (1991), 'Networks of innovators: a synthesis of research issues', *Research Policy*, vol. 20, no. 5.

Howell, D.R. (1994), 'Information technology and the demand for skills: a perspective on the US experience', paper presented at the OECD conference on Employment and Growth in the Knowledge-Based Economy, Copenhagen, November 1994.

Industry Canada (1993), 'Knowledge, technology and employment trends', memo by Pat Murray, July.

Industry Canada (1994), 'Employment growth in Canada', memo by N. Stephens.

Katz, L.F. and K.M. Murphy (1992), 'Changes in relative wages 1963–1987: supply and demand factors', *Quarterly Journal of Economics*, February.

Krueger, R.B. (1993), 'How computers have changed the wage structure: evidence from micro-data, 1984–89', *Quarterly Journal of Economics*, February.

Lauritzen, F. (1994), 'Technology, education and employment', paper presented at the OECD conference on Employment and Growth in the Knowledge-Based Economy, Copenhagen, November 1994.

Lundberg, E. (1961), *Produktivitet och räntabilitet: Studier i kapitalets betydelse inom svenskt näringsliv*, Stockholm: Studieförbundet Näringsliv och Samhälle.

Lundvall, B.-Å. (ed) (1992), *National Systems of Innovation: Towards a Theory of Innovation and Interactive Learning*, Pinter Publishers.

Lundvall, B.-Å. (1995), 'The Global Unemployment Problem and National Systems of Innovation', in D. O'Doherty (ed.), *Globalisation, Networking and Small Firm Innovation*, London: Graham and Trotman.

Lundvall, B.-Å. and B. Johnson (1994), 'The learning economy', *Journal of Industry Studies*, vol. 1, no. 2, December, pp. 23–42.

Nonaka, K. (1991), 'The knowledge creating company', *Harvard Business Review*, Nov.–Dec.

OECD (1992), *Technology and the Economy – The Key Relationships*, Paris.

OECD (1994a), *The OECD Jobs Study – Facts, Analysis, Strategies*, Paris.

OECD (1994b), *The OECD Jobs Study – Evidence and Explanation, Part I*, Paris.

OECD (1994c), *Manufacturing Performance: A Scoreboard of Indicators*, Paris.

Pavitt, K. (1991), 'What makes basic research economically useful?', *Research Policy*, vol. 20, no. 2.

Polanyi, M. (1958/1978), *Personal Knowledge*, Routledge and Kegan Paul.

Rosenberg, N. (1982), *Inside the Black Box: Technology and Economics*, Cambridge: Cambridge University Press.

von Hippel, E. (1994), 'Sticky information and the locus of problem solving: implications for innovation', *Management Science*, no. 40.

PART II

Innovation and Technological Development

3. The evolutionary approach to technological change: a framework for microeconomic analysis

Luis E. Arjona Béjar

The idea of a perspective in economics that would draw on ideas from the theory of evolution is not new. However, it has mainly been since the early 1980s that the use of evolutionary analogies in economics has flourished, and the work of different authors has converged towards the building up of a common set of concepts and analytical tools. Scholars working on the area of technological change have put forward concepts akin to the evolutionary approach. Most of these contributions come from research on innovation and diffusion in the Schumpeterian tradition and from the product life cycle literature. In this chapter, I argue that these concepts can be put together coherently in an evolutionary framework and provide the foundations for the analysis of the development of specific technologies.

The term 'evolutionary' has spread considerably in recent times and it is often used in works that have little in common regarding their theoretical perspective. Therefore, it is convenient to start by stating briefly, in Section 1, what in our view the main tenets of an evolutionary approach are. Section 2 provides a selective review of a series of ideas from the literature on technological change. This section is an effort to articulate those ideas in a framework that is useful for the empirical study of specific technologies. In Section 3, I employ this framework in order to highlight the link between the so-called technology theories of international trade and the notion of international trade as an aspect of the spatial dimension of the diffusion of innovation. Two technologies from the polyethylene and photocopying equipment industries are used to illustrate that the patterns of international trade can be fruitfully analysed from an evolutionary perspective.

1. THE EVOLUTIONARY APPROACH IN ECONOMICS

The central concern of the evolutionary perspective is to explain economic change. It sees the economy as a complex evolving system, which is open in the sense that the outcomes of its development are not predictable. The diversity and mutability of the different components of the system and the pressure exerted on them by selective forces that emerge both from within and from outside the system are the fundamental elements shaping the course of economic change.

There is a major difference between the evolutionary approach and the equilibrium perspective that dominates most of economic analysis. The latter looks at the way in which the actions of independent agents coordinate and sees no inherent tendency to change in the economy. In evolutionary thinking, in contrast, the economy is seen as a system in continuous change and the problem is to understand the mechanisms by which it changes.

While discussing the evolutionary approach in economics it is useful to compare it with the application of evolutionary ideas in biology, since the latter offers an invaluable source of concepts and analogies, given the more advanced degree (at both the theoretical and the empirical level) to which evolutionary explanations have been used in biology[1].

In economics, as in biology, evolution is seen as primarily driven by two mechanisms: one that introduces novelty in the system and creates variety, and another that selects on the basis of the diversity of the entities within the system. Regarding novelty, in the social domain, one may think of habits and routines as an equivalent to genes, and of the mechanisms that provoke changes in them as the analogue of those behind genetic variation. With respect to the mechanisms of selection, the institutional settings of economic systems (and at a more basic level the natural environment itself), will act in favour of or against the behaviour associated with those routines. In this way, selection will change the diffusion of routines and modes of behaviour in populations of individuals and organizations. According to this idea, which has been traced back to Veblen, socio-economic evolution is seen 'as a selection process working on institutions as units of selection' (Hodgson, 1993, pp. 126, 132). The essential element of this analogy is that routines, like genes, are depositories of information and the means to transmit it: actions and thoughts are sustained and structured by routines and habits that operate on behaviour as a set of instructions.

As in the natural world, diversity is essential for selection to operate, and the generation of diversity is fundamental for evolution. However, in contrast with biological evolution, in which genetic variation occurs at a slow pace, in human systems the introduction and spread of novelty take place at a much faster rate. The difference with respect to the natural world is not only a question of speed. In economic systems, the mechanisms that generate variety play a much more important role in driving the evolutionary process. The innovative and imitative activities that create and modify habits, routines and institutions are, above all, the result of purposeful behaviour. The fact that we are dealing with individuals and organizations with intentions, which acquire and interpret information and are capable of thinking and learning, is a central element that distinguishes evolution in economics from that in biology. New behaviour seeks, in general, to be adaptive. Therefore, the environment influences the process of creation of variety. Furthermore, individuals and organizations innovate not only keeping the present conditions of their environment in mind, but also anticipating changes in it.

Routines, as genes, replicate themselves. However, in routines there is not a clear physical mechanism like that of genetic duplication. There is, instead, a social mechanism that involves imitation and learning. As many authors have pointed out, there is an important Lamarckian element in socio-economic evolution. Adaptive behaviour is learnt, fixed in routines and carried in the memory of individuals and organizations. These routines are transmitted from one generation to the next and play an important role in shaping subsequent behaviour.

Regarding the selection environment, it is important to stress not only that it affects the creation of variety, but that, by the same token, the introduction of new behaviour produces changes in the environment itself. The implications of these have been summarized by Allen and Lesser by noting that 'evolution generates diversity and diversity drives evolution' (Allen and Lesser, 1991, p. 165).

The most important specificity of evolution in human systems is its institutional dimension[2]. Economic evolution takes place at different levels. It can be observed at the level of technologies, firms, industries, market structures and other socio-economic institutions, and at the level of the economic systems as a whole. A key concept, on which the theory of evolution in biology elaborates, is that of species. There is not, however, an equivalent concept in economics. Taxonomic classifications in economics have to follow a different logic, one that is appropriate for the different levels at which evolution takes place. The concept of institution, broadly defined as 'commonly held patterns of behaviour and habits of thought, of a routinized and durable nature, that are associated with people interacting in groups or larger collectives' (Hodgson, 1993, p. 253) is fundamental. This concept cannot only be the basis to elaborate taxonomies at different levels of evolution, but may also serve to establish links between these different levels. Furthermore, organizations, as materialized and organized forms of institutions, are elementary units on which to base the population approach that is essential for evolutionary analysis. The criteria by which a population can be defined may vary according to the specific purposes of the analysis and there is no need, as in biology, to tie ourselves to a single concept like that of species.

2. TECHNOLOGICAL CHANGE AS AN EVOLUTIONARY PROCESS

Technology and the Definition of Industry

The definition of technology adopted here is a broad one. Technology includes the material elements employed and obtained in the production process, the individual and collective knowledge and skills of the people who participate in it and the elements of organization that articulate it.

The distinction between technique and technology is an important one. Techniques refer only to the artifacts involved in the production process. However, the changes that one observes at the level of artifacts are only one aspect of more fundamental changes in the knowledge, skills and decision rules of both the individual and institutional elements of the organization that deploys a technology.[3] When looking at technology, I shall distinguish three dimensions that overlap in different degrees: the knowledge, the routine and the artifact dimensions of technology. The understanding of these three dimensions and of how they interrelate provides crucial insights into the analysis of technological change. It is at the level of artifacts, i.e. in the techniques, where the manifestation of technological change is more evident. However, it is necessary to look into the parallel changes that occur at the level of knowledge and routines in order to assess the significance of such changes, understand the process by which they come about and identify the determinants of their rate and direction.

The artifact dimension of technology relates to a transformation process in which energy and materials of one form gain value by transforming them into energy and materials of a different form (Metcalfe and Boden, 1991, pp. 710–11). When a specific technology is considered at this level, three aspects of it are made evident: the transformation process itself, its product, and the services that the latter provides to its user. On this basis, as Saviotti and Metcalfe have proposed, it is possible in principle to characterize technologies by representing each of these three aspects by means of interrelated multidimensional characteristics' vectors (Saviotti and Metcalfe, 1984).

The knowledge dimension of technology refers to a body of concepts and theories that enable the design and operation of the process of production. This knowledge conveys an understanding of the process, of its relationship with the needs it satisfies and (of fundamental interest to us) of potential directions for further development of the technology. This last idea has been advanced in different ways by researchers in the area of technological change[4]. Dosi has expressed it through the generic notion of technological paradigm that he defines as a '"model" and a "pattern" of solution of *selected* technological problems based on *selected* principles derived from natural sciences and on *selected* material technologies ... [which] ... embodies strong presumptions on the directions of technical change to pursue and those to neglect' (Dosi, 1982, p. 152, italics in the original). The recognition of this, less visible, aspect of technology is crucial for the study of the individuals and organizations involved in the process of technological change.

The third element of our triad is the routine dimension of technology. Organizations develop routines associated with specific technologies. There are two important aspects of the routine dimension of technology. First, the formation of routines is essential for the command of a technology and for the mere existence of the required skills and problem-solving strategies. The formation of habits of thought, action, interaction and communication is an integral part of the learning process and a requisite for the existence of the collective competence of the organization. From this perspective, following Nelson and Winter, the specific technology that an organization commands can be conceived as a (complex) routine (Nelson and Winter, 1982, pp. 14–17). The other important aspect of routines is the element of inertia that they carry with them. Inertia is essential in preserving variety and is of fundamental importance for the evolutionary process: for the selection mechanism to operate, variety has to be stable relative to the speed with which selection operates (Metcalfe, 1989, pp. 57, 62).

The concepts above allow us to think about technology at different levels of abstraction. The focus on the knowledge dimension and the use of concepts like that of technological paradigm, for instance, can be applied from the level of a specific technology, as it exists within an organization, to the level of general fields of technology that apply to whole branches of economic activity. In order to have a theoretical framework operative for empirical analysis, it is necessary to distinguish between these different levels of abstraction (Hagerdoorn, 1989, pp. 95–8).

At the most concrete level we can think of technologies as they exist within each individual firm. Technologies are largely firm-specific. Firms compete by championing specific designs and develop capabilities to be effective in the context in which they operate. To refer to technology at a more general level we will introduce Nelson and Winter's concept of technological regime (Nelson and Winter, 1982, pp. 258–59), interpreted as a set of basic design parameters associated with key aspects of a specific technology. The cognitive element of this concept has been emphasized by Metcalfe and Boden. Following these authors, a technological regime consists of a 'hard core of fundamental scientific and engineering principles' adhered to by a group of firms that gives coherence to their technological activities (Metcalfe and Boden, 1991, p. 714).

The concept of technological regime leads us immediately to the question of the definition of industry. By industry we will understand the population of business organizations that carry out the production and commercialization of the products associated with a technological regime within which all operate. Therefore, the industry is a population of business units that is defined by the technology that is common to all of them.[5]

Finally, it is possible to move to an intermediate level of abstraction between the notion of technological regime and the specificity of each firm's technology and to distinguish a few competing design configurations within an industry. These design configurations are different 'operational routes' to the design and production of specific artifacts (Metcalfe and Boden, 1991, pp. 714–15). They are a set of particular technological solutions to the problems defined by the regime, which have emerged, diffused and survived in the industry. In this context, each of the specific technologies of individual firms in an industry will correspond to one of these design configurations (Georghiou *et al.*, 1986, pp. 33–5). The notion of design configuration is a key concept; it allows us to deal with technological diversity within the industry and helps to highlight similarities and differences in the technological routines of the firms.

Technological Change and the Development of an Industry

A most important achievement of the research on technological change has been its contribution to a clearer perception of the close relationship between innovation, diffusion and industrial development. Recent research has called our attention to three important facts: first, that innovation is a rather continuous process that shapes the process of diffusion of a technology, while the latter, in turn, modifies the conditions on which further innovation takes place;[6] second, that the environment in which a technology develops is continuously shaped and, to a certain extent, created by the processes of innovation and diffusion themselves (Freeman, 1990; Hagerdoorn, 1989; Amendola and Bruno, 1990); and finally, and of particular interest to the present discussion, that the firms and the characteristics of the industry co-evolve with the technology (Nelson, 1992).

There are two major streams in the literature of technological change that have converged to considerably increase our understanding of the relationship between the development of a technology and that of its associated industry. The first is the study on the relationship between the life cycle of a product and the different stages of the development of an industry. The second is the research on innovation and diffusion of innovation in the Schumpeterian tradition.

The product life cycle hypothesis rests, as the term suggests, on an analogy with the life cycle of living organisms in biology.[7] The basic idea is that of a pattern of development that follows a series of stages: birth, growth, maturity and decline. From the perspective of the innovation and diffusion aspects of technological change, the life cycle expresses itself in two superimposed patterns of innovation and diffusion. With respect to innovation, the early stage represents a fluid period with frequent changes in the design of the product. This is followed by a tendency towards standardization in which the emphasis shifts towards process innovations that seek to exploit economies of scale and reduce costs. A slow-down in innovative activity characterizes the mature stage. Finally, the decline phase is usually related to the emergence of a new technology that displaces the old one. Regarding the process of diffusion that runs in parallel, the pattern followed during the life cycle can often be approximated by an S-shaped trajectory in measures of market penetration. That pattern represents the different rates at which such penetration occurs during the introduction, growth and maturity phases.

The basic scheme of the product cycle presented above has been subsequently refined as studies of innovation have brought additional elements to the surface. First, a sharp dichotomy between product and process innovation has proved to be inadequate. There are instances, such as cost reduction innovations, that convey significant changes in both process and product design. That is the case, for instance, with the introduction of new plastic materials to replace metals in airframe construction (Sahal, 1985, pp. 64–6). A second point is that, as several authors have pointed out, the biological metaphor can often be misleading. There may be changes in the economic environment, or significant innovations within the regime, which can lead to dematurity, and to a reversal in the slow-down of the diffusion of a technology. A pattern of diffusion different from the S-shaped pattern suggested above may result from these changes (Iwai, 1984; Abernathy and Clark, 1985; Durand, 1992). The major innovations in the automobile industry that followed the oil shocks of the 1970s offer a good example of this kind of dematuration effect. Furthermore, during its diffusion, the technology changes, different designs compete in the market and new generations of artifacts displace old ones. Thus, the path of diffusion of a technology that one observes is an aggregate of curves corresponding to different design configurations.

The question of the maturity of a technology is central to the analysis of the co-evolution of technology and industry. There are limits to how much a given technology can be improved and it is important to bear in mind the limits defined by a technological regime when judging innovations. This is necessary in order to distinguish whether we can talk of dematuration or, rather, of the emergence of a new regime. It is also important to stress that, as Georghiou *et al.* have pointed out, maturity is largely a socio-economic phenomenon that depends on the collective expectations of those involved in developing a technology with respect to the profitability of attempting further developments (Georghiou *et al.*, 1986, p. 58).

The emergence of a dominant design is a theme intimately related to the ideas presented above. According to the dominant design hypothesis, the 'fluid' period in the development of a technology, characterized by active experimentation in product technology, comes to an end with the emergence of a dominant design (Abernathy and Utterback, 1978; Clark, 1985). This dominant design incorporates a number of basic choices that are no longer reviewed in subsequent designs but are only refined and elaborated upon.[8] This hypothesis has received confirmation from several case studies; however, as Utterback and Suárez note, they have been limited to assembly products (Utterback and Suárez, 1993, p. 2). Although its universal applicability is still open to question,[9] the dominant design concept offers a useful guide for the analysis of the development of technology, which can be directly related to the concept of design configuration introduced earlier. There may be different designs coexisting in an industry. A single dominant design may emerge in some cases with complete or virtual elimination of others, but this will not necessarily happen in every industry. One reason for this is that markets are not homogeneous and different configurations may enjoy advantages in different niches. Nonetheless, regardless of whether a single design imposes itself or more than one coexist, the general idea of some configurations being abandoned while elements of design become firmly established with the development of a technological regime is a plausible generalization.

The evolutionary approach offers a rich theoretical framework to integrate the ideas presented above. The emergence and evolution of a technology and of its associated industry are shaped in a competitive process in which the driving forces are selection and the generation of variety. In this context, the ability of competitors to adapt, to anticipate market conditions and to exploit the development potential of the design configurations that they champion is the key aspect in their competitive performance, rather than their static allocative efficiency. At each point in time, the requirements of the market and its price structure both act as devices that guide innovative activity and exert selective pressure. In this way, they favour some routes of technological development and hamper others. The different success of competing firms translates into different profitability and growth. For some firms, repeated failure will eventually lead to bankruptcy. For others, there will be scope for adaptation and survival. The size and number of firms in an industry and the diffusion of different routines among them are all outcomes of the same evolutionary process that drives technological development.

As was noted earlier, it is not only technology and market structure that change. The selection environment is not immutable: innovation and diffusion redefine the conditions under which subsequent market selection will take place. Both firms and customers learn, and the concepts of product and user needs are formed and reshaped (Clark, 1985). There is, thus, the broader issue of the formation of the industry and its context.[10]

3. INNOVATION, DIFFUSION AND INTERNATIONAL TRADE

The model of technological and industrial evolution outlined above is of direct relevance to the debate on the role of technological change in international trade.

Posner's technology gap and Vernon's product life cycle theories are perhaps the best known statements on the relationship between technological change and international trade. Posner stressed the fact that, following the introduction of a new product in one country, its consumption in other countries will usually precede the establishment of production facilities abroad. These lags of production with respect to consumption give rise to trade flows. In this way, continuous innovation can be a constant source of international trade (Posner, 1961). Vernon, on the other hand, emphasized the link between the life cycle of the product and the changes in the relative weight of the different factors that determine the location of production: as the technology matures and product and process innovation fade away, labour costs become more important than proximity to suppliers and markets (Vernon, 1966). Subsequently, Vernon reconsidered his model to allow for a changed institutional setting in which transnational firms had the possibility of separating innovative and production activities and exploiting, from the outset, the advantages offered by different locations (Vernon, 1979).

Most of the debate around these theories has centred on the empirical relevance regarding the role of technological change as a factor that explains international trade.[11] Important as this may be, this leads us to a rather static analysis of the technology–trade relationship. Furthermore, too much stress on that issue has tended to obscure a basic message of these trade theories, namely that changes in trade flows are one aspect of the spatial dimension of the diffusion of innovation. It is this view of the relationship between trade and technological change that will be explored in this chapter.[12]

The application of the framework outlined above to the study of international trade allows us to explain it as the outcome of evolutionary processes. Trade flows inform us about the geographical dimension of the co-evolution of a technology and its industry. In the remainder of this chapter I analyse the changes in trade flows associated with two innovations. This analysis has three main purposes: first, to exemplify how concepts like technological regime and design configuration can be given empirical content; second, to provide an illustration of their usefulness in the study of the trade associated with specific technologies; and third, to show what is involved in the application of an evolutionary framework to the empirical analysis of trade flows.

Two words of caution are necessary in relation to the scope and the aims of the cases presented in the following pages. First, I do not attempt to explore all the aspects of the application of the framework presented in Section 2, but only to illustrate the use of some important concepts. Second, I shall limit myself to looking at some salient facts about trade flows and seeing how the evolutionary approach helps in understanding them. A full evolutionary explanation of the trade flows would amount to identifying and placing in their historical context the different elements relative to the technology, the firms and the environment that have converged to shape the co-evolution of the technology and the industry that is behind the patterns of trade. Space precludes any attempt at such an explanation.

The two cases analysed here are indirect electrostatic photocopying (IEP) and linear low density polyethylene (LLDPE). The first is an innovation that gave origin to a new technological regime and corresponds to an assembly type of industry. The second was a major innovation within an existing regime and corresponds to a chemical processing industry. In a nutshell, the IEP case corresponds to a situation in which, about a decade after the emergence of the new technological regime, major changes occurred in the location of production, which considerably altered the patterns of international trade. These changes occurred during the fluid period of the development of the technology: new design configurations were being introduced and the markets for the product were being created. The course followed by the diffusion of IEP, and in particular its spatial dimension, was shaped in a competitive struggle. The outcome of this struggle depended on the innovative performance of the firms in product, process and market practices. The differences in the national environments where the firms were located clearly played an important role. The LLDPE case, on the other hand, is an example of a major innovation that emerged within a mature technological regime. This maturity contributed to patterns of diffusion and trade in LLDPE significantly different from those followed by other types of polyethylene resin introduced earlier. Both the maturity of the technologies associated with the polymerization of ethylene and their uneven diffusion in different parts of the world have been fundamental in shaping the spatial dimension of the diffusion of LLDPE. The country of origin of the innovation and the competitive moves of both innovating and imitating firms have also been important. Government intervention and contingencies, such as the fluctuations in the prices of oil and other hydrocarbons, have been equally important.

In what follows, the two innovations will be discussed in separate sections. In each case, I start by presenting some trade facts associated with them. Afterwards, I analyse briefly the characteristics of the technology and its development, and assess the factors that have contributed to generate the trade patterns observed.

Indirect Electrostatic Photocopying

The first automatic IEP machine was introduced by Xerox in the US in 1959. It represented a major breakthrough for the convenience copying of documents on plain paper. For ten years, Xerox retained a monopoly in the technology. The innovation was very successful and during that period the company experienced enormous growth.[13] The international diffusion of IEP went in parallel with the internationalization of Xerox. Two joint ventures, Rank Xerox in the UK and Fuji-Xerox in Japan, formed the backbone for its expansion in the Eastern hemisphere. Initially, the machines were produced in the US and exported abroad. In 1965 major manufacturing facilities were established in the Netherlands and six years later production facilities were established in Japan. Although there is no information available about the trade between the US company and its associates in other countries, the establishment of new manufacturing sites obviously had an impact on trade flows.

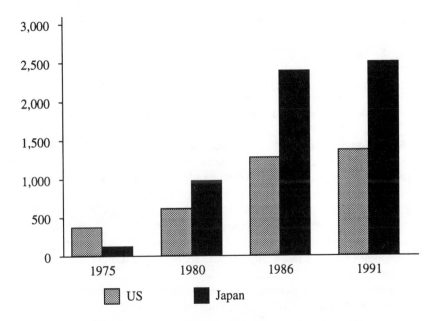

Sources: Elaboration on Wolfman, 1993 and Japan, MITI, 1991 and 1993.

Figure 3.1   Output of IEP equipment in Japan and in the US (000 units)

Of more interest here is the fact that in the 1970s, with the lapse of Xerox basic patents, several firms from the US, Western Europe and Japan entered the industry. Relatively soon, the competitive balance shifted in favour of the Japanese manufacturers and, although Xerox retained the largest share of the market, the second half of the 1970s and the early 1980s witnessed the withdrawal of most US and Western European manufacturers and an increase in the market share of Japanese firms. As a result, Japan has become the largest producer and exporter of photocopiers in the world (see Figure 3.1 and Table 3.1).

Table 3.1   Share of major exporters of photo- and thermo-copying apparatus in total market economy exports (%)

	1980	1986	1991
Japan	43	62	42
Netherlands	13	11	16
West Germany	13	8	10
France	3	4	8
US	6	4	7
UK	15	5	6
Hong Kong	1	2	4
Total ($m US)	2,314	3,692	6,208

Source: Elaboration on UN Yearbook of International Trade Statistics, various years.

Regarding the nature of the innovation, the significance of IEP was not only a question of technical superiority with respect to other copying technologies. The IEP innovation represented, in our terminology, the introduction of a new technological regime in reprography and the birth of a new industry. The technology relied on an entirely different knowledge base and required a different set of skills from those of other copying technologies.[14] The latter were based on photochemistry and used specially coated papers. Duplicating technologies relied on mechanical devices for the application of dyes and inks on paper. The heart of IEP technology was the application of the principles of photoconductivity and electrostatics to the reproduction of images. Although IEP displaced other technologies in convenience copying, it was above all market-creating.

The entry of firms in the 1970s meant more than a simple increase in supply and in the number of competitors. It brought a great deal of diversity to the industry. One dimension of this diversity was increased technological variety. Although Xerox had made considerable improvements to the technology, it had pursued a relatively narrow line of development. The core elements of IEP technology are the photoconductor and the development subsystems. In the Xerox copiers, the photoconductor was based on a selenium drum photoreceptor and the development subsystem on a dual dry insulating toner applied with a magnetic brush. Several of the new entrants introduced new design configurations in these subsystems (see Table 3.2). These new design configurations represented different approaches to the basic problem of the IEP process of creating and developing a latent image from an original for its subsequent transfer to paper. Each of these new designs had a different potential in relation to the most relevant techno-economic aspects of the process such as copy quality, manufacturing costs, machine speed and reliability. This is one reason why different design configurations coexist in the market.[15] In the photoconductor system, for instance, organic mono-layered drums are preferred at the low end of the market because of their low costs. In the high-volume, high-speed segment, in contrast, multi-layered organic photoreceptors in a belt configuration are preferred since they last longer, allow improved paper handling, which increases reliability, and make it possible to use a flash exposure system, which saves time. Consequently, different configurations appear with different frequency in the various segments of the market.

Table 3.2   Main photoconductor and development systems introduced in the early 1970s

Photoconductor system	Company and year	Development system	Company and year
Cadmium sulphide drum	Canon (1970)	Liquid toner	Canon (1972)
Organic belt mounted on drum	IBM (1970)	Dry monocomponent toner	3M (1972)
Zinc oxide master	3M (1972)	Dry dual conductive toner	Kodak (1975)
Organic belt	Kodak (1975)		

The innovation brought about by entry was not limited to the basic subsystems of the IEP process. Another aspect of innovation was the introduction of features such as reduction capabilities, document feeders and other devices aimed to capture specific niches of the market. Entry also brought new marketing and distribution practices. Against the practice introduced by Xerox of renting the copy equipment, some firms introduced outright sale and distribution through networks of dealers. In that way, the firms were able to enter the market without having to undertake the high investment involved in building the organization required to compete with Xerox on its own terms.

In relation to the patterns of trade described above, the early trade flows of IEP equipment can be clearly identified as a technology gap type of trade. This trade rested on the monopoly enjoyed by Xerox on the basis of its patent rights. However, the technology gap theory does not help us to understand the rise of Japan as a major exporter. Regarding Vernon's product cycle theory, it would be inadequate to interpret the shift of IEP production to Japan as a corroboration of the predictions of the model. This shift does not fit a pattern in which, once the technology offers little potential for further innovation and for the exploitation of economies of scale, the production emigrates to a low-wage location. A relatively low wage gave an advantage to Japanese producers; but equally important were their significant innovation in product and process technology and the considerable expansion in their scale of production relative to that of their competitors (Ghazanfar, 1984). IEP technology was far from being mature when Japanese firms established their domination on the industry.[16] If one is searching for a confirmation of Vernon's hypothesis, it is more plausible to look at more recent trends such as the location of labour-intensive refurbishing activities in low-wage countries.

The success of the Japanese firms in the photocopier industry rested on two basic elements: first, on their ability to produce copiers of comparable quality to those of their competitors but at a much lower cost, and second, on their perception of the potential of outright sale in the low-speed, low-price segment of the market. In fact, the entry of Japanese firms contributed to a considerable expansion of that segment of the market.

In order to understand the shift in trade patterns in favour of Japan, it is necessary to look at the different factors relative to the firms, the environment and the technology that contributed to a superior market performance of the Japanese firms during the period in which that shift occurred. The ability of the firms to either develop or acquire the technological knowledge associated with design configurations competitive in that segment of the market was an important element behind their success. The relatively low wages of Japan compared with the US and Western European competitors gave, no doubt, an important cost advantage to Japanese firms. Equally important was the particularly efficient combination of methods of production and product design that has been characteristic of the success of Japanese firms in other assembly industries such as the automobile industry and consumer electronics. This efficiency in manufacturing was largely related to conditions specific to the Japanese environment: as has been documented in many studies, the basis of these production methods extends beyond the individual firm into the various companies participating in the production chain (Goto, 1982; Freeman, 1987; Odagiri and Goto, 1993). Characteristics specific to the Japanese environment are also likely to have influenced the ability of the firms to perceive the potential of the low end of the market, which led them to focus on that segment on a large scale. It has been suggested that the extended and acute need for efficient methods of document reproduction, dictated by the complexity of the Kanji characters on which Japanese writing is based, contributed to creating awareness in Japanese firms about the potential of the market.[17]

The important role played by elements shared by Japanese firms should not obscure the relevance of diversity. In spite of common national advantages, not all Japanese firms have performed equally well: as in Europe and the US, some have left the market. In the case of successful firms, the key elements for success have been different. Canon and Ricoh, the two firms that have captured the largest market shares, illustrate this point. Canon's outstanding innovative performance was a distinctive characteristic from the outset. The firm entered the industry with its own proprietary technology in the basic photoconductor and development subsystems, and has continued to be very innovative. This has been an important factor behind its success. In 1981, for instance, Canon introduced the personal copier, which opened a segment of the market in which it retains over 50 per cent. In the case of Ricoh, distribution agreements with Savin, Kalle and Nashua played an important role in building up the significant market share that the firm gained soon after its entry. Ricoh obtained its basic technology through licensing. Its partners also contributed to the acquisition of technology as part of the distribution deals: Savin's proprietary technology on liquid developments was used in most Ricoh's machines during the 1970s, and an organic photoconductor developed by Hoechst (Kalle's parent company) was

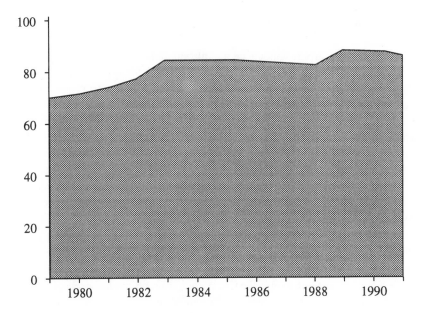

Source: Elaboration on data provided by Dataquest.

Figure 3.2   Share of Japanese manufacturers in total placements of photo-
copiers in Western Europe (%) (shares from data of units placed)

also used in some of Ricoh's copiers. However, as Ricoh gained more technological autonomy and knowledge of overseas markets, it started to increasingly distribute its copiers overseas through its own distribution network.

It is important to stress that the pattern of diffusion of IEP technology that led to the concentration of productive capacity in Japan was shaped by the competitive struggle of the mid 1970s, in which Japanese producers enjoyed the various advantages mentioned above. Some of these initial advantages have been affected by changes such as the strengthening of the yen and the increase in wages in Japan. However, through their presence in the industry, the firms have built technological competencies and a market position that have proven resilient to changes in the environment that contributed to their initial advantage. In 1985, for instance, the EEC established anti-dumping duties on Japanese copiers, which eroded their competitiveness in that market. However, it is significant that this was followed by the establishment of manufacturing sites by Japanese producers in the region rather than by the emergence of new local competitors. Although the contribution of Japanese exports to the Western European market has fallen, the share of Japanese firms in that market has not been weakened by the imposition of tariffs (see Figure 3.2).

Linear Low Density Polyethylene

In 1977, Union Carbide announced the introduction of a low pressure process to produce low density polyethylene (LDPE). The process offered substantial reductions in plant costs, space and energy consumption with respect to the conventional high pressure processes.[18] Soon it became apparent that Union Carbide's was as much a process as a product innovation: the process delivered an LLDPE, which at the time of introduction was superior to conventional LDPE in various characteristics. Furthermore, those characteristics were among the most relevant for the applications that made up the largest share of the LDPE market. It was estimated that LLDPE would impose a threat to 70 per cent of that market. In response, several of the main contenders in the LDPE industry developed their own proprietary LLDPE technologies.

Investment in LLDPE capacity has followed, however, a very different pattern from the one that characterized the polyethylene technologies that preceded it. Both LDPE and high density polyethylene (HDPE) experienced their earliest and greatest diffusion in the US, Western Europe and Japan. Polyethylene production has been traditionally concentrated in these regions, which have enjoyed significant trade surpluses with the rest of the world. These three regions are also home to the major companies that own and have developed the various proprietary technologies for the production of polyethylene. Nevertheless, although there has been a considerable penetration of LLDPE in the US, the share of capacity using new LLDPE technology in Western Europe and Japan is below the world average.[19] Important petrochemical complexes with LLDPE plants have been built in other countries. In particular, considerable export-oriented LLDPE capacity was built in Canada and Saudi Arabia during the 1980s. As a consequence there was a weakening in the surplus position in polyethylene trade of Western Europe, Japan and, to a lesser extent, the US. Regarding trade in LLDPE, the US and Western Europe developed a significant deficit with Canada and Saudi Arabia, respectively (see Figure 3.3 and Table 3.3).

Table 3.3   Trade balances in polyethylene, 1988 (000 tonnes)

Country / Region	LLDPE	Total polyethylene
United States	–384	212
Canada	480	590
Latin America	–5	–313
Western Europe	–150	150
Middle East	460	804
Africa	–7	–222
Japan	–15	144
Other Far East	–400	–1,509

In relation to the nature of the innovation, in contrast with IEP, LLDPE did not inaugurate a new technological regime. It represented, instead, a widening of the trajectory of development of the technology to produce HDPE, that is, that associated with the low pressure polymerization of ethylene based on organo-metallic catalysts. The key aspects of Union Carbide's LLDPE technology had already been applied to polyethylene production and were established areas of research.[20] In spite of this, the particular combination of them by Union Carbide produced a very significant innovation, which brought into more direct competition two technologies that had remained relatively separated as product groups with little market overlap: LDPE and HDPE. Furthermore, it made it possible to build plants that can switch from the production of one type of resin to the other.

Two facts have been decisive for the pattern of development followed by LLDPE technology and its market: first that the process technologies of both the regime from which LLDPE emerged and that whose major markets it was threatening were considerably developed already and, second, that the LLDPE innovation was mainly of a market-stealing type and created few new applications. Thus, although LLDPE fostered some new developments, it did

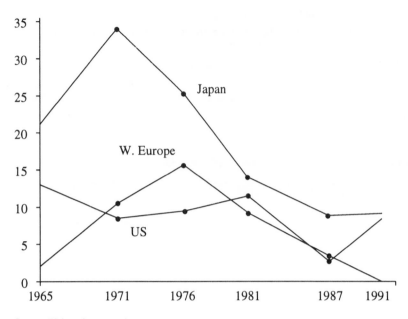

Source: Elaboration on various sources (see Arjona, 1994, p. 327).

Figure 3.3   Polyethylene trade balance/production ratios (%) (ratios from data in weight units)

not introduce a major change in the pace of innovation and market growth in polyethylene as a whole. Rather, it has been the conditions dictated by the state of development of the technological regimes associated with the polymerization of ethylene that have marked the pace and direction of the development of LLDPE technology.

Table 3.4   Average logarithmic rates of growth of polyethylene production, 1965–89 (%)

	1965–69	1970–74	1975–79	1980–85	1985–89
US	11.7	9.4	6.8	3.3	2.0
Western Europe	22.1	15.1	4.6	3.4	3.2
Japan	22.6	11.1	0.7	0.8	3.7
World	18.1	12.7	6.5	4.8	4.0

Source: Elaboration on UN Yearbook of Industrial Statistics, various years, and Predicasts 1982 (from data in weight units).

There are, in a word, indications of maturity in polyethylene technologies: there is little scope for further innovation-led growth in the markets of the regions where polyethylene technologies have had their greatest diffusion.[21] Since the mid 1970s, the broad pattern in the polyethylene industries at a worldwide level has been one of a slow-down in the rate of growth (see Table 3.4). In the US, Western Europe and Japan, polyethylene production shows clear signs of the retardation phenomenon observed by Burns (1934) and Kuznets (1954).

The cost structure of polyethylene production changed dramatically in the 1970s. This change was partly because of many years of increases in plant scale, which reduces the weight of the fixed component of unit costs, but was due mainly to the increases in the price of oil. The main raw material, ethylene, passed from representing 30 per cent of the costs in 1972 to 70 per cent ten years later, with the corresponding reduction in the importance of fixed costs. Therefore, the considerable savings in this component of costs achieved by Union Carbide's gas phase process had a relatively minor impact on unit costs. At the level of the applications, the technologies to process the LLDPE and the products for which it was used were basically the same as those for conventional LDPE. In summary, LLDPE contributed little to the expansion of the polyethylene markets in the way of new applications, and the same can be said regarding the expansion via cost reductions that translate into lower prices.

Table 3.5   New polyethylene plants in developing countries that started to operate from 1979 onwards (capacity in 1992)[a]

	Share (%)
LL[b]	43.0
LDPE	28.8
HDPE	28.2
Total (000 tonnes/year)	5 618

Notes:
a   data for Algeria, Argentina, Brazil, China, India, Israel, Mexico, Qatar, S. Korea, Saudi Arabia, Singapore, Taiwan, Turkey, Venezuela.
b   Includes LLDPE and LL/HDPE capacities.

Source: Elaboration on various sources (see Arjona, 1994, p. 295).

The maturity of the two technological regimes associated with the polymerization of ethylene and the fact that they had experienced a considerable diffusion in the US, Western Europe and Japan are intimately related to the changes in the patterns of international trade. In the past, with relatively fast growth in these regions, and capacity being built usually ahead of demand, export markets were a natural way out for excess production. With changed conditions and the growth slow-down in those regions, capacity has been increasingly being built near the faster growing markets in the rest of the world and in countries with natural resources. This new capacity is serving regional markets, to which the surplus regions exported in the past, and is the main force behind the loss of grip in world markets of the traditional exporters. Strong political will to establish or expand petrochemical production and a disposition of the companies with the technology to license and/or invest in less developed countries have been important factors in these changes in the location of investment.[22] Considerable new polyethylene capacity was built during the 1980s, mainly in the Far East, the Middle East and South America. LLDPE technology has been actively licensed and accounts for a great share of this new capacity (see Table 3.5).[23] This has caused the greater penetration of LLDPE technology in several countries of these regions compared with Western Europe, Japan and even the US.

In relation to the trade in LLDPE, the launching of important export-oriented projects, based on natural resources availability, contributed to the trade deficits of the US and Western Europe. At the time that LLDPE was being introduced to the market, oil prices were particularly high. The availability in Canada and Saudi Arabia of cheap ethane feedstock for the production of ethylene made them attractive locations for LLDPE capacity. Another important factor that contributed to the projects was that investment in petrochemicals was actively promoted by local governments (Chapman, 1991, pp. 185–86). The new Canadian and Saudi Arabian petrochemical complexes have had significant effects on trade flows. With the production facilities and the associated infrastructure in place, there is a basis for continued expansion, even though the high oil prices that contributed to the projects have not remained at that level.

The important point is that the developments in Canada and Saudi Arabia have not been echoed elsewhere. There are no signs of a new trend leading to a reversal of trade patterns in which the traditionally surplus countries would become large net importers of polyethylene. Although an increase in oil prices could unleash similar projects in other locations with ethane availability, there are not many places in the world with large supplies of unexploited gas. It is true that there is a tendency towards the contraction of the polyethylene trade surplus of the traditional exporters. However, a major reversal of trade flows has not occurred even in the case of Western Europe and Japan, which depend considerably on oil imports. Oil continues to be imported in large quantities for energy use (which represents the largest share of its consumption). Given the considerable development of the oil tanker industry, transport costs are relatively low and the availability of oil in other countries does not represent a major advantage. The economies derived from the existing infrastructure, such as ethylene pipelines, the proximity to markets and suppliers, and the fact that firms based on these regions own the technology and continue developing it are created advantages that make firms in the advanced regions very resistant to competition from producers from abroad.

A point about the diffusion of LLDPE that merits consideration is the greater penetration of this innovation in the US compared with Western Europe. Four main factors contributed to this difference in penetration. First, the country of origin of the innovation appears to have played an important role. Second, differences in the characteristics of the petrochemical industries of the two regions (type of feedstock, number and size of firms, presence of the public sector) contributed to a stronger recession in the Western European industry during the early 1980s which explains, in part, a different attitude towards investment in LLDPE. Third, the different timing of the introduction of LLDPE in the two regions also corresponded to a different situation in the prices of oil and the situation in Europe was less conducive to stimulating investment in the new technology. Finally, differences in the patterns of polyethylene consumption and in the technology employed by plastic processors contributed to the tendency in Western Europe to consume less LLDPE and to a greater resistance to invest in machinery to process it. In summary, a technology gap combined with differences in the environment of the two regions and differences in oil prices generated different patterns of diffusion of LLDPE technology in the US and Western Europe.

I conclude this discussion of LLDPE innovation by noting that my analysis of trade has relied considerably on the insights provided by the theories of Posner and Vernon. In fact, polyethylene was identified long ago by Hufbauer, in his study of synthetic materials, as a clear example of technology gap trade (Hufbauer, 1966). The different timing in the diffusion of polyethylene has been central to the analysis. The insights of the product life cycle model, on the other hand, have also been useful and have helped us to understand the broad trends in the international location of polyethylene capacity. However, as various authors who have applied this framework to the analysis of petrochemicals have noted, this requires us to introduce additional elements to Vernon's basic scheme (Stobaugh, 1970; Auty, 1988; Chapman, 1991). In particular, it is necessary to consider important elements like the dynamics of the different regional markets, the role of government intervention, and contingencies such as the fluctuations in oil prices.

CONCLUDING REMARKS

In this chapter I have presented elements of an evolutionary framework for the study of technological change at a micro level. Such a framework was applied to the analysis of the patterns of trade associated with two innovations. I have established, in two specific cases, how the emergence and change in the patterns of trade relate to the introduction of innovations and to their international diffusion.

A comparison between the two cases illustrates the relevance of the nature of an innovation in relation to existing technologies. Whether an innovation inaugurates a new technological regime or not is of fundamental importance for the subsequent development of the technology and of its industry. The major changes in the competitive balance in the photocopier industry during the 1970s, for instance, were largely the outcome of technological competition within the fluid period of a new regime. Major changes in the technology and in the industry were witnessed in those years. The changes in trade flows were an expression of those more fundamental changes. The LLDPE innovation, in contrast, did not represent a new regime. In spite of the considerable impact that LLDPE had in the polyethylene industries, the course of their development was mainly driven by the maturity of the two technological regimes associated with polyethylene production. Regarding the geographical dimension of the diffusion of LLDPE and of its associated trade flows, these are also largely explained by the maturity of the two polyethylene regimes and by their uneven international diffusion.

The analysis of the two cases also makes it clear that, although important, a focus on technology alone is insufficient for understanding the evolution of trade flows. A key message that emerges from the two exercises is that one ought to look at a series of interlocking factors relative to the technology, to the firms in the industry and to the national and international environments. This is an essential part of an evolutionary analysis.

Regarding the old debates on the role of technology in international trade, the two cases presented above have served to illustrate that, although the relevance of the predictions of Posner's and Vernon's theories may vary in different situations, the basic idea behind these theories of looking at the spatial aspect of the diffusion of technology to explain trade flows retains its methodological value.

The analysis of innovation and diffusion has traditionally been based implicitly or explicitly on a supply/demand perspective. Thus, the factors that affect technological change are grouped according to whether they correspond to the demand or the supply forces of the market. This way of proceeding offers a convenient way of analysing how they impinge on the behaviour of producers and buyers, and has produced valuable insights. However, it has a major shortcoming: it makes us look at these phenomena of an equilibrium perspective, as the market-coordinated outcome of two forces acting independently from each other. The perspective that we adopted here was to look at the factors behind technological change as relative to three key elements of the evolutionary process: the technology itself, the population of firms, and the selection environment. This way of proceeding unveils a crucial dimension of the way in which these factors operate which is absent in a market equilibrium perspective: namely, how they interact through the mechanisms of variety and selection.

NOTES

This chapter draws on the work for my Phd thesis at the University of Manchester. I am highly indebted to Stan Metcalfe for his supervision. Thanks are due to Pilar Díaz, Klaus Nielsen, Björn Johnson, Kurt Unger and an anonymous referee for their helpful comments on earlier drafts. I am also grateful to Consejo Nacional de Ciencia y Tecnología for financial support.

1. There are, however, limits to the extent to which one can make use of biological analogies in economic and social sciences. This is due not only to the fact that the theory of evolution in biology remains a highly controversial subject (see Mani, 1991), but also because of the specificities of socio-economic systems that arise from their human nature.
2. The market, which acts as a selection environment, for instance, is an institution supported itself by other institutions. The latter facilitate and regulate the exchange of commodities. (See Hodgson, 1988, pp. 176–9).
3. Layton has offered a useful image of technology as a spectrum of activities and objects with ideas at one end, techniques at the other and design in the middle (Layton, 1974, pp. 37–8).
4. Rosenberg's (1976) 'focusing devices', Sahal's (1981, 1985) 'technological guideposts', Nelson and Winter's (1982) 'technological regimes' and Dosi's (1982) 'technological paradigms' are concepts very close in meaning which have been put forward to capture this idea.
5. The definition of industry used here is of course arbitrary; different criteria can be used to render an equally valid definition. The merit of our definition rests on its usefulness in empirical analysis. Regarding our concept of firm, it is more restricted than the meaning conveyed in the everyday use of the word. We will be using the terms firm and business unit as equivalent, but, in practice, this equivalence only holds occasionally. Modern firms are usually an aggregate of business units forming a larger organization.
6. Georghiou *et al.* (1986), for instance, present a series of case studies in which this interrelationship is explored. This contrasts with the early studies of innovation and diffusion which tended to regard them as relatively separate stages of technological change.
7. The life cycle hypothesis was present in the writings of Vernon (1966) and Hirsch (1967) on international trade. For a clear early presentation of the product life cycle ideas see Muller and Tilton (1969).
8. Although, as presented above, the image created by this description is one of superiority of the dominant design which triumphs over competing alternatives, there are other ways in which a dominant design becomes established. There is the possibility of 'locked-in' phenomena in which factors other than strict technological merit play an important role in the establishment of a dominant design.
9. See the discussion on this topic in Nelson, 1992, pp. 9–10.
10. The co-evolution of institutions related to an industry is a complex process that involves not only the firms but institutions such as governmental agencies, universities, engineering associations, regulations and other institutions in the technology support system. (See Perez, 1983).
11. See, for instance, the contributions by Hufbauer and by Gruber and Vernon, and the comments on them in Vernon (ed.) 1970.
12. The relationship between the diffusion of innovation and international trade was emphasized long ago by Metcalfe and Soete (1984). However, this has been a rather neglected area of research.

13. Between 1959 and 1974, Xerox sales increased from 33 million US dollars to 3.6 billion (Hunger *et al.*, 1986, p. 448).
14. An exception is the closely related direct electrostatic photocopying process known as 'electrofax'. This technology branched from the same paradigm from which IEP emerged. The major disadvantage of this process relative to IEP is the use of paper coated with zinc oxide instead of plain paper.
15. Another reason is that although there are firms that compete on the basis of more than one configuration, there is also a tendency to concentrate on the promotion and development of one or a limited number of them.
16. The two main Japanese competitors, Ricoh and Canon, for instance, have moved away from the configurations in the basic photoconductor and development subsystems that were at the heart of the copiers on which they based their challenge in the market. This is indicative of the fact that the regime was still being actively developed at the time when Japanese producers gained a significant market share in this industry.
17. Interview with a Rank-Xerox executive.
18. Capital investment was estimated to be 50 per cent of that required for an equivalent LDPE high pressure plant, and energy savings were estimated to be 75 per cent.
19. By 1992, the share of LLDPE plants in world polyethylene capacity was 27 per cent. But while the share of LLDPE in polyethylene capacity was 37 per cent in the US, it was only 16.5 per cent in Western Europe and 18 per cent in Japan.
20. The three key elements of the innovation were: aionic polymerization of ethylene with modified chromium based catalysts; the use of butene-1 comonomer to introduce branching in the polymer and reduce its density; and the reliance on a gas-phase process.
21. A similar trend has been found for petrochemicals as a whole, and there is evidence of a decline in innovative activity in these industries (Walsh, 1984). In this respect, it is important to note that the maturity of polyethylene technologies is part of a wider phenomenon: the maturity of the technology system to which they belong (petrochemicals broadly defined). This technology system is a constellation of technological and economically related innovations (Freeman and Perez, 1988, pp. 46–7).
22. Union Carbide, for instance, has been withdrawing from the production of polyethylene outside the US, while at the same time it has become very active in the licensing of its polyethylene technology. The royalties from this activity have been an important element for the profitability of its polyethylene business (Bower, 1986, pp. 100–4).
23. The capacity of plants that have started to operate since 1979 in the countries to which Table 3.5 refers represents 70 per cent of the aggregate polyethylene capacity operating in those countries. This reflects the enormous increase in polyethylene capacity that has taken place there in the last fifteen years.

REFERENCES

Abernathy, W.J. and K.B. Clark (1985), 'Innovation: Mapping the winds of creative destruction', *Research Policy*, 14, 3–22.

Abernathy, W. and J.M. Utterback (1978), 'Patterns of innovation in technology', *Technology Review*, 7, 40–7.

Allen, P.M. and M. Lesser (1991), 'Evolutionary human systems: Learning, ignorance and subjectivity', in Paolo Saviotti and Stan Metcalfe (eds), *Evolutionary Theories of Economic and Technological Change: Present Status and Future Prospects*, Harwood Academic Publishers, pp. 160–71.

Amendola, M. and S. Bruno (1990), 'The behaviour of the innovative firm', *Research Policy*, 19, 419–33.

Arjona, Luis (1994), *Essays on the Study of Technological Change and International Trade*, unpublished PhD thesis, University of Manchester, Faculty of Economic, Social and Legal Studies.

Auty, R.M. (1988), 'The economic stimulus from resource-based industry in developing countries: Saudi Arabia and Bahrain', *Economic Geography*, 64, 209–25.

Bower, Joseph (1986), *When Markets Quake: The Management Challenge of Restructuring Industry*, Boston, Mass.: Harvard Business School.

Burns, Arthur F. (1934), *Production Trends in the United States since 1870*, New York: National Bureau of Economic Research.

Chapman, Keith. (1991), *The International Petrochemical Industry: Evolution and Location*, Basil Blackwell.

Chemical Intelligence Services (1987), *Chem Facts Polyethylene*, Dunstable.

Chemical Intelligence Services (1993), *Chem Facts Polyethylene*, Dunstable.

Clark, K.B (1985), 'The interaction of design hierarchies and market concepts in technological evolution', *Research Policy*, 14, 235–51.

Dosi, G. (1982), 'Technological paradigms and technological trajectories: A suggested interpretation of the determinants and directions of technical change', *Research Policy*, 11, 147–62.

Durand, T. (1992), 'Dual technology trees: Assessing the intensity and strategic significance of technological change', *Research Policy*, 21, 361–80.

Freeman, Christopher (1987), *Technology Policy and Economic Performance: Lessons from Japan*, London: Frances Pinter.

Freeman, C. (1990), 'Diffusion: Spread of new technology to firms, sectors, and nations', in Heertje Arnold (ed.), *Innovation, Technology and Finance*, Basil Blackwell, pp. 38–70.

Freeman, C. and Perez, C. (1988), 'Structural crisis of adjustment: business cycles and investment behaviour', in G. Dosi *et al.* (eds), *Technical Change and Economic Theory*. London and New York: Pinter Publishers, pp. 38–66.

Georghiou, Luke, J. Stanley Metcalfe, Michael Gibbons, Tim Ray and Janet Evans (1986), *Post-Innovation Performance: Technological Development and Competition*, London: Macmillan.

Ghazanfar, Agha (1984), *An Analysis of Competition in the Office Reprographics Industries in the United Kingdom (1880–1980): A Case Study of Technological Change, New Entry and End Game Strategies, and Creative Destruction*, unpublished PhD thesis, University of London, London Graduate School of Business Studies.

Goto, A. (1982), 'Business groups in a market economy', *European Economic Review*, 53–70.

Hagerdoorn, John (1989), *The Dynamic Analysis of Innovation and Diffusion: A Study in Process Control*, New York and London: Pinter Publishers.

Henderson, R.M. and K.B. Clark (1990), 'Architectural innovation: The reconfiguration of existing product technologies and the failure of established firms', *Administrative Science Quarterly*, 35, 9–30.

Hirsch, Seev (1967), *Location of Industry and International Competitiveness*, Oxford: Clarendon Press.

Hodgson, Geoffrey M. (1988), *Economics and Institutions: A Manifesto for a Modern Institutional Economics*, Cambridge: Polity Press.

Hodgson, Geoffrey M. (1993), *Economics and Evolution: Bringing Life Back into Economics*, Cambridge: Polity Press.

Hufbauer, G.C. (1966), *Synthetic Material and the Theory of International Trade*, London: Gerald Duckworth & Co.

Hunger, D., T. Conquest and W. Miller (1986), 'Xerox Corporation: Proposed diversification', in Alan Rowe, *et al.*, *Strategic Management: A Methodological Approach*, pp. 447–66.

Iwai, K. (1984), 'Schumpeterian dynamics: An evolutionary model of innovation and imitation', *Journal of Economic Behaviour and Organization*, 5, 159–90.

Japan, MITI (1991), *Statistics on Japanese Industries*.

Japan, MITI (1993), *Statistics on Japanese Industries*.

Kuznets, Simon (1954), *Economic Change: Selected Essays in Business Cycles, National Income and Economic Growth*, London: William Heinemann Ltd.

Layton, E. (1974), 'Technology as knowledge', *Technology and Culture*, 15, 31–41.

Longley, Roger (1991), *Petrochemicals: An Industry and its Future*, London: The Economist Intelligence Unit, Special Report No. 2067.

Mani, G.S. (1991), 'Is there a general theory of biological evolution?', in P. Saviotti and J.S. Metcalfe (eds), *Evolutionary Theories of Economic and Technological Change: Present Status and Future Prospects*, Harwood Academic Publishers, pp. 31–57.

Metcalfe, J.S. (1989), 'Evolution and Economic Change', in A. Silberston (ed.), *Technology and Economic Progress*, Macmillan, pp. 54–84.

Metcalfe, J.S. and M. Boden (1991), 'Innovation strategy and epistemic connection: An essay on the growth of technological knowledge', *Journal of Scientific and Industrial Research*, 50, 707–17.

Metcalfe, J.S. and L. Soete (1984), 'Notes on the evolution of technology and international competition', in M. Gibbons *et al.* (eds), *Science and Technology Policy in the 1980s and Beyond*, London and New York: Longman, pp. 270–96.

Muller, D. and J. Tilton (1969), 'Research and development as barriers to entry', *Canadian Journal of Economics*, 2, 570–9.

Nelson, Richard (1992), *The Co-Evolution of Technology and Institutions*, Columbia University, September, mimeo.

Nelson, Richard R. and Sidney Winter (1982), *An Evolutionary Theory of Economic Change*, Cambridge, Mass.: Cambridge University Press.

Odagiri, H. and A. Goto (1993), 'The Japanese system of innovation: Past, present and future', in R. Nelson (ed.), *National Innovation Systems*, New York and Oxford: Oxford University Press, pp. 3–21.

Perez, C. (1983), 'Structural change and the assimilation of new technologies in the economic and social system', *Futures*, vol. 15, no. 5, 357–75.

Posner, M.V. (1961), 'International trade and technical change', *Oxford Economic Papers*, 13(3), 323–41.

Predicasts (1982), *World Plastics to 1995*, Predicasts Inc.

Rosenberg, Nathan (1976), *Perspectives on Technology*, Cambridge: Cambridge University Press.

Sahal, D. (1981), 'Alternative conceptions of technology', *Research Policy*, 10, 2–24.

Sahal, D. (1985), 'Technological guideposts and innovation avenues', *Research Policy*, 14, 61–82.

Saviotti, P.P. and J.S. Metcalfe (1984), 'A theoretical approach to the construction of technological output indicators', *Research Policy*, 13, 141–51.

Stobaugh, R.B. (1970), 'The neotechnology account of international trade: The case of petrochemicals', *Journal of International Business Studies*, 2(2), 41–60.

Utterback, J.M. and F.F. Suárez (1993), 'Innovation, competition, and industry structure', *Research Policy*, 22, 1–21.

Vernon, R. (1966), 'International investment and international trade in the product cycle', *Quarterly Journal of Economics*, 80(2), 190–207.

Vernon, Raymond (ed.) (1970), *The Technology Factor in International Trade*, New York: National Bureau of Economic Research.

Vernon, R. (1979), 'The product cycle hypothesis in a new international environment', *Oxford Bulletin of Economics and Statistics*, 41, 255–67.

Walsh, V. (1984), 'Invention and innovation in the chemical industry: Demand-pull or discovery-push?', *Research Policy*, 13, 211–34.

Wolfman, Lydia (1993), *Wolfman Report on the Photographic and Imaging Industry in the United States*.

4. The glocalization of technology

Marc Humbert

The main argument of this chapter is that although there is a genuine trend towards the globalization of the process of technology creation this is not leading to a 'de-societalization' of the innovation processes. Innovation processes will remain societal processes of which the presence of strong international differences provides confirmation. However, these differences are not limited to these processes but concern the whole societal organization and its workings. Moreover, innovation processes are the result of an interaction between different societal systems on the one hand and physical systems which are common to every society on the other hand. This complex framework hosts the challenging process of the globalization of technology and helps to turn it into opportunities for local and national systems. This is because it leads to the development of a better articulation between the global and the local dimension of technology creation or to the emergence of what we could call the *glocalization* of technology. After assessing the present state of the globalization of technology, I shall discuss the argument of embeddedness of innovation processes within national systems and then, as a conclusion, I shall spell out what are, from my point of view, the challenges and opportunities brought by what I have termed the glocalization of technology.

GLOBALIZATION OF TECHNOLOGY

Globalization as a challenge to nations seems to be a new way of discussing older themes such as the threat of multinationals to the autonomy of national economies. A quarter of a century ago, Ronstadt (1977) tried to assess the importance of R&D conducted abroad by US multinationals. Many articles were published at the end of the 1970s on the topic (for example, Mansfield *et al.*, 1979), and Madeuf could write on the international technological order (Madeuf, 1981). Since that time a lot of work has been done about an evolving phenomenon which is sometimes termed techno-globalism (for example, Petrella, 1989; OECD, 1992). In order to assess the importance of this evolution I shall try to define its components and then take some key data from research already published. Finally I shall discuss recent trends.

Techno-globalism: What Does it Mean?

I shall start with Archibugi and Michie's (1995) taxonomy. They proposed three categories of techno-globalism: *global exploitation of technology* – that which could be measured by the extensions of patents in foreign markets; *global technological collaboration* – measured by the number of inter-firm R&D agreements and the number of co-authored scientific papers; *and global generation of technology* – that which could be measured by patents granted in the USA to firms applying from outside their home country.

The first category represents the first historical step towards the globalization of technology and it now seems obvious to any innovative firm that it has to protect its innovation, not only in its home country but also abroad. To be sure, the 'quality' of the laws on intellectual property rights is not constant across the world and the opportunities available in each market and the threat of competitors also varies. This already advanced process of global exploitation of technology means something more: technology is now acknowledged as universal and could be diffused globally to potential users throughout the world. In fact technology transfer or diffusion has spread widely not only through patents' extension, but through exports of capital goods, licences, technical assistance, even exports of goods and phenomena such as imitation and reverse engineering. The proportion of nation-specific or 'monocultural' technologies (see Humbert, 1991b) has become very low, even if, in some cases, minor adaptations due to lack of international standards or harmonization are necessary to turn these technologies into products ready for any markets. However, this 'globalization' remains mainly concentrated within the countries (USA, Japan and the European Union) of the triad (see Humbert, 1993).

The second category raises something relatively new that can be divided in two. First we have the phenomenon of technological collaboration. To be sure, among academics this is no news, since people have worked together for ages, and a lot of discoveries and inventions have always been the result more of team-work than of any individual task. But until recently firms have researched and developed innovations in their own laboratories, with the utmost possible secrecy, jealously patenting their inventions (and even, sometimes, not patenting them for fear of leakages, preferring instead quick exploitation). However, in recent years, firms have entered into R&D agreements, sometimes with funding by a government agency for a significant part of the costs. The most famous case is the Japanese VLSI project in the mid 1970s, this has been followed by EEC programmes such as ESPRIT and EUREKA, which are international programmes, and by the semi-conductor project in the USA. Such projects, at a national level, still flourish in many areas. For example, Germany launched a project of inter-firm R&D with firms from the steel industry, the automotive industry and the chemicals industry, along with universities, scientific institutes and government (BMFT) to find alternative processes to welding. The project was conducted from July 1987 to the end of 1990, with DM 9.8 million provided by the ministry (BMFT) out of a cost of DM 20 million. The project was a success and has demonstrated the efficiency of inter-firm R&D collaboration (Häusler *et al.*, 1994). Mowery and Teece (1993) have also noted that 'during the past 15 years, U.S. industrial research has been in the throes of a restructuring that is changing the position of industrially funded in-house research within the corporate innovation process [as...] R&D collaboration with U.S. industry have expanded in importance recently'.

The second part of this category is the extension abroad of technological collaborations. Here again this move is obvious among academics where internationalization has led for a long time to the interexchange of students, postdoctoral researchers and professors, and to the development of international journals and international programmes. However, international agreements between firms in R&D are not so ancient. The first study on this phenomenon was published by Mariti and Smiley in 1983. This study and further ones have clearly linked this phenomenon with the emergence of new rules of the game for competition in world markets (see, for example, Mytelka, 1991). We may note in particular that firms, in collaborative agreements, are searching complementary assets to boost rapid technological progress (Teece, 1986). Indeed the most impressive fact is the extremely rapid growth in the number of agreements after 1980. The largest database on technology cooperation agreements is that of MERIT-CATI (see Hagedoorn and Schakenraad, 1988), which has compiled data on new materials, biotechnology and information technologies since 1970. It clearly shows a surge in the early 1980s which is confirmed up to now.

Archibugi and Michie's third category, global generation of technology, is more questionable. First of all we should consider that a process of innovation which includes international technological collaboration (i.e. the second category) is a genuine process of global generation of technology. In fact, under their third category the authors asked the old question recalled at the beginning: are foreign firms doing R&D in host countries? The answer to this first question is 'yes' and has been for a long time, but is this phenomenon more and more widespread and what is the proportion between R&D at home and abroad? What is the proportion of local to foreign R&D at home? The case of foreign R&D is a case of collaboration as usual in a given country where a foreign-owned laboratory is employing both foreign and local people with both foreign and local links of all kinds (with other firms, universities, government agencies, etc.). Is there a case of technology generation? This is, more precisely, the question posed by the authors in this category and they adopt the idea that we can only have a positive answer when a patent is granted to the foreign laboratory. As a matter of fact this is restrictive for two reasons. First, as we have argued above, doing R&D abroad is a case of a global technological activity and the firm will pursue it only if it is productive. In any case, there will be a technological return even without patents. Second, while according to the management of the firm the applications of patents may be a more or less centralized operation, research resulting in patents may be conducted through collaboration between teams in various countries including one in the firm's home country. Hedlund (1994) and Howells (1995) have pointed out that transnational corporations are increasingly organizing cross-border teams to develop in-house international R&D projects. Moreover, it seems that there is an old

Table 4.1   Globalization of technology

	Principal means	Principal results
Global exploitation of technology	exports of goods	diffusion
	exports of capital goods	transfer
	exports of licences	imitation
	exports of technical assistance	reverse engineering
	extension abroad of patents	
	production facilities abroad	
Global collaboration in technology	cross-border technico-economic networks	discovery
	in basic research	invention
	in precompetitive research	design
	close to markets	innovation
	international joint ventures	technology out-sourcing
	R&D abroad by MNEs[a] (greenfield, takeover, or upgrading)	
	patenting from abroad by MNEs[b]	

Notes: (a)   MNEs = multinational enterprises.
　　　(b)   As an incentive to boost the efficiency of overseas laboratories.

practice of international technology out-sourcing by multinational firms (Chesnais, 1992) as they search to benefit from access to knowledge available in all forms in their host countries (see Humbert, 1990). Doing so they internationalize or globalize their in-house process of technology creation even if resulting patents are delivered to the parent company. So, doing R&D abroad is an important step away from techno-nationalism, and worldwide dispersed patenting would be a clear criterion to assess if a firm is fully globalized but it is not a requisite to state that the process of globalization of technology is on its way. Somehow patenting from abroad can be seen as one of the results expected from R&D abroad which is already a form of a global process of technology creation. Table 4.1 gives a synthetic view of my argument in two categories: global exploitation of technology and global cooperation in technology. I shall now turn to look for some empirical evidence about this process, first taking stock of studies giving information about the importance of R&D abroad and then of the importance of patenting from abroad by multinational firms.

R&D Abroad

In 1989 Casson *et al.* studied the international distribution of the laboratories owned by 500 major firms (Casson *et al.*, 1992, p. 181). Out of a total of 904 laboratories, 463 are located in the USA with a foreign dependence ratio of 39 per cent, that is to say, 181 of these 463 laboratories are foreign-owned. Out of the total 904 laboratories, 406 are owned by US firms and 124 of them are located abroad, which shows an international ratio of 31 per cent. This is a little below the general mean which is 39 per cent.

These data give an average of a relatively high level of globalization of technology. In an earlier survey, for 1982, 792 of the world's largest industrial companies indicated that 30 per cent of their production was located abroad and 12 per cent of their R&D expenditures (Dunning, 1994, p. 72). These figures are weaker, suggesting a growth between 1982 and 1989, but these figures surely depend on the respective sizes of home and overseas laboratories. Although we do not have many time-series, data presented by Peters (1992) provides evidence of a trend towards a growing number of firms setting up new R&D laboratories outside their home base. Most studies confirm the domination of a small number of countries as home countries for multinationals and as host countries for R&D expenditures and foreign-owned laboratories as well. The location of R&D abroad varies not only across countries but also among industries. Data from Cantwell and Hodson (1990) show an increase between 1966 and 1982 and also great differences between industries: the share of R&D expenditures of US multinationals located abroad is more than 13 per cent in food products, pharmaceuticals, motor vehicles and aircraft, and a mere 3.3 per cent in electrical equipment. A specific study of 20 automobile firms – the main makers of automobiles – by Miller (1994) shows that 25 per cent of R,D&E (Engineering) personnel are located abroad and Miller indicates that Japanese car makers are developing multi-regional strategies which would lead to dispersed R,D&E facilities.

Patenting from Abroad

Papanastassiou and Pearce have established data on the share of US patents of the world's largest firms attributable to research in foreign locations, outside the home country of the parent company (1994, p. 118). For almost all home countries this share has increased significantly from 1970 to 1990. For US-based companies it has risen from 5 per cent to 8 per cent, for French-based companies, from 8 per cent to 16 per cent. UK-based companies now have a proportion of nearly 50 per cent and are in the same range as companies based in small countries like Belgium, Switzerland, Belgium or Canada. Conversely, Japanese-based companies show a significant move towards the reduction of patents coming from research in foreign locations, from 2.6 per cent to 0.9 per cent. According to the authors this can be explained, in spite of a wide development of the internationalization of Japanese enterprises, because of the extreme speed of growth of technological activities in Japan. On the whole, the share of research abroad by the world's largest firms has grown slowly from 10.35 per cent to 11.22 per cent. As for the data quoted above, there are strong differences between industries: food products, chemicals, pharmaceuticals, mechanical, engineering, building material, coal and petroleum products have a share higher than 14 per cent whereas textiles, aerospace and measuring instruments are below 4 per cent.

I would add, concerning this theme of patenting, that this measure understates the recent evolution of the phenomenon. Research needs time to give birth to something which can be patented, then there is a lapse of several months, even years, before the patent is granted. Therefore it is interesting to examine recent trends in greater detail.

Recent Trends

At a global level, the globalization of technology was first led by US multinational enterprises but in recent years the lead has been taken by Japanese multinational enterprises. According to many studies (for example, Warrant, 1991), US multinationals began to do R&D abroad in the 1960s with a rapid growth around 1970 establishing their R&D facilities principally in Europe. Japanese firms have started to organize R&D abroad only since 1985 (see Guelle, 1989; she draws upon a study conducted in 1988 by the Japan Development Bank on 437 Japanese multinationals). A big firm like Hitachi only started very recently to do R&D abroad. Tsutomu Kanai, Hitachi President, stated in 1993:

> I believe that foreign input in our R&D programmes is not only desirable but crucial. As you know, since 1989 Hitachi has established seven overseas R&D bases including Dublin, Düsseldorf and Milan and these are helping to greatly further our level of basic research. These have been responsible for some remarkable technological breakthroughs such as the development of a single-electron memory device which we developed jointly with Cambridge University.[1]

Japanese firms have established R&D operations independently and through international joint ventures, principally in the United States. A publication by MITI in 1987 (quoted from Mowery and Teece, 1991, Table 6) states that out of 135 international research joint ventures involving Japanese firms from 1982 to 1987, 93 (69 per cent) were established in the United States as against 13 in the UK, 9 in Germany, 7 in France, and 5 in Italy. A more recent study by the US Department of Commerce shows for the years 1989 and 1990 that Japanese firms have established 448 links with US firms among which 23 were research joint ventures and 65 R&D and product joint ventures (Mowery and Teece, 1991, Table 8). This is an apparent growth which has already led to a significant level of global collaboration in technology. In some fields the stock of existing R&D facilities owned by Japanese firms is very impressive. A study by Ganther and Dalton (1991) gives a list of more than 70 major Japanese research laboratories in electronics within the United States, more than half of them established since 1988. A study by Sigurdson (1992) confirms that the internationalization of Japanese R&D is well on its way.

Despite these clear trends it is difficult to state that the processes of technology creation are globalized and many studies underline facts of non-globalization. Patel and Pavitt (1991) have established (based on a sample of 686 among the world's largest manufacturing firms) that their technological activities have remained concentrated in their home country, and their paper has found a large audience. In fact it was based – as many papers are – on patenting, from abroad or otherwise, in the United States, and for the years 1981 to 1986. All the critics above stand by their results. Using the same bases, the studies surveyed by Granstrand, Håkanson and Sjölander (1993) led them to the same conclusion: 'despite increasing internationalization, there are still no signs of far-reaching "denationalization", that is loss of national features .... There is a long way to go towards genuine globalization of industry and technology' (Grandstrand *et al.*, 1993, p. 425). However, many have already taken this direction and Pavitt himself recommends following the path. In a paper on internationalization of technological innovation, he stated as a conclusion: 'some British firms have recognised the importance of person-embodied knowledge transfers and have established R&D laboratories in Japan. More generally, we should increase the flow of British scientists and engineers to Japanese universities and related institutions' (Pavitt, 1992, p. 122). To be sure, this path represents a change from micro-cultures and national cultures to an international or global culture, and this is a crucial change. Thus limits to globalization (see, for example, Storper, 1992) are coming principally from the defence of those national or micro-cultures which prefer to consider that innovation processes are still societal processes, strictly embedded within their cultural borders. However many, such as Jessop, Nielsen and Pedersen (1993, p. 229), believe that 'national economic space is no longer the most obvious starting point for pursuing economic growth, technological innovation or structural competitiveness'.

INNOVATION PROCESSES WITHIN NATIONAL SYSTEMS

The common reality of the innovation process is far from a genuinely globalized process and that has led many scholars to focus on the embeddedness of this process. A new way of thinking has been introduced by Freeman (1987) coining the expression 'national system of innovation'. For him and his followers, nations do or should monitor their specific processes of innovation. Another stream of thought coming from regional and geographic studies has emerged in the field in so far as they were tempted to discuss more in-depth spatial themes by referring to industrial organization categories.[2] They pointed out the territorial embeddedness of technology and the proper dynamics of territories as localized systems of innovation.

I shall briefly present a few points, guided by these two approaches, to underline their contribution to the understanding of the innovation process. To be sure, the process is clearly embedded within societal systems and to grasp its complete societal dimension with a more institutionalist and evolutionary approach, we have to go a little further building up on the results of these previous analyses.

The notion of national systems of innovation was used first by Freeman (1987) but the discussion of this notion spread widely after the publication of two books, one edited by Nelson (1993) and the other by Lundvall (1992) who had been working for a long time with a team at Aalborg University on something very close to this notion (see Lundvall 1985). A lot of papers have been published since, building on these earlier contributions, for example, by Patel and Pavitt (1994). Table 4.2 shows four definitions of a national system of innovation. My purpose is not to focus on the (actual) differences between these definitions but rather to point out that all definitions are a stimulating attempt

1. to locate the analysis of innovation processes in a conceptual framework, where not only markets but also institutions play a crucial role and where history matters;
2. to explain jointly high technology breakthroughs, incremental innovation, technology diffusion and transfer, and organizational innovations;
3. to stress differences between countries' economic performances and link them to the importance of technological capabilities and the diversity of national patterns, especially of national technological trajectories.

We may start with the issue of international differences in performance, as this strongly supports the idea that there are nation-specific ways of doing everything, especially innovation. However, this does not ensure that every innovation process will appear to be generated by a community of actors pertaining to a single nation.

Table 4.2   Four definitions of a national system of innovation

---

Freeman (1987, pp. 1 and 4)

Network of institutions in the public and private sectors whose activities and interactions initiate, import, modify and diffuse new technologies.

   [In an application to Japan, key roles are played by:]
*   government policy (particularly MITI);
*   corporate R&D, especially in relation to imported technology;
*   education and training;
*   general structure of industry [and business atmosphere]

Nelson and **Rosenberg** (1993, pp. 4–5 and 15)

A set of institutions whose interactions determine the innovative performance of national firms....

   A set of institutional actors that, together, plays the major role in influencing innovative performance ...

   [This is] not limited to ... firms at the forefront of world's technology, or to institutions doing the most advanced scientific research [but depends on] the factors influencing national technological capabilities. The term '*innovation*' [encompasses] the processes by which firms master and get into practice product designs and manufacturing processes that are new to them, if not to the universe or even to the nation. ... [Thus, there is] no sharp guide to just what should be included in the innovation system, and what can be left out.

Table 4.2 continued

Technological advance proceeds through the interaction of many actors; some of the key interactions [are] between component and systems producers, upstream and downstream firms, universities and industry, and government agencies and universities and industries.

Lundvall (1992, pp. 2 and 12–15)

A system of innovation is constituted by elements and relationships which interact in the production, diffusion and use of new, and economically useful, knowledge and a national system encompasses elements and relationships, either located within or rooted inside the borders of a nation state.

We may make a distinction between a system of innovation in the narrow sense and a system of innovation in the broad sense. The narrow definition would include organisations and institutions involved in searching and exploring – such as R&D departments, technological institutes and universities. The broad definition [...] includes all parts and aspects of the economic structure and the institutional set-up affecting learning as well as searching and exploring – the production system, the marketing system and the system of finance present themselves as sub-systems in which learning takes place.

Determining in detail which sub-systems and social institutions should be included, or excluded, in the analysis of the system is a task involving historical analysis as well as theoretical considerations.... [Thus] a definition of the system of innovation must, to a certain degree, be kept open and flexible. ... In the real world the state and the public sector are rooted in national states, and their geographical sphere of influence is defined by national borders. The focus upon *national* systems reflects the fact that national economies differ regarding the structure of the production system and regarding the general institutional set-up. Specifically, we assume that basic differences in historical experience, language and culture will be reflected in national idiosyncrasies in:

- internal organisation of firms;
- interfirm relationships;
- role of the public sector;
- institutional set-up of the financial sector;
- R&D intensity and R&D organisation.

Missing among these elements is the national education and training system .... An important task for future research is to integrate education and training systems and innovation systems in one single analytical framework.

Table 4.2 continued

Patel and **Pavitt** (1994, pp. 79–80)

The national institutions, their incentive structures and their competencies, that determine the rate and direction of technological learning (or the volume and composition of change-generating activities) in a country....

['Change-generating' activities are] activities such as product design, production engineering, quality control, staff training, research and/or the development and testing of prototypes and pilot plan. Four sets of institutions – and of related activities – are widely recognised as central features of national systems of innovation in all countries:

- business firms, especially those investing in change-generating activities;
- universities and similar institutions, providing basic research and related training;
- a mixture of *public and private institutions*, providing general education and vocational training;
- governments, financing and performing a variety of activities that both promote and regulate technical change.

International Differences in Performance

As a matter of fact the various approaches to National Systems of Innovation have only one point in common (see point (3) above) that obviously leads to a 'national' approach. Lundvall, Nelson and Rosenberg, and others have cautiously developed their 'national' approaches and acknowledge that 'the internationalization of business and technology erodes the extent to which national borders, and citizenship, define boundaries that are meaningful in analyzing technological capabilities and technical advance' (Nelson and Rosenberg, 1993, p. 17). However, Nelson and Rosenberg underline that there still are striking differences: 'Japanese firms in the semiconductor business tend to be different than American, German, or French firms. The university systems are different and play different roles in national R&D systems. The development paths of Korea and Taiwan have been very different and so too are their present organization of industry and structure of R&D' (*ibid.*, p. 18). Lundvall puts it similarly: 'it must be recognised that important elements of the process of innovation tend to become transnational and global rather than national'; however, 'national systems of production', according to him, have been playing a crucial role for a very long time. 'The modern nation states in the Western world – not necessarily the new states in the former colonies – have worked as "engines of growth"' (ibid.).

More generally this approach addresses an old question – why growth rates differ – in a new manner, by focusing on technology. In fact this is not completely new. Michalet and Delapierre (1978) had already pointed out the importance of national scientific and technological capabilities, building on the 'neo-technology' theories of international trade which had focused since the early 1960s on the technological gap between countries. The extension of the role of technology as the key to national wealth began during the 1970s. Strange has conceptualized the crucial role, in competition between nations, of the 'knowledge structure' (Strange, 1994/1988) and Lundvall states that 'the most fundamental resource in the modern economy is knowledge' (Lundvall, 1992, p. 1). Porter (1990), Kogut (1993) and Fagerberg (1994) among others address the same questions why are some nations wealthier than others? – and search in the same (black?) box of technology to shed some light on another question – what should one do when enduring a 'negative' shift of competitive advantage? All scholars dealing with these questions show 'national' specific patterns; e.g. van Hulst, Mulder and Soete (1991, p. 258) 'can distinguish three patterns in the technology-export relationship' and 'this division coincides with Ergas' [1987] classification of technology policies'. If the analysis of technology policies by Western countries in economic literature has only in recent years spread widely (not before the 1980s), the effort to promote technological capabilities and international transfer of technology in the Third World is a very old theme in development studies (cf. Lall, 1993). Moreover, policy-makers, even in Western countries, have effectively contributed, by their interventions, to shaping 'national patterns' and 'national trajectories'. Had markets been free everywhere, differences between countries could have been reduced to different relative price scales, explained by different national endowments of production factors. The real world of nations is more complex and there are not only markets – not really free – but organizations, institutions, etc., that build national patterns – this is the common point (1) (see above) of the approaches in terms of national systems of innovation. McKelvey follows this argument to state that if 'the organization of capitalist society differs in different nations', then there are 'implications for how, why and when innovation occurs' (McKelvey, 1992, p. 7).

Nations as Societal Systems Embedding Technological Trajectories

McKelvey underlines that the key problem is to explain differences 'among capitalist countries' and that explanations 'lie in specific differences in the workings of market-based societies' (McKelvey, 1992, p. 3). Therefore we must elaborate on how a societal system works, and first of all define what it is and then try to explain the way innovation processes may emerge from it. We would have to refer to theoretical background in order to use the word 'system' as a concept and not as an equivalent for 'set'. Here we will just say that simple sets are not systems; only a complex of dynamically interactive elements capable of self-organization, replication and evolution with sufficient autonomy can be called a system. A group of people living together have established structures, rules and the ways to behave within this framework. These structures along with the workings of this group of people gather the characteristics that must be assessed as constituting or not constituting a system. Therefore we could consider this group of people as a societal system in the sense of the systemic theory. Regarding any human groupings living on a territory and sharing common history and values, Bancal (1974) states that a societal system can exist and last only as long as a few permanent functions are continuously performed within this society, all of them simultaneously.

Among them, but not always *'primus inter pares'* as it is in market-based societies, the economic function plays a leading role in organizing and promoting 'change-generating activities' (see the quotation from Patel and Pavitt in Table 4.2), upgrading the scientific and technological capabilities of the society and the efficiency of the production apparatus of the society. To be sure, political, cultural and ethical functions are also responsible for shaping the patterns of the structure and evolution of this apparatus including its technological trajectory. These functions are performed in a nation-specific way, giving birth to formal and informal institutions rooted in a common history. Thus, people in a given society share the same habits when doing business, delineating and conducting new projects; they have been educated within the same structures and having followed the same curriculum can refer to the same basic knowledge and values. Moreover, their new technical and industrial projects will be supported, as usual, by a well-known, nation-specific financial framework. Ouchi (1980) identifies such social groups at an infra-national level, as 'clans', and many academics specializing in Regional Studies believe that such groups are common at local levels (e.g. Bianchi and Bellini, 1991, quoting Ouchi). Lundvall uses the word 'tribes' to underline this importance of mutual trust and solidarity that seem compulsory to launch new projects.[3] However, as language, culture, basic knowledge, routines, and formal institutions are usually shared at the level of the nation, he prefers to support national and not local systems of innovation.

Thus, nations are the societal systems that master, as far as they can, production apparatuses and 'national' technological trajectories. Nevertheless, this is not exactly the same as postulating that every innovation is generated by a national system of innovation. This issue was raised by Lundvall himself who states 'Processes of innovation transcend national borders and sometimes they are local rather than national' (Lundall, 1992, p. 4). Rather than an *'a-priori'* choice, the best way to address this issue could be the one opened up by

McKelvey (1992, p. 8), that is, 'instead of analyzing how a national system produces innovation, we ask to what extent an innovation process builds up or is part of a national system', or, may I add, of a global, national, local system or apparatus of production. To tackle this open question I shall now try a bottom-up approach starting with an elementary innovation process, firstly by using direct references to literature on national systems of innovation and then by attempting to elaborate on this approach.

Scope of the Relevant Community of Actors Involved in an Innovation Process

Literature on National Systems of Innovation can be used to identify the relevant community of actors for a given process of innovation. Lundvall (1992) focuses on the user–producer interaction as the main source of innovation. This means that the bulk of the process lies within a few places, a few firms, and that proximity can play a crucial role for information exchange, feedback, and the transfer of tacit knowledge. In this sense, we might have expected Lundvall to be more 'local'-oriented as he seemed earlier when he stated that 'geographical and cultural distance ... might play an important role' in the case of incremental and an even more important one in the case of radical innovations (Lundvall, 1991, p. 17). It seems that within local places with a clearly delimited employment area, with a cluster of related firms, innovation processes based essentially on user–producer relationships can flourish. However, limitations of such local processes are obvious. Unlike Lundvall, I believe that user–producer relationships, within a limited area, will be efficient for incremental innovations, diffusion of processes that have been developed elsewhere, but will hardly be able to give birth to the design of entirely new processes, or radical innovations. Since the end of the nineteenth century the main structures of production have been built on technologies nurtured by science and scientific knowledge. Thus, most evolution has involved key industries and their relations on a scope very far from localized user–producer relationships. Moreover, to rely on this kind of relationship could lead to a kind of 'producer-lock-in' according to McKelvey (1992, p. 5), when a producer is unable to gather information on the latest technical opportunities.

How should we consider innovations such as the transistor, the TGV (the French high speed train), the jet aircraft? Should they be attributed to the administrative area where either the laboratory that got the patent, or the facility that produced the first units are situated? If we take into account the whole societal process which, in each case, led to an innovation, we will see clearly that key interactions have involved people, institutions and societal 'functions' working on a national basis rather than on a strictly located area. There is a broad consensus to acknowledge that in production and in technology there are 'national' ways – the American model, the German model, the British model, the French model, etc. Each nation has its way of interacting, as a societal system, with, let's say, physics, and of conducting processes leading to new products and to new processes of production. These processes involve people belonging to the same community. Is it always a national community which is the relevant one for a given process?

Studying the evolution of shoe-making machinery in the United States, Nelson and Rosenberg (1993, p. 15) consider that the relevant community was national, using technology 'different than in Europe, because of physical proximity, and because of shared language and culture'. Even in the case of the same technology, for example, the Bessemer steel technology, studies have shown, 'different national communities at work, with some international exchange, but with the bulk of the interaction among nationals'.[4] In most fields of technical advances, during the nineteenth century and until World War II, the relevant players, or community of actors at work, have been national. Truly sub-national communities are the exception, but there are well known examples of localized production and innovation systems, in the watch industry, or in the glazed ceramic sets. In virtually all such cases these communities have eventually endured harsh times from outside technical advances in their industry or in related ones and had to rely on their insertion within a national societal system to try to get through. Conversely there were also, in the past, some examples where the relevant communities were international. According to Nelson and Rosenberg (1993, p. 17), 'the early history of radio was one of transnational activity, involving inventors and companies in Great Britain, the United States and Western Europe, all building on each other's work. The development of synthetic fibres involved similar transnational interactions ... [so that] the idea that there were in these fields nearly disjoined technological communities does not ring right'.

This observation of a variety of examples of innovation processes leads us to agree with what can be taken as a key statement by Nelson and Rosenberg (1993, p. 15): 'The important interaction, the networks, are not the same in all industries or technologies'. It is widely accepted that the intensity of innovation activities varies greatly across industries. The concentration is high. For example, in 1982 among the innovations launched in the United States, 38 per cent were in two sectors (computers and office equipment (SIC 361, 362, 364 and 367) and measuring and controlling devices (SIC 382)) out of a distribution in 17 sectors (see Feldman, 1994, p. 117). This is linked with differences in amounts of R&D expenditures and to the classification (adopted worldwide) of high, medium and low technology sectors. Moreover, it is a strong argument for exploring the idea that innovation processes not only are a part of the workings of a national system but depend on industry-specific characteristics that are, to a certain extent, linked to the nature of the industry, that is to say to its role of transforming things that are subjected to the laws of physics. This argument contributes to the weakening of the link between technology and national systems.

CONCLUSION: CHALLENGES AND OPPORTUNITIES

National systems are challenged by the emerging phenomenon of globalization, and the challenge is not restricted to trade in goods and services or to the use of production facilities abroad by multinational companies. Techno-globalism is challenging innovation processes which are confined to national systems.

Innovation processes require more than the sole user–producer relationships. When studying a given innovation and searching to describe the whole historical process from the first idea to its existence and its possible diffusion – through the market or other means – Callon (1991, p. 196) states that such a process is hosted by a technico-economic network. According to him such a technico-economic network is a coordinated set of heterogeneous actors: public laboratories, technical research centres, enterprises, financial institutions, users and public authorities which collectively participate in the design, elaboration, production and distribution-diffusion of goods and services production processes, some of them through market transactions. Undoubtedly, and as Bell and Callon acknowledge (Bell and Callon, 1994, p. 76), a technico-economic network belongs to the category of meso-systems (Humbert, 1985) or intermediate systems (neither local nor national).

Nowadays, more and more technico-economic networks are cross-border networks (see Imai and Baba, 1991) where interactions concern people, firms and institutions located in specific places but in different countries. Figure 4.1 illustrates a segment of a cross-border network in the information technology sector. Every actor in such a network can contribute to various networks or meso-systems whilst remaining an actor of its nation viewed as a societal system. However, in cross-border technico-economic networks the innovation process results from an interaction between people, firms, institutions which are citizens of various countries. In this sense, it is a case where globalization of technology is challenging national systems of innovation.

Most of the leading industries which are reshaping the world of industry by their evolution and their interactions have some characteristics in common. They are technology-intensive with cross-border networks, they endure a fierce rivalry among a few giant firms which compete for world markets, international and intra-industry trade counts as a high proportion of production and is growing rapidly, international flows of direct investment are increasing, international alliances and agreements and not only joint ventures are more and

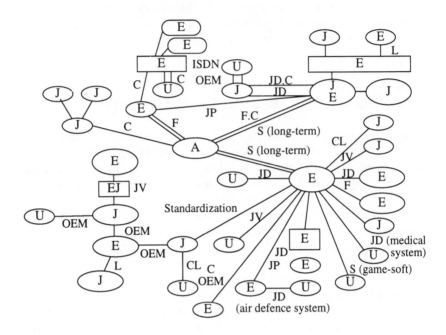

Figure 4.1   A segment of a cross-border network in the IT industry

Notes:

J: a Japan-originated firm	JV: Joint Venture
E: a Europe-originated firm	JP: Joint Production
JD: Joint Development	L: Licensing
CL: Cross Licensing	F: Franchising
S: Subcontracting	C: Capital participation
ISDN: Integrated Services Digital Networks	OEM: Original Equipment Manufacturer
U: a US-originated firm	

more numerous, governments act to boost the transformation of the apparatus of production located in their territory, attracting foreign direct investment, subsidizing some local actors, devising strategic trade, industry, and technology policies. Therefore such industries form meso-systems at the world level and interactions between them shape the world technological and industrial trajectory. The main challenge facing a societal system lies in the fact that its national or territorial technico-industrial trajectory does not fit that of the world's. This is exactly what Guerrieri and Tylecote establish when they search for the determinants of national competitive advantages. 'Success in a given sector is largely determined by the degree of fit between: (i) what technological progress in a given sector requires, in terms of internal and external structural and cultural characteristics; (ii) what characteristics are already prevalent in that country and sector' (Guerrieri and Tylecote, 1994, p. 49). Therefore, what can a national system do? To answer this question it is necessary to shed some light on three points on which I have previously put forward some arguments.

First, what kind of specificity does a specific societal system want? Is there a need for a specific technology and science as Lyssenko dreamt? Societal differences are at stake even in the field of science and technology. However, we may recall that it seemed that there were two clear-cut different alternatives or regimes: market or planned economies. Today it is obvious that both needed more or less the same technologies, the same technical changes, and that one has been definitely superior to the other in the field of technical efficiency and economic performance. Less developed countries that are keen on getting industrialized may try to escape democracy but not 'capitalist' technologies (as Lenin said that building socialism needed electricity and soviets). Every country is wanting to catch up with the world level of technology; even 'the advanced capitalist economies must move up the technical hierarchy and specialize in the new core technology if they are to maintain employment and growth' (Jessop *et al.*, 1993, p. 236). To be sure, technology is not by itself a societal goal, but a means to reach what are these 'specific' goals, employment, growth perhaps, or more generally to make one's way towards specific societal values or culture (see Humbert, 1991a). Among advanced capitalist economies themselves we can observe differences in growth rates; however, there are parallel trends and some convergence as illustrated by the intensification of intra-industry trade between these countries. Had they built strongly differentiated systems, especially concerning innovation, the outcome would have displayed a wide range of specialized economies. On the contrary, industrialized countries are increasingly producing and exchanging the same products made from the same technologies. They all want the new core technologies that are globally created.

This leads to the second point: how nation-specific is a technology? Many such as Dalum, Johnson and Lundvall (1992, p. 311) underline that 'technology ... does not exist by itself, but is embedded in an institutional set-up'. However, it is difficult to wipe out the possibility of transferability of technologies from one country to another and, furthermore, to recognize that there is no need to reinvent the wheel: 'to borrow and absorb technical knowledge developed and already used abroad often involves more limited efforts than to develop it from scratch' (*ibid.*). Thus we must consider that the 'institutional set-up' embedding the 'wheel' is largely shared by countries round the world, that is to say that there is an actual degree of freedom of technology *vis-à-vis* its national system of birth. As a matter of fact, 'it is obvious and well known that in most nations only a small part of the total technical learning is really home spun' (*ibid.*, p. 310). Then (i) the link between a nation and a technology is not exclusive; (ii) usually a nation uses technologies spun abroad. So we come to our third point.

How easily can a societal system benefit from a technology not invented at home? In the past, most societal systems were fairly closed and therefore differentiated, producing technologies adapted to very specific contexts; most less developed countries claimed that there were not real transfers of technology from industrialized countries and a strand of literature pointed out the need for appropriate technologies. Many underlined that MNEs were transferring old technologies or at least technologies far behind the technology frontier and that the transfer was not complete and was usually overpriced. Recently, the globalization of technology has opened the boxes, technologies are less and less adapted only to unique contexts and MNEs are no longer reluctant to conduct R&D abroad, not only in industrialized countries but also in LDCs (see Reddy and Sigurdson, 1994), thanks also to the extension of decentralization permitted by the development of information and communication technologies (see Howells, 1995). However, we must distinguish between technologies that can be imported and innovation capabilities that must be home grown as an outcome of the workings of a societal system. What remains as a difficulty is not to import but to transform foreign sources of technologies (whatever their form – capital goods, licences, direct investment) so far as contribute to a genuine upgrading of the industrial technology development. The impact of inward technology transfer on local competitiveness depends on 'the overall effort to exploit foreign sources of technology [which is linked to] the creation of a skilled production and technical labor force' (Mowery, 1993, p. 51). As Lall puts it, 'foreign investment is an effective means of transferring the results of innovation, but not necessarily the innovation capability itself.' That is to say, 'there is no substitute for indigenous capability development effort, and technological transformation cannot be a passive process based on open doors' (Lall, 1993, p. 93). Everywhere local areas and local processes can grasp the opportunity of international flows of knowledge and technology, provided that they have previously developed basic capabilities to exploit them. This *'importance of domestic capabilities for monitoring and absorbing foreign research'* (Mowery, 1994, p. 128) is that of the glocalization of technology and this is how one can turn the challenge of globalization into opportunities.

These opportunities for glocalization imply changes for national systems and the way they are considered. First they must be clearly conceptualized as open systems of innovation, as Bellon put it (Bellon and Niosi, 1994). This openness is an opportunity to stimulate changes; conversely, closed systems may prefer stability and coherence with permanent institutional patterns and they can resist and present 'limits to how fast changes can be introduced without damaging the coherence' (Johnson, 1992, p. 43) especially when change is not incremental but radical. Openness is a guarantee against rigid habits and routines, and it nurtures flexibility and ability to change and therefore to innovate. Moreover, interaction with abroad is essential for a society willing to develop the apparatus of industrial production located on its territory towards more competitiveness and technical efficiency. As Vázquez Barquero (1994, p. 202) puts it, 'A territory cannot be developed if new firms do not start up and the existing firms do not develop, be they endogenous or exogenous to the local productive system'. This clearly recognizes the role that foreign investment can play, and its implication in the improvement of the local apparatus of production and the local innovation capabilities. Such a role for exogenous actors is also played via local firms using other foreign resources: Héraud *et al.* (1995) state, based on a survey, that the key relationships of the more innovative SMEs in Alsace are international. As a matter of fact 'transterritorial networks can overcome constraints of territory' (de Bresson and Amesse, 1991, p. 370). Moreover, air coming from abroad can enhance the home system of innovation. In a study carried out for UNCTAD, Leong (1994, p. 273) presents the example of Singapore where 'the presence of transnational companies' R&D facilities helps to generate secondary R&D activities among the local supporting industries and also train a pool of local manpower in R&D work. In a similar way Vázquez Barquero (1994, p. 214) concludes from his study about the impact of the presence of a multinational in Spain that 'Citroën has contributed towards defining a local environment, more open to receiving and adapting new ideas and technologies'. To be sure, local facilities of more or less global firms are involving national actors in global generation of technology, and therefore these actors are becoming the best agents for change in the national innovation system. A world of interdependent national systems is presumably superior to a world of independent, autocentric, innovation systems, superior in its ability to generate more changes, more radical innovations. In the meantime it implies more competition and because they are afraid of it or the lack of a level playing field many countries are tempted to develop a strong techno-nationalism. When such a tendency concerns countries like the United States it is a serious threat to the development of the technological capacities in more or less all countries due to the level of interdependence already achieved. For example, the USA wanted to stop cooperation with Japan, arguing that 'Japanese public agencies and firms do not contribute to the global pool of scientific knowledge in proportion to the economic benefits that they derive from it' (Mowery, 1994, p. 125). By and large, every country fears that the other plays as a free rider, capturing the economic returns of innovation processes nurtured by its national funds, infrastructure, etc. Stopping cross-border flows of technology for this reason could lead to negative effects for a host of innovation processes. Conversely, enhancing international cooperation and liberalization of technological activities 'would be conducive to strengthening the innovation [meso-]systems of participating national entities' (Foray, 1994, p. 31). However, states have still their role to play, as Jessop *et al.* (1993, p. 237) put it: 'states must get involved in managing the process of internationalization and creating the most appropriate frameworks for it to proceed ... [with] new legal forms for cross-national cooperation and strategic alliances ... promoting technology transfer'. In such contexts not only can localized processes of innovations benefit from the tendency towards globalization of technology, but this tendency, and its challenge, may give birth to new localized processes of innovation, to new localized technico-economic networks – a phenomenon which I have termed 'glocalization' of technology.

NOTES

A first draft of this chapter was presented at the 1994 Annual Conference of EAEPE in Copenhagen. This is a shortened version that has been revised, benefiting from stimulating comments and helpful suggestions from Björn Johnson and Klaus Nielsen. I would also like to thank two anonymous copy-editors who took care that this text is written in correct English. However I remain solely responsible for any mistakes, confusions or omissions.

1. *Financial Times*, Friday September 17 1993. He also gives an example of a new fund investment system developed by the Belgian branch of Kredietbank, based on software produced by a collaboration between Hitachi UK and the UK subsidiary of an American firm, Hewlett Packard.
2. A conglomerate of social scientists with a new wave of regional studies principally by economists, led in France by Aydalot (1984) and his team 'GREMI', in Italy by political scientists, drawing on the theme of the third Italy (Bagnasco, 1977) and its interpretation by economists in terms of Marshallian industrial districts (Becattini, 1979) and in the United States by geographers like Malecki (1980). There were also sociologists who brought about the 'network' approach as did Camagni (1991).
3. He used this term in a lecture he gave at our research centre (CERETIM, May 1995).
4. Nelson and Rosenberg (1993, p. 15) quote Allen, R.C. (1983), 'Collective Invention', *Journal of Economic Behaviour and Organization*, 1(4), pp. 1–24, and Morison, E. (1966), 'Almost the greatest invention', in E. Morison (ed.), *Man, Machines and Modern Times*, Cambridge, Mass., MIT Press.

REFERENCES

Archibugi, D. and J. Michie (1995), 'The globalisation of technology: new taxonomy', *Cambridge Journal of Economics*, 18, 121–40.

Aydalot, P. (ed.) (1984), *Crise et espace*, Paris: Economica.

Bagnasco, A. (1977), *Tre Italia: La problematica territoriale dello sviluppo economico italiano*, Bologna: Il Mulino.

Bancal, J. (1974), *L'économie des sociologues*, Paris: PUF.

Becattini, G. (1979), 'Dal Settore industriale al distretto industriale: alcune considerazioni sull'unità d'indagine dell'economia industriale', *Rivista di Economica e Politica Industriale*, 1.

Bell, G. and M. Callon (1994), 'Réseaux technico-économiques et politiques scientifiques et technologiques', *STI Revue*, 14, 67–126.

Bellon, B. and J. Niosi (1994), 'Des systèmes nationaux d'innovation ouverts', *Revue Française d'Economie*, 1, 79–130.

Bianchi, P. and N. Bellini (1991), 'Public policies for local networks of innovators', *Research Policy*, 20, 487–97.

Bresson, C. de and F. Amesse (1991), 'Networks of innovators: a review and introduction to the issue', *Research Policy*, 20, 363–79.

Callon, M. (1991), 'Réseaux technico-économiques et irréversibilités', in R. Boyer, B. Chavance and O. Godard, *Les figures de l'irréversibilité en économie*, Paris: EHESS, pp. 195–230.

Camagni, R. (ed.) (1991), *Innovation Networks: Spatial Perspectives*, London: Belhaven.

Cantwell, J. and C. Hodson (1990), 'The Internationalisation of Technological Activity and British Competitiveness', Working Paper Series B, vol. III, University of Reading,

Casson, M., R.D. Pearce and S. Singh (1992), 'Global integration through the decentralisation of R&D', in M. Casson (ed.), *International Business and Global Integration*, Basingstoke: Macmillan.

Chesnais, F. (1992), 'National systems of innovation, foreign direct investment and the operations of multinational enterprises', in B.-Å. Lundvall (ed.), *National Systems of Innovation*, London: Pinter.

Dalum, B., B. Johnson and B.-Å. Lundvall (1992), 'Public policy in the learning society', in B.-Å. Lundvall (ed.), *National Systems of Innovation*, London: Pinter.

Dunning, J.H. (1994), 'Multinational enterprises and the globalization of innovatory capacity', *Research Policy*, 23, 67–88.

Ergas, H. (1987), 'Does technology policy matter?', in B. Guile and H. Brooks (eds), *Technology and Global Industry*, Washington: National Academy Press.

Fagerberg, J. (1994), 'Technology and international differences in growth rates', *Journal of Economic Literature*, XXXII, 1147–75.

Feldman, M.P. (1994), *The Geography of Innovation*, Dordrecht: Kluwer.

Foray, D. (1994), 'Accessing and expanding the science and technology knowledge-base: an integrated approach to European innovation and technology diffusion policy', paper presented at the Journée d'étude *Les politiques technologiques régionales*, Saint-Etienne, 19 May.

Freeman, C. (1987), *Technology and Economic Performances: Lessons from Japan*, London: Pinter.

Freeman, C. and J. Hagedoorn (1995), 'Convergence and divergence in the internationalization of technology, in J. Hagedoorn (ed.), *Technical Change and the World Economy*, Aldershot: Edward Elgar.

Ganther, P.A. and D. Dalton (1991), *Japanese Affiliated Electronics Companies and U.S. Technological Development: 1990 Assessment*, Washington: US Dept. of Commerce.

Granstrand, O., L. Håkanson, and S. Sjölander (eds) (1992), *Technology Management and International Business: Internationalisation of R&D and Technology*, Chichester: Wiley.

Granstrand, O., L. Håkanson, and S. Sjölander (eds) (1993), 'Internationalization of R&D – a survey of some recent research', *Research Policy*, 22, 413–30.

Guelle, F. (1989), 'L'internationalisation et la délocalisation de la R&D des grands groupes japonais', *Revue d'Economie Industrielle*, 47, 197–208.

Guerrieri, P. and A. Tylecote (1994), 'National competitive advantages and microeconomic behaviour', *Economics of Innovation and New Technology*, vol. 3, 49–76.

Hagedoorn, J. and J. Schakenraad (1988), 'Inter-firm partnerships and co-operative strategies in core technologies', in G. Dosi and C. Freeman (eds) *New Explorations in the Economics of Technical Change*, London: Pinter.

Häusler, J., H.W. Hohn and S. Lütz (1994), 'Contingencies of innovative networks: a case study of successful interfirm R&D collaboration', *Research Policy*, 23, 47–66.

Hedlund, G. (1994), 'A model of knowledge management and the N-form corporation', *Strategic Management Journal*, 15, 73–90.

Hedlund, G. and J. Ridderstråle (1994), 'International development projects: key to competitiveness, impossible or mismanaged?', Institute of International Business, Stockholm, mimeo.

Héraud, J.A., R. Hahn, A., Gaiser and E. Muller (forthcoming), 'Réseaux d'innovation et tissu industriel: une comparaison Alsace/Base Wurtemberg', in B. Haudeville, J.A. Héraud and M. Humbert, *Technologie et performances économiques*, Paris: Economica.

Howells, J. (1995), 'Going global: the use of ICT networks in Research and Development', *Research Policy*, 24, 169–84.

Hulst, N. van, R. Mulder and L. Soete (1991), 'Exports and technology in manufacturing industry', *Weltwirschaftliches Archiv*, heft 2, Band 127, 246–389.

Humbert, M. (1985), 'Propositions méthodologiques pour une analyse des méso-systèmes', in J. de Bandt, and M. Humbert, 'Les filières de production ou la mésodynamique des relations Nord-Sud', *Cahiers du CERNEA*, 16 (June).

Humbert, M. (1990), 'Systemic competition of firms and nations in oligopolies', paper given at international conference *Merger Oligopoly and Trade*, Aix-en-Provence, 21–22 June.

Humbert, M. (1991a), 'Perdre pour gagner? Technique ou culture, Technique et culture', *Espace Temps*, 45–46, 53–61.

Humbert, M. (1991b), 'The globalisation of technology as a challenge for industry and society', colloque international *MASTECH*, Lyon, 9–12 September.

Humbert, M. (ed.) (1993), *The Impact of Globalisation on Europe's Firms and Industries*, London: Pinter.

Imai, K., and Y. Baba (1991), 'Systemic innovation and cross-border networks, transcending markets and hierarchies to create a new techno-economic system', in OECD, *Technology and Productivity: The Challenge for Economic Policy*, Paris: OECD.

Jessop, B., K., Nielsen and O.K. Pedersen (1993), 'Structural competitiveness and strategic capacities: rethinking the state and international capital', in S.-E. Sjöstrand (ed.), *Institutional Change: Theory and Empirical Findings*, Armonk, N.Y.: M.E. Sharpe.

Johnson, B. (1992), 'Towards a new approach to national systems of innovation', in B.-Å. Lundvall (ed.), *National Systems of Innovation*, London: Pinter.

Kogut, B. (ed.) (1993), *Country Competitiveness: Technology and the Organizing of Work*, New York: Oxford University Press.

Lall, S. (1993), 'Policies for building technological capabilities: lessons from Asian experience', *Asian Development Review*, 11 (2), 72–103.

Leong, L.M. (1994), 'Industrial districts in developing countries: case study of Singapore', in UNCTAD, *Technological Dynamism in Industrial Districts: An Alternative Approach to Industrialization in Developing Countries?*, New York: UN, pp. 267–86.

Lundvall, B.-Å. (1985), *Product Innovation and User-Producer Innovation*, Aalborg: Aalborg University Press.

Lundvall, B.-Å. (1991), 'Technological revolutions and the spatial division of labour', paper presented at the North American Regional Science Conference, New Orleans, November.

Lundvall, B.-Å. (ed.) (1992), *National Systems of Innovation*, London: Pinter.

Madeuf, B. (1981), *L'ordre technologique international: Production et transfert*, Paris: La Documentation Française.

Malecki, E.J. (1980), 'Dimensions of R&D location in the United States', *Research Policy*, 16, 29–42.

Mansfield, E., D. Teece and A. Romeo (1979), 'Overseas Research and Development by U.S. based firms', *Economica*, 46, 187–96.

Mariti, P. and R.H. Smiley (1983), 'Co-operative agreements and the organisation of industry', *Journal of Industrial Economics*, XXXI (4), (June).

McKelvey, M. (1992), 'Technology embedded in nations? Genetic engineering and technological change in national systems of innovation', paper presented at EAEPE fourth conference, November, Paris.

Michalet, C.A. and M. Delapierre (1978), 'The Impact of Multinational Enterprises on National Scientific and Technological Capacities in the Computer Industry', mimeo.

Miller, R. (1994), 'Global R&D networks and large-scale innovations: the case of the automobile industry', *Research Policy*, 23, 27–46.

Mowery, D.C. (1993), 'Inward Technology Transfer and Competitiveness: The Role of National Innovation Systems', Working Paper no. 93–19, CCC, Berkeley.

Mowery, D.C. (1994), 'Balancing benefits and obligations within the global R&D system: the changing position of Japan', in D.C. Mowery (ed.), *Science and Technology Policy in Interdependent Economies*, Dordrecht: Kluwer.

Mowery, D.C. and D.J. Teece (1991), 'The Changing Place of Japan in the Global Scientific and Technological Enterprise', CCC Working Paper no. 91-16, Berkeley.

Mowery, D.C. and D.J. Teece (1993), 'Strategic Alliances and Industrial Research', CCC Working Paper no. 93–6, Berkeley.

Mytelka, L. (ed.) (1991), *Strategic Partnerships: States, Firms and International Competition*, London: Pinter.

Nelson, R. (1991), 'Recent Writings on Competitiveness: Boxing the Compass', CCC Working Paper no. 91-18, Berkeley, University of California.

Nelson, R. (ed.) (1993), *National Innovation Systems*, Oxford: Oxford University Press.

Nelson, R. and N. Rosenberg (1993), 'Technical Innovation and National System', in R. Nelson (ed.), *National Innovation Systems*, Oxford: Oxford University Press.

OECD (1992), *Technology and the Economy: The Key Relationship*, Paris: OECD.

Ouchi, W. (1980), 'A Framework for understanding organizational failure', in J.R. Kimberley and R.N. Miles (eds), *The Organizational Life Cycle*, San Fransisco: Jossey Bass.

Papanastassiou, M. and R. Pearce (1994) 'La mondialisation de l'innovation et l'organisation de la R&D dans les multinationales', in F. Sachwald (ed.), *Les défis de la mondialisation*, Paris: Masson.

Patel, P., and Pavitt, K. (1991), 'Large firms in the production of world's technology: an important case of "non-Globalisation"', *Journal of International Business Studies*, 1st quarter, 1–21.

Patel, P. and K. Pavitt (1994), 'National Innovation Systems: why they are important, and how they might be measured and compared?', *Economics of Innovations and New Technology*, 3, 77–95.

Pavitt, K. (1992), 'Internationalisation of technological innovation', *Science and Public Policy*, 19, 119–23.

Peters, L.S. (1992), 'Technology management and the R&D activities of multinational enterprises', CSTP-RPI paper.

Petrella, R. (1989), 'Globalisation of technological innovation', *Technology Analysis and Strategic Management*, 1 (4), 393–407.

Porter, M. (1990), *The Competitive Advantage of Nations*, London: Macmillan.

Reddy, P. and J. Sigurdson (1994), 'Emerging patterns of globalisation of corporate R&D and scope for innovative capability building in developing countries?', *Science and Public Policy*, 21 (5), 283–94.

Ronstadt, R.C. (1977), *Research and Development Abroad by US Multinationals*, New York: Praeger.

Sigurdson, J. (1992), 'Internationalizing R&D in Japan', *Science and Public Policy*, 19 (3), 134–44.

Storper, M. (1992), 'The Limits to Globalization: Technology Districts and International Trade', *Economic Geography*, 68(1), 60–93.

Strange, S. (1994), *States and Markets* (1st edn 1988), London: Pinter.

Teece, D.J. (1986), 'Profiting from technological innovation: implications for integration, collaboration, licensing and public policy', *Research Policy*, 15, 285–305.

Vázquez-Barquero, A. (1994), 'The integration of external firms within local productive systems: some lessons from the Spanish experience', in G. Garofoli and A. Vázquez-Barquero (eds), *Organisation of Production and Territory: Local Models of Development*, Pavia: Giarmi Inculano.

Warrant, F. (1991), 'Transnationalisation de la R&D: essai de synthèse', *Nouvelles de la Science et de la Technologie*, 9, 15–28.

5. Technological performance and variety: the case of the German electronics industry

Uwe Cantner, Horst Hanusch and Georg Westermann

1. INTRODUCTION

In this chapter we present an investigation into the perceived heterogeneous performance of firms – as measured by efficiency indicators – within certain industrial sectors. Such analyses have a longstanding tradition in public sector economics[1] as well as for the private sector.[2] The neoclassical explanation of such differences relies either on the concept of 'market failures' – which is apparent in the concept of X-inefficiency[3] or in several oligopoly models in industrial organization[4] – or on other 'breakdowns' such as product differentiation,[5] spatial market fragmentation,[6] and 'institutional split'.[7] Inefficiencies measured on the basis of these concepts are mainly referred to as technical (and allocative) inefficiencies measured against a single given best practice technology.

Recent advances in the economics of technological change, however, increasingly stress that the industry structure may also be the result of the coexistence and competition of several different technologies.[8] Moreover, this diversity is a major force pushing forward technological progress. For empirical analyses this implies that a variety of technologies, i.e. production functions, is to be expected and several best-practice technologies might be identified.

Consequently, the analytical procedure we employ has to take into account that, contrary to traditional frontier-production analysis, there may exist more than one best-practice technique. Since traditional neoclassical econometric approaches to frontier production functions determine only a single best-practice technology – at least at the outset – these methods are not suitable for our problem. Instead, we suggest a non-parametric approach, the linear programming approach[9] or Data Envelopment Analysis (DEA),[10] to investigate technological performances and variety. This method does not require a special type of production function, nor does the applicability depend on the existence of general equilibrium conditions. Quite the contrary, based on the broad definition of Leontief-type production functions this procedure allows us to detect a large number of specific Leontief-functions each representing a certain 'technology' defined and approximated by specific input ratios. Moreover, these functions can be compared with each other leading to a number of best-practice technologies as well as measures of technical inefficiencies. Both will be used to define certain technology fields with one or several technology leaders and a larger number of technically backward firms.

Applying this method, our empirical analysis focuses on the electronics sector in Germany. We are able to detect several best-practice technologies as well as a measure for technical inefficiency. Coupled with a traditional cluster analysis technology leaders can be assigned to specific 'technology fields'. Relating those results to the firm-specific R&D-capital stocks on the one side and to the patenting activities of the firms on the other, it is shown that these technology indicators are able to explain the perceived intra-industry heterogeneity.

We proceed as follows: Section 2 delivers the theoretical foundation of our analysis. Moreover the DEA method is introduced which is well suited to perform an efficiency analysis within the theoretical framework of the modern approach to innovation and new technology. Section 3 delivers our results with respect to technical inefficiency which then are related to R&D and patent activity in Section 4. Section 5 concludes our investigation.

2.   THEORETICAL BASIS AND ANALYTICAL MODEL

Technological Variety – A Theoretical Foundation

The following discussion presents arguments explaining the heterogeneous technical performance of firms within a sector. Production techniques are defined by various combinations of production factors which may differ among firms.

The modern theory of innovation explains differences or asymmetries between firms by their respective technical performance. Emphasis is placed on the fact that opportunities of and advances in technology (tend to) dominate any economic determinants of a firm's choice of technique.

Traditional neoclassical production theory, however, does not share this view. Instead, the path of technological progress is seen as mainly being determined by changes in relative factor prices where the technological possibilities are open and known to all economic agents. Consequently, assuming a well functioning market mechanism, firm heterogeneity within a sector is not to be expected. Diversity, nevertheless empirically observable, is then explained by market failures, or other breakdowns.

This neoclassical concept of factor-price induced technological progress has been challenged by the well-known Salter (1960) and Fellner (1961) critique. Salter (1960, p. 43) notes that 'when labor costs rise, any advance that reduces total costs is welcome and whether this is achieved by saving labor or capital is irrelevant'. Moreover, Ahmad (1966, p. 345) states that 'only technological considerations and not a change in the relative price of the factor may influence the nature of invention, even if there exists the possibility of choosing from different kinds of invention'.[11] Modern innovation theory attempts to develop these aspects further.

Here, a major point of criticism focuses on the standard neoclassical assumption that technological knowledge is considered as a public good, implying technological uniformity between firms.[12] Instead, the modern approach distinguishes between public knowledge on the one hand and private, often tacit, technological knowledge on the other. It is this private good character of technological know-how that allows firms to develop along a technological path that is often described as cumulative, selective and finalized.[13] Consequently, although different firms may belong to the same branch, although they are technologically tied to common – public good – principles, and although they are engaged in the production of the same class of goods, they nevertheless differ with respect to their specific production technology.

The reason for building up a private stock of technological knowledge leading to technological diversity is found in the conditions by which technological progress is accomplished at the level of the firm. The technological capability that a firm acquires is determined by its past investments and learning effects as well as its own R&D engagements. Conversely, these capabilities are decisive for further successful technological improvements as well as the successful adoption of new techniques developed elsewhere. This implies (a) that further technological advances are mainly determined and constrained by the technique(s) that a firm has been using in the past and (b) that the firm's search for new solutions is characterized by bounded rationality and local learning effects.

Technological know-how also has a public good character which allows for locally constrained spillover effects. Technological progress exhibiting both private and public good aspects is often labelled 'localized technological progress'.[14]

A major consequence of this view is that relative factor prices play only a minor role for the development of new technologies. Considering the standard textbook isoquant, only a (small) number of all possible techniques along an isoquant are practised, and substitution processes – which are to be considered as resource-using search processes – due to changes in relative factor prices are not costless.

Therefore, if the technological opportunities of a firm are great, search efforts will be devoted to innovation, not to substitution.[15] In this case of local technological advances, the development path of a firm will be characterized by fairly constant factor input ratios, independent of the prevailing relative factor prices. Furthermore, transition to new techniques caused by changes in the relative factor prices will not be reversible, i.e. technological change is characterized by irreversibilities.With this theoretical background, we make the following characterization of a firm's productive activities to be used in the subsequent investigation:

I.   An industry consists of firms employing different production functions, each representing a particular firm-specific technique. Since these techniques are the outcome of localized technological progress, we consider the resulting techniques – at least in the short run – to have at the outset zero elasticity of substitution. This suggests assuming for each firm a Leontief-type production function – at least in the short run. Firm heterogeneity is then represented by the diversity of different Leontief-production functions, i.e. different factor input combinations and thus different firm-specific techniques.

II. In the medium and long run the assumption of a localized technological change does not imply that the development path is characterized by a constant factor input ratio. We rather suggest a development path contained within elastic barriers[16] allowing for a range of input ratios. Phenomena like the increasing mechanization of the production processes are thus taken into account.

With this characterization of the firm, the technical performances within an entire sector may be described with reference to the nature of the technological know-how. To the extent that the know-how is a private good, we suggest the following first structural element (I), an element of *technical dominance*:

I.   Due to different firm-specific technical approaches there may appear more than one best-practice technique dominating other techniques. Best-practice techniques cannot be ranked as unequivocally better or worse because they differ in their respective relative factor use. Firms applying these techniques are interpreted as technology leaders. The technological frontier of a sector consequently consists of these best-practice techniques.

In so far as the technological know-how possesses a public good character, an additional structural element (II) appears, an element of *horizontal technological variety*:

II. Due to the (local) spillover effects of localized technological change, firms applying similar techniques are bound together by common technological principles and constitute a 'technology field'.

Combining (I) and (II) suggests the coexistence (and therefore variety) of several technology fields dominated by best-practice technology leaders. Within those technology fields less-than-best-practice techniques can be ranked relative to the respective technology leaders. Observed differences can be represented by a standard measure of technical inefficiency[17] and are caused by

(a) inefficient use of inputs, given a specific technique;
(b) the fact that the firm-specific technological know-how may differ within a specific technology field.

Empirical analysis aiming at detecting intra-sectoral heterogeneity has to take account of both (I) the relative technical performance of firms and (II) technological variety. The next section will introduce a method suitable for this purpose.

The Analytical Model

The analytical approach we apply is non-parametric and based on a linear programming procedure. In operations research and management science this analysis has become well known as the Data Envelopment Analysis (DEA),[18] whereas in the economics literature on frontier production functions it has diffused much more slowly.[19] From here on, we will refer to this procedure as DEA.

DEA allows us to compute an index for relative technical (in)efficiency for each firm within a sample. The choice of a non-parametric approach helps to take account of technological variety by allowing for several parametrically different production functions. Principally this procedure relies on the traditional index numbers of productivity analysis. For each firm j ($j = 1,...,n$) a productivity index h_j is given by:

$$h_j = \frac{u^T Y_j}{v^T X_j} \tag{5.1}$$

Here Y_j is an s-vector of different outputs and X_j an m-vector of different inputs of firm j; s-vector u and m-vector v contain the aggregation weights u_r ($r = 1,...,s$) and v_i ($i = 1,...,m$) respectively.

In (5.1), h_j is nothing other than an index of *total factor productivity*. The respective aggregation functions (for inputs and outputs respectively) are of à linear arithmetic type as also employed in the well-known Kendrick-Ott productivity index.[20] There, however, by special (general equilibrium) assumptions the aggregations weights, u_r and v_i, are given exogenously.

DEA does not rely on such assumptions, in particular it is not assumed that all firms in the sample have a common identical production function. The specific aggregation weights are determined endogenously and can differ from firm to firm. They are the solution to a specific optimization problem (as discussed below), and therefore they are dependent on the empirical data of our sample.

The basic principle of DEA is to determine the indexes h_j in such a way that they can be interpreted as efficiency parameters. The (relatively) most efficient firms of a sample should be characterized by an h-value equal to unity, all less efficient firms by an h-value of less than unity. The following constrained maximization problem is used to determine such an h-value for a particular firm l, $l \in \{1,...,n\}$, out of the sample:

$$\max h_l = \frac{u^T Y_l}{v^T X_l}$$

$$s.t.$$

$$\frac{u^T Y_j}{v^T X_j} \leq 1; j = 1,...,n;$$

$$u, v > 0. \tag{5.2}$$

Problem (5.2) determines h_l of firm l subject to the constraint that the h_j of all firms of the sample are equal or less to 1. The constraints provide that h is indexed on [0,1]. Moreover the elements of u and v have to be strictly positive. This requirement is to be interpreted that for all inputs and outputs there exists a positive value.

Since we employ linear arithmetic aggregation functions for inputs and outputs, (5.2) is to be rendered as a problem of linear fractional programming. To solve such optimizations, there exist a number of methods, the best known of which is Charnes and Cooper (1962). They suggest transforming (5.2) into a standard linear programme by claiming for the denominator in the objective function to be constant. The resulting linear programme can then be solved by the simplex algorithm:

$$\max \mu^T Y_l$$

s.t.

$$\mu^T Y_j - \omega^T X_j \le 0; j = 1,...,n;$$

$$\omega^T X_l = 1$$

$$\mu, \omega > 0 \tag{5.3}$$

Y_l and X_l are the r- and s-vectors of outputs and inputs respectively of firm l. In (5.3) the vectors μ und ω are the transformed aggregation weights which also have to be strictly positive.

Problem (5.3) represents a version of efficiency analysis which is known as the 'Production'- or 'Efficiency Technology'-form: here, one attempts to maximize the output of firm l where input is normalized, the solution is to be positive, and the efficiency indexes[21] of all firms are restricted to [0,1]. The dual to (5.3) is known as the 'Envelopment'-form since here a frontier function (containing several linear parts) can be determined. This obviously relates our analysis to the one of Farrell (1957). The corresponding dual programmme then reads:[22]

$$\min \Theta_l$$

s.t.

$$Y_r \lambda_l \ge y_{rl}; r = 1,...,s;$$

$$\Theta_l x_{il} - X_i \lambda_l \ge 0; i = 1,...,m;$$

$$\lambda_l \ge 0 \tag{5.4}$$

y_{rl} and x_{il} are the output r and input i of firm l respectively. Y_r and X_i are the n-vectors of outputs s and inputs m. The parameter Θ_l to be minimized expresses the percentage level to which the inputs of firm l have to be reduced proportionally, in order to produce efficiently. With $\Theta_l = 1$ the respective firm belongs to the efficient firms on the frontier. The n-vector λ_l states the weights of all (efficient) firms which serve as reference for firm l. For the efficient firm l (with $\Theta_l = 1$), we obtain 1 for the lth element of λ_l and 0 for all other elements.

Using the 'Envelopment'-form of (5.4) it is easy to select efficient and inefficient firms directly. Principally, the Pareto-Koopmanns criterion is employed which allows us to compare vectors. The linear programming procedure as performed by (5.4), however, may result in selecting a firm as DEA-efficient although it is clearly dominated by another firm on the frontier. This may happen when the parts of the frontier are parallel to one of the axes. To avoid such results the linear programme in (5.4) has to be modified as follows:

$$\min \Theta_l - \varepsilon e^T s_l^- - \varepsilon e^T s_l$$

$$s.t.$$

$$Y_r \lambda_l - s_l^- = y_{rl}; \ r = 1,...,s;$$

$$\Theta_l x_{il} - X_i \lambda_l - s_l^+ = 0; \ i = 1,...,m;$$

$$\lambda_l, s_l^+, s_l^- \geq 0 \tag{5.5}$$

This modification provides that for all firms, which are on the frontier ($\theta_l = 1$) but which are dominated by other firms of the frontier, the respective slacks (s_l^+ for excess inputs, s_l^- for output slacks) are taken into account in the objective function.[23] Vector e^T contains only elements 1.[24] ε is a positive constant smaller than any other variable of the programme. This guarantees that slacks are only taken into account when a strictly convex envelope has already been determined.[25]

For efficiency analyses additional to θ one has to take into account remaining slacks. Only then is a clear-cut selection of efficient and inefficient firms possible. For simple qualitative statements this procedure is sufficient. For a quantitative analysis, however, it would be helpful to combine the proportional reduction θ_l as well as s_l^+ and s_l^- into a single measure. This is done by a method suggested by Ali and Lerme (1990).

As is known from index numbers for total factor productivity the input factors have to be aggregated in a single number. Similarly, in DEA the respective weights are given by the marginal productivities of the input factors of the reference firm. These marginal productivities are the solution of the primal programme (5.3). Using the marginal productivities of the respective reference firms (determined by the non-zero elements of the vector λ_l) one can weight the inputs on the one hand and the s_l^+ and s_l^- of firm l on the other hand. The ratio between both delivers the amount of the additional inefficiency. Subtracting this measure from θ_l delivers an adjusted aggregate measure of inefficiency ι_l. In our empirical analysis below we rely solely on ι_l.

3.   DATA SET, PROCEDURE OF INVESTIGATION AND EMPIRICAL RESULTS

Data Set and Procedure of Investigation

The data we analyse in this section refer to 39 German electronic firms of different sub-branches and are taken out of the annual reports of these firms. This source covers balance sheet and profit and loss account data of German manufacturing firms since 1980. The data set we use here is time consistent in the sense that we have neither entries nor exits of firms over the whole period of investigation,

1985 to 1991. All firms under consideration are of the legal form 'shareholders' company'. In order to compute the efficiency score 't', we define some suitable variables for inputs and output.

As an output measure we construct a 'total output' consisting of the sum of 'total sales', 'inventory changes', and 'internal used firm services' from the profit and loss accounts. This output is deflated by a composed price index for German investment goods.

On the input side we distinguish between 'capital', 'labour', and 'material'. 'Capital' is captured by the balance sheet position 'fixed assets' (net value at the beginning of the year). Since we have no information about the age structure of capital this measure is not deflated. For 'labour' we compute the effective worker hours per year by multiplying the number of workers of a firm by an index of effective worker hours for the German machinery industry. 'Material' consists of the deflated profit and loss position 'raw materials and supplies'.

Our empirical analysis proceeds in three main steps. The first one is related (a) to the technological structure, (b) to the dynamics of this structure, and (c) to the aspect of technological variety. For this investigation the efficiency scores of DEA are used and interpreted.

In a second step our efficiency indices will be related to firm-specific R&D. For this data we rely on a database of the Stifterverband. From our 39 firms above there are only 26 firms which have reported their R&D.

Finally, we also relate our productivity results to the patenting activity of the firms. The respective patent data are drawn from the database of the European Patent Office. These data, however, do not cover the whole period of our investigation but only the years 1985 to 1988.

Technical Efficiency

According to our route of investigation detailed above, the first step of our investigation attempts to answer the following questions on the productivity structure of our sample:

1. Which firms are efficient in a particular year?
2. Is the set of efficient firms stable over time?

The results show that in a year-by-year analysis there are only two firms that are continuously members of the efficient set. Other firms lose their leading position after some years or appear only for a short period on the frontier. The number of efficient firms is varying from 3 to 8 firms per year with a slightly increasing tendency.

From this result we learn that the structure of the technological frontier changes quite rapidly. One can imagine some of the facets on the frontier vanishing and others appearing from period to period. We assume that only the technologically best firms stay on and leave their mark for a longer time.

With respect to the dynamics of the above described technological structure we ask the following questions:

3. Do the inefficient firms get closer to the frontier during time, i.e. is there a catch-up?
4. Has technological progress been driven by the efficiency leaders?
5. Compared to the 'all-time best frontier' does the efficiency of the whole sector increase?

These questions lead to dividing the sample of firms into two subgroups. The first one includes only the efficient firms, the other one consists of the not-efficient firms. Figure 5.1 shows the average year-by-year ι-value of the inefficient group (NEFFSTAT) together with the average year-by-year ι-value of the efficient firms (EFFSTAT) (which, of course, has to be 1,0 by definition). To obtain a measure of the movement of the frontier we compute another average ι-value for the efficient sub-sample (EFFDYN) as a comparison with the 'all-time best-practice' frontier.

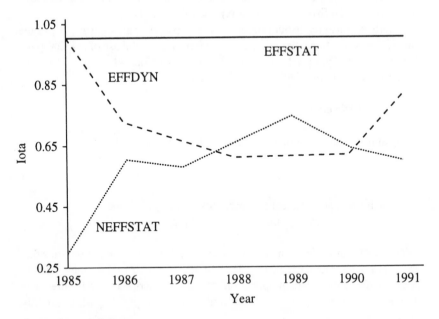

Source: Own calculations.

*Figure 5.1	Average efficiency series electronics sector*

Figure 5.1, for the period from 1988 to 1990, shows that the increasing relative efficiency of the inefficient firms is not affected by a movement of the frontier. This is obvious because from 1988 to 1990 the actual frontier's efficiency compared to the all-time best frontier does not change. The inefficient firms do really catch up.

With respect to the 'all-time best-practice' frontier for the efficient firms at least from 1986 a slightly but obviously increasing tendency can be noticed. Consequently, the year-by-year efficiency leaders are pushing forward the technological development.

Another calculation not shown in Figure 5.1 is the following: the average t values for the group of inefficient firms (calculated in the same way with reference to the 'all time best-practice' frontier) show as well an increasing trend from 0.30 (1985) to 0.37 (1991) for the electronics sector. Therefore, the sector shifts towards more technical efficiency.

Finally we want to take account of technological variety. The following three questions are addressed with respect to this issue:

6. What are the differences between the efficiency leaders?
7. Do the efficiency leaders define 'technology fields' within one branch?
8. How does the technological efficiency and importance of these 'technology fields' develop over time?

In the year 1985 we discover three electronics firms with an t-value of 1,0. Closer inspection of the input structure of these firms shows clearly that some of them differ extremely in the proportions of the use of the three inputs necessary to produce one unit of output. Therefore, it seems obvious that there exists more than one efficient 'technology' in order to produce electronics goods. The different proportions of inputs used here will help us to define different 'technologies' – each one characterized by a certain input ratio.

The fact that we detect some firms quite successfully applying extremely differing 'technologies' leads to the question whether it is possible to define them as the protagonists of different 'technology fields'. This seems plausible because DEA evaluates the inefficient firms using the facets of the frontier built up by linear combinations of the efficient ones. So we apply the λ values delivered by DEA to group the inefficient firms around the year-by-year technology leaders. To verify this assignment defined by the DEA method, we additionally ran a traditional cluster analysis (K-means) using input ratios as factors. This delivers six different clusters of input ratios which we label 'technology fields', F1 to F6. For these fields the DEA assignment is confirmed by 85 per cent. Moreover, in four of the six clusters more than one efficient firm joins the same 'technology field'.

With respect to the input ratios technology field F2 and even more F6 can be characterized as high capital-intensive. In field F1 and more intensely in field F3, we find a high material-intensity. An intensive use of labour, differing only in the extent (F5's labour intensity is higher), is a characteristic of the clusters F4 and F5.

Table 5.1 gives an account of the number of firms joining the six technology fields. It is evident that the main fields are F4 and F5 where the importance of the first is increasing, the one of the latter decreasing over time.

Table 5.1   Number of firms in each technology field (F1–F6)

Field	F1	F2	F3	F4	F5	F6
Year						
1985	2		1	5	30	1
1986	3	1	2	8	25	0
1987	2	1	2	9	25	0
1988	3	1	2	14	19	0
1989	3	1	2	17	16	0
1990	4	2	1	18	14	0
1991	3	2	2	22	10	0

Source: Own calculations.

The average ι-value (as measured against the all-time best-practice frontier) of the technology fields could give an account of the technological level of these fields.[26] Table 5.2 delivers these measures for each field and each year.

Table 5.2   Average ι for each technology

Field	F1	F2	F3	F4	F5	F6
Year						
1985	0.779	–	1.0	0.369	0.304	0.398
1986	0.579	0.459	0.926	0.313	0.280	–
1987	0.665	0.490	0.927	0.336	0.291	–
1988	0.675	0.513	0.835	0.358	0.276	–
1989	0.759	0.523	0.777	0.327	0.313	–
1990	0.772	0.442	0.782	0.326	0.289	–
1991	0.727	0.502	0.845	0.393	0.271	–

Source: Own calculations.

Here, however, one has to be very cautious as (in a cross-section comparision) this value tends to be higher for a lower number of firms. Taken this into account, comparing F4 and F5 suggests that the (average) technological level of F5 is constantly higher than the level of F4 with an increasing tendency only in the latter. A reason for this result might be that we find technological progress only in F4, that F4 is denser in the sense that the inefficient firms are closer to the leaders and/or that well performing firms of F5 leave this technology and enter into F4. The latter argument will be investigated further in the next steps.

Table 5.3 shows the number of movements between the respective fields during the period 1985–91. Evidently most of the movements occur between technology fields F4 and F5. This again furthers the observation that the technologies in F1, F2, F3 and F6 are rather extreme and cannot be easily applied by 'outsiders'. As to the comparison of the main fields F4 and F5, 20 firms move from F5 to F4 and only 3 move the other way round. Therefore, F4 seems to be more attractive.

Table 5.3   Movements between technology fields during the period 1985–91

	to	F1	F2	F3	F4	F5	F6
from							
F1				3		1	
F2					1		
F3			2				
F4				1		3	
F5			3	1	20		
F6				1			

Source: Own calculations.

Concerning any gains or losses of moves between fields, Table 5.4 gives an account of the change of the average ι-value of the moving firms. These numbers, however, have to be interpreted carefully. A switch from F5 over into technology field F4 leads to a slight increase of relative technical efficiency.

A contrary result is found for a 'jump' from F4 to F5. One reason for this is the fact that the gap between the technology leaders and the followers in F5 is larger compared to F4 which makes the latter more attractive. A deeper investigation into why some firms nevertheless change from F4 to F5 has to be accomplished in further steps.

Economic reasons as well as reasons of dynamic efficiency have then to be considered. However, four of the ten technology switches do fit into the concept

Innovation and technological development

of 'elastic barriers' (David, 1975) where a switch into a considerable different technology is accompanied by a loss of technical efficiency.

Table 5.4   Average ι change of moving firms

	to	F1	F2	F3	F4	F5	F6
from							
F1				0.011		0.266	
F2					0.630		
F3		−0.090					
F4			−0.099			−0.092	
F5		−0.045	0.038		0.044		
F6			0.060				

Source: Own calculations.

4.   TECHNICAL (IN)EFFICIENCY AND TECHNOLOGICAL PROGRESS

In this section we focus on the relationship between the inefficiency measures obtained in the previous paragraph and proxy variables for the firm specific technological progress. Is the relative efficiency position of firms – at least partly – determined by its technological performance?

To make the latter concept operational for empirical analyses one can distinguish between technology input measures such as R&D expenditures and technology output indicators such as patents. We will use both in the following analysis, well aware of the apparent difficulties, in connection with both indicators, of giving a satisfactory account of the technological performance on the firm level. Let us start with R&D expenditures.

R&D Expenditures and Relative Efficiency

In order to relate our ι-measures to R&D expenditures we apply traditional OLS where ι is the dependent variable and the R&D capital stock and other measures are independent. Some qualifications concerning these measures have to be made. One is related to ι when it is used in regression analyses in the following form:

$$\iota = Z\beta + \varepsilon \tag{5.6}$$

Z is the matrix of independent variables and β is the vector of regression coefficients and ε is the vector of error terms. Since the efficiency scores are restricted on $[0,1]$ the error term ε is dependent on Z and thus biased and inconsistent estimates for β are to be expected. A proof of this is found in Holvad and Hougaard (1993) who suggest correcting for this by transforming ι onto an unrestricted range:

$$\ln\left(\frac{1-\iota}{\iota}\right)$$

(5.7)

Consequently the dependent variable is unrestricted and OLS can be applied. For interpreting the regression results, however, one has to keep in mind that the sign of the estimates for the β values is related to the transformed and not the original ι, where the sign is just opposite.

In our estimation we related different independent variables with our efficiency measure. One of these is the R&D capital stock, RDS_t, which we use instead of yearly R&D expenditures, RD_t because R&D expenditures cannot be expected to improve productivity at once but only after a certain lapse of time and because technological progress is considered as a cumulative activity.

We suggest therefore that the technological level of a firm which is supposed to have a positive impact of productivity can be approximated by the accumulated R&D expenditures of the past. For this reason we calculate this stock for each firm by the perpetual inventory method where we apply degressive depreciation by a rate of 15 per cent:[27]

$$RDS_t = RDS_{t-1}*0.85 + RD_t.$$

(5.8)

The measured relative inefficiency of firms naturally has more than one determinant.[28] In the context of our analysis we are mainly interested in whether technological factors can be attributed to determine the relative position of firms. The following OLS results are therefore to be taken as to test the sign of the investigated relations rather than as an estimate of a complete theoretical model. Therefore, we proceed step-by-step adding technological and other related variables. Here we include RDS/L as the R&D capital stock per labour; K/L, the capital/labour ratio takes into account the effects of an increasing mechanization of the production process; RD/Y is the R&D intensity; the time variable ETP should cover non-specified trend effects such as exogenous technical progress; finally in certain runs we include dummy variables DCL for the respective technology fields in order to catch technology specific fixed effects.

For RDS/L, ETP we expect a negative coefficient because R&D and exogenous technical progress should improve the relative position of a firm with respect to the all-time best-practice frontier. RD/Y is expected to have a positive sign because the R&D expenditures in year t are assumed to increase productivity only in later years. The coefficient of K/L can have either sign; however, whenever process innovations are embodied in investment the sign should be negative.[29]

Table 5.5   Regression results for the electronics sector

Variant	const.	RDS/L	K/L	RD/Y	ETP	DCL	R^2
1	7,600	–0,00047					0,08
	(82.562)	(–3.964)					
2	7,298	–0,00054	0,00001				0,09
	(32.090)	(–4,229)	(1,453)				
3	7,441	–0,00118	0,00001	0,73618			0,21
	(34,620)	(-6,796)	(0,693)	(5,089)			
4	7,432	–0,00118	0,00001	0,73772	0,0034		0,21
	(30,588)	(–6,748)	(0,627)	(5,037)	(0,076)		
5		–0,00116	0,00001			sign.	0,81
		(–13,09)	(0,845)				
6		–0,00119	0,00001	0,4215	0,0269	sign.	0,82
		(–14,01)	(0,865)	(1,600)	(1,199)		
7	7,410	–0,00117	0,00001				0,85
only F4	(36,073)	(–20,34)	(1,548)				
8	7,193	–0,00117	0,00001	2,802	0,0046		0,87
only F4	(31,046)	(–21,195)	(2,057)	(3,290)	(0,199)		
9	7,977	–0,0008	0,00000				0,15
only F5	(74,36)	(–3,930)	(0,151)				
10	7,871	–0,003	0,00001	1,317	0,0068		0,25
only F5	(67,86)	(–4,358)	(0,724)	(3,361)	(0,497)		

Source: Own calculations.

Table 5.5 delivers our results for the coefficients, the t-values (in parenthesis) and the R^2 measures for various model variants. For variants 1 to 4 the estimates for the RDS/L coefficient are significant and as expected negative. Thus, the accumulated R&D capital stock has a considerable positive impact on the firms relative position towards the all-time best-practice frontier.

The mechanization variable K/L is positive in sign but not significant. Since the electronics sector – as compared, for example, to machinery[30] – is considered mostly as a sector not heavily dependent on technical progress embodied in investment, this result seems plausible. The estimate for R&D intensity shows a significant positive sign which is to be interpreted that increasing current R&D expenditures do not improve a firm's relative position. The fact that electronics firms on average invest high R&D funds per output unit with no immediate positive effect on efficiency clearly shows up here. Finally, exogenous technical progress is not significant here. These results are more or less consistent with the description of the electronics sector by Pavitt (1984). There, electronics is considered as rather a science-based sector relying very much on its own R&D efforts in a cumulative fashion.

Including dummies for the various technology fields improves the results considerably: R^2 increases to about 0,81. Investigating the most 'crowded' technology fields 'F4' and 'F5' (characterized by comparably low K/L ratios of all technology fields within this sector) leads to a slight improvement for 'F4' and a drastic decline in the regression fit of 'F5'. These results suggest that our technology fields are significantly different.

Patenting Activity and Relative Efficiency

In a final step we consider the output of innovative activities, patents. We capture the patent activities of the firms in our sample by simply counting the number of patents they raised within a certain period for the German market. The data are taken from the 1991 publication of the INPADOC database by the 'Ifo-Institut für Wirtschaftsforschung'.[31]

Aware of the well-known difficulties in accounting for and weighting patents[32] we accept the rough procedure of Ifo and consider only those firms (a) who have applied for patents in at least two countries and (b) who had at least five applications during the years 1985–88. The relatively high costs for patenting abroad can be used as a yardstick (and lower bound) for the importance of the patents.

We are also aware of the fact that between patenting and a possible increase in productivity a certain amount of time has to pass. This time lag should be not longer (or even shorter) than the one between R&D expenditure and productivity change. By comparing the patents of the years 1985 to 1988 with the efficiency measures of the year 1991, we lag our data between three and six years.

For the above mentioned period we select from our sample ten electronics firms with patent activities for Germany and at least one other country. This very small number and the fact that exactly weighting the patents was not possible until now prevents us from performing regressions to relate them to efficiency measures. So we simply divide our sample in a patenting and a non-patenting group of firms and concentrate on the differences between these subsamples. And even without a precisely measured relationship our results are remarkable.

Table 5.6   Efficiency of patenting and non-patenting firms in 1991

	Electronics
average efficiency of patenting firms	0.46
average efficiency of non-patenting firms	0.40
percentage of efficient firms within patenting firms	10%
percentage of efficient firms within non-patenting firms	3%

Source: Own calculations.

In Table 5.6 we show that the average efficiency of the patenting firms is higher than the average efficiency of non-patenting firms. The percentage of technology leaders is three times higher in the patenting sample than in the non-patenting group.

Finally, we take account of the relevance of patenting for the respective technology fields. Table 5.7 gives an overview. The main result for electronics is that concerning the more 'crowded' fields F4 and F5, the former has a higher average efficiency (see Table 5.2) and leads also in the percentage of patenting.

Table 5.7   Patenting and technology fields in electronics

techn. field	patenting firms	non-patenting firms	total	% patenting
F1	0	3	3	0
F2	0	2	2	0
F3	0	2	2	0
F4	9	13	22	41
F5	1	9	10	10
total	10	29	39	26

Source: Own calculations.

This simple calculation supports the results for R&D given above by indicating a positive correlation between patenting (as the ouput of R&D) and the relative efficiency of a firm.

5.   CONCLUSION

This chapter has delivered an empirical study on technical performance and diversity within the German manufacturing sector 'Electronics' for the years between 1985 and 1991. Based on concepts from modern innovation theory we employ a non-parametric linear programming procedure, DEA, which allows us (a) to compute an index for the relative technological and technical inefficiency of firms and (b) to determine certain technology fields differing by their relative use of input factors.

Our study shows that it is possible (a) to find a structure of technical inefficiencies characterized by several technological leaders and (b) to detect several technology fields taking into account technological diversity. A dynamic analysis delivers (c) that the total efficiency of the sectors improves over time and (d) that there are differences among the respective technology fields.

These results are related to measures of firms' technological performance. We argue that the efficiency position of firms is dependent on their respective technological performance. This result seems to be independent of whether we use the R&D capital stock as technology input measure or patenting activity as a technology output proxy.

Although our results do very much confirm the notion that technological progress is an important determinant of firm performance some qualifications necessarily have to be made. First, all we know about the technology of a firm is deduced from a very rough procedure, e.g. technologies are distinguished by their factor input ratios. An analysis related to more technical aspects would be very much appreciated here. For future work we consider using more information on the production structure as well as qualitative innovation data to improve our results. Second, it is obviously quite crucial for our results how the factor 'capital' is defined. Vintage effects, capacity utilization, technical life cycle, etc. are not considered yet. Some improvement on this is expected whenever longer time series data completed with more reliable investment figures are available. Last but not least, the analysis of efficiency scores has to be worked on in order to distinguish between the top firms which are as yet not comparable ($\iota = 1$). Those improved measures might then help – in a longer times series analysis – to compare different technology fields and their comparative development directly.

ACKNOWLEDGEMENTS

We are very grateful to the 'Stifterverband für die Deutsche Wissenschaft' who made it possible to relate our results on relative firm productivity to firm-specific R&D expenditures. We are especially grateful to Christoph Grenzmann from the SV-Wissenschaftsstatistik in Essen/Germany who provided technical assistance as well as the computations which are presented in Section 4.

Moreover, we thank Jean Bernard, Giovanni Dosi and Angelo Reati for their remarks and suggestions, as well as Klaus Nielsen and Andrew Tylecote for their careful editing. Remaining errors are still our responsibility.

Finally, financial support by the European Commission for the SPES project 'Comparative Economics of R&D: The Case of France and Germany' as well as by the DAAD programme PROCOPE is gratefully acknowledged.

NOTES

1. See, for example, Bös (1988), Hanusch and Cantner (1991), and Cantner *et al.* (1995).
2. See, for example, Caves and Barton (1990).
3. See, for example, Crew *et al.* (1971) and Leibenstein (1976).
4. For inefficiencies accruing from entry barriers see, for example, Brandner and Spencer (1985); Mankiw and Whinston (1986). On the effects of excess capacity see Caves *et al.* (1979).
5. See, for example, Carlsson (1972).
6. See, for example, Moomaw (1981, 1985).
7. See Caves and Barton (1990).
8. See, for example, Dosi (1988); Nelson and Winter (1982).
9. For an overview see Färe *et al.* (1993).
10. See Charnes and Cooper (1962, 1985). For an excellent overview see Charnes *et al.* (1994).
11. It should be noted here that also Pasinetti (1981) shows in a Sraffian framework that the choice of technique depends only on technical factors and is totally independent of economic factors (there the wage rate).
12. As a by-product, the use of the concept 'representative agent' is justified.
13. See Dosi (1988).
14. See Atkinson and Stiglitz (1969).
15. See Antonelli (1994).
16. See David (1975).
17. With our assumption of short-run Leontief type production functions allocative (in)efficiency is only a minor problem because a specific technique is optimal for a considerable range of relative factor prices.
18. See Charnes and Cooper (1962, 1985); Charnes *et al.* (1994).
19. See Färe *et al.* (1993).
20. See Kendrick (1956) and Ott (1959).
21. The ratios are stated here as differences which are not allowed to be positive.
22. See Charnes *et al.* (1986).
23. The variable ε has to be smaller than any other measure of the optimization. This implies especially that first the frontier has to be determined and then the slack variables can enter the basic solution.
24. Of course, one should here distinguish two vectors e^T for inputs and output respectively which contain *s* and *i* elements respectively. To ease notation we do not take account of this. Further analysis is not affected.
25. This condition is equivalent to the statement that the aggregation weight or prices of the primal programme are to be strictly positive.
26. For this measure see Forsund and Hjalmarsson (1987); Carlsson (1972).
27. The rate 15 per cent is very often used in empirical investigations where R&D capital stocks are used. For computing (5.8) we use all available past R&D expenditures of firms. For the initial period, however, the starting R&D capital stock is approximated by $RDS_0 = RD_0/(0.15 + g)$, where g is the growth rate of GNP. See, for example, Meyer-Krahmer and Wessels (1989).
28. For a discussion of these aspects see, for example, Caves and Barton (1990).
29. It would be interesting to include here investment data in order to take into account vintage effects. As yet, our data do not allow us to take this into account.
30. See Cantner *et al.* (1996).
31. See Faust and Buckel (1991).
32. See, for example, Pavitt (1985), Griliches (1990) or Kleinknecht (1993).

REFERENCES

Ahmad, S. (1966), 'On the theory of induced invention', *Economic Journal*, vol. 76, pp. 344–57.

Ali, A.I. and C.S. Lerme (1990), *Data Envelopment Analysis Models: A Framework*, Working Paper, School of Management, University of Massachusetts at Amherst.

Antonelli, C. (1994), 'Localized technological changes: a model incorporating switching costs and R&D expenses with endowment advantages', in Y. Shionoya and M. Perlman (eds), *Innovation in Technology, Industries, and Institutions*, Ann Arbor: University of Michigan Press, pp. 75–89.

Atkinson, A. and J.E. Stiglitz (1969), 'A new view of technological change', *Economic Journal*, vol. 79, pp. 573–8.

Bös, D. (1988), 'Introduction: recent theories on public enterprise economics', *European Economic Review*, vol. 32, pp. 409–14.

Brandner, J.A. and B.J. Spencer (1985), 'Tacit collusion, free entry and welfare', *Journal of Industrial Economics*, vol. 33, pp. 277–94.

Cantner, U., H. Hanusch and G. Westermann (1995), 'Effizienz, öffentlicher Auftrag und Deregulierung', *Jahrbücher für Nationalökonomie und Statistik*, vol. 214(3), pp. 257–74.

Cantner, U., H. Hanusch and G. Westermann (1996), 'Detecting technological performance and variety – an empirical approach', in E. Helmstädter and M. Perlman (eds), *Behavioural Norms, Technological Progress and Economic Dynamics: Studies in Schumpterian Economics*, Ann Arbor: University of Michigan Press, pp. 223–46.

Carlsson, B. (1972), 'The measurement of efficiency in production: an application to Swedish manufacturing industries 1968', *Swedish Journal of Economics*, vol. 74, pp. 468–85.

Caves, R.E. and D.R. Barton (1990), *Efficiency in U.S. Manufacturing Industries*, Cambridge: MIT Press.

Caves, R.E., J.P. Jarrett and M.K. Loucks (1979), 'Competitive conditions and the firm's buffer stocks: an exploratory analysis', *Review of Economics and Statistics*, vol. 61, pp. 485–96.

Charnes, A. and W.W. Cooper (1962), 'Programming with linear fractional functionals', *Naval Research Logistics Quarterly*, vol. 9, pp. 181–6.

Charnes, A. and W.W. Cooper (1985), 'Preface to Topics in Data Envelopment Analysis', *Journal of Operations Research*, 2, pp. 59–94.

Charnes, A., W.W. Cooper and R.M. Thrall (1986), 'Classifying and characterizing efficiencies and Inefficiencies in Data Envelopment Analysis', *Operations Research Letters*, vol. 5(3), pp. 105–10.

Charnes, A., W.W. Cooper, A.Y. Lewin and L.M. Seiford (1994), *Data Envelopment Analysis: The Theory, the Method and the Process*, Boston: Kluwer Academic.

Crew, M.A., J.W. Jones-Lee and C.K. Rowley (1971), 'X-Efficiency Theory versus Managerial Discretion Theory', *Southern Economic Journal*, vol. 38, pp. 173–84.

David, P. (1975), *Technical Choice, Innovation and Economic Growth*, Cambridge: Cambridge University Press.

Dosi, G. (1988), 'The Nature of the Innovative Process', in Dosi *et al.* (1988), pp. 221–38.

Dosi, G., C. Freeman, R. Nelson, G. Silverberg and L. Soete (1988), *Technical Change and Economic Theory*, London and New York: Pinter.

Färe, R., S. Grosskopf and C.A.K. Lovell (1993), *Production Frontiers*, Cambridge University Press.

Farrell, M.J. (1957), 'The Measurement of Productive Efficiency', *Journal of the Royal Statistical Society*, Series A, vol. 120, pp. 253–81.

Faust, K. and E. Buckel (1991), 'Ifo-Patentstatistik, im Wettbewerb um die Technologie von morgen', *Unternehmensreport 1991*, München: Ifo-Institut für Wirtschaftsforschung.

Fellner, W. (1961), 'Two propositions in Theory of Induced Innovation', *Economic Journal*, vol. 71, pp. 305–8.

Forsund, F.R. and L. Hjalmarsson (1987), *Analysis of Industrial Structure: A Putty-Clay Approach*, Stockholm: Almqvist & Wiksell International.

Griliches, Z. (1990), 'Patent statistics as economic indicators: a survey', *Journal of Economic Literature*, vol. XXVII, pp. 1661–1707.

Hanusch, H. and U. Cantner (1991), 'Produktion Öffentlicher Leistungen, Effizienz und Technischer Fortschritt', *Jahrbuch für Nationalökonomie und Statistik*, vol. 208(4), pp. 369–84.

Holvad, T. and J.L. Hougaard (1993), *Measuring Technical Input Efficiency for Similar Production Units: A Survey of the Non-Parametric Approach*, European University Institute, Florence, EUI Working Paper, ECO 93/20.

Kendrick, J.W. (1956), 'Productivity trends: capital and labor', *Review of Economics and Statistics*, vol. 38, pp. 248–57.

Kleinknecht, A. (1993), 'Why do we need new innovation output indicators?', in A. Kleinknecht and D. Bain, *New Concepts in Innovation Output Measurement*, New York: St Martin's Press, pp. 1–9.

Leibenstein, H. (1976), *Beyond Economic Man: A New Foundation for Microeconomics*, Cambridge, Mass.: Harvard University Press.

Mankiw, N.G. and M.D. Whinston (1986), 'Free entry and social inefficiency', *Rand Journal of Economics*, vol. 17, 1986, pp. 48–58.

Meyer-Krahmer, F. and H. Wessels (1989), 'Intersektorale Verflechtung von Technologiegebern und Technologienehmern', *Jahrbuch für Nationalökonomie und Statistik*, vol. 206(6), pp. 563–82.

Moomaw, R.L. (1981), 'Production efficiency and region', *Southern Economic Review*, vol. 48, pp. 344–57.

Moomaw, R.L. (1985), 'Firm location and city size: reduced productivity advantages as a factor in the decline of manufacturing in urban areas', *Journal of Urban Economics*, vol. 17, pp. 73–89.

Nelson, R.R. and Winter, S.G. (1982), *An Evolutionary Theory of Economic Change*, Cambridge, Mass., and London: The Belknap Press of Harvard University Press.

Ott, A.E. (1959), 'Technischer Fortschritt', in *Handwörterbuch der Sozialwissenschaften*, Bd. 10, Stuttgart, pp. 302–16.

Pasinetti, L. (1981), *Structural Change and Economic Growth*, Cambridge: Cambridge University Press.

Pavitt, K. (1984), 'Sectoral patterns of technical change: towards a taxonomy and a theory', *Research Policy*, vol. 13(6).

Pavitt, K. (1985), 'Patent statistics as indicators of innovative activities: possibilities and problems', *Scientometrics*, 7, pp. 77–99.

Salter, W. (1960), *Productivity and Technical Change*, Cambridge: Cambridge University Press.

Shionoya, Y. and M. Perlman (eds) (1994), *Innovation in Technology, Industries, and Institutions*, Ann Arbor: The University of Michigan Press.

6. High R&D intensity without high tech products: a Swedish paradox?

Charles Edquist and Maureen McKelvey

INTRODUCTION

This chapter argues that a paradox is visible in the Swedish economy. The paradox has to do with the fact that while, on the one hand, a high proportion of the Gross Domestic Product (GDP) is spent on formal research and development (R&D), on the other hand, the Swedish economy produces only a below average percentage of R&D-intensive products relative to total manufacturing, compared to the average for the OECD countries. There thus seem to be problems in translating R&D results into R&D-intensive products, having to do, we argue, with specific Swedish factors at the firm and national levels.

Formal R&D is considered an indicator of input into knowledge creation and technical development and is therefore seen to be an indicator of innovativeness. There are therefore important reasons why such a paradox is a problem for Sweden and for other countries facing a similar situation. One reason is that both the old growth account literature and the modern economics of innovation identify knowledge and innovation as the main sources of productivity growth. The relative level of knowledge and technology embodied in industrial products therefore matters for a country's economic growth.

Although R&D can be used for many different types of low, medium and high tech products as well as for more basic research, Sweden is an interesting case because many have perceived it as a medium to high tech country. At least up until the early 1990s, Sweden was generally perceived as a successful economy, finding a successful, middle road of welfare capitalism. Moreover, Sweden has often been heralded as 'high tech' due to, for example, innovative ways of organizing manufacturing, extensive use of advanced production machinery, and a high percentage of GDP spent on R&D. In fact, research has shown that Swedish industry does use advanced production technologies extensively, for example in the engineering industry, which accounts for about half of manufacturing (Edquist and Jacobsson 1988).

Products are another matter. The specialized industrial structure of Sweden has been heavily based on 'refined' natural resources like paper and pulp, mining and engineering (Edquist and Lundvall, 1993). These are not high tech products, but Sweden has nevertheless had an aura of a medium to high tech country.

Sweden as a whole and particularly Swedish firms devote considerable resources to R&D. As a whole in the late 1980s, Sweden spent approximately 2.8 per cent of GDP on R&D, which is on par with the leaders such as Japan and the USA; many other small countries tend to invest a lower percentage (SIND, 1990a). Firms spend the majority (68 per cent) of this total R&D. Swedish industrial R&D is clearly dominated by a few large, multinational firms.

In this chapter, we analyse the performance of the Swedish economy in relation to the OECD average for R&D-intensive production relative to manufacturing as a whole. The figures are presented in the Appendix along with those for the performance of Germany, Japan, the Netherlands and the United States. The cross-country comparisons for each R&D-intensive sector show the proportion of R&D-intensive products in manufacturing compared to the OECD average. Our comments are, however, mainly restricted to explaining the apparent paradox in the Swedish economy.

This analysis is novel in two ways. Firstly, we specifically distinguish between use of high tech in production processes and its incorporation as R&D-intensive products. As argued below, the OECD definition of high tech products is used in order to enable international comparisons. Secondly, most comparative analyses of countries' competitive performance, such as Michael Porter's (1990) work, analyse exports. We analyse production within the country rather than exports. This approach is based on theoretical work in the economics of technical change which argues that it is production and development of technologies which lead to significant long-term positive externalities such as cumulative development of knowledge. Export data only imperfectly reflect this.

THEORETICAL CONSIDERATIONS

The fact that countries specialize in production and then trade different goods and services comes as no surprise to economists. In fact, classical and neoclassical international trade theorists have long stressed that differences between countries in terms of relative prices, availability of resources (land, labour) and market structures explain countries' specialization. Countries produce different goods, whereupon they trade internationally those where they have an advantage. However, in these theoretical constructions, particularly neoclassical theory, technology is an exogenous variable.[1] According to this logic, it makes no difference whether a country is specialized in low, medium or high tech goods, as long as they participate in international trade. Everyone benefits anyway.

In contrast, contemporary research on the economics of technical change starts from different assumptions and comes to different conclusions. Based on evolutionary economic theory, firms are assumed to differ in their knowledge about, and use of, various resources including knowledge and technology.[2] Firms are seen to have varying capabilities to develop, monitor and use technology and knowledge. They do not know which techniques are most efficient. Instead, they must invest in search, R&D or innovation processes to discover which technical alternatives are (potentially) possible in order to develop and choose among alternatives.

In the economics of technical change tradition, technology is endogenously generated within the economy rather than an external factor. Firms are the ones who often develop technologies of relevance for economic activities, sometimes in interactions with other organizations such as universities. The development and diffusion of technology is often local, tacit and cumulative within individuals, firms and countries (Dosi, 1988).

These assumptions about technology and knowledge in the economics of technical change have significant implications for analysing patterns of national production specialization and for linking high tech to economic growth and to productivity growth. Firms, and hence countries, have differing abilities to find and translate technology and knowledge into economic innovations, in the sense of new or improved products and production processes. In particular, Dosi, Pavitt and Soete (1990) conclude that whether or not firms in a specific country will be able to innovate, and in which industrial sectors, depends on initial conditions in firms, the organization of markets, and technological capabilities as well as on institutions affecting actors' capabilities and decisions about these conditions. Related research on 'national systems of innovation' has similarly indicated significant differences among countries in terms of ability to innovate and in terms of institutions and organizations.[3]

Because the economics of technical change perspective emphasizes a dynamic view of the economy, technical change is assumed to modify the economic playing rules by creating more efficient processes and more attractive products. Innovation, rather than price differences, is central. Therefore, if a country is specialized in technologies/sectors with higher opportunities to innovate, its longer-term economic prospects are better than those of countries specialized in less innovative sectors. It matters whether a country produces bulk goods competing on price or specialized products competing on quality, uniqueness or other qualities which enable temporary monopoly rents. In the latter case, countries have a better probability of achieving productivity growth and hence economic growth.

Although the specialization of production is only one of many factors influencing labour productivity, we argue that the relative percentage of R&D-intensive goods in industrial production can be linked to productivity growth. The reason is that labour productivity is an indicator, which measures efficiency of the manufacturing process in price terms. Productivity and productivity growth indicate a ratio between value added (or sales) and employees (or number of hours worked). Thus, productivity can increase because the production process has become technically more efficient (and requires less labour) and/or because an improved/new final product can be sold at a higher price.

There are two theoretical reasons as to why these propositions about a relationship between productivity and R&D-intensive goods are important when analysing Sweden's (or other countries') production specialization.

The first is that if technological competence and capability do build cumulatively in an economy in interactions between firms and organizations, then a country which is relatively low tech will tend to stay so, and vice versa. Countries will tend to develop along specific 'trajectories' or paths of industrial specialization and technological competencies.

Secondly, if production of high tech products tends to create more positive externalities in an economy compared to low tech products, then countries specialized in high tech will tend to be in a better position to capture future returns arising from the dynamic creation of resources and rents (Tyson, 1992). In contrast, countries which lose a high tech specialization of production should be worried about the future economic health of their economy. Our analysis of the apparent Swedish paradox is based on these theoretical arguments.

CONCEPTUAL SPECIFICATIONS

Analysis of the level of R&D-intensive goods in Sweden and other countries requires international comparisons. A first question, then, is what constitutes an R&D-intensive good and industrial sector? It has already been argued that industrial R&D indicates the amount of resources devoted to technological innovation. R&D expenditures are resources spent on formal search activities. Other types of learning such as interactive learning within and between firms and development of tacit knowledge are usually not included in such figures. R&D expenditures have therefore been criticized as an inadequate measure of innovation. They are, however, still a useful measure partly because R&D expenditures do indicate intent to innovate and partly because international, comparative statistics are available.

Our study discusses the R&D intensity of industrial sectors. In turn, R&D intensity is often taken as an indicator of 'high, medium and low technology'. In a first classification, the OECD defined high tech industries as those which on average spend 4 per cent or more of sales value on R&D. Those industries which spend between 1 per cent and 4 per cent are medium tech and those spending less than 1 per cent are low tech.[4] This classification is used here.

The OECD criteria can then be used to identify industrial sectors as used in statistical databases. The ISIC (International Standard Industrial Classification) system uses three-digit numbers to denote broad industrial sectors. These three-digit categories in turn consist of several four-digit industrial product groups. According to the OECD's criteria, the following sectors/product groups were high tech in the ISIC, revision 2:

ISIC 3522	Drugs and Medicine
ISIC 3825	Office Machinery and Computers
ISIC 383	Electrical Machinery and Components[5]
ISIC 3845	Aerospace
ISIC 385	Technological Goods (Scientific Instruments)

These ISIC categories constitute the industries defined as R&D-intensive (high tech) in this chapter.

The OECD definition categorizes industries which can be seen to be, on average, high, medium or low tech across the eleven largest OECD economies. The purpose of taking an international average is that the categories can then be used to make comparisons among countries. Here we use these international categories to compare individual countries, especially Sweden, to the OECD average. However, because the categories are internationally determined, the percentage spent on R&D in each sector may or may not hold for each individual country. Thus, international comparisons can be made using the OECD classification, but individual deviations – in this case for Sweden – should be pointed out.[6]

These five industrial sectors thus consist of groups of products. As mentioned, we have made a conceptual distinction between technology used as process technology and the products which the industrial sector manufactures. Product technologies means what is produced and sold. Process technologies are used to make goods and services. It is a question of how things are manufactured. Only product technologies are analysed here.[7]

The importance of producing improved or new products goes beyond the price competition of equilibrium analysis. In a situation of dynamic Schumpeterian competition, the innovating firm can capture temporary monopoly rents for new and improved products. This gives firms incentives to innovate. In a dynamic sector – and hence in a dynamic economy – new and improved products are more important as a means of competition than price reductions (resulting, for example, from improved process technologies).

However, used alone, R&D expenditures say nothing about the efficacy of the innovation process nor about the level of technology used in production. For example, Pavitt has shown that in some capital-intensive, large-scale industries such as paper and pulp, where the process technology is advanced, the process technology is developed by upstream machine producers because they are better able to capture the economic benefits than the paper mills (Pavitt, 1984). Assuming that the paper and pulp industry does not invest much in R&D to develop their final products, the products sold by the machine producers would be more R&D-intensive than the products sold by the paper and pulp industry. In this example, the machinery is defined as a product technology when designed and sold by machinery makers, but it is a process technology when used by paper and pulp manufacturers.

Finally, we would like to point out that our analysis of the relative level of technology in products is preliminary. We have taken R&D intensity as a proxy for innovative effort, even though technology is also developed in other ways. We have taken R&D-intensive industries as a proxy for high tech products, even though there are discrepancies between products and industrial sectors; there are high tech products in low tech sectors and vice versa. Nevertheless, we have presented arguments as to why these are reasonable indicators.

THE SWEDISH CASE IN AN INTERNATIONAL COMPARISON

Trends in the R&D-intensive industrial sectors in Sweden during the past twenty years are here compared with the OECD average and with four other countries, namely Germany, Japan, the Netherlands and the United States. These comparisons can be found in the Appendix, which includes six figures. Figure 6.1 compares the Swedish share of R&D-intensive goods in production and in exports relative to the OECD average. Figures 6.2 to 6.6 illustrate developments in the five countries for each R&D-intensive sector listed above.

The Appendix to this chapter also contains a description of the STAN database – which is the source of the figures – and the equation used. Our comments will be restricted to Sweden but the reader should particularly note developments in Japan which has increased its specialization in the high tech product groups.

Figure 6.1 shows the Swedish share of exports and production of R&D-intensive products in manufacturing as a percentage of the OECD average from 1970 to 1990. The percentage of R&D-intensive goods in Swedish *exports* rose from the early 1970s to 1978, thereafter decreased, and then rose again at the end of the 1980s. Figure 6.1 also gives information about the relative specialization of Sweden in *production* of R&D-intensive sectors. Whereas exports showed an increase for several years at the end of the 1980s, the increase in relative production was minor. At the aggregate level of all R&D-intensive goods as a percentage of manufacturing, the Swedish percentage was at 71 per cent in 1990 (see Figure 6.1). In that this is well below 100 per cent, Sweden is not specialized in production of high tech products, relative to other industrialized countries. In fact, the general trend is that Swedish industry has become decreasingly specialized since 1975.

Figures 6.2 to 6.6 show each country's production as a percentage of the OECD average in the various R&D-intensive sectors. From the mid 1970s, the Swedish trend has been negative for three of the five R&D industrial sectors, namely, Office Machinery and Computers (ISIC 3825), Electrical Machinery and Components (ISIC 383), and Aerospace (ISIC 3845).[8] For these three sectors, Sweden was above, just at or just below the OECD average during the early to mid 1970s but subsequently became less specialized. Sweden's share of Technological Goods (ISIC 385) has been around 50 to 70 per cent of the average during the period but ended in a positive direction. By the early 1990s, Sweden was thus not specialized in any of these four high tech sectors.

There is, however, one exception to this generally negative Swedish trend, namely Drugs and Medicine (ISIC 3522). Sweden has gone from well below the OECD average in 1970 (44 per cent) up to and above the OECD average (104 per cent) in 1990 and has thus become specialized. This new area of specialization differs significantly from Sweden's previous specialization in the engineering and paper and pulp industries. A very interesting question demanding further research is therefore why and how Sweden has managed to specialize in Drugs and Medicine during this period.

In the other R&D-intensive industries which lie nearer Sweden's traditional specialization, Sweden has increasingly been left behind, relative to other industrialized countries. The empirical material presented in the Appendix thus indicates that despite large investments in R&D, the Swedish industrial structure has not been successfully (re)oriented towards R&D-intensive sectors during the past twenty years.

In order to argue that Sweden's relatively low and decreasing proportion of R&D-intensive goods in production, compared to the OECD average, affects economic growth and productivity growth, it is necessary to present some additional data. This data should preliminarily indicate whether or not a relationship between growth and productivity on one hand and R&D-intensive products on the other can be identified.[9]

One indicator of dynamic competition is whether the markets for high tech products have been growing equally as fast, faster or slower than for manufacturing as a whole. If the markets are growing faster, then this indicates that firms which successfully compete in these markets can expand production, thereby potentially stimulating growth and employment. For the period 1974–88 both in Sweden and in the OECD as a whole, market growth for each of the five R&D-intensive products was greater than for manufacturing as a whole.[10] In fact, the market which grew the fastest, Office Machinery and Computers (ISIC 3825), was the industrial sector in which Sweden most dramatically lost its position (see Figure 6.3). Japan dramatically increased its specialization in this sector from the early 1980s. A growing market indicates new market opportunities, which seem to be related to technical opportunities.

A study done by the Swedish Industrial Board (SIND, 1990b) about the dynamism of high tech firms corresponds to expectations that dynamic competition and growing markets rely on firms performing R&D.[11] SIND classified Swedish firms as high, medium and low tech based on R&D intensity. Although there are some exceptions, the SIND study generally indicates that large investments in R&D by firms led to a (much larger) growth in volume of production, as measured by increase in value added. This relationship between R&D and growth in value added is explainable if one assumes that R&D leads to new or modified products, for which market growth is rapid and which command a higher price in a situation of dynamic competition. Similar relationships held for the relationship between R&D and (absolute) productivity in the SIND study.

The relationship between R&D and productivity growth which showed up at the individual firm level in Sweden is generally supported at the industrial sector level for 1974–88. In a previous paper, we showed that in general in Sweden, productivity growth in R&D-intensive sectors was higher than for manufacturing as a whole (Edquist and McKelvey 1992, Chapter 4).[12] This was the general trend, although there were some exceptions.

Sweden seems to get, however, a decent return from its R&D investments, as indicated by some output measures. For example, Pavitt and Patel indicate that the number of patents per capita that Sweden takes in the USA is on par with those large countries which are innovation leaders (Pavitt and Patel, 1988; Edquist and McKelvey, 1992).[13] Sweden also has a positive technology trade balance, a figure which includes expenditures for patents, licenses, royalties, and know-how. In 1987, Sweden had a net positive balance of 562 million SEK and in 1989, a net positive balance of 821 million SEK (SCB, 1991). These sketchy output measures thus indicate that R&D investments in Sweden do lead to novelties valuable in that they can be protected as patents and/or sold as knowledge, know-how, etc. Of the R&D which is performed in Sweden, Swedish firms do seem to reap benefits, as indicated by innovation indicators. They do not, however, seem to have translated that knowledge into R&D-intensive products.

The question remains, to what extent is the Swedish phenomenon a paradox? Should we have expected that a high intensity of R&D results leads to the production of R&D-intensive products? It is a paradox if R&D is taken straight off the bat as an indication of innovativeness. The paradox may, however, be mostly apparent. In particular, R&D is an input measure of intent to innovate; an attempt to create something new. It says nothing about how efficiently those resources are used in the R&D process nor about whether the knowledge and technologies being developed are likely to be attractive on a market. We may be dealing with an apparent paradox, caused by an over-reliance on R&D indicators in the economics of technical change tradition.

There are two sides of the paradox, the high R&D intensity and the low specialization in R&D-intensive products. Specialization has already been discussed at length and we will return to it in our concluding remarks. Let us therefore focus on some characteristics of the former side. Part of the paradox may be explained by the orientation and efficiency of the R&D performed within Sweden. Firstly, one might imagine that the high percentage of GDP spent on R&D reflects government spending on basic research. However, this hypothesis does not hold, as firms perform 68 per cent of the gross expenditures on R&D (OECD, 1993). Of the total industrial R&D, the majority goes to product innovations.

Another reason may be the relatively high R&D intensity of Swedish industrial sectors which are internationally considered medium tech industries. Two sectors in particular seem to pass the criterion. The medium tech sector Engineering (ISIC 382) minus the high tech sector Office Machinery and Computers (ISIC 3825) spent 5.8 per cent of sales on R&D in 1987 and 4.1 per cent in 1991. Transport Equipment (ISIC 384) also spent significant amounts on R&D. This category includes both aerospace (high tech) and automobiles (medium tech). Swedish industrial statistics do not provide separate R&D statistics for the aerospace and automobile industries, but the broader Transport Equipment (ISIC 384) spent 6 per cent of sales on R&D in 1987.[14] Because of the firms' mix of products, it is thus not clear whether the Swedish automobile industry alone – without aerospace – would be high or medium tech, although another analysis of Sweden (NUTEK, 1995, p. 28) has placed automobiles as high tech. Even very low tech sectors like Paper and Pulp Products may spend relatively more in Sweden on R&D as a percentage of sales than the OECD average.

A third reason for the high R&D intensity has to do with the Swedish structure of production. Both production and R&D expenditures are heavily dominated by large, multinational firms. Between ten and fifteen firms account for over 50 per cent of industrial R&D, and firms with more than 1000 employees account for almost 80 per cent of the total industrial R&D.

Swedish firms have tended to keep a large percentage of their total R&D – up to 70-80 per cent – within Sweden while placing production abroad. In other words, if their R&D investments were spread out over the world production activities of these Swedish multinational firms, then their R&D intensity would be lower. The level of R&D in Sweden may thus reflect the Swedish economy's reliance on large engineering firms placing production abroad – rather than on Sweden's unusually high innovative opportunities in medium tech sectors. Firms have thus, in some sense, made Sweden a knowledge producer without domestically translating that knowledge into economic value. However, these large firms have recently increasingly moved R&D abroad, thereby opening the possibility of a changing situation in the future (Cantwell, 1994; Håkanson and Nobel, 1993). This is reflected in the fact that 1987 was a peak for investment in industrial R&D as a percentage of sales in Sweden, after which it has dropped.

Although these various factors explain part of the apparent Swedish paradox of high R&D intensity without high tech products, it is still troubling that Sweden has mostly either remained de-specialized or lost specialization in the high tech products during the past twenty years. There seem to be particular Swedish circumstances which, by contributing to the problem, create a political/economic situation in which this paradox could arise.

CONCLUDING REMARKS

The apparent paradox of high R&D intensity without specialization in R&D-intensive products in Sweden is a phenomenon requiring additional explanation and discussion. The reasons why Sweden has become increasingly de-specialized in production of R&D-intensive products, with the notable exception of Drugs and Medicine, include both firm-specific and national contextual factors, such as political and institutional factors.

As mentioned, both Sweden's production structure and Sweden's industrial R&D infrastructure are heavily dominated by large firms. These firms account for the majority of industrial R&D, and their decisions to invest, or not invest, in new products and sectors strongly affect the Swedish industrial structure. Small Swedish firms have not been able to exploit R&D-intensive products and grow rapidly into larger firms to an extent similar to that in the USA. Nor have large firms diversified as in Japan.[15] Although there are some notable exceptions, it seems that these existing, large Swedish firms stick close to existing products when innovating and producing.

According to David Teece (1988), this is rational behaviour because a firm's 'core business' is mutually dependent on its knowledge base. Because of the cumulative knowledge base and firms' existing complementary assets, such as marketing, those new products which firms choose to take to market will tend to be close to their previously successful products. If, due to national contextual factors, Swedish firms continue to be profitable by producing old products, then this results in a lack of structural change, which is in turn a partial explanation of why Sweden is below the OECD average in high tech products.

According to these ideas about firm behaviour, we should expect that Sweden as a whole should remain specialized in its traditional pattern of industrial production. As that specialization has tended to be fairly medium to low tech – paper and pulp, steel, mechanical engineering, etc. – it is not so surprising that Sweden is not currently specialized in high tech products. There are, however, reasons to be concerned about developments in Sweden, particularly since relative high tech specialization has decreased.

To understand why Swedish firms particularly lack incentives to change, national contextual factors which support and/or hinder innovation in Sweden must be included in our analysis. A full analysis of the various factors constituting the Swedish system of innovation cannot be presented here, but it is clear that the Swedish state has played a key – if unfortunate – role in reducing firms' incentives to innovate during the 20-year period studied here.

In particular, the Swedish state gave substantial economic support to ailing mature industries during the 1970s and early 1980s and devalued the Swedish crown several times from 1976 to 1982. Devaluations enabled existing firms to make substantial profits from mature products. In addition, financial speculation became common due to deregulated financial markets in the 1980s. These factors reduced the incentives to innovate. This seemed to keep the Swedish economy rolling for a while, but Sweden currently has very serious industrial structural, unemployment and government budget problems. This indicates that government policies which were intended to be immediate, apparent solutions turned out to help cause longer-term problems. The missing pressures in Sweden to innovate and to renew the industrial structure are therefore a partial explanation for the Swedish ailment.

The lack of incentives to exploit product innovations, which would have led to structural change, has contributed to the current economic crisis, which became apparent by 1991. Sweden shifted rapidly from being a model economy successfully balancing market pressures and supporting a welfare state to just another example of a national economy with deep problems. The Swedish crisis has included a rate of official unemployment (8–12 per cent) not seen since the Great Depression; a decrease in industrial output and industrial employment of about 20 per cent from 1989 to 1993; and a yearly government budget deficit at about 13 per cent of GDP.

Another depreciation of the Swedish crown has also occurred. Although the Swedish government and the Central Bank tried very hard in 1992 to defend the currency, the economic crisis and financial speculation forced them to abandon the fixed exchange rate. The floating crown promptly sunk, with a depreciation of about 20–25 per cent against the currencies of the major industrial countries. Depreciation has once again enabled a surge in exports and in profits of those large Swedish firms involved in exports, particularly of traditional products like paper and pulp.

This made traditional Swedish goods relatively less expensive abroad, and sales are not due to larger increases in efficiency and productivity relative to competing countries. Thus, the apparently positive trends of export growth and sky-rocketing profits in Sweden in 1994–95 are primarily based on the depreciation. Indeed, a major part of the rising capital investments in 1994 and 1995 have been going to traditional sectors like steel and forest-based industries. It has simply become more profitable to export the same old products, produced in the same old way. Once again, Sweden seems to be making another loop in the vicious circle of short-term solutions and short-term surges which aggravate the longer-term, structural problems.

The Swedish phenomena analysed here are interesting because, as we have argued, some technologies/sectors allow more opportunities to innovate than others. Innovations seem to be a vital, if partial, cause of productivity growth and economic growth. Therefore, from a perspective of the economics of technical change, a dynamic economy requires continuous reconstitution of products, firms and industries. If a country is specialized over time in sectors with high innovative opportunities, then its longer-term economic prospects are better than those of countries specialized in less innovative sectors. An economy which does not change falls behind. This is the basic reason why it matters in which industrial sectors countries are specialized.

APPENDIX

This chapter makes an international comparison of R&D-intensive manufacturing sectors from the early 1970s to the early 1990s. The comparison is between individual countries – Sweden in particular – and the OECD average. Such an analysis requires long-term, internationally compatible statistics. We therefore decided to use the OECD STAN (STructural ANalysis for industrial statistics) database. In STAN, data from the older OECD COMTAP (Compatible Trade and Production) database and other sources has been converted and estimated to be comparable across time and countries. We used the 1994 version.[16]

Our calculations are based on production in countries. In contrast, it is most common to use some index of export specialization to analyse countries' production specialization (Dalum, 1992; Porter, 1990). The most common one is the Basalla index. This chapter instead analyses the production structure, using a similar index. Our argument is that production offers the best indicator of potential positive externalities involved in developing commercially relevant technologies. Actual production ensures more positive externalities, both in the immediate and longer-term periods. Export specialization reflects production specialization only in an imperfect manner.

More specifically, the following figures compare the percentage of R&D products in countries' manufacturing as a percentage of the average of OECD countries. The basic formula is:

$$\frac{Y_{ij} / Y_m}{Y_{ijO} / Y_{mO}}$$

where

Y_{ij} is output, current prices, of R&D-intensive sector i in country j
Y_m is output, current prices, of total manufacturing in country j
Y_{iO} is output, current prices, of R&D-intensive sector i in the OECD
Y_{mO} is output, current prices, of R&D-intensive sector i in the OECD.

The OECD average is defined as 1.00, or 100 per cent. If a country is above the average (1.00), it is defined as specialized and if below the average, it is not specialized.

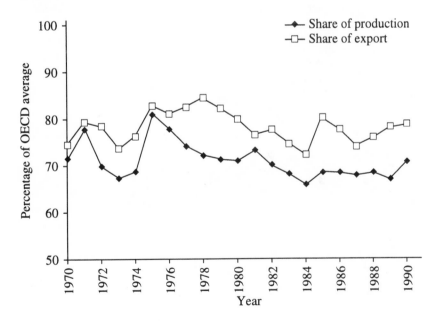

Figure 6.1   Share of export and of production of manufacturing products in R&D-intensive industries (as % OECD average) (Sweden), 1970–90

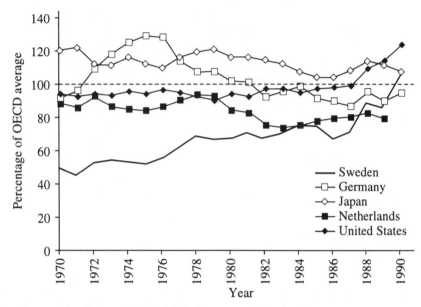

Figure 6.2   Share of ISIC 3522 (Drugs and Medicine) of manufacturing production in five countries (as % OECD average), 1970–90

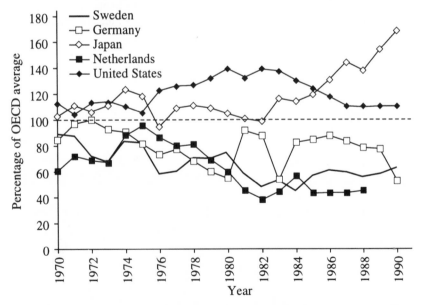

Figure 6.3   Share of ISIC 3825 (Office Machinery and Computers) of manufacturing production in five countries (as % OECD average), 1970–90

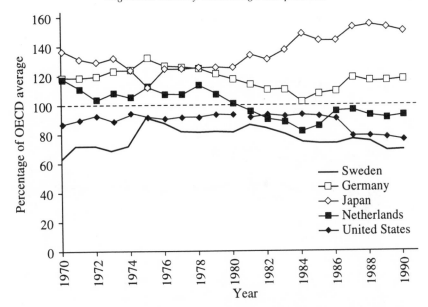

Figure 6.4   Share of ISIC 383 (Electrical Machinery and Components) of manu-
facturing production in five countries (as % OECD average), 1970–90

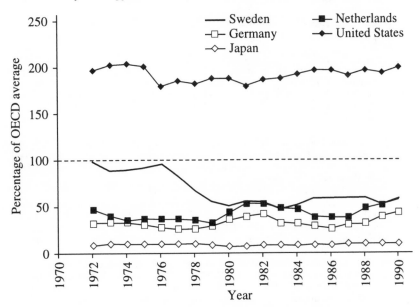

Figure 6.5   Share of ISIC 3845 (Aerospace) of manufacturing production in
five countries (as % OECD average), 1970–90

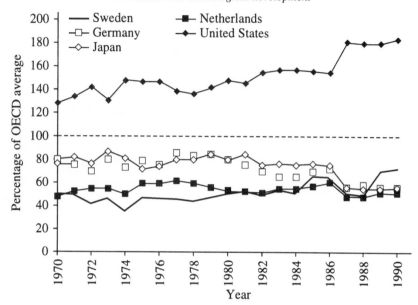

*Figure 6.6   Share of ISIC 385 (Technological Goods) of manufacturing
production in five countries (as % OECD average), 1970–90*

NOTES

François Texier has given valuable help in updating the analysis and figures. We also received valuable comments at the EAEPE conference in Copenhagen in 1994. The data has not been revised since the original book submission in 1995. We would therefore like to point out that Sweden has increased production in telecommunications, which may affect the sector Electrical Machinery and Computers positively.

1. The new trade theories and the new growth theories also increasingly take technology into account. They have been criticized, however, for retaining an oversimplified view of technology and for sticking too closely to the general equilibrium analysis from which they were mutated (Dosi, Pavitt and Soete, 1990).
2. Nelson and Winter (1982) is the seminal work in this field.
3. Two influential books have recently been published on national systems of innovation, namely Lundvall (ed.) 1992 and Nelson (ed.) 1993. Edquist (1993) outlines various approaches to systems of innovation, including national, sectoral and regional ones. McKelvey (1991, 1994) critically analyses several approaches, whereas McKelvey (1993) analyses Japan in terms of institutions supporting innovative activities.
4. In 1994, the categories were revised and changed to four categories – high, medium-high, medium-low and low tech sectors (OECD, 1994, p. 231). In this classification, the high tech sectors only include those with more than 10 per cent of R&D expenditures/production.
5. ISIC 383 can be divided into three high tech product groups at the four-digit numbers ISIC 3831 (Electrical Industrial Machinery), ISIC 3832 (Radio, TV and Communication Equipment), and ISIC 3839 (Electrical Apparatus) and one lower tech product group ISIC 3833 (Household Appliances).

6. In Sweden between 1981 and 1991, the first four R&D-intensive industries listed above spent more than 4 per cent of sales value on R&D, as expected from the OECD definition of high tech. In the fifth sector, Technologial Goods, the main product is Scientific Instruments. During the 1970s and 1980s, the Swedish scientific instrument industry spent more than 4 per cent, but declined to 2.7 per cent in 1989 and further declined to 1.9 per cent in 1991. Thus during the twenty years analysed here, Scientific Instruments has fallen below the 4 per cent cut-off. (Based on SCB, 1983, 1985, 1989, 1991 and 1993.)

7. The making of new or improved products may or may not be closely dependent on process technology. The degree of dependence between product and process technologies can vary among different products and industrial branches.

8. For Electrical Machinery and Computers one explanation for the decline is that Sweden was specialized in electro-mechanical products in the 1970s but did not manage to make the transition to electronic products. Note, moreover, that Figure 6.5 indicates that the United States is extensively specialized in Aerospace, relative to the OECD average. This skews the distribution for the other countries.

9. Research on the relations between R&D and productivity includes numerous contributions, of which two notable ones include Bailey and Gordon (1988) and Nelson (1981).

10. See Edquist and McKelvey, 1992, Chapter 4. In that work, Table 17 shows that in both current and constant prices, all five of the R&D-intensive sectors had faster market growth in Sweden than for manufacturing as a whole. Table 18 shows that the annual growth rate in total OECD imports, current prices, was also higher for R&D-intensive goods than for manufacturing as a whole.

11. See also Edquist and McKelvey, 1992, Figure 3.14 and pp. 67–9. SIND uses the same classification as the rest of this chapter, but they classified *firms* as high to low tech whereas this chapter discusses industrial *sectors* as high to low tech.

12. Based on Swedish industrial statistics, we calculated productivity growth in Sweden for manufacturing as a whole and for each of the five R&D-intensive sectors for the periods 1974–80 and 1980–88. We calculated productivity in four ways: as sales value divided by number of employees (Tables 20 and 22) and as value added divided by number of employees (Tables 21 and 22). We calculated them in both current and constant prices. We would like to point out that the category 'manufacturing as a whole' includes the R&D-intensive sectors.

13. American patents can be considered an indicator of various countries' contribution to the global pool of knowledge.

14. According to the 1987 annual report, the Volvo group as a whole spent 5 per cent of sales on R&D and the Saab group spent 7.3 per cent of invoicing on R&D. However, both industry groups include products in the higher and medium tech segments of the transport industry. The Volvo group included automobiles, trucks, buses, motors for marine and industry, aircraft engines, food products and other. Saab included automobiles, trucks, buses, aerospace, advanced materials, automation and military and control engineering. Neither the firms' annual reports nor official statistics specify how R&D expenditures are distributed among product groups.

15. Analysis of USA based on Mowery and Rosenberg (1993) and of Japan on Goto and Odagiri (1993).

16. OECD, DSTI (STAN/Industrial) 1994. The countries included as the OECD average in STAN are Australia, Belgium, Canada, Denmark, Finland, France, Germany, Italy, Japan, Netherlands, Norway, Sweden, the United Kingdom and the United States.

REFERENCES

Archibugi, D. and M. Pianta (1992), *The Technological Specialization of Advanced Countries*, Kluwer.

Bailey, M. and R. Gordon (1988), 'The productivity slowdown, measurement issues, and the explosion of computing power', *The Brooking Papers on Economic Activity*, XIX:2, pp. 347–420.

Cantwell, J. (1994), 'Introduction: transnational corporations and innovatory activities', in J. Cantwell (ed.), *Transnational Corporations and Innovatory Activities*, Routledge.

Dalum, B. (1992), 'Export specialisation, structural competitiveness and national systems of innovation', in Lundvall, B.-Å. (ed.).

Dosi, G. (1988), 'Sources, procedures and microeconomic effects of innovation', *Journal of Economic Literature*, XXVI(3) (September).

Dosi, G., K. Pavitt and L. Soete (1990), *The Economics of Technical Change and International Trade*, Harvester Wheatsheaf.

Edquist, C. (1993), 'Systems of innovation – a conceptual discussion and a research agenda', paper presented at workshop 'Globalization versus National or Local Systems of Innovation', organized by the EUNETIC Network at BETA in Strasbourg, March 11–12.

Edquist, C. and S. Jacobsson (1988), *Flexible Automation: The Global Diffusion of New Technology in the Engineering Industry*, Basil Blackwell.

Edquist, C. and B.-Å. Lundvall (1993), 'Comparing the Danish and Swedish systems of innovation', in R. Nelson (ed.), *National Systems of Innovation*, Oxford University Press.

Edquist, C. and M. McKelvey (1992), 'The Diffusion of New Product Technologies and Productivity Growth in Swedish Industry', Consortium on Competitiveness and Cooperation (CCC), CCC Working Paper no. 19–15, Berkeley, Cal.: UC, Center for Research in Management. Originally published in Swedish in SOU 1991:82.

Goto, A. and Odagiri, H. (1993), 'The Japanese system of innovation: past, present, and future', in R. Nelson (ed.), *National Systems of Innovation*, Oxford University Press.

Håkanson, L. and R. Nobel (1993), 'Foreign research and development in Swedish multinationals', *Research Policy*, 22, 373–96.

Ingenjörsvetenskapsakademien (IVA) (1989), *Forskning och Utveckling i Utlandet: En Studie av Svensk Multinationella Företag IVA PM 1989:1*, Stockholm: IVA.

Lundvall, B.-Å. (ed.) (1992), *National Systems of Innovation: Towards a Theory of Innovation and Interactive Learning*, Pinter.

McKelvey, M. (1991), 'How do national systems of innovation differ? A critical analysis of Porter, Freeman, Lundvall and Nelson', in G. Hodgson, and E. Screpanti (eds), *Rethinking Economics: Markets, Technology and Economic Evolution*, Edward Elgar.

McKelvey, M. (1993), 'Japanese institutions supporting innovation', in S.-E. Sjöstrand (ed.), *Institutional Development and Change: Theory and Empirical Findings*, Sharpe.

McKelvey, M. (1994), 'National systems of innovation', in M. Tool, W. Samuels and G. Hodgson (eds), *Handbook of Evolutionary and Institutional Economics*, Edward Elgar.

Mowery, D. and N. Rosenberg (1993), 'The US national system of innovation', in R. Nelson (ed.), *National Systems of Innovation*, Oxford University Press.

Nelson, R. (1981), 'Research on productivity growth and productivity differences: dead ends and new departures', *Journal of Economic Literature*, vol. XIX (September), pp. 1029–64.

Nelson, R. (ed.) (1993), *National Systems of Innovation*, Oxford University Press.

Nelson, R. and S. Winter (1982), *An Evolutionary Theory of Economic Change*, The Belknap Press of Harvard University Press.

Norgren, L. (1989), *Kunskapsöverföring från universitet till företag: En studie av forskningens betydelse för de svenska läkemedelsfsretagens produktlansering 1945–1984*, PhD thesis, Allmänna Förlaget.

NUTEK (1995), 'Svenskt näringslivs teknologiska specialisering' Bilaga 11 till Långtidsutredningen 1995. Finansdepartementet.

OECD (1993), *Main Science and Technology Indicators*.

OECD (1994), *Science and Technology Policy: Review and Outlook*.

Pavitt, K. (1984), 'Sectoral patterns of technical change: towards a taxonomy and a theory', *Research Policy*, 13, pp. 343–73.

Pavitt, K. and P. Patel (1988), 'The international distribution and determinants of technological activities', *The Oxford Review of Economic Policy*, 4.

Porter, M. (1990), *The Competitive Advantage of Nations*, Macmillan.

Statistiska centralbyrån (SCB) (1983), *Forskningsstatistik – Teknisk och naturvetenskaplig forskning och utveckling i företagssektorn 1981 U 27*.

Statistiska centralbyrån (SCB) (1985), *Forskningsstatistik – Teknisk och naturvetenskaplig forskning och utveckling i företagssektorn 1983 U 14*.

Statistiska centralbyrån (SCB) (1989), *Forskningsstatistik – Teknisk och naturvetenskaplig forskning och utveckling i företagssektorn 1987 U 14*.

Statistiska centralbyrån (SCB) (1991), *Forskningsstatistik – Teknisk och naturvetenskaplig forskning och utveckling i företagssektorn 1989 U 14 SM 9101*.

Statistiska centralbyrån (SCB) (1993), *Forskningsstatistik – Teknisk och naturvetenskaplig forskning och utveckling i företagssektorn 1991 U 14*.

Statens industriverk (SIND) (1990a), *Svensk högteknolgisk industri och dess export* SIND 1990:4.

Statens industriverk (SIND (1990b), *Industrin till år 2000 – ett tillväxtdecennium?* Bilaga 18 till Långtidsutredningen 1990. För Finansdepartementet, Norstedts Tryckeri.

Teece, D. (1988), 'Technological change and the nature of the firm', in G. Dosi *et al.* (eds), *Technical Change and Economic Theory*, Pinter.

Tyson, L.A. (1992), *Who's Bashing Whom? Trade Conflict in High-Technology Industries*, Institute for International Economics.

PART III

The Theory of the Firm and Relations
between Firms

7. Black boxes, grey boxes: the scope of contracts in the theory of the firm

Margherita Turvani

OVERVIEW AND INTRODUCTION

In the 1960s Fritz Machlup (1967) reviewed the state of the theory of the firm. In comparing the cornerstones of orthodox marginalist theory with the main currents of thought at the time, namely the behavioural and managerial approaches, he identified 'twenty-one concepts of the firm'. He argued that the various possible 'visions' were in any case always 'fictions', representations of complex phenomena which we devise according to our theoretical and practical aims.

If we tried to repeat Machlup's exercise today, we would certainly have to lengthen the list of concepts considerably. New 'visions' of the firm have been put forward and fresh problems placed on the agenda. Economists have marshalled their troops, and once again the arena is the theory of the firm. On one side stands the contractual or transaction cost perspective, on the other the competence or evolutionary perspective[1].

Visions, we know, have the advantage of concentrating people's attention and giving strength and unity to ideas (and theory), but they may also hide important features. Visions focus our thinking giving rise to hierarchical priorities in theorizing: some concepts will play the role of the protagonist in the story. Some others will play the role of supernumerary, fading in the background.

Leaving the metaphor, entering the arena requires a sizable effort to understand the origin of the controversy between the evolutionary and transaction cost perspectives. Perhaps the story needs to be revised anyway, although my aim in this chapter is not so ambitious. Much more modestly I will offer some critical reflections on one of the cornerstones of the modern theory of the firm: the notion of contract and its scope in organizing human activity.

Understanding the specificity and the organizational complexity of the firm is far from being reached. The black box has been opened, but a new box has been found inside: the contract.

The new box may not appear as black as the old one, but it still looks grey. Quite an effort has been devoted by economists into making it transparent, yet, for example, the notion of the incomplete contract is hazy, becoming the grey part where all 'tosh' is dumped. Williamson (1993, p. 147) has called 'tosh' that which can be distinguished from the 'essential', where the latter 'involves an examination of the rational core', while 'tosh' is the remaining 'superfluous rituals, rules of procedure without clear purpose'. He believes that 'a place should be made for "tosh", but "tosh" should be kept in its place' (ibid.). Of course, such a distinction is rather arbitrary, leading to misunderstanding between the modern, competing visions of the firm. Which 'rationality' stands behind the use of contracts as means of organizing human economic activity?

I think that we may look at it from two different perspectives: one, which I call foresight, mainly develops issues of calculability; the other, which I name farsight, focuses on liquidity and on precautionary behaviour. To shed light on what I see as a critical divide in assessing the scope of contracts in organizing economic life, we need to move 'uncertainty' from the background of the scene to the foreground, assigning it the role of the hero in the story.

When such a perspective is consistently assumed, we may realize that many of the controversies in the arena of the theory of the firm constitute a revised edition of a historical controversy: the one between Coase and Knight.

To be sure, foresight and farsight of economic agents will develop as complementary strategies to deal with pervasive uncertainty in human life. Yet the first kind of behaviour has received much more attention in the literature. Focusing on farsight, instead, implies a new perspective, one in which the future, ignorance, even non-awareness are not such irresistible threats to human action and rationality. The impossibility of devising a complete design for an organization which is capable of responding permanently and exhaustively to the need to control the future, because of the very nature of human knowledge, allows discretion for the application of human judgment and the definition of new objectives providing the basis for the evolution of economic life and, if we wish to be optimistic, for 'improving the quality of life through changes in the form of organization of want-satisfying activity' (Knight, 1971, p. ix).

In this chapter, in the first section I discuss the notion of the firm as a nexus of contracts. I reappraise three seminal contributions: Knight's *Risk, Uncertainty and Profit*, Coase's 'The Nature of the Firm', and Simon's 'A Formal Theory of the Employment Relation'. I summarize some of the arguments that were developed in Turvani (1995). I build a link between Knight and Simon: both of them were proposing a different perspective from the Coasean vision. Knight's concept of judgment is combined with Simon's concept of liquidity of resources, allowing the firm to evolve even within its nexus of contracts. To them, the firm's reason for existence is not simply found in transaction costs, but has to be found in the way human beings deals with cognitive and decision processes.

The scope of contract, as it appears in these two visions, seems quite different: according to my own view, Knight and Simon emphasize a human attitude in dealing with uncertainty that I call farsight, while Coase refers to a more common notion of foresight. Specifically, this may imply a new perspective in looking at the labour contract, shedding light on the specificity of the employer–employee relationship. If we place it in a context of uncertainty, the distinctive feature that appears is not the imposition of constraints in behaviour but its ability to promote discretion thereby allowing degrees of freedom for the firm acting in a competitive market.

In the second section I discuss the notion and the scope of contracts. Contracts, between individuals and between firms, are not simply 'quid pro quo' devices. Rather they function by providing and limiting individual responsibilities. When uncertainty emerges, incomplete contracting will result, posing the issue of identifying an entity able to assume and to guarantee non-contractible outcomes. Incomplete contracts pose the problem of the role of the vacuum, that is, anomie that we may see in firms. The nexus of contracts therefore may appear as half full or half empty, according to the perspective we are assuming. If we assume a Coasean perspective, then the nexus of contracts appears as half empty, posing a huge variety of problems of design and enforcement as we know from the principal–agent literature. If we assume an evolutionary perspective, which we may derive from a Knightian theory of the firm, the contractual vacuum leaves room for agents' entrepreneurial judgment. Markets and firms may, as a result, be seen as complementary institutions: they interact in producing a flow of information in the constant attempt to fill the knowledge gap, which is at the very root of the contract incompleteness.

In the third section I elaborate the notion of non-contractible outcomes, connecting them to the cognitive problems that agents face in running economic processes when uncertainty is present. I return to the distinction between farsight and foresight as the two strategies at hand to govern agents' interaction. Their feasibility and appropriateness are then discussed.

CONTRACTING IN KNIGHT, COASE, AND SIMON

The idea of contrasting Knight's vision with that of Coase is obviously not mine. In his seminal work of 1937, Coase himself often argues with Knight. Coase's criticism focuses on the personal role of Knight's entrepreneur as opposed to the impersonal nature of the contractual tool.[2] Simon's argument fits in nicely with the controversy, since focusing on the employer–employee relationship directly addresses the issue of 'the nature of contracts'.

What follows may appear too sketchy; however, my purpose is to stress the contrasts between what I interpret as different perspectives of the nexus of contracts underlying the existence of the firm.[3]

Knight's Vision

Agents have to deal with a cooperative production process: we must look at 'free enterprise as a system or method of securing and directing cooperative effort in a social group' (Knight, 1971, p. x). Due to the division of labour, there is interdependence among individuals. If the social system is seen as a mechanical arrangement in the spirit of Robinson Crusoe-style economies in which each individual takes all the others as given in what Knight describes as his or her 'own private economy', then there is no specific organizational problem. Even in the presence of change, recourse may be made to a non-organized form of production: there may be forms of individual learning by trial and error, but the production process will still take place automatically. Can joint production be organized by resorting to free contracts? This raises the problem of team production, that is, the problem of identifying the contribution of separate production forces. However, in the absence of uncertainty, the coordinator guaranteeing the joint effort may be paid with the share made available by cooperation.[4]

What happens when uncertainty is introduced? The division of labour dramatically raises the problem of interdependency: organization modalities are banal if an economic system reflects the ideals of competition and perfect knowledge, but they become crucial when human action is developed in a context of irreducible uncertainty. The division of labour may lead to a strong complementarity among agents and processes: the solution of the coordination problem cannot rely solely on the available knowledge. In the presence of uncertainty every decision is laden with consequences and, even if agents may have common interests, they have to anticipate the actions of others. Writing contracts within this system of interrelations implies that uncertainty must be explicitly taken into account. Insurance markets will not be the tool best suited to deal with uncertainty. Risky situations – that is, situations to which probabilities are assigned which are therefore insurable – need to be distinguished from situations of true uncertainty.[5] According to Knight, free enterprise solves this problem by assigning authority to a single person who exercises judgment, therefore assuming responsibility for non-contractible outcomes (the process of cephalization). The employment relationship is the distinctive feature of free enterprise in that it enables limited responsibility to be exercised in exchange for a guarantee on the residual responsibilities supplied by the entrepreneur.

The transparent, impersonal nexus of contracts, therefore, provides the environment necessary for entrepreneurial action to emerge and to stiffen. 'Judgment' appears and by doing so shows the importance of personal knowledge and cognition.

'So long as we adhere to the fundamental condition already emphasized, that men *know exactly what they are doing*, that no uncertainty is present, other elements of reality ... merely complicate the process of adjustment without changing the character of the result' (Knight, 1971, p. 94). 'With the introduction of uncertainty – the fact of ignorance and necessity of acting upon opinion rather than knowledge, ... doing things, the actual execution of activity becomes in a real sense a secondary part of life; the primary problem or function ... is deciding what to do and how to do it' (Knight, 1971, p. 268).

Accordingly, the use of contracts within the firm is rather seen as a tool to enhance decision processes about what to do and how to do it, instead of as a tool to execute detailed activities, according to some exogenous division of labour, or set of transactions. Decision-making processes do not take place mechanically: calculation is no longer adequate. Agents will set about systematically searching for information: a collective process of producing knowledge is set in motion. Contracts, in this perspective, serve the purpose of facilitating and distributing decision processes among agents, providing some guarantee against uncertainty and eventually producing profit.[6]

Coase's Vision

Here again the accent is placed on the problem of understanding the reasons why the firm exists in a specialized exchange economy. Coase basically sees the problem as that of understanding why a certain set of exchanges or transactions, to use his language, are enclosed within something called the firm and not dissolved in the market. There ensues a search to discover why subjects are induced to create alternative forms of managing a set of transactions. The various organizational forms of transaction may be compared in terms of costs. What distinguishes the forms of coordination, however, is not only a different cost, but also a different degree of consciousness.

Coase agrees with Knight in interpreting the authority relationship as an efficient and socially beneficial tool, but he sees the advantages of such forms of governance mainly in terms of the reduction of the transaction costs: 'The main reason why it is profitable to establish a firm would seem to be that there is a cost of using the price mechanism. The most obvious cost of "organizing" production through the price mechanism is that of discovering what the relevant prices are' (Coase, 1937, p. 390). Of course someone might specialize in selling this information, but the 'costs of negotiating and concluding a separate contract for each exchange transaction which takes place on a market must also be taken into account ... A factor of production (or the owner thereof) does not have to make a series of contracts with the factors with whom he is cooperating within the firm, as would be necessary, of course, if this cooperation were as a direct result of the working of the price mechanism. For this series of contracts is substituted one,' (Coase, 1937, p. 391).

Thus the advantages in terms of what Coase describes as transaction costs are clear: the firm is an artifact built with the purpose of reducing the costs of coordination and control:[7] it is nothing more than a set of exchanges which are rearranged in a different form. Choosing to coordinate production in the firm rather than resorting to the market is only a question of price or expediency and the entrepreneur's decision-making is reduced to calculation.[8] Entrepreneurship is basically a question of make-or-buy choices: 'Management merely reacts to price changes, rearranging the factors of production under its control' (Coase, 1937, p. 405).

Entrepreneurial activity is thus the managing of a production function which may be organized via firms or market: they therefore appear as two alternative modes of governing transactions since 'the entrepreneur has to carry out his function at less cost ... because it is always possible to revert to the open market if he fails to do this' (Coase, 1937, p. 392).

Accordingly, contracts serve the purpose of reallocating transactions between firms and markets, the well-known make-or-buy choice, emphasizing issues of feasibility and calculability, implicitly assuming that 'what to do and how to do it' is a minor problem in economic life.

Simon's Vision

Simon's work, focusing on the employer–employee relationship, directly addresses the issue of the nature of contracts. He approaches organizations from the inside, that is, trying to understand why a standard contract (the sale contract) may be replaced by a different contractual arrangement (the employment contract) generating the peculiar features of the employer–employee relationship. In what conditions will an employment relationship be rationally preferred to a sale contract? Simon's analysis, therefore, sets out to cast light on the conditions which bring labour transactions into the administrative process, thus removing them from the market. But what are 'the most significant features of the administrative process, i.e. the process of actually managing the factors of production, including labor'? (Simon, 1951, p. 293). The main difference between the two contractual forms resides in the domain of authority and Simon offers an explanation of what he calls 'the area of acceptance', i.e., a worker's attitude to complying.[9]

The employment contract contains the agreement concerning the worker's willingness to accept the authority of an employer in exchange for a wage. This arrangement does not contain a specific and detailed description of the reciprocal promises and performances. The set of these preliminary agreements, which are subject to contract, is thus vague: in a context of uncertainty, the most important feature of the employment contract is that it is 'advantageous to postpone decision ... in order to gain from information obtained subsequently' (Simon,

1951, p. 304). The employment contract, as an incomplete specified contract, can thus give rise to a relationship dominated by 'long-run rationality'. The employment contract reflects a preference for liquidity, both in the event of 'contingencies' and to deal with the problem of the interdependency between reciprocal behaviours. The labour contract veils the employer–employee relationship. Indeed, the idea of an incomplete contract implies that we must allow for some 'vacuum of contracts' , an area in which contracts are silent. The nexus of contracts preserve an area of anomie which, I claim, mantains some degree of liquidity in human resources. Accordingly, contracts, labour contracts especially, do not only serve the purpose of creating and governing routinized (administrative) behaviour but they enhance discretion. The impersonal role of contracts is combined with the idiosyncratic nature of knowledge and cognition.

THE SCOPE OF CONTRACTS: OR IS THE GLASS HALF FULL OR HALF EMPTY?

The firm is no longer a 'black box' represented by a production function. It emerges as an organization form. The technological construction, as in the neoclassical view, is substituted by a governance structure. Yet the object of analysis is not organization but the variety of exchanges between individuals, called transactions. The problem thus arises of investigating the origins of the variety of transactions, seeking the reason why exchanges depart from the ideal model of spot market exchange. Transaction costs, that is, market usage costs, thus lay the basis for a theory of differentiation of institutions.[10]

'Contractual men', taking into account the presence of transaction costs, will sign any sort of contracts, seen as 'sophisticated' exchanges: the economy and, in particular, production will be organized by contracts, thus giving rise to the firm.

According to Williamson such a perspective offers a new vision to focus on important yet neglected issues: 'Pin making – how to organize (more generally, how to govern) the "eighteen distinct operations" (transactions) made famous by Adam Smith (1776) – rather than how many pins to make and at what price – becomes the object of the analysis' (1995, p. 6).

This is the well-known Coasean perspective. To paraphrase Knight, contractual men are mainly concerned with the problem of 'doing'. 'How to do it', the technological problem of discovering and defining, i.e., learning, the 'eighteen distinct operations' is beyond the scope of the analysis, and the same is true for the 'what to do' problem, the market problem, that is, which one of the 'eighteen distinct operations' should be performed. Eventually, the 'how' and 'what to do' problems appear in a weak form, in the choice of the most feasible (efficient) contractual form for doing.

What happens when contractual men have to deal with the three problems of 'what', 'how' and 'doing' simultaneously? Which contract may do the job?

Historically, we have assisted with the gradual framing of economic operations by law, thus gradually filling up 'an area of legal vacuums'.[11] The development of institutions, and the institution of contract among them, have been recognized as being among the main sources of economic growth (North, 1991).

Freedom of contract means that parties are free to abstain from stipulating a given contract or from including a given clause based on their own judgment. Moreover, only economic operations which can (and must) be governed by law may be the subject matter of a contract. 'Can' involves both the description and the enforcement of agreements. If we conceive of the contract as a promise, the parties need to be able to define the contents of the promise and, also, to obtain the respect of the promise itself. The promise should be sustainable, that is, not in contradiction with more general principles, and should be feasible, that is, it should be described in some detail to allow parties to define their expectations and the enforcer to judge, should disputes arise.

Corresponding to this freedom is the responsibility for the commitments assumed: *pacta sunt servanda*. Contracts, between individuals and between firms, are not simply 'quid pro quo' devices. They function in that they provide and limit individual responsibilities.

The contract makes the assumption of commitments an obligation once they have been freely accepted, but if responsibilities are not clearly identified, the contract can neither be respected nor enforced, that is, even if parties are not opportunistic, it would be hard to fulfil the promises and to connect *ex ante* intentions to *ex post* outcomes. Here the issue of uncertainty becomes subtle and pervasive.

The inability of agents to buy full protection against uncertainty, in economic literature, is generally explained in terms of moral hazard, the weakening of incentives that accompanies the shifting of risks, rather than in terms of Knightian uncertainty. But it is recognized that 'insurance as customarily defined covers only a small range of events relevant to the economic world: much more important in shifting risks are securities, particularly common stocks and money' (Arrow, 1962, p. 144). These forms of guarantee stand as a shield against non-insurable risks.[12] Liquidity, the non-commitment of resources to any specific purpose, reflects agents' precautionary behaviour, when it is advantageous to postpone decisions, to benefit from knowledge and information that agents do not as yet hold.

We may then look at incomplete contracting from two different perspectives: the glass could be half full or half empty. If we assume a Coasean perspective, then the nexus of contracts appears as half empty, because markets do not provide all the information required, posing a huge variety of problems of design and enforcement. If we assume an evolutionary perspective, such as we may derive from a Knightian theory of the firm, the vacuum in contracts offers the opportunity to preserve some liquidity, in a changing world, allowing the exercise of 'judgment', that is, the production of a firm's idiosyncratic knowledge.

FORESEEING OR FARSEEING?

The Knowledge Gap

The contrast in attitudes to the kinds of cognitive problems that agents face in running a specialized economy seems to be the watershed between theories of the firm. Again the controversy between Coase and Knight may be illuminating.

The contrast between the two authors comes out very sharply if we deal with the role of knowledge in production. For Knight, much of the decision-making process which takes shape in the firm is based on entrepreneurial judgment. Knowledge acquisition and production is not a straightforward process and above all does not completely and definitively unravel the knots of uncertainty. The 'amount of uncertainty ... may be reduced in several ways ... It is possible, at a cost, to increase control over the future.' But this 'is complicated by the fact that the use of resources in reducing uncertainty is an operation attended with the greatest uncertainty of all. If we are uncertain as to the results of ordinary business operations we are doubly so as to the results of expenditures ... looking toward the increase of knowledge and control' (Knight, 1971, pp. 347–8).

On the contrary according to Coase, knowledge may be easily acquired on the market in the form of specialized services: 'Every business buys the services of a host of advisors. We can imagine a system where all advice or knowledge was bought as required. Again, it is possible to get a reward from better knowledge or judgment not by actively taking part in production but by making contracts with people who are producing' (Coase, 1937, pp. 400–1). The cognitive problem is reduced to a search problem. Agents are simply looking for prices. The costs of using the price mechanism are the costs 'of discovering what the relevant prices are' (Coase, 1937, p. 390).

This search activity and, eventually, reallocation according to price changes, defines the role of the entrepreneur: 'The above analysis would also appear to have clarified the relationship between initiative or enterprise and management. Initiative means forecasting and operates through the price mechanism by the making of new contracts' (Coase, 1937, p. 405).

By signing new contracts, however, it is not clear how the knowledge gap may be filled: the nature of the problem at stake is not solely a matter of efficiency (the prohibitive costs associated with designing, signing and enforcing contracts) but it is a matter of fact, that is, no fully specified contract can be signed. Incompleteness of contracts calls for a guarantor.[13]

More recently, Arrow has emphasized the pervasive nature of uncertainty, connecting it to the incompleteness of markets: 'A complete general equilibrium system, as in Debreu, requires markets for all contingencies in all future periods. Such a system could not exist. First, the number of prices would be so great that the search would become an insuperable obstacle: that is, the value of knowing prices of less consequence, those on events remote in time or of low probability, would be less than the cost so that these markets could not come into being. Second, markets conditional on privately observed events cannot exist by definition ... We certainly know that many – in fact, most – markets do not exist ... there is a gap in the information relevant to an individual's decision, and it must be filled by some kind of conjecture' (Arrow, 1987, p. 209).

Knight reappears. Judgment and conjecture are the keys for understanding the entrepreneurial function: uncertainty appears as a residual because of the failure of the insurance market, that is, it cannot be absorbed by writing ordinary insurance contracts. Yet more compelling appears to be the case of uncertainty arising from the knowledge gap, i.e., the impossibility of exhaustive classification of all the possible states of the world.

'When the categories of knowledge themselves are unknown, they cannot form the basis of interpersonal agreement or market exchange' (Langlois and Cosgel, 1993, p. 460): the definition of individual responsibility becomes fuzzy. We may easily see 'cephalization' i.e., the concentration of responsibility, as a viable way to lighten the burden of complex interactions, as Knight saw it. It is then possible to reconstruct responsibilities through delegation: when responsibility is concentrated it is identified by definition or rather by an agreement between the parties. It can then once more be decentralized, i.e., distributed according to judgment.

If, when facing a knowledge gap, the agents can no longer assume full responsibility for their commitments, the relief[14] may be found in building an institution, a guarantor, where the ultimate responsibility is assumed, allowing individuals limited responsibility: vacuums in contracts cease to be a threat and become an opportunity for entrepreneurial activity.

Thus the consolidation of uncertainty referred to by Knight occurs, in the firm's production of guarantees, not only for the parties involved, but for the whole set of economic operations, thus enabling the market to operate at a lower cost and to expand.[15] In a highly interdependent world, every form of uncertainty control must tackle the problem of recognizing individual responsibilities: the role the entrepreneurial firm performs, with respect to the market, is not so different in nature from the role of the joint stock company with respect to the spread of firms as organization forms.

Looking at the 'nature' of the firm from this perspective implies that markets and firms are never alternatives but always complementary. The two governance mechanisms do not stand as two available solutions to the problem of coordinating the division of labour, but each of them requires the existence and the functioning of the other.[16] Markets operate via contracts, yet coordination by contracts requires firms, where entrepreneurial judgment fills the necessary vacuum in contracts, improving the functioning of markets as coordination device. In the real market economy, competition, although creating opportunities for firms, threatens their very existence, because the areas of uncertainty spread. On the other hand firms, by protecting individuals from the continuous impact of uncertainty, also protect and allow the expansion of the market.

Knight's intuition was right: the high degree of specialization attained by our economies is mainly the outcome of a particular form of organization – the firm.[17]

Foreseeing

When agents face a knowledge gap,[18] specialization, that is, the increase in interdependency between agents, poses compelling cognitive problems. Contractual men need contracts to facilitate exchange as soon as we leave the ideal spot market exchange, yet contracts cannot do the job.

How can agents understand and foresee their fellow men's actions? Economists look for an answer in Adam Smith's hint, i.e., his parable of human passions and interests. This story tells us that we may foresee human behaviour if we understand what kinds of interests are moving people and if we believe that pursuing interests overcomes passions. In modern economic language we may say that we can foresee human conduct if individuals are able to rationally pursue their own interests, that is, they are able to behave according to a means-ends rationality. A strong concept of rationality is generally adopted meaning that rationality is the optimal choice among given alternatives under some external constraints. Accordingly contractual men may sign contracts, the issue being that of transaction costs and overall computational competence.

Unfortunately, this notion of rationality cannot solve all the relevant economic problems. Human agents do not only face choices among given alternatives. It is even more important to understand how alternatives are created, that is, how human knowledge develops and what role should be attached to ignorance. Contractual men are not only ignorant about some future contingencies but, at any moment of time, they cannot solely rely on the available knowledge to anticipate some future state of the world which will be the outcome of agents interacting with each other. New markets will emerge, some will disappear. New information will flow, being produced by human agents' actions: it needs to be exchanged and, far more compelling, the new knowledge needs to be interpreted to be used.[19] The information problems that agents face appear compelling: the Knightian notion of uncertainty seems to arise out of human problem solving.[20]

Organization theorists and more recently quite a few economists subscribe to the major findings of a line of research that, since the 1950s, has been developed to understand decision processes in organization, by scholars such as Cyert, March, and Simon. Human agents follow different patterns of behaviour according to the decision problem they face. Solving a choice problem may assume different patterns: on one side we can place a choice behaviour among well known and defined alternatives, on the other we place a research behaviour that characterized all the situations in which it is important to find out what the alternatives are. This second pattern is widely diffused and applies to all choices that take place in an uncertain environment, where the problem to be solved has not yet been defined with the proper detail and behaviour is focused to fill the knowledge gap.[21] In these situations, calculation and search are not sufficient, since it is often not clear what kinds of information we are looking for; further agents must develop abilities to recognize what is relevant to the solution of the problem at hand, that is, they must develop an adequate level of competence within the problem space. To set problems clearly and to solve them implies various degrees of learning and the generation of new knowledge, which requires specialization in cognitive skills, that is, the creation of 'competence'.[22]

Farseeing

Contractual men may adopt and combine both these patterns of behaviour in signing contracts, relying on two different strategies or forms of rationality. Assuming a calculative strategy would lead one to take into account as many contingencies as one's knowledge and forecasting ability will allow, eventually including new contingencies as new information becomes available. Human foresight and transaction costs will be the constraints.

Conversely, a farsighted strategy would imply preserving some degree of freedom in contracts, an area in which the contracts are silent.

Modern institutional economics works in both directions. Foreseeing is predominant in principal–agent theory: there interaction between agents is dealt with in purely contractual terms focusing on incentive design. Transaction cost analysis focuses on a semi-strong form of farsight, in Williamson's word 'calculativeness':

> Transaction cost economics ... concedes that comprehensive contracting is not a feasible option (by reason of bounded rationality), yet maintains that many economic agents have the capacity to look ahead, perceive hazards, and factor these back into contractual relation, thereafter to devise responsive institutions. In effect, limited but intended rationality is translated into incomplete but farsighted contracting, respectively.

The concept of contract out of which transaction cost economics works is therefore that of incomplete contracting in its entirety, which has the appearance of a contradiction in terms. In fact, such a concept of contract presents healthy tensions to which both economics and organization theory can productively relate. (Williamson,1996, p. 9)

Williamson claims that 'calculativeness' is a form of farseeing since transaction hazards may not be mitigated by relying neither exclusively on *ex ante* incentive alignment nor on insurance. The key feature of his vision has to be found in the idea of 'governance': 'If a contract becomes maladapted, by reason of an unanticipated disturbance, it is easy for the parties to get relief by turning elsewhere, or do they need to work through the problem together?' (Williamson, 1996, p. 4). Accordingly 'the study of governance is concerned with the identification, explication and mitigation of contractual hazards in all of their forms' (p. 5). The notion of 'governance structure' appears more sophisticated than the notion of 'nexus of contracts'; the focus is not on designing exchanges between contractual men, but on a system of safeguards, a set of bounds that agents assume to force themselves, with incentives and sanctions, to avoid the costs of breaking the promise.

This exercise of 'calculativeness' implies an effort in foresight, in identifying hazards, and farsight too, devising the necessary remedies. An agent's farsightedness, here, refers to some precautionary behaviour.

However, in this framework, to run a firm, to do the job of conceiving an efficient governance structure, lawyers and economists are needed, not an entrepreneur.

Again, what is at stake here is the idea of knowledge gap that agents face, that is, if all hazards can be somehow treated as risks and be contracted for, or some uncertainty will always persist, requiring 'judgment', to use Knight's word, or 'conjectures' in Arrow's, or 'problem-solving' in Simon's words. Signing the most sophisticated contract will not rule out uncertainty. Who will bear the responsibility and guarantee for it? The lawyer, the economist, the entrepreneur? The answer, of course, is the entrepreneur. But, still, may we read the incomplete contracting between employer and employee uniquely in terms of precautionary behaviour?

Is the rationale for incomplete contracting to be found in a need for flexibility or should we look elsewhere? Are agents' preferences for liquidity simply the answer to their need for flexibility?

Here the notion of liquidity becomes crucial: while flexibility means that we can reallocate resources, presumably with some optimality, to pursue a new goal, liquidity properly means that some resources will not be allocated to any precise end but will be kept liquid, that is, idle. Liquidity obviously may serve the purpose of flexibility but the two notions are not identical.

Labour contracts are incomplete in that the contents of the preliminary agreement may be redefined as more information gradually becomes available. Incompleteness may also imply that some elements need not be defined at all. By making the contents of a contract explicit over time, the use of resources may be allocated and reallocated, that is, some flexibility will obtain. But the labour contract preserves liquidity in the use of internal resources. Leaving aside, as the occasion requires and the notion of incompleteness implies, the definition of some terms in the contract this implicitly means there is no exhaustive allocation, or more precisely some resources might not be committed to a particular use: they may remain idle or will be used according to discretion.[23]

If the parties are free to redefine the terms of effective transactions in the administrative process, there may yet remain areas not subject to contracting. These areas represent the vacuum of contract at any moment in time and stand for the existence of an area of discretion, an area in which there are no definite administrative procedures.

Incomplete labour contracts thus allow for some degree of liquidity. This area of 'vacuum of contracts', that is, an area not covered by any contract, may be reconnected to an economic reason for discretion (transaction costs), but there could be a 'vacuum', a real ignorance in the administrative process. Liquidity preference is therefore a strong form of farsighted behaviour. It reflects the possibility of benefiting from information flows which gradually become available, allowing for flexibility. But liquidity stands for the need to safeguard environments of anomie, that is, lacking rules, because the knowledge production process can never be fully described and regulated.[24]

If the division of labour is necessarily accompanied by the division of knowledge, if human cognitive activities are far more complex than choosing among known alternatives, and if agents must engage in problem solving, thereby creating new knowledge, then the vacuum in contracts in the firm may serve the purpose of leaving areas for the autonomous solution to problems and judgment is spread within the organization: knowledge of 'time and place' (von Hayek, 1945) is continuously elaborated and used, creating unique competencies, differentiating individuals as much as organizations.[25]

ACKNOWLEDGEMENT

The author gratefully acknowledges the research support of Murst (40%), 'Istituzioni, crescita, sviluppo economico'.

NOTES

1. For a history of evolutionary theory in economics see Hodgson (1993) and Nelson (1995). For a presentation and appraisal of these two approaches see Foss (1993).

2. More recently Coase (1988) has called into question his own thinking, criticizing the purely contractual view of the firm which neglects an important function of the firm: organizational coordination. This comment was taken up by Aoki (1990), who, following Coase's suggestions, has inquired into the difference in organizational costs for various firms, that is, the factors whereby the performances of individual firms constitute a limit to the dissolving of the firm on the market.

3. Reappraising the Knight–Coase debate is not purely an issue of history of economic thought. I do agree with Langlois and Cosgel (1993, p. 456) that 'Knight's oft-misunderstood analysis of the firm has much to contribute to today's literature'. See also the recent contributions of Barzel (1987), Boundreaux and Holcombe (1989), Foss (1993), Gunning (1993), and Leroy and Singell (1987).

4. This is a key idea in the important work by Alchian and Demsetz on team production (1972). Their work states the market-hierarchy continuity and their logical equivalence. Indeed the parties involved in team production are always free to dismiss each other (just as the grocer may be dismissed by the client) and the organizational problem is a purely technological problem. Alchian and Demsetz are echoing Knight's view when he deals with the problem of coordination in the absence of uncertainty: 'There might be managers, superintendents, etc., for the purpose of coordinating the activities of individuals. But under conditions of perfect knowledge and certainty such functionaries would be laborers merely ... without any responsibility of any sort' (Knight, 1971, pp. 267–8).

5. It is worth remembering what Stigler has to say in his introduction to a 1971 edition of *Risk, Uncertainty and Profit*: 'I find the book of Knight intensely interesting for a reason somewhat removed from the theory ... it explains as no other work does the crucial importance of uncertainty, and its inevitable consequence, ignorance, in transforming an economic system from a beehive into a conscious social process with error, conflict, innovation and endless spans of varieties of change. The full yield of this vision has hardly begun to be reaped by modern economics' (Stigler, 1971, p. xiv).

6. Concentrating all the responsibilities in one specific figure, creating the entrepreneurial function, is not primarily a consequence of the fact that in the world there are many individuals with different abilities for coping with risks and therefore prepared to unload their responsibility concerning judgment of uncertainty on someone who is remunerated for this service. Obviously, the specialization process among individuals is also based on individual inclinations. Nonetheless, ordinary forms of insurance are not the most relevant feature of the firm. On this subject Knight is very clear: the entrepreneur does not receive rewards for his services, but the results of his judgments are appropriated, once all payments have been made, including those related to the various forms of insurance he provides, which are implicitly or explicitly referable to the contracts he has stipulated.

7. Market usage costs are actually the usage costs of the contractual system governing market transactions, that is, primarily contract-law usage costs. In fact, apart from the more elementary forms of exchange – spot exchanges – economic agents can make use of more sophisticated contractual forms enabling quid pro quo exchanges to take place. The reference point, however, remains the external functioning of markets able to supply a relevant range of prices for the transaction. The evaluation of the advantages of contractual forms thus relies on the price mechanism. This implies that the relevant set of prices already exists for the purposes of defining the transaction.

8. 'If a workman moves from department Y to department X, he does not go because of a change in relative price, but because he is ordered to do so' (Coase, 1937, p. 387). But why should the workman give up his right to 'observe' the market? Is it because the coordinator has better knowledge? Is it because it is efficient in term of transaction cost to hire someone to do the planning? This seems to be Coase's answer: but if this is the case then labour becomes the principal and the coordinator is the agent.

9. For a review and discussion of the role of authority in organization see Dow (1994) and Menard (1995).

10. However, what is acknowledged is the logical equivalence rather than the complementary between market and hierarchy: 'firms and markets are alternative modes of governance and

the allocation of activity between firms and markets ... is something to be derived' (Williamson, 1996, p. 6).

11. Although there has been a gradual contractualization of economic operations, the phenomenon of contract avoidance still exists. This is what Williamson (1985), referring to the debate between jurists in America, calls the recourse to private ordering. The explanation of this contract avoidance lies above all in the high usage costs of the contract and in the possibility of resorting to other forms of relationships between parties and other systems of sanctions. From this point of view the firm would seem to constitute an important case of contract avoidance, because under the roof of stipulated formal contracts with factors of production, de facto contractual relationships are concealed, sets of promises between the parties supported by internal systems of sanctions and guarantees. The incomplete nature of the employment relationship, for example, may thus be explained in terms of a greater efficiency with de facto contractual systems compared to legal contractual systems. The peculiarity of the employment relationship has also implied the development of specific contractual law, labour law as opposed to commercial contract law, as Masten (1988) argued.

12. These means do not only offer an opportunity for diversification but also stand as a warrant.

13. For a discussion of the meaning and role of ignorance, that is, what we describe as knowledge gap, see Loasby (1976). In some circumstances, when agreement or consensus on the facts is more important than the actual certainty about them, authority may relax the constraints due to the incompleteness of knowledge.

14. I say relief because firms do not properly solve this problem. They only assume the responsibility to deal with it. Therefore all the problems treated, for example, by the principal–agent literature are extremely important.

15. On this subject see North's very illuminating work on the analysis of inter-institutional relations, reduction in transaction costs and the development of the division of labour and of the market.

16. In my opinion this perspective has interesting implications regarding interactions between law and economics. The first one is that we cannot have a clear-cut separation between institutional environment (sets of laws) and institutional arrangements (organizational forms), considering the former as given and therefore allowing a static comparative analysis of the latter, as in Williamson (1993), because the two are continuously interacting. As a matter of fact firms do change their organization (and size) continuously as long as markets and laws change the boundaries and the amount of risks that may be shifted. The second one is that of course we must discharge Posner's idea that laws (common law) do reflect an efficiency perspective: on the contrary we do have bad laws and they have poor effects on economic organizations. See Atiyah (1986).

17. Authority in this context is a way by which agents simplify both the incentive and the cognitive problem they are facing, laying the base for a more decisive division of labour.

18. Using Keynes' words, we are facing a problem of ignorance. 'We are dealing still with a system in which the amount of the factors employed was given and the other relevant facts were known more or less for certain ... At any given time facts and expectations were assumed to be given in a definite and calculable form'. But 'the expectation of life is only slightly uncertain. Even the weather is only moderately uncertain. The sense in which I am using the term is that in which the prospect of a European war is uncertain, or the price of copper and the rate of interest twenty years hence ... About these matters there is no scientific basis on which to form any calculable probability whatever. We simply do not know' (Keynes, 1937, pp. 212–14).

19. As Arrow (1962) has shown, the market for information and knowledge is rather imperfect: information is indivisible and is produced at a cost, yet its value is not fully appropriable; once available, information may be reproduced with negligible costs. Underinvestment in information production may result and yet information will leak from the owner through markets, undermining the very existence of the market for knowledge; but above all at any moment in time 'most markets do not exist' leaving the individuals with a knowledge gap that need to be handled.

20. Knight's idea that it is not possible to describe every possible risk, assigning it some probability, according to Arrow (1951), needs to be connected to an idea of uncertainty arising out of the processes the human mind adopts in solving problems. Due to the features

and the limits of human cognitive capabilities, agents will work by grouping events into categories, therefore simplifying the duty at hand. It will result in some uncertainty in the relations among events, instead of invariance.

21. The literature accepts the existence of diversified patterns of action and problem-solving activities, recalling the distinction between different cognitive situations that agents face when uncertainty is present, proposed by Knight. As we saw he distinguished between the problem of doing, of what to do, and how to do. In real economic life, however, such a distinction is not clear-cut: 'doing' in firms, always requires the solutions to the three problems simultaneously. Within innovative firms, doing is a matter of creating new knowledge and learning, as Vincenti (1990) has so nicely shown in his analysis of the development of the modern aircraft.

22. The evolutionary theory of the firm proposed by Nelson and Winter (1982) elaborates on this perspective; more recently many have worked on the idea that firms do develop specific competence (Dosi and Egidi, 1991). See also Langlois (1993). The capability to develop new knowledge is certain if we focus on innovative behaviour of firms: not only is quite a large amount of resources devoted to this purpose but firms do learn 'by doing' and 'by using' (Rosenberg, 1994).

23. This is what Penrose claims (1959). A firm's ability to grow or change is precisely due to the existence of free resources in the firm. The present chapter, in common with much of the recent literature on the theory of the firm, owes a large debt to Penrose's work. March also stresses this aspect, speaking of organizational slack, and devotes much of his work to organizational learning.

24. This anomie, or lack of rules, necessarily leads to a vacuum of responsibility. And this provides another reason for the firm's management to assume 'unlimited' responsibility and for it to be conferred on an authority. Moreover, it is precisely widespread and indelible irresponsibility which makes the problems of incentives and motivation within organizations so pervasive.

25. Here the notion of agency is slightly different from that normally assumed in the principal–agent models. The contents of the contract are not defined according to contingencies, but rather as a transfer of authority (see Schanze, 1987). Delegation concerns the assigning of objectives and the responsibility for realizing them (with the transfer of possible resources required). If we look at delegation as a form of decentralized problem-solving activity than we may say that entrepreneurial and innovative activities are spread accordingly within the organization. See Egidi and Turvani (1994). To have some nice examples of how innovative behaviour and knowledge production is spread within organizations see Vincenti (1990).

REFERENCES

Alchian, A. and H. Demsetz (1972), 'Production, information costs and economic organization', *American Economic Review*, 62, pp. 777–95.

Aoki, M. (1990), 'The participatory generation of information rents and the theory of the firm', in M. Aoki, B. Gustafsson and O. Williamson (eds), *The Firm as a Nexus of Treaties*, London: Sage.

Aoki, M., B. Gustafsson and O. Williamson (1990) *The Firm as a Nexus of Treaties*, Sage.

Arrow, K. (1951), 'Alternative approaches to the theory of choice in risk-taking situations', *Economica*, 19, pp. 404–37.

Arrow, K. (1962), 'Economic welfare and the allocation of resources for invention', in F. Lamberton (ed.), (1971), *Economics of Information and Knowledge*, Penguin.

Arrow, K. (1987), 'Rationality of self and others in an economic system', in R. Hogarth and R. Reder (eds), *Rational Choice*, University of Chicago Press.

Atiyah, P.S. (1986), *Essays on Contract*, Oxford: Clarendon.

Barzel, Y. (1987), 'Knight's moral hazard theory of organization', *Economic Inquiry*, vol. XXV (January).

Boundreaux, D. and R. Holcombe (1989), 'The Coasian and Knightian Theories of the Firm', *Managerial and Decision Economics*, vol. 10.

Coase, R. (1937), 'The nature of the firm', *Economica*, 4, pp. 386–405.

Coase, R. (1988), 'Lecture on "The Nature of the Firm": Influence', *Journal of Law, Economics and Organization*, 4, pp. 33–47.

Coase, R. (1992), 'The institutional structure of production', *American Economic Review*, vol. 82, no. 4.

Commons, J. (1924), *Legal Foundation of Capitalism*, Macmillan.

Demsetz, H. (1988), 'The theory of the firm revisited', *Journal of Law, Economics, and Organization*, vol. 4, no.1.

Dosi, G. and M. Egidi (1991), 'Substantive and procedural uncertainty', *Journal of Evolutionary Economics*, 1, pp. 145–68.

Dow, G. (1994), 'Authority relations in the firm: review and agenda for research', paper presented to *'Transaction Cost Economics and Beyond'*, Rotterdam, 6–7 June.

Egidi, M. and M. Turvani (eds) (1994), *Le ragioni delle organizzazioni economiche*, Rosenberg & Sellier.

Foss, N.J. (1993), 'Theories of the firm: contractual and competence perspectives', *Journal of Evolutionary Economics*, 3.

Gunning, P. (1993), 'Entrepreneurists and firmist: Knight vs. the modern theory of the firm', *Journal of the History of Economic Thought*, 15 (Spring).

Hodgson, G. (1993), *Economics and Evolution: Bringing Life back into Economics*, Polity.

Jensen, M. and W. Meckling (1976), 'Theory of the firm: managerial behaviour, agency cost, and capital structure', *Journal of Financial Economics*, 3, pp. 305–60.

Keynes, J.M. (1937), 'The general theory of employment', *Quarterly Journal of Economics*, 51, pp. 209–23.

Knight, F.H. (1923), 'The ethics of competition, *Quarterly Journal of Economics*, pp. 579–624.

Knight, F.H. (1971), *Risk, Uncertainty and Profit*, University of Chicago Press.

Langlois, R. (1993), *Capabilities and Coherence in Firms and Markets*, The University of Conneticut W.P. 94–151.

Langlois, R. and M. Cosgel (1993), 'Frank Knight on risk, uncertainty, and the firm: a new interpretation', *Economic Inquiry*, vol. XXXI, pp. 456–65.

LeRoy, S. and L. Singell (1987), 'Knight on risk and uncertainty', *Journal of Political Economy*, vol. 95, no. 2.

Loasby, B.J. (1976), *Choice, Complexity and Ignorance*, Cambridge University Press.

Loasby, B.J. (1991), *Equilibrium and Evolution*, Manchester University Press.

Machlup, F. (1967), 'Theories of the firm: marginalist, behavioural, managerial', *American Economic Review*, vol. 62, pp. 1–33.

Malmgren, H.B. (1961), 'Information, expectation and the theory of the firm', *Quarterly Journal of Economics*, 75, pp. 399–421.

March, J.G. and H. Simon (1958), *Organizations*, Wiley.

Masten, S. (1988), 'A legal basis for the firm', *Journal of Law, Economics and Organization*, 4 (Spring), pp. 181–98.

Menard, C. (1995), *Inside the Black Box: The Variety of Hierarchical Forms*, ATOM W.P. 95–01.

Milgrom, P. and J. Roberts (1989), *The Economics of Modern Manufacturing: Technology, Strategy and Organization*, CEPR-Stanford, no. 162.

Nelson, R. (1995), 'Recent evolutionary theorizing about economic change', *Journal of Economic Literature*, vol. XXXIII (March).

Nelson, R. and S. Winter (1982), *An Evolutionary Theory of Economic Change*, Cambridge, Mass., The Belknap Press of Harvard University Press.

North, D. (1991), 'Institutions', *Journal of Economic Perspectives*, Winter, pp. 97–112.

Penrose, E. (1959), *The Theory of the Growth of the Firm*, Oxford: Blackwell.

Polanyi, M. (1962), *Personal Knowledge*, Harper and Row.

Rosenberg, N. (1994), *Uncertainty and Technological Change*, CEPR, Stanford University.

Salais, R. (1989), 'L'analyse economique des convention du travail', *Revue Economique*, 40.

Schanze, E. (1987), 'Contract, agency and the delegation of decision making', in G. Bamberg and K. Spreman (eds), *Agency Theory, Information and Incentives*, Springer.

Shackle, G.L. (1995), *Uncertainty in Economics*, Cambridge University Press.

Simon, H. (1951), 'A formal theory of the employment relation', *Econometrica*.

Stigler, G. (1971),'Introduction', in K. Knight (ed.), *Risk, Uncertainty and Profit*, Chicago: University of Chicago Press.

Turvani, M. (1995), 'The Core of the Firm: the Issue of the Employer–Employee Relationship' in J. Groenewegen (ed.), *Transaction Cost and Beyond*, Kluwer Academic.

Vincenti, W. (1990), *What Engineers Know and How They Know It*, Johns Hopkins Press.

von Hayek, F. (1945), 'The use of knowledge in society', *American Economic Review*, vol. 35, no. 4, pp. 519–30.

Williamson, O.E. (1985), *The Economic Institutions of Capitalism*, Free Press.

Williamson, O.E. (1993), 'Calculativeness, trust and economic organization', *Journal of Law and Economics*, vol. XXXVI, April.

Williamson, O.E. (1996), *The Mechanism of Governance*, Oxford: Oxford University Press.

Williamson, O., M. Watcher and J. Harris (1975), 'Understanding the employment relation: the analysis of idiosyncratic exchange', *Bell Journal of Economics*, 6, pp. 250–80.

Winter, S. (1982), 'An essay on the theory of production', in S. Hymans (ed.), *Economics and the World Around It*, Michigan University Press.

8.   Governance of transactions: a strategic process model

Bart Nooteboom

THEORETICAL PERSPECTIVE

My purpose in this chapter is to provide a framework for the analysis and design of relations between firms. I aim to analyse the different factors that determine dependence between partners, in the form of a coherent scheme that provides the basis for an analysis and description of the process of strategic interaction in a relation, and the evolution of that relation in time, as a function of conditions such as the market and technology, and strategic orientations of the partners. The overall framework is claimed to have general validity for strategic interaction between firms, but its details are specific for vertical relations between suppliers and contractors. The interaction studied deals with the tension that arises in relations between advantages due to values that the parties involved offer each other (cooperation), and risks due to mutual dependence (conflict). Strategic interaction may indicate the use of a game-theoretic model, but while some use of that approach is made in analysing aspects of the problem, it is expected to be inadequate to deal with the complexities involved in the development of the relation. Instead, to allow for complexity and dynamics of the relation, the framework aims to provide the basis for simulation.

The framework incorporates elements from Transaction Cost Economics (TCE): 'relation specific investments' yield switching costs; 'bounded rationality' yields opportunities for opportunism; 'legal governance and private ordering' constrain such opportunities. It also incorporates elements that derive from sociology rather than economics: institutions (including socially inculcated ethical norms) also constrain opportunities for opportunism; trust, bonding and habituation constrain the inclination towards opportunism; learning forms a crucial dimension of the value of interaction.

The 'New Institutionalist' theory of TCE has effected a shift in the study of the boundaries of firms, although it does not quite satisfy its earliest ambition (going back to Coase, 1937) of giving a *sufficient* explanation of the existence of firms (Hodgson, 1993; Pitelis, 1993, 1994; Dietrich, 1993). Nevertheless, particularly in the work of Williamson (1975, 1985) it provides a useful and fruitful perspective. Its fruitfulness has been shown both in the theoretical debates that it has triggered and in successful empirical research.

But it is not complete. It is a framework for comparative static analysis and lacks a dynamic perspective, because it does not take learning into account. According to TCE the advantage of outside sourcing lies in the mobilization of market incentives, and specialization as a means to achieve economies of scale, as a source of efficiency. This view of specialization is limited, in that the tacit assumption, typical of neoclassical economics, is that perception, knowledge and competence are not path-dependent, and are objective and 'given'; available like goods on a shelf in the shop of technology, to be had at the going price, as a basis for rational choice. Since learning is not part of the theory, it is blind to the possible role of transactional relations in shifting perception, knowledge and preference, or, more generally, development of competence, which can also entail shifts in the presence or perception of opportunism (Johanson and Mattson, 1987; Hodgson, 1993; Nooteboom, 1992, 1993b; Foss, 1993; Dietrich, 1993).

We adopt a fundamentally different theory of knowledge (Hodgson, 1988, 1993; Nooteboom, 1992, 1993b). A crucial value of transaction relations lies in complementarity of knowledge, competence and access to other resources. Different firms, with different histories, in different contexts of markets and technologies, have developed different perspectives and cognitive competences that cannot be easily and instantaneously adopted or transferred. Therefore, linkages with other firms are sought to gain access to competencies, including cognitive competencies, that are lacking in one's own firm (Nooteboom, 1992, 1993b).

Transactions are viewed as embedded in relations that develop in time. This view has been advocated for a number of years in marketing by the International Marketing and Purchasing Group (IMP) (see Hakansson, 1982, 1987; Hagg and Johanson, 1983; Easton, 1989). Exchange leads to mutual adaptation, which entails investment in a relation. As a result of this, bonding between the actors develops, trust is generated, and a lasting relation emerges (Johanson and Mattson, 1987; Easton, 1989). The differences between TCE and IMP are close to those identified by Foss (1993): TCE is oriented towards efficiency of contracting, given certain competencies, and IMP is oriented towards competence building.

Our criticism of TCE is fundamental in that it proposes to reintroduce a Neo-Institutionalist sociological perspective, which was present in the 'Old Institutionalism' of Veblen and Commons (Hodgson, 1993). It is sociological in the sense that it considers the development and interactiveness of relations, while TCE sticks to the methodological individualism of standard (neoclassical) economics and focuses on transactional events rather than on transactional relations (Hodgson, 1993). Neo-institutionalism also reintroduces the role of institutions as culturally embedded forces that constrain and guide conduct, and thereby limit opportunism.

The inclusion of the perspective of learning and interaction constitutes a major attraction of the IMP perspective. However, if the IMP view is taken to imply a rejection of the TCE view as a whole, it runs the risk of throwing out the baby with the bathwater. Doubtless, in the present turbulent conditions firms require networks of relations, and trust forms an important dimension in such relations. But there are risks as well: trust is not unbounded, it cannot be taken for granted, and it may break down. From the TCE perspective, the investments in relations that the IMP approach recognizes, as an instrument of bonding which generates trust, are at risk since they are likely to be relation-specific.

TCE has contributed greatly by specifying rigorously what the nature and extent of risk in transactions is: if there is opportunism, and bounded rationality makes it impossible to foresee it and to foreclose its undesirable consequences, then one runs the risk of either the loss of investment to the extent that investments are relation-specific, or 'hold-up' situations as a consequence of the resulting dependence. Next, TCE has provided indications of how to construct schemes for 'governing' transactions in such a way that risks are reduced: in bilateral private ordering the use of different guarantees to compensate for one-sided transaction-specific investments (cross-ownership of assets, hostages, guaranteed price, volume or period of purchase), and counter-measures to guard against invalid use and expropriation of such guarantees; in infrequent transactions: trilateral governance, with some third party acting as an arbitrator. These concepts are of theoretical and practical use, and it is a waste to ignore them. Both trust and opportunism are likely to arise in transaction relations, and neither should be ignored. Therefore, in spite of the differences between the two outlooks (TCE and IMP), we should seek to integrate them. That is the theoretical point of departure of the present chapter (this position was argued before in Nooteboom, 1993b).

SOURCES OF COOPERATION

From the literature on trust (Williams 1988; Gambetta 1988), Nooteboom (1995b) adopted four sources of cooperation, as illustrated in Table 8.1.

Table 8.1   Sources of cooperation

	macro	micro
egotistic	coercion or fear of sanctions from some authority (god, law)	material advantage or 'interest'
non-egotistic	ethics: values/norms of proper conduct	bonds of friendship, kinship or empathy

Economics, including New-Institutionalist TCE, focuses on the egotistic sources, while Neo-Institutionalism aims at incorporating the non-egotistic sources. I propose that trust belongs to the second category: it cannot be reduced to egotistic motives, and its core lies in the renunciation of such motives on the basis of ethics or emotions. I take the following position on cooperation and trust. A more extensive discussion can be found in Nooteboom, 1995b.

> X is willing to engage in cooperation with Y ... , even if this makes X dependent, if X has a more or less well grounded belief, in the form of a subjective probability, that Y will cooperate in the sense of not mis-using such dependence. This belief may be based on (perceived) available *opportunities* for misuse on the part of Y, Y's *incentives* towards misuse, and Y's *propensity* to employ the opportunities. Inclination to use opportunities for defection is related to trust, which has its basis in ethics, kinship, friendship or empathy.
>
> My definition of (behavioural) trust would now be as follows: X trusts Y to the extent that X chooses to cooperate with Y on the basis of a subjective probability that Y will choose not to employ opportunities for defection that X considers damaging, even if it is in the interest of Y to do so. The trustworthiness of Y depends on Y's true propensity to employ those opportunities. (1)

Note that (1) indicates that trust relates to a choice not to defect in spite of both a motive and an opportunity to do so, and that trust is related to a propensity, not a certainty: it may not be resistant to golden opportunities.

Here, 'defection' is closely related to the concept of opportunism, as employed in TCE: 'interest-seeking with guile', and to make the connection with TCE I shall equate the two. Thus I shall speak of 'opportunities for opportunism', and the *'inclination'* to employ them. We may define power as opportunities to act against someone's interest in a way that they cannot control. Thus power is close to opportunities for opportunism. Trust is then associated with the voluntary submission to power on the belief that it will not be exercised. From Table 8.1 we may adopt three basic dimensions in the governance of relations: material (self-)interest; opportunities for opportunism; inclination towards opportunism.

As we shall see, material interest includes the elements from TCE that come under the heading of 'relational contracting': making it in the interest of both parties not to engage in opportunism. Governance through opportunities for opportunism includes what in TCE is called 'legal contracting': blocking opportunistic actions by formal, contractual means supported by law. Governance by trust, through limitation of inclinations to employ opportunities for opportunism, is of course absent from TCE.

As indicated in Table 8.1, trustworthiness can be based on institutions in the form of ethical rules or norms, or on emotional bonds. I propose that sheer habituation may also cause opportunities for opportunism to be foregone, if only because these opportunities are not noticed. These determinants of trustworthiness are mediated by character and affected by the duration of a relationship. A long-lasting relationship creates its own institutions, bonds and habits, and for this reason one may aim for a lasting relationship to build up norms/values, habituation and bonds of friendship or empathy. As pointed out by Hirschman (1984), trust is not a scarce commodity that is used up: it may grow with its usage. In contrast with TCE, we do not assume opportunism as a prior, exogenous condition, but as a factor that should be endogenous; that depends on the conditions and the evolution of the relationship.

Furthermore, different people, with different characters, are not equally susceptible to sources of trustworthiness. The question of course arises as to what 'character' means on the aggregate level of an organization. This issue of aggregation of traits is too complex to treat fully here. I shall leave it at this: with culture as a mechanism to constrain and guide behaviour in an organization, and hence an organization-specific institution, it makes sense to talk about organizational traits, although they are subject to greater or lesser variation as

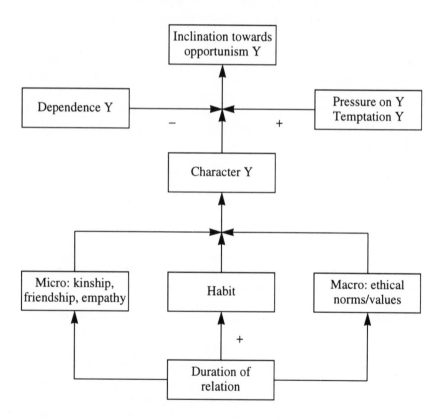

Figure 8.1   Inclination towards opportunism

a function of the individuals in the organization that one is dealing with. This variation depends on the 'tightness' of the culture.

Finally, trustworthiness is conditional upon outside pressure, degree of temptation ('golden opportunity') and dependence on the partner. Outside pressure refers in particular to competitive pressure: if a firm is under high pressure, there will be more pressure to employ opportunities for material advantage.[1] Given a golden opportunity, moderately trustworthy people succumb to temptation. Thus it is wise not to submit one's partners to such temptation. When one is highly dependent on the partner, one will be more careful not to set off a cycle of opportunism and retribution. The conditions for trustworthiness or its inverse of 'inclination towards opportunism' are summarized in Figure 8.1. In this figure, the position of 'character' requires a comment. The figure may suggest that character is *determined* by ethical norms/rules, bonds of friendship/kinship and habit. While that may be true, up to a point, what I want to illustrate with the figure is that the effects of bonds, ethics and habit are *mediated* through character. To illustrate this, the arrow of causality is drawn through rather than to 'character'.

We now proceed to develop an overall causal scheme of governance, which indicates how partners in a relation become dependent upon each other, and how they may govern the risks of such dependence.

A GENERAL MODEL OF GOVERNANCE

Let us consider a relationship between X and Y, and analyse it from the perspective of X. We propose that material interest consists of two parts: perceived value of the partner Y to X (VYX) and the costs to X of switching to a different partner (SWX). It is those two factors taken together that make it in X's interest to engage upon and maintain a relationship with Y, and thereby make X captive and dependent to some extent; susceptible to what Williamson called 'hold-up'. To cover this we define a variable CAPX (captiveness X) = VYX + SWX. From the perspective of Y we have the corresponding variables VXY, SWY, CAPY (value of X to Y, switching costs and captiveness of Y).

For the value of the partner we take the relative value: value relative to the next best alternative. Such value may have many dimensions, which depend on the specific type of relation involved. In the Appendix (Figure 8.6) the relevant dimensions are indicated for a subcontracting relationship. Note that in view of the importance of other firms as external sources of learning, innovative capacity and network position of the partner form part of his value. Continuity of the partner (in the sense of his robustness to failure and intention towards on-going cooperation) is part of his value as well. Connected to this, the institutional setting in which the partner is embedded will form part of his evaluation.

When the relative value of the partner is negative (VYX < 0), one would prefer the alternative on the basis of material interest. But in that case one may be prevented by switching costs from breaking away from the relationship, unless the value of the partner is so low that total captiveness becomes negative (CAPX < 0). Then an alternative to Y becomes so much more attractive that it pays to incur the switching costs. Note that even then a switch need not occur immediately. One may accept temporary set-backs for the sake of renewed success in the future. Thus the view of the value of the partner should not be myopic, but should include expected value of the relation in the future, as indicated before.

Switching costs have several causes. First, to search and evaluate a novel partner entails search costs. Note that with a greater value of the partner one has more to lose with breaking the relationship, so that the value of Y to X contributes to X's switching costs. It will be more difficult to find a better or equal alternative, and meanwhile one suffers loss of quality or loss in the form of high replacement costs.

Second, there is the well known cause of 'transaction-specific assets' from TCE: when an investment is specific to a relationship, then discontinuing the relationship causes a loss of the residual value of investment, with the need to reinvest in a similar asset for another partner. Specific investments may not be symmetric between partners, but switching costs may be redistributed between partners as part of governance, as set out in TCE: by shared ownership of the asset; guarantees from the least dependent party to the other; posting hostages. Guarantees may take the form of long-term contracts, severance payments, etc. The determinants of switching costs are specified in more detail in the Appendix (Figure 8.7).

X is vulnerable to possible opportunistic conduct to the extent that he is captive (CAPX > 0), but vulnerability also depends on other factors: opportunities to Y for opportunistic conduct (OOY), and Y's inclination to employ such opportunities (IOY). The first is part of TCE, but the second is not, as already discussed. The factors that determine inclination towards opportunism (IOY) have also already been discussed (see Figure 8.1).

As set out in TCE, opportunities for opportunism (OOY) are determined by the constraints of legal contracts and opportunities for the monitoring required to impose those constraints. When one has little access to information about the partner ('information asymmetry'), opportunities for monitoring Y are limited and Y's opportunities for opportunism are correspondingly widened. When there is external uncertainty or 'volatility' concerning contingencies that are relevant to the relation, unforeseen events may occur that cannot be covered in the contract and yield novel opportunities for opportunism. Note that under present conditions of rapid change in technologies and markets volatility is high. For a full representation of the determinants of the opportunities for opportunism, see the Appendix (Figure 8.8).

Summing up: the dependence of X (DEX), in the sense of vulnerability to opportunism, is determined by captiveness (CAPX) due to the partner's value (VYX) and switching costs (SWX), and the partner's opportunities and inclination to opportunism (OOY, IOY). Each of these variables forms a necessary condition: if any of them is zero, there is no risk of dependence (DEX = 0). The simplest way to express this mathematically is the following multiplicative specification:

$$DEX = CAPX.OOY.IOY \qquad (2)$$

The model is summarized in Figure 8.2.

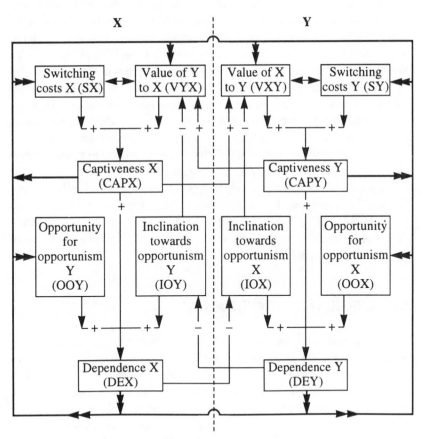

Figure 8.2   Interaction between X and Y

Note that the model is symmetric for X and Y. For Y we have that its dependence (DEY) follows from its captiveness (CAPY = VXY + SWY), X's opportunities for opportunism (OOX) and his inclination towards opportunism (IOX): DEY = CAPY.OOX.IOX.

In the figure, the single lines indicate causality: how variables are affected by other variables. At any one moment in time, this causation applies to the given governance structure. But both parties can engage in actions to modify the governance structure by trying to change one or more of the underlying variables. This is indicated by double lines, in what engineers would call a 'control loop'. Some comments are in order. We see lines of causality from the value of the partner to one's captiveness (VYX → CAPX; VXY → CAPY), but also lines from the partner's captiveness to his value (CAPY → VYX; CAPX → VXY). The latter serves to indicate that value is not myopic: in the evaluation of one's partner one takes into account his intention to continue the relation in the future, and his captiveness supports such intention. This is not all: trustworthiness also affects expected future value of the partner (IOY → VYX; IOX → VXY). We also see a line of causality running from dependence of an actor to his inclination towards opportunism (DEY → IOY; DEX → IOX). This expresses the fact that one will be less inclined towards opportunism to the extent that one is dependent on the partner (in particular: more dependent on him than vice versa). In the control loop, note that while it is primarily the ultimate outcome of (perceived) dependence (DEX, DEY) that triggers adjustment to governance, captivity (CAPX, CAPY) may already trigger such action.

The model is quite general: it may be applied to a wide range of relationships. By way of experiment it has for example been tried on marital relations (Nooteboom, 1993d). In the Appendix the submodels that underlie the basic variables for a subcontracting relation are substituted, to yield a full model of subcontracting (Figure 8.9).

STRATEGIES OF GOVERNANCE

Now we use the model for a systematic exploration of strategies for modifying governance structure, along the 'control loop' of Figure 8.2. This is connected with the distinction that Hirschman (1970) made between 'exit' and 'voice'. If one disagrees with something in a relationship, one can seek to get out (exit), or one can voice one's objections to seek improvement of the relationship. The scheme can be used ex ante, for the analysis or design of contracts, and ex post, for the governance of an on-going relationship. Here we focus on the latter: strategies for the governance of an on-going relationship.

Attempts to revise governance structure may be triggered from within the relationship, by actions of the partners, but also by external events. For example, when for X a more attractive partner enters the scene, the relative value of Y may drop below zero. This may trigger X to take actions towards breaking up the relationship. Changes of relative value may also be caused by changes in market conditions or technology, or by shifts of ownership, as when a partner merges with or is taken over by some other firm, or by changes in the network in which the partner is embedded. A change of technology may affect specificity of investments: for example, information technology has widened opportunities for flexible production. A change in the law, technology of monitoring (information and communication technology) and volatility of conditions may change opportunities for opportunism. Changing competitive pressure, personnel changes or changes of ownership may modify inclinations towards opportunism.

With the model presented in Figure 8.2, we can take into account the effects of actions on the position of the partner, the implications for his/her actions, and the implications of that for one's own position. That is what makes the interaction strategic, in the original, military sense of taking into account the fact that one has an intelligent counterpart who, unlike nature, adjusts his/her actions to one's own. Therefore, an analysis of the position of party X should include the position of counterpart Y. In this respect, the analysis resembles the approach from game theory. Note that the system is recursive: dependence of Y on X affects dependence of X on Y; it reduces the advantage of opportunism for Y and thereby reduces Y's inclination to opportunism. Thus an iterative process of mutual adjustment can arise, which lasts until the relationship falls apart or an equilibrium in mutual adjustment occurs, which may be comparable to the concept of a Nash equilibrium in game theory: given the conduct of the other party one cannot improve one's own position with respect to some aspiration level. Note that there may be multiple equilibria, depending on where one starts and what strategic orientations parties take, or no equilibrium because parties get locked into a circle of adjustment, or because the relation explodes, or because meanwhile conditions have changed concerning opportunities that arise, legal rules, technology and its implications for specificity of assets, and so on. While we use game theory to explore equilibria under specific conditions, in an analysis of comparative statics, we have no ambition to analytically determine Nash equilibria for *time paths* of the relationship as a whole. Even if that were technically possible, which is doubtful, it would either lack relevance for its excessive demands on the rational powers of the protagonists, or would impose too many constraints on the adjustment of parameters that represent perception, knowledge and opportunism, and on the occurrence of external events, or both. For an analysis of the evolution of the relationship we prefer simulation as a tool.

Again we take X as the focal partner. According to the scheme in Figure 8.2, one can try to modify the basic variables that determine captiveness and dependence, as follows:

V.   governance by value: change the relative value of the partner (VP), or the value which one offers to the partner (VO)
S.   governance by switching costs: change one's own switching costs (SO) or those of the partner (SP)
R.   legal governance: change one's own opportunities for opportunism (OO), or those of the partner (OP)
I.   governance by trust: change the inclination towards opportunism of oneself (IO) or of the partner (IP)

While TCE focuses on S and O, the IMP group emphasizes V and I. This basic scheme is further developed in Table 8.2. We do not consider all logical possibilities, but restrict the analysis to pronounced, frequently arising instruments. Not all the underlying factors constitute instruments. Laws and norms cannot easily be influenced. A change of law requires political action via some collective such as an industry association. A change of ethical norms or values either takes a long time or requires that one move to a different institutional environment. It is also difficult to influence the volatility of conditions.

Note that the different items of strategy are not independent, and can weaken or reinforce each other. Taking formal, legal measures can destroy the atmosphere of a relationship, increasing the inclination towards opportunism. More generally, the disadvantage of adversarial actions is that they can call forth similar reactions, resulting in a destructive chain reaction which leads to the collapse of the relationship. However, a cooperative action, such as increasing the dependence of the partner by increasing one's worth for him, can entail further specific investments, which increases the risk of opportunistic conduct. However, this need not be the case for all cooperative action: e.g. investment in a reputation of reliability, by means of decent conduct, would also benefit alternative or potential future relationships. But the point is that in a package of measures one should heed their consistency, not to destroy in one move what has been built up in another. One of the uses of the scheme is to explore consistency in a package of governance. The optimality of a package depends on the situation, and in particular on the strategic posture of the other side.

We can proceed by analysing for each of the actions indicated in Table 8.2 the effects on the basic variables in Figure 8.2: value, switching costs, opportunities and inclination for opportunism. This yields only first-order effects, which can be traced manually. But these have further effects, in a chain of actions and reactions. An analysis of these chains of action, on the basis of a simulation model, will be presented in a later paper.

Table 8.2   Instruments

Influence value:

VPH increase value of the partner, by investing in his competence; this will generally entail specific investments; the aim can be to improve the value of a relationship that for reasons of switching costs must be continued

VPL decrease the value of the partner, by detracting from his competence

VOH increase one's own value for the partner, also in general by specific investments; the aim can be to make the partner more dependent, thus reducing one's own dependence

VOL accept that one's own value is lowered by the partner's actions, or lower one's value oneself, to make oneself less attractive, in order to extricate oneself from an undesirable relationship.

Influence switching costs:

SOL1 lower one's own switching costs (and simultaneously lower the value of the partner), by shifting share of volume to alternative partners; this diversifies risk of dependence

SOL2 the same, by searching for or developing alternative partners with higher value

SOLPH1 lower own switching costs and increase those of the partner by selling a share of the ownership of specific assets

SOLPH2 the same, by obtaining additional guarantees from the partner (as compensation for specific assets)

SOHPL1 accept demands from the other side to buy a share of specific investments

SOHPL2 accept demands from the other side to give guarantees

SPH increase switching costs of the partner by demanding a hostage

SOH increase own switching costs by offering a hostage

SOPL lower switching costs of both sides by switching to a more flexible technology, or by means of standards for contracts, procedures or techniques (e.g. EDI)

Influence opportunities for opportunism:

OPL1 reduce the room for the partner, by narrower legal or other formal contractual constraints, with corresponding sanctions

OPL2 the same, by more control of his activities

OOL1 accept demands for less room for oneself

OOL2 the same, so that own activities are subjected to closer control

OOH1 increase own room by looser constraints

OOH2 the same, by limiting control

Influence inclination to opportunism:

IPOL 'bonding' by such investments in the relationship that institutional elements such as norms, or characteristics such as emotions, or pure habituation reduce the inclination to opportunism (briefly: invest in 'atmosphere')

IOH give evidence of a greater inclination to opportunism by show of indifference, antipathy, animosity or loss of norms, so that the other party sees a higher risk of opportunistic conduct.

STRATEGIC INTERACTION

On the basis of the inventory of strategic actions (Table 8.2), we will now analyse processes of strategic interaction. The actions indicated in Table 8.2 can be classified in several ways, for example, in a cooperative or adversarial way, depending on whether or not one takes the interest of the partner into account. They can be aimed at reinforcement or weakening of the relation. This yields a two-by-two table, as illustrated in Table 8.3.

Table 8.3   Typology of strategy (for X)

	fastening	loosening
adversarial	constrain partner (CAPY+, OOY−) block alternatives hostages restrict actions close monitoring *binding*	reduce own constraints (SWX−, OOX+) reduce values (VYX−, VXY−) decrease own bonding (IOX+) *breaking up*
cooperative	increase values (VYX+, VXY+) increase bonding (IOX−, IOY−) increase own constraints (SWX+, OOX−) increase spec. assets (SWX+, SWY+) *making attractive*	reduce switching costs (SWX−, SWY−) decrease bonding partner (IOY+) *setting free*

Notes:
A cooperative strategy also is: *submission;* that is, accept an aggressive strategy (binding, breaking up) of the partner, for example, by accepting constraints (OOX−, SWX+).
+ means that a variable is increased; − that it is decreased.

The different types are given names that indicate what we call 'strategic orientation'. With 'binding' one binds the partner to the relationship by restricting his room for action, and increasing his captiveness. With 'making attractive' one creates a bind by making oneself more attractive to the partner, making further specific investments and by strengthening emotional and normative bonds. With 'breaking up' one increases one's own freedom at the cost of the other side, by increasing one's own room for opportunism, and extricating oneself from control and shifting the burden of the relation to the other side by one-sided specificity, guarantees and punishments of defection. With 'setting free' one increases room for alternatives for both sides, by reciprocal engagement of multiple relations, preparing for alternatives and facilitating switching. With 'submission' one surrenders to 'breaking up' by the other side.

The next question is: which strategies are preferable under different conditions? Game theory provides a means for at least a partial, comparative static analysis, for sensible options for action under different conditions. We consider some situations that are interesting because they often occur:

A. Both sides wish to continue the relation because the relative value of the partner is positive for both. How do they deal with the temptation of opportunistic conduct, to take advantage of each other's dependence?
B. Both sides have lost interest and have found more attractive alternatives elsewhere, and prolong the relationship only because of switching costs. How do they arrive at disentanglement? Or will they try tò give the relationship a new boost of value?
C. One side (X) has more attractive alternatives, and wishes to continue the relationship only because of switching costs. His relative value to the other (Y), however, is still positive. Will X try to extricate himself from the relationship, and if so, how will the other side react? Will any attempt be made to improve the relationship?

Without further specification of variables (pay-offs) we cannot deduce determinate outcomes, but in a game-theoretic framework we can explore the directions of choice.

Our intuition tells us that with symmetric dependence a cooperative strategy is likely, and in case of asymmetry the least dependent party may act aggressively. The game tree (in 'extensive form') for situation A is given in Figure 8.3.

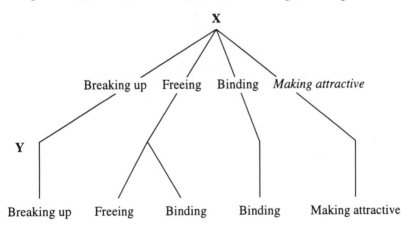

Figure 8.3   Situation A: VYX > 0; VXY > 0

For both parties X and Y the relative value of the partner is positive: VXY > 0 and VYX > 0, so that they are in a strategically equivalent position. That already excludes the strategy of submission: there is no reason for it. Since X has an interest in the relationship, it is not likely that he would opt for a 'loosening' action. He might be tempted to 'break up': one-sided guarantees and ownership of specific assets at the disadvantage of the partner, and one-sided room for opportunism. There is no reason for Y to accept that, if we assume that he knows X's interest in the relationship. X might consider an action of 'freeing', if he wants to diversify risks or sources of information, and leaves the same room for Y. Y might go along with that, with a similar reaction of freeing. This depends on a trade-off between risk of leakage of competitive advantage and profit in access to more varied sources of competence. Problems arise if this is asymmetric between partners. If freeing is attractive for X but not for Y, then Y will probably respond with 'binding'. If X seeks to bind Y, Y is likely to respond in the same fashion. Thus there emerges a tug-of-war in which both sides try to limit each other's scope with formal contractual means and controls, and demand for hostages. Finally, X may opt for 'making attractive'. It is to be expected that Y will reciprocate this constructive, trust-inducing strategy. Both sides have an interest in the relationship and are prepared to invest further in it. Y could, however, interpret X's action as a show of weakness and might be tempted to 'break up', but then X would repay with a similar action, and taking that into account, Y is more likely to respond cooperatively. Summing up: taking into account the likely reactions of Y, one of the cooperative actions is the most likely for X. If both sides want to diversify they wind up at 'freeing'. If one of them does not, they are likely to wind up at reciprocal 'making attractive'.

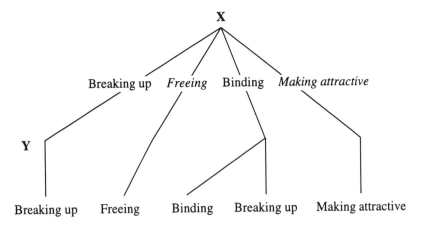

Figure 8.4   Situation B: VYX < 0; VXY < 0; CAPX > 0

The game tree for situation B is given in Figure 8.4. Here also, the two sides are in a strategically equivalent position, which again virtually excludes a 'submissive' response to an aggressive action. We again consider the options for X. Since X would obtain more value from another partner (VYX < 0), one might see no reason not to try 'breaking up'. But Y is then likely to retaliate with the same action. They will soon find that it is more fruitful to both adopt a 'freeing' strategy. A 'binding' strategy by X is not likely. If he does adopt it, Y will retaliate with the same strategy, or with a strategy of breaking up. In either case, X does not get any closer to his objective. A more viable alternative to 'freeing' would be 'making attractive': try to give the relationship a new perspective. This is viable if Y responds in the same fashion. Whether a symmetric action of freeing or making attractive emerges depends on what costs less: mutually improving value or incurring switching costs.

In cases A and B we see that the intuition that in symmetry of strategic position strategic actions will tend to be cooperative is confirmed. We now consider situation C, where there is asymmetry of position: for one side the value of the partner is positive, and for the other negative. This game is illustrated in Figure 8.5.

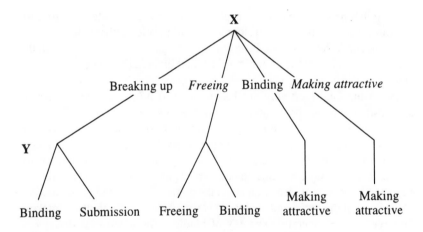

Figure 8.5   Situation C: VYX < 0; CAPX > 0; VXY > 0

X has more attractive potential partners, but is held back from getting out by switching costs. The least likely action for X is 'binding'. If he should choose it nevertheless, Y would probably react by 'making attractive', thereby trying to reduce X's inclination to get out. But X is more likely to consider a loosening strategy. How would Y react if X took 'breaking up'? Y is not in a sufficiently strong position to retaliate with the same action. He could contemplate 'making attractive', at the risk that the expected damage of X walking out is further increased (by the loss of additional specific investments for making himself more attractive). Y is likely to try 'binding', but if he has few means for that, 'submission' may be the only option left. An alternative option for X is 'freeing'. Then also Y may react with 'binding'. However, given X's threat that he may resort to breaking up, Y may more wisely choose to go along with 'freeing'. If X expects that, he may go for the 'freeing' strategy. If X expects Y to react by binding, he will resort to breaking up. X also has the alternative of 'making attractive'. Y would no doubt welcome the attempt at revitalizing the relation, and would cooperate in the same fashion. This is perhaps a likely scenario only if Y has such good means to bind X that there is no way for X to get out without heavy damage. If, on the other hand, Y has only limited means for binding, nothing stops X from devolving switching costs on Y, and Y can only submit until for him also ending the relation is best. If Y cannot make it impossible for X to get out, but can make things quite difficult, an outcome of mutual freeing is most likely.

A LIFE CYCLE OF RELATIONSHIPS

A relationship is not instantly in place, and sooner or later it will end. Relationships are subject to development; a 'life cycle' perhaps, with a start, middle and end. Perhaps there is an analogy to marital relationships, with the stages of courtship, engagement, marriage and divorce (Nooteboom, 1993d). The question is how one can govern the different stages. How does one initiate a relationship, and (certainly not less important) how does one govern its ending, when the time has come, and how does one prepare for that?

The beginning of a relationship is not simple in so far as one does not yet know what its potential is, and yet relationship-specific investments are required. In love relationships the dedication of love helps; blind to risk and visionary of the partner's unbounded value. In business relations, as in marriages of reason, one depends more on information about the partner's value, and his reputation. On the basis of the preceding analysis it is straightforward to think of 'making attractive', as a cooperative strategy of binding. An adversarial strategy of 'binding' is not suitable to encourage the partner to help the relationship blossom. Such an adversarial approach would consist of one or more of the following actions: legal or other formal contractual limitations of the room for action (OPL), or demand for hostages (SPH). These actions make the partner shy away, because he is asked to accept switching costs before being able to assess the value of the relationship. It would arouse an atmosphere of suspicion, with claims and counter-claims of formal assurances and guarantees, whereby the relationship is locked into formalisms which inhibit its development, while (especially at the beginning of a relationship) its bounds are difficult to indicate, and scope for development is desired. Nevertheless such action may be required to limit one's own switching costs, and may be warranted if it is clear that such costs are highly one-sided and risk-sharing is needed to embark upon the relationship. Then the partner is perhaps prepared to 'submit'. One should be careful not to try and specify too much at the beginning. As game theory (repeated games, see Axelrod, 1984) teaches us, if it is known beforehand when the relationship will end, the seeking of short-term advantage will prevail and will frustrate cooperation. It is precisely the open-endedness of the relationship that yields the preparedness to make sacrifices. 'Making attractive' entails investment in good atmosphere and shared norms and values (IPOL), investment in the value of the partner (VPH) or one's own value to the partner (VOH).

A next step in the cooperative strategy is that one proceeds to reinforce the value one has for the partner ('making attractive'), and thereby to bind him, at the cost of the smallest possible transaction-specific investments. This stage requires the willingness, in case of asymmetry of specific investments at the cost of the partner, to take some share in it, and/or to provide some guarantees for continuity, on the condition that the partner provides sufficient openness to allow for control against misuse. Characteristic of this stage is the development of a shared language, procedure and code of conduct, for further cooperation. This requires specific investment from both sides, which contributes to symmetry of specificity, and thus to the equilibrium and hence stability of the relationship. In marital relations this can be described as courtship that develops into engagement.

When thus the cooperation develops and bears fruit, the basis arises for further investment ('making attractive') and giving guarantees for continuity ('submission'). We find ourselves in situation A described in the last section. Continuation of mutual 'making attractive' is plausible. Bonds become stronger, and habituation and trust arise. Mutual dependence has been or is confirmed by the exchange of hostages, in the form of knowledge of each other's technology and markets, people stationed at each other's locations in teams of joint production or development, investment in each other's competence. Thus we see a step-by-step development. It is important not to make the steps too big, and to make their success clearly visible.

As the relationship develops, its boundaries become more visible. The risk grows of the potential of the relationship becoming exhausted, and new, more attractive alternatives emerging. One should be alert to this, and take measures in time. Not to be ambushed by defection, it becomes time to define the boundaries of the relationship, and to rearrange guarantees. The basis for this is better than at the start: the value of the relationship has proved itself, but so have its limitations. In a cooperative approach, partners aim to make it mutually clear to what extent the relationship can be strengthened, and also when a more attractive alternative arises. But one can also try to agree on what one does not expect from each other and where partners will let each other free.

A sensitive point is reached if one party sees one or more attractive alternatives, and sees the end of the relationship nearing, while for the other the relative value of the partner remains positive. We are then in position C as described above. The party with defection in mind is tempted to hide that fact. He no longer wants to invest in the relationship but is tempted to let the other side continue to do so, and reduce his own switching costs, in the preparation for escape. Explorations of new relationships are hidden. If the other side finds out, and still perceives positive value of the partner, and/or faces high switching costs, he will grasp all means to 'bind' the partner. If that happens, the other partner will tend to react by 'breaking up'. A bitter battle develops of binding and breaking up. For the side that wants to extricate himself, that can cost much aggravation, money and time, and it can have negative effects on his reputation as a partner. In view of the problems of the battle of breaking up/binding, which also apply to the party that wishes to step out, it is interesting to see whether there may be a viable cooperative strategy of dissolution: 'freeing', as discussed before. As the party who wishes to get out, one can try to resist the temptation to hide one's inclination to loosen the relation, on the argument that in the end the costs of that approach are higher than the returns. This implies that one announces one's dissatisfaction and will to loosen the relationship, is open concerning the reduction of commitment (SOL1) and the development of alternatives (SOL2), and helps the partner to cope without too much damage (SOPL). The partner also obtains the time to reduce switching costs, by stopping transaction-specific investments and looking for alternatives. However, if the side that wants to continue the relationship is able to effectively bind the partner who wants to get out, they are more likely to wind up in mutual 'making attractive', to give new impetus to the relationship.

It is also possible that situation B arises: both partners see attractive alternatives, and then are likely to arrive at a cooperative strategy of mutual 'freeing'. It is also possible that both sides wish to continue the relationship (situation A), but in a looser fashion, with a certain amount of diversification of relations. In that case also, the outcome of mutual 'freeing' is likely. Contracting relations may have this outcome as a matter of course: after a while, some specialty becomes a commodity. A product that was specific for some advanced user becomes more generally accepted, and the specialty turns into a commodity, with multiple users and less transaction-specific investments. Or a specialized production process develops into a more widely applicable process, as a 'dominant design'. Or standards that at first were proprietary and varied between producers evolve to industry standards (e.g. in computer software, and communication standards for EDI).

CONCLUSIONS

Using elements from transaction costs economics and other approaches, I have developed a process model of strategic interaction, which provides a basis for analysing contracts and strategies of 'governance', depending on the circumstances and the stage of development of a relationship. The scheme can in principle be used by firms to design their relationships and explore possible actions. The intention is to develop the model further into a simulation model by attaching quantifiable parameters to the different causal relations in the scheme, and calibrating them in cooperation with firms, concerning their actual positions and relationships. This will serve to further explore the typology of situations and strategies in more detail.

APPENDIX: DETAILS OF THE MODEL

Figure 8.6 gives a further elaboration of the determinants of the value of a partner, in the case of subcontracting relationships. Value depends on the share that the partner has in the relevant volume of production or input. We summarize this as 'percentage volume X'. Under conditions of rapid change concerning technology and markets, the value of the partner further depends on his technological capability, which here includes the level of quality, delivery time and costs. Of increasing importance is the value of the partner as a source of know-how, or more generally competence, concerning technology, markets, politics, and the innovative capability of the partner. This is taken as part of 'technological capability'. Also important is the reliability of quality, delivery time and costs. In so far as it is relevant, value also includes the capacity to manage and integrate activities. For a 'main supplier': the capacity to integrate activities from second-tier suppliers, including logistics, vendor rating and quality control. Next, flexibility may be important, concerning production volume, personnel, time, organization, specifications of the product, configuration of production. Network position, i.e. connections through the partner with further sources or markets, may also be important. Network position entails a number of aspects. One is indirect access via the partner to sources beyond. The term 'source' is taken in the general sense of 'resource'. That includes materials, components, machinery and equipment, services, but also labour, reputation, legitimation, permits and licences, sources of capital and markets. A relationship which at first sight is risky or unprofitable can at further sight be wise because one expects to gain access through the partner to a new market. The consequences of the rupture of a relationship are graver to the extent that it leads to the blocking of access to sources. Another threat to network position can lie in the

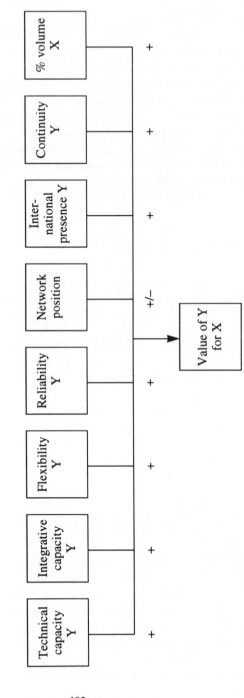

Figure 8.6 Value of Y to X

fact that a customer or supplier can also have contacts with competitors. Sensitive information on technology, product or process may leak to a competitor. Internationalization of the partner is closely related to network position, but perhaps deserves separate mention. It can be of great importance that the partner can offer presence in different market segments, in different countries. For a supplier that may offer an opportunity to penetrate widely in different markets. If proximity of supply is important to the user, and the user produces in different places, it is important that the supplier is represented at different locations. Finally, it is of importance how long the relationship is expected to last: one is less inclined towards opportunism if one expects the advantages of cooperation to last. The strength of this effect depends on the reputation of the partner and his perceived will, and behind that his advantage, to continue the relationship. Continuity also depends on mishaps. Without any design, the relationship can be broken by business failure or takeover of the partner. Firm size also has an effect on the dimensions of value. Small firms usually have fewer products in more restricted markets, and therefore are more vulnerable to business failure, and can be taken over more easily. Small firms often have a lesser capability to integrate activities, because they often cannot afford infrastructure in the form of knowledge of procedures, specialist support and investments in quality control, R&D facilities, EDI, distribution channels. On the other hand they are often more flexible, creative and innovative. Their international presence is often restricted. For a further discussion of firm size effects in transaction costs see Nooteboom (1993a); on the strengths and weaknesses of small firms in innovation see Nooteboom (1994).

The factors that determine switching costs are specified in Figure 8.7. Switching entails the following costs: loss and recommitment of new relation-specific investments, possible penalties for breach of contract or other guarantees given to the partner (imported from the variable 'opportunities for opportunism'), injury to a hostage supplied to the partner. The risk of loss of specific investments is determined by the product of three factors: the percentage of volume involved in the relationship, the extent to which transactions entail specific investments, and the share that one has in their ownership. We recall that by his own specific investments the partner also can become dependent. However, symmetry of dependence is not guaranteed. Guarantees can be given and received, mostly as compensation for one-sided specific investments. Hence they can have a positive or a negative net effect on switching costs. A special type of guarantee can be at issue if by leaving a partner his continuity and thereby employment are at risk. One may then be held liable for the loss of employment. Then risk depends on the percentage of the total production *of the partner* that is involved in the transactions, because that is what determines the risk of discontinuity of the supplier in case the transactions are discontinued. However, another reason

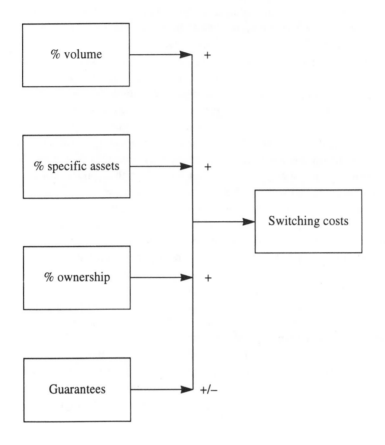

Figure 8.7   Switching costs

for wanting to maintain not one exclusive relationship but a diversity of contacts could be that it enhances the role in learning that relationships play (Nooteboom, 1992, 1995a). One may mobilize a different technology to reduce asset specificity. One option is the employment of more flexible production methods, in machinery or its configuration, so that with fewer switching costs one can produce a modified product. Another possibility is to shift the so-called 'uncoupling point' in production to a point further downstream in the production process. Specificity of investments (in equipment, people, procedures, etc.) is then limited to a smaller part of the whole process. Taken to the extreme, this leads to the assembly of different products from standard components. In other words: it is possible to produce highly specific products without highly specific investments (Nooteboom, 1993c).

Figure 8.7 indicates actions that one can take to reduce switching costs or the consequences of opportunistic actions. For example, if production by the supplier requires a specific asset, the user may participate in its ownership and finance, to thus participate in the risk. This has a limit, probably at 50 per cent ownership. If the user participates for more, and that results in transfer of decision making to the user, the latter may transfer it to an alternative supplier, to the detriment of the supplier considered. In that case the supplier would not be wise to retain less than 50 per cent ownership. An alternative to financial participation is that the user provides guarantees concerning the duration, volume, frequency or price of purchase, so that the supplier can be more confident of recouping his investment. Or the user can commit himself to refund part of the remaining value of the asset in case he breaks the relationship prematurely. The provision of such guarantees often requires the provision of counter-guarantees against misuse. This may require an agreement on information exchange, or monitoring by a third party, to verify compliance with the conditions for the guarantees. Note that guarantees can go in both directions, so that the net effect on switching costs can be positive or negative. One may also diversify risk over a greater number of partners. A possible measure also is the provision of a hostage, which is characterized by the condition of asymmetric value: it has intrinsic value for the giver but not for the receiver, so that the first will exert himself to keep to the agreement, and the second is not tempted to expropriate it, and not hesitant to jeopardize it. The function of hostage may be fulfilled by know-how, technology or knowledge, possibly in

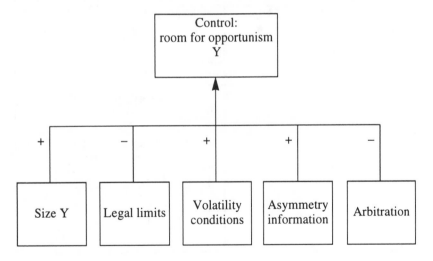

Figure 8.8   Room for opportunism (for Y)

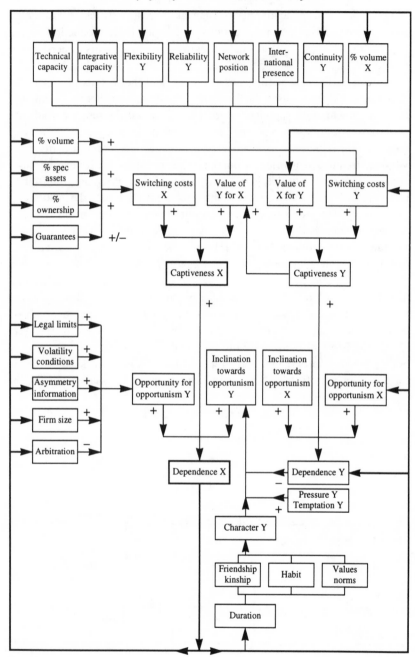

Figure 8.9   Relation management (by X)

the form of a patent or licence, of value to the giver but not the receiver, and which can leak to competitors if the giver does not keep to his commitments. Note that there is a relationship between switching costs and opportunities for opportunism, for which the causes are indicated in Figure 8.8. The boundary between the two may not always be clear.

Legal contracting is used to limit opportunities for opportunism. The possibilities here depend on the law ('legal limits') and its enforcement. Enforcement depends on possibilities for monitoring conduct, which are limited to the extent that information is asymmetric. Possibilities for foreseeing all relevant contingencies in a contract depend on the volatility of conditions. Control for unforeseen conditions and monitoring can both be enhanced by making use of a third party arbitrator. Firm size is also relevant, because of effects of scale on transaction costs (Nooteboom, 1993a). A larger firm in general has more discretion and a wider reach, with access to a wider market, more sources, more advisors within and outside the firm, a higher level of education and experience, and more political clout. As a result, the expectation is that a larger firm has more room for opportunism. Or in other words: a larger firm is more difficult to control. On the other hand, a larger firm for the same reasons is also more conspicuous, and may be more vulnerable to loss of reputation. Small, fly-by-night operators have little to lose and may therefore be less reliable. Firm size also has an influence on the availability of information. Because in smaller firms there is less need for formal information systems, because much supervision and control can be direct, and because there are effects of scale in setting up information systems, smaller firms have less documented information, and are therefore less accessible to monitoring from outside. This gives disadvantages at all stages of transactions: contact, contract and control. For a further discussion of effects of scale on transaction costs, see Nooteboom (1993a) and Nooteboom *et al.* (1992).

Substitution of the submodels in Figures 8.1, 8.6, 8.7 and 8.8 in the general model of Figure 8.2 yields a detailed model of governance of subcontracting relations shown in Figure 8.9.

NOTE

1. In an earlier version of the model this consideration was absent. In attempts at application, contacts in the highly competitive automotive industry judged the model to be 'too soft and trusting', while contacts at the Dutch gas monopoly judged it to be 'unduly suspicious of opportunism'. This could be explained by taking into account that pressure reduces trustworthiness.

REFERENCES

Axelrod, R. (1984), *The Evolution of Cooperation*, New York: Basic Books.
Coase, R.H. (1937), 'The nature of the firm', *Economics*, N.S., 4, 386–405.

Dietrich, M. (1993), *Transaction Cost Economics and Beyond: Towards a New Economics of the Firm*, London: Routledge.

Easton, G. (1989), Industrial Networks – a Review, 5th IMP conference, pp. 161–82.

Foss, N.J. (1993), 'Theories of the firm: contractual and competence perspectives', *Journal of Evolutionary Economics*, 3(2), pp. 127–44.

Gambetta, D. (ed.) (1988), *Trust: Making and Breaking Cooperative Relations*, Oxford: Basil Blackwell.

Hagg, I. and J. Johanson (1983), *Firms in Networks*, Business and Social Research Institute, Stockholm, Sweden.

Hakansson, H. (ed.) (1982), *International Marketing and Purchasing of Industrial Goods: An Interaction Approach*, Chichester: Wiley.

Hakansson, H. (ed.) (1987), *Industrial Technological Development – A Network Approach*, London: Croom Helm.

Hirschman, A.O. (1970), *Exit, Voice and Loyalty: Responses to Decline in Firms, Orpnisations and States*, Cambridge, Mass.: Harvard University Press.

Hirschman, A.O. (1984), 'Against parsimony: three easy ways of complicating some categories of economic discourse', *American Economic Review*, 74, 88–96.

Hodgson, G.M. (1988), *Economics and Institutions*, Cambridge: Polity Press.

Hodgson, G.M. (ed.) (1993), *The Economics of Institutions*, Aldershot: Edward Elgar.

Johanson, J. and L.G. Mattson (1987), 'Interorganisational relations in industrial systems – a network approach compared with the transaction cost approach', *International Studies of Management and Organization*, 17, no. 1.

Nooteboom, B. (1992), 'Towards a dynamic theory of transactions', *Journal of Evolutionary Economics*, 2, pp. 281–99.

Nooteboom, B. (1993a), 'Firm size effects on transaction costs', *Small Business Economics*, 5, 283–95.

Nooteboom, B. (1993b), 'Transactions and networks: do they connect?', in J. Groenewegen (ed.), *Dynamics of the Firm: Strategies of Pricing and Orpnisation*, Aldershot: Edward Elgar.

Nooteboom, B. (1993c), 'An analysis of specificity in transaction cost economics', *Organization Studies*, 14, pp. 443–51.

Nooteboom, B. (1993d), 'Relations in industry and marriage' (in Dutch), *Economisch Statistische Berichten*, 22/29 December, pp. 1175–9.

Nooteboom, B. (1994), 'Innovation and diffusion in small business: theory and empirical evidence', *Small Business Economics*, 6, 327–47.

Nooteboom, B. (1995a), 'Cost, Quality and Learning Based Governance of Transactions: Western, Japanese and a Third Way', paper at EGOS symposium, Istanbul, 6–8 July 1995.

Nooteboom, B. (1995b), *Trust, Opportunism and Governance: A Process and Control Model*, School of Management & Organization, Groningen University, P.O. Box 800, 9700 AV, Groningen, the Netherlands.

Nooteboom, B., P.S. Zwart and T. Bijmolt (1992), 'Transaction costs and standardisation in professional services to small business', *Small Business Economics*, 4, 141–51.

North, D.C. (1990), *Institutions, Institutional Change and Economic Performance*, Cambridge University Press.

Pitelis, C. (1993), *Transaction Costs, Markets and Hierarchies*, Oxford: Basil Blackwell.

Pitelis, C. (1994), 'On the nature of the firm', in A. van Witteloostuijn (ed.), *Market Evolution: Competition and Cooperation across Markets and over Time*, Kluwer Academic Publishers.

Williams, B. (1988), 'Formal structures and social reality', in D. Gambetta (ed.), *Trust: Making and Breaking Cooperative Relations*, Oxford: Basil Blackwell, pp. 3–13.

Williamson, O.E. (1975), *Markets and Hierarchies: Analysis and Antitrust Implications*, New York: The Free Press.

Williamson, O.E. (1985), *The Economic Institutions of Capitalism: Firms, Markets, Relational Contracting*, New York: The Free Press.

9. Schumpeterian banker–entrepreneur interaction and the spontaneous evolution of bank–industry networks: why institutional endowments matter

Thomas Marmefelt

INTRODUCTION

Schumpeter (1911) considered credit essential to innovation. The entrepreneur would not be able to innovate without a banker extending credit which would provide the required additional purchasing power. In a world of uncertainty and bounded rationality, the institutional forms of interaction between bankers and entrepreneurs become crucial to the innovation process. If bankers and entrepreneurs institutionalized their interaction within a bank–industry network, then the banker would provide more credit at lower costs, thus improving innovativeness. The bank–industry network is based on mutual trust and network commitment, where the banker's learning-by-financing about the entrepreneur's innovative skills and new potential innovations is more efficient. Both debt and equity instruments could be used, because the distinction is between informed finance and arm's-length finance.

Learning-by-financing is the function upon which the bank–industry network is founded. Institutions provide heuristics reducing uncertainty (Hodgson, 1989). Banks may informationally capture high quality firms through a low-cost, on-going history of financial information production (Fama, 1985; Sharpe, 1990). Historically evolved mutual trust decreases transaction costs (Lundvall, 1991). As moral values decrease decision-making costs (Etzioni, 1988), network commitment is essential for the sustainability of mutual trust and thereby the networks. Network commitment, thus, represents a resolute behaviour of pragmatic rationality, in the sense of Sugden (1991). An industrial finance convention with long-term bank–industry links and mutual understanding allows for greater industrial flexibility (Rivaud-Danset and Salais, 1992).

In this chapter, I will analyse Schumpeterian banker–entrepreneur interaction as an evolutionary Stag Hunt game; evolutionary because the banker and the entrepreneur interact strategically as satisficing agents in a world with uncertainty and bounded rationality and Stag Hunt because they would be better off by cooperating within a bank–industry network, but only if both of them do so.

The two evolutionary stable strategies of this game are, using Sugden's (1986) definition of convention, the spontaneously evolved conventions of industrial innovation finance: (i) the bank convention with bankers and entrepreneurs cooperating within bank–industry networks and (ii) the bond convention with independent bankers and entrepreneurs.

My purpose is to show theoretically how bank–industry networks, based on mutual trust and network commitment, evolve spontaneously due to learning-by-financing only when the institutional endowments – network commitment and developed banking – are sufficient, and that some collective action might be necessary to make the spontaneous evolution of bank-industry networks feasible. This explains why some financial systems are bank-oriented with strong bank–industry networks, while others are market-oriented with weak bank–industry networks.

Witt (1989) identifies two conjectures for analysis of the propagation process of economic institutions, the Smith-Menger-Hayek conjecture of spontaneous order and the Olson-Buchanan-Tullock conjecture of collective action, but the former may need the latter. New institutional economics[1] follows the spontaneous order conjecture by focusing on function rather than intention, but requires sufficient institutional endowments to sustain the function. Insufficient institutional endowments require collective action – the design of privileged groups (Olson; 1965, Sandler, 1992) – to start the spontaneous evolution. Learning-by-financing, the function explaining bank–industry networks, requires institutional endowments, such as developed banking and a preference for network commitment.

THE BANK–INDUSTRY NETWORK AS A SPONTANEOUS ORDER IN AN EVOLUTIONARY STAG HUNT GAME

A functionalist-evolutionary explanation[2] of why bank–industry networks exist requires that Elster's (1979) five criteria are fulfilled. The bank–industry network is an institution explained by its function learning-by-financing for bankers and entrepreneurs if and only if: (1) learning-by-financing is an effect of the bank-industry network; (2) learning-by-financing is beneficial for bankers and entrepreneurs; (3) learning-by-financing is unintended by the actors producing the bank–industry network; (4) learning-by-financing is unrecognized by the banker and the entrepreneur; and (5) learning-by-financing maintains the bank–industry network by a causal feedback loop passing through the decision-making of bankers and entrepreneurs.

With banker–entrepreneur interaction as an evolutionary Stag Hunt game, the population of bankers and the population of entrepreneurs interact strategically, each individual player following a strategy which is a fixed satisficing rule due to uncertainty and bounded rationality. There are no attempts to form a club in order to design a network. Learning-by-financing is a function, not an intention. The bankers and the entrepreneurs choose their respective strategy and the viability of each strategy depends on its relative fitness in the own population, given the strategy mix of the other population. The criteria above are, thus, fulfilled and the network evolves by strategic interaction between satisficing agents in the Stag Hunt game, not by design.

Considering institutions as spontaneously emerged order in a world with uncertainty and bounded rationality implies that an institution is a convention having evolved through a process of social interaction. A convention is, thus, an evolutionary stable strategy, ESS, in an evolutionary game with two or more possible ESSs (Sugden, 1986).[3]

Modelling banker–entrepreneur interaction and its institutionalization would, therefore, require an evolutionary game with at least two ESSs, something which is the case for the Stag Hunt game, based on Rousseau's story of the stag hunt, which is an intermediary game between the Prisoners' Dilemma and the Coordination game (Ullmann-Margalit, 1977). Basically, it argues that while hunters may individually catch rabbits, they would all be better off if all of them would cooperate in order to hunt a stag.

There are two evolutionary stable strategies, ESSs,[4] each one corresponding to a convention: individual rabbit hunting and collective stag hunting, the latter being the preferred convention which requires cooperation. How does this game relate to banker–entrepreneur interaction? Essentially the collective stag hunt represents banker–entrepreneur interaction within a bank–industry network where the banker's lower information costs, due to historically evolved private information, decrease the financing costs of the entrepreneur. He/she may then obtain more credit to realize further innovations. Individual rabbit hunting, however, represents arm's-length interaction between bankers and entrepreneurs, giving the maximum security level,[5] but not the big entrepreneurial rents.

The private information of the bank–industry network will be produced only as long as both the banker and the entrepreneur cooperate with mutual trust. Defection when the other party cooperates would, unlike the Prisoners' Dilemma, not give the highest payoff, since the mutual trust and thereby the creation of private information are destroyed. Hence, the evolution of bank–industry networks should be seen as a Stag Hunt game.

Bankers and entrepreneurs play a two-person random pairing game between a member of the population of bankers and a member of the population of entrepreneurs. There are two strategies, Strategy 1 being network-oriented and Strategy 2 being independent-minded. The banker chooses between Strategy 1 (informed) of being a network bank and Strategy 2 (arm's length) of being an independent bank, behaving like a market investor in the latter case. Similarly, the entrepreneur chooses between Strategy 1 (reliable) of staying within the network and Strategy 2 (unreliable) of taking the credit as a temporary link with the banker. Set the payoffs of independent bankers and entrepreneurs to unity and let u > 1 denote the payoff of the network banker and v > 1 the payoff of the network entrepreneur. This gives the payoff structure of the Stag Hunt game illustrated in Table 9.1.

Table 9.1   Banker–entrepreneur interaction as a Stag Hunt game

Entrepreneur Banker	1 (Reliable)	2 (Unreliable)
1 (Informed)	*u,v*	0,1
2 (Arm's length)	1,0	1,1

Let *p* denote the proportion of bankers using strategy 1 (informed) in the population of bankers and q the proportion of entrepreneurs using strategy 1 (reliable) in the population of entrepreneurs. Then the population dynamics of the pair (p,q) represent the institutional dynamics of banker–entrepreneur interaction guiding the evolution of bank–industry networks.

The payoff matrix of Table 9.1 and the shares of network-oriented bankers and entrepreneurs, *p* and *q* respectively, lead to a system of two differential equations describing the population dynamics of bankers and entrepreneurs.

Let us assume Malthusian dynamics, so the growth rate of a strategy is equal to its relative fitness. Hence, a strategy grows as long as its fitness is higher than the average fitness of the population (Friedman, 1991). Therefore, the growth of informed bankers becomes:

$$\dot{p} = p(uq - 1)(1 - p) \qquad (9.1)$$

and the growth of reliable entrepreneurs:

$$\dot{q} = q(vp - 1)(1 - q) \qquad (9.2)$$

Equation (9.1) shows that the proportion of informed bankers in the population of bankers is stable only when $p = 0;1$ or $q = 1/u$. Similarly, equation (9.2) shows that the proportion of reliable entrepreneurs in the population of entrepreneurs is stable only when $q = 0;1$ or $p = 1/v$.

As shown by Friedman (1991), the ESSs of a game whose population dynamics are given by a system of differential equations are stable equilibria identified through a local stability analysis of the Jacobian created by this system.

Let us, therefore, carry out a local stability analysis of the system consisting of equations (9.1) and (9.2), studying the determinant and the trace of the Jacobian. The determinant of the Jacobian of the system of equations (9.1) and (9.2) is:

$$\det J = (uq - 1)(1 - 2p)(vp - 1)(1 - 2q) - uvpq(1 - p)(1 - q) \qquad (9.3)$$

while the trace of the Jacobian is:

$$\operatorname{tr} J = (uq - 1)(1 - 2p) + (vp - 1)(1 - 2q) \qquad (9.4)$$

The results of the local stability analysis of the five equilibrium points are summarized in Table 9.2. Hence, dynamic analysis (local stability analysis) gives the two ESSs of the Stag Hunt game: $(p = 0, q = 0)$ and $(p = 1, q = 1)$, each one corresponding to a convention: (i) the bond convention with independent banks and firms $(p = 0, q = 0)$ and (ii) the bank convention with bank–industry networks $(p = 1, q = 1)$. There are, in addition, two unstable equilibria, $(p = 0, q = 1)$ and $(p = 1, q = 0)$, as well as a saddle point, $(p = 1/v, q = 1/u)$.

Table 9.2   Results of the local stability analysis

Equilibrium	det J		tr J		Result
$(p = 0, q = 0)$	1	[+]	−2	[−]	ESS
$(p = 0, q = 1)$	$u - 1$	[+]	u	[+]	unstable
$(p = 1, q = 1)$	$v - 1$	[+]	v	[+]	unstable
$(p = 1, q = 1)$	$(u - 1)(v - 1)$	[+]	$2 - u - v$	[−]	ESS
$(p = 1/v, q = 1/u)$	$-(1 - 1/v)(1 - 1/u)$	[−]	0		saddle point

The institutional dynamics of banker–entrepreneur interaction converge for all points to the right of the line $((p = 0, q = 1);(p = 1/v, q = 1/u);(p = 1, q = 0))$, that is, the line between the two unstable equilibria and the saddle point, to the bank convention and for all points to the left of this line to the bond convention.

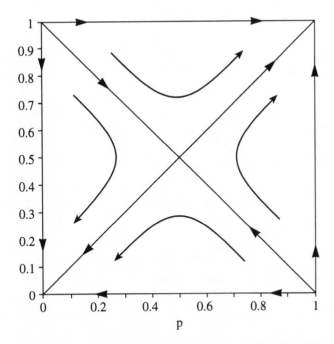

Figure 9.1   Institutional dynamics of banker–entrepreneur interaction when
u = v = 2

Figure 9.1 shows the institutional dynamics when the bank convention has twice the payoff of the bond convention, a payoff structure for which the probability of convergence to the bank convention is equal to the probability of convergence to the bond convention.

When the relative payoffs increase, as in Figure 9.2, the critical levels of informed bankers and reliable entrepreneurs required for an institutional dynamic towards the bank convention decrease, because both the banker and the entrepreneur have a higher relative fitness within a bank–industry network.

As the relative payoffs of the bank convention have increased, the probability of convergence to the bank convention is considerably larger than the probability of convergence to the bond convention. Hence, the spontaneous evolution of bank–industry networks depends on the relative payoffs of the bank convention compared to the bond convention, but these payoffs are dependent on the institutional endowments.

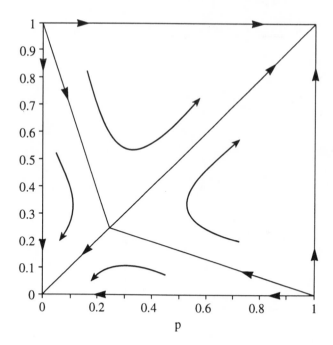

Figure 9.2   Institutional dynamics of banker–entrepreneur interaction when
u = v = 4

INSTITUTIONAL ENDOWMENTS, COLLECTIVE ACTION, AND THE VIABILITY OF A BANK–INDUSTRY NETWORK

A developed banking system and a historically evolved preference for network commitment are crucial institutional endowments. A developed banking system is, of course, essential for the willingness of the entrepreneur to turn to the banker, but the commitment between banker and entrepreneur after an initial successful cooperation determines the possibilities for learning-by-financing.

Network commitment may be seen as a Becker (1992) habit, but if agents have pragmatic rationality, then network commitment represents a resolute behaviour, in the sense of Sugden (1991), a Kantian self-imposed law or a Humean desire to stick to past behaviour of commitment. Moral sentiment induces commitment (Frank, 1988), but moral sentiment is in itself a historically evolved convention, an underlying satisficing rule.

How are the payoffs affected by network commitment? Using a collective action approach (Olson, 1965; Sandler, 1992), the relative payoffs of network bankers and entrepreneurs in the Stag Hunt game may be endogenized. Collective action problems are not limited to Prisoners' Dilemma games and any game structure is applicable to more than one configuration of costs, technology of public supply, and tastes (Sandler, 1992).

Hence, the bank–industry network has to be regarded as a privileged group where the network-specific information, the private information obtained by network banks, is a public good for network members only. The network produces joint products, giving a private utility, entrepreneurial rents and interest payments divided within the network, as well as a public utility, the institutional endowments of developed banking and network commitment. Initial property rights are not neutral, thus contradicting the Coase theorem (Kahneman, Knetch, and Thaler, 1990).

Suppose that each unit of network-specific information, for an entrepreneur, yields one unit of private utility and k units of public utility. Let E denote the ratio of bank convention entrepreneurial rents to bond convention entrepreneurial rents and R the ratio of bank convention interest payments to bond convention interest payments. E and R, thus, indicate the ratio of value of information to value of diversification.

A network banker holds equity shares of the entrepreneur's firm, because there is a minimum equity share that a bank has to hold in the firm to maintain a stable customer relationship between bank and firm as well as a legal maximum share (Aoki, 1988). Assume that the banker holds the minimum share needed to maintain the network learning-by-financing, σ, and market investors the rest. Hence, the network banker's private utility depends, in addition to interest payments, R, on the entrepreneur's utility according to the banker's share of corporate equity, σv. If the public utility is determined by summation of the private utilities, then the utility of the network banker becomes:

$$u = R + \sigma v + k(E + R) \qquad (9.5)$$

where the utility of the network entrepreneur is:

$$v = E + k(E + R) \qquad (9.6)$$

A developed industrial banking system with strong bank–industry networks and efficient learning-by-financing implies that E and R are high, something which increases the relative payoffs of the bank convention. These payoffs depend, however, not only on the return of the banker and the entrepreneur, but also on the institutional endowments' increasing the public utility within the network through a higher k.

Learning-by-financing evolves over time, making $E > 1$ and $R > 1$, as the relative value of information becomes higher, but does not exist initially, so that $E_0 = R_0 = 1$. Institutional endowments with k > 0 are therefore necessary for a spontaneous evolution of bank–industry networks and learning-by-financing.

When the institutional endowments are insufficient, public utility becomes nonpositive, so that k ≤ 0. This situation requires collective action, designing the bank–industry network as a fully privileged group. Collective action transforms the payoff structure of the Stag Hunt game as shown in Table 9.3.

Table 9.3   Banker–entrepreneur interaction as a symmetric fully privileged Stag Hunt game

Entrepreneur Banker	1 (Reliable)	2 (Unreliable)
1 (Informed)	2,2	0,1
2 (Arm's length)	1,0	–1,–1

This payoff structure gives another dynamic system of the evolution of network-oriented bankers and entrepreneurs:

$$\dot{p} = p(1 - p) \tag{9.7}$$

$$\dot{q} = q(1 - q) \tag{9.8}$$

The system given by equations (9.7) and (9.8) have, as shown in Table 9.4, four equilibria, but only one ESS: ($p = 1$, $q = 1$), that is the bank convention, while the bond convention ($p = 0$, $q = 0$) is an unstable equilibrium, ($p = 1$, $q = 0$) and ($p = 0$, $q = 1$) being saddle points.

Table 9.4   Results of the local stability analysis

Equilibrium	det J		tr J		Result
($p = 0$, $q = 0$)	1	[+]	2	[+]	unstable
($p = 0$, $q = 1$)	–1	[–]	0		saddle point
($p = 1$, $q = 0$)	–1	[–]	0		saddle point
($p = 1$, $q = 1$)	1	[+]	–2	[–]	ESS

This gives the institutional dynamics in Figure 9.3. The bank convention is the dominant strategy, because bank–industry networks have been established by design, making them a fully privileged group.

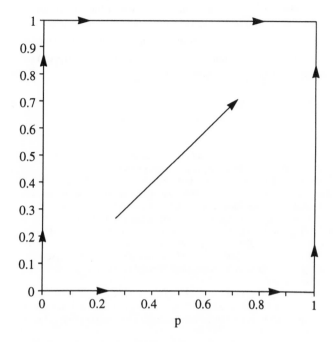

Figure 9.3   Institutional dynamics of banker–entrepreneur interaction when the bank convention is fully privileged

CONCLUSIONS

Schumpeter considered credit essential to innovation. The institutional forms of interaction between bankers and entrepreneurs, therefore, become crucial for the innovation process. Within the bank–industry network, the banker produces more private information through the more efficient learning-by-financing about the entrepreneur's innovative skills, making more credit available at a lower cost.

Analysing Schumpeterian banker–entrepreneur interaction as an evolutionary Stag Hunt game, I provide a functionalist-evolutionary explanation of why bank–industry networks actually exist in a world with uncertainty and bounded rationality. The evolutionary game gives two evolutionary stable strategies, corresponding to the two spontaneously evolved conventions of industrial innovation finance: (i) the bank convention with bankers and entrepreneurs cooperating within bank–industry networks and (ii) the bond convention with independent bankers and entrepreneurs.

Bank–industry networks evolve spontaneously only when the institutional endowments – network commitment and developed banking – are sufficient, otherwise some collective action might be necessary to make the bank convention feasible as a convention of industrial innovation finance through the design of bank–industry networks as a fully privileged group.

NOTES

1. See, for example, Ullmann-Margalit (1977), Schotter (1981), Axelrod (1984), and Sugden (1986) who all use game theory to explain the evolution of institutions or rules.
2. See, for example, Langlois (1986) for a comparison between functional explanations focusing on why institutions exist and causal-genetic explanations focusing on how they have emerged. Although both are valuable, the former opens up scope for a comparison between spontaneous order and collective action through the connection between function and intention.
3. Sugden's definition is, therefore, broader than the one used by Lewis (1969) which is limited to established conventions. For Sugden it is sufficient that everyone conforms and expects everyone else to conform to a regularity of behaviour, but Lewis requires in addition that everyone conforms on condition that the others do. Hence, following Sugden, a convention may arise in other than coordination games.
4. An ESS fulfils two conditions: (i) being the best response to itself and (ii) being uninvadable.
5. As may be observed from Table 9.1, the lowest payoff of the informed banker and the reliable entrepreneur is 0, while an arm's-length banker and an unreliable entrepreneur always receive 1, regardless of what the other player does.

REFERENCES

Aoki, Masahiko (1988), *Information, Incentives, and Bargaining in the Japanese Economy*, Cambridge: Cambridge University Press.

Axelrod, Robert (1984), *The Evolution of Cooperation*, New York: Basic Books.

Becker, Gary S. (1992), 'Habits, addictions, and traditions', *Kyklos*, 45, 327–46.

Elster, Jon (1979), *Ulysses and the Sirens: Studies in Rationality and Irrationality*, Cambridge: Cambridge University Press.

Etzioni, Amitai (1988), *The Moral Dimension: Toward a New Economics*, New York: Free Press.

Fama, Eugene (1985), 'What's Different about Banks?', *Journal of Monetary Economics*, 15, 29–39.

Frank, Robert H. (1988), *Passion within Reason: The Strategic Role of the Emotions*, New York: Norton.

Friedman, Daniel (1991), 'Evolutionary games in economics', *Econometrica*, 59, 637–66.

Hodgson, Geoffrey M. (1989), 'Post-Keynesianism and institutionalism: the missing link', in J. Pheby (ed.), *New Directions in Post-Keynesian Economics*, Aldershot: Edward Elgar.

Kahneman, Daniel, Jack Knetch and Richard Thaler (1990), 'Experimental tests of the endowment effect and the coase theorem', *Journal of Political Economy*, 98, 1325–48.

Langlois, Richard N. (1986), 'Rationality, institutions, and explanation', in R.N. Langlois (ed.), *Economics as a Process: Essays in the New Institutional Economics*, New York: Cambridge University Press.

Lewis, David K. (1969), *Conventions: A Philosophical Study*, Cambridge, MA: Harvard University Press.

Lundvall, Bengt-Åke (1991), 'Explaining Inter-Firm Cooperation and Innovation: Limits of the Transaction Cost Approach', mimeo, Institute for Production, Aalborg University, March.

Olson, Mancur (1965), *The Logic of Collective Action*, Cambridge, MA: Harvard University Press.

Rivaud-Danset, Dorothée, and Robert Salais (1992), 'Les conventions des financement des entreprises. Premières approches théorique et empirique', *Revue française d'économie*, 7:4, 81–120.

Sandler, Todd (1992), *Collective Action: Theory and Applications*, Ann Arbor: University of Michigan Press.

Schotter, Andrew (1981), *The Economic Theory of Social Institutions*, New York: Cambridge University Press.

Schumpeter, Joseph A. (1911), *Theorie der wirtschaftlichen Entwicklung: Eine Untersuchung über Unternehmengewinn, Kapital, Kredit, Zins und den Konjunkturzyklus*, 4th edn, Munich and Leipzig: Duncker & Humblot, 1935.

Sharpe, Steven A. (1990), 'Asymmetric information, bank lending, and implicit contracts: a stylized model of customer relationships', *Journal of Finance*, 45, 1069–87.

Sugden, Robert (1986), *The Economics of Rights, Cooperation, and Welfare*, Oxford: Basil Blackwell.

Sugden, Robert (1991), 'Rational choice: a survey of contributions from economics and philosophy', *Economic Journal*, 101, 751–85.

Ullmann-Margalit, Edna (1977), *The Emergence of Norms*, Oxford: Clarendon Press.

Witt, Ulrich (1989), 'The evolution of economic institutions as a propagation "process"', *Public Choice*, 62, 155–72.

PART IV

Markets, Economic Systems and
the Role of Moral Norms

10. Varieties of capitalism and varieties of economic theory

Geoffrey M. Hodgson

The twentieth century has been dominated by the ideological polarization between capitalism and socialism. Strikingly, what has emerged out of the recent collapse of the Eastern Bloc is the view that we are now at 'the end of history' (Fukuyama, 1992). It is widely held that liberal-democratic capitalism is the normal or ideal state of affairs: once established and refined it cannot be surpassed.

I challenge this view here – but not by arguing for the feasibility or superiority of a socialist or any other alternative to capitalism. Essentially, pronouncements of the 'end of history' ignore the tremendous variety of forms of capitalism itself. In addition, a theoretical blindness to the immense variety within the modern system is curiously engendered by influential economic theorists from both right and left. In particular, although both Karl Marx and Friedrich Hayek have contributed an enormous amount to our understanding of how capitalist systems function, they both sustain a view of a singular and purified capitalism.

Furthermore, there is no unique or optimal combination of subsystems and institutions within capitalism that will necessarily triumph over other combinations. Although not all capitalisms are equal in performance, the advantages or efficiencies of one type of capitalism over another are typically dependent on their historical path and context and thereby none can be said to be ultimately superior to all the others.

The views of the American institutional economists, particularly Thorstein Veblen, provide an important counter to the differing approaches of Marx, Hayek and other authors on these questions. This chapter is about the theoretical and conceptual tools required to perceive and understand the actually existing variety of different forms of capitalism.

THE UNIVERSALITY OF NEOCLASSICAL ECONOMICS

Instead of the characteristic features of a given economic system, the starting point of neoclassical economics is the ahistorical, abstract individual.[1] The features and institutions that characterize a given economy do not form part of its core analysis. In starting from allegedly universal and ahistorical concepts, neoclassical economics fails to become rooted in any specific socio-economic system. Its very generality becomes a barrier to a deeper understanding of capitalism or other systems. Instead of attempting to confront a particular economy, or *real* object, it becomes confined to a remotely abstract and artificial *idea* of an economy.

Lionel Robbins (1932) encapsulated this approach with his famous but ahistorical definition of economics as the 'science of choice'. The economic problem becomes one of the allocation of scarce means in the pursuit of given ends. Individuals are assumed to have fixed and given utility functions and they exchange resources with each other to maximize their own utility. It is alleged that a wide range of social and economic phenomena can be analysed in these terms.

The door is thus opened to what is described by its practitioners as 'economic imperialism': the invasion of other social sciences with the choice-theoretic methods of neoclassical economics, informed by the presumed universality of such ideas as scarcity, competition and rational self-interest.[2] Yet scarcity and competition are not so universal as the economic imperialists presume.[3]

The Hidden, Ideological Specifics

In a direct attack on neoclassical economics, Marshall Sahlins (1972) shows that tribal economies differ from capitalism in that they do not generate ever-increasing wants. Tribal, hunter-gatherer societies in tropical regions are faced with such an abundance of food and other necessities that resources are, for practical purposes, unlimited. Thus, against the neoclassical view, it is possible for there to be vast resources and scarce wants.

The limitation of the neoclassical concept of scarcity is also, but perhaps more appropriately, exhibited with respect to the issue of information and knowledge. Information is a peculiar commodity because if it is sold it can be still retained by the seller. Neither skills nor knowledge are given or limited, because of the phenomenon of 'learning by doing'. As Albert Hirschman (1985, p. 16) points out, 'Use of a resource such as a skill has the immediate effect of improving the skill, of enlarging (rather than depleting) its availability'.

Especially in the growing and knowledge-intensive economies of modern capitalism the so-called 'law' of scarcity is thus broken. Even if neoclassical economics abandons its universalist claims and applies itself to a more limited set of types of economic system it still ill-fits the modern age.

The concept of the utility-maximizing individual in a world of scarcity that is seemingly typified in a capitalist society is frequently extended without warranty by neoclassical economics to all forms of socio-economic system. Although neoclassical economics often claims to be universal, by stressing individualism, scarcity and competition its analysis reflects dominant ideological conceptions found in Europe and America in the modern age.

However, ideology does not necessarily correspond with reality. It is inaccurate to suggest that neoclassical economics strictly represents a capitalist or market economy (Hodgson, 1992a). It is admitted – even by leading exponents – that neoclassical economic theory does not satisfactorily encompass money, markets or firms![4] Neoclassical economics is not only strictly inaccurate but also insufficiently specific. The irony is that by attempting to erect a universal analysis of socio-economic behaviour, neoclassical economics ends up basing itself on a specific set of concepts seemingly associated with an individualistic and competitive market economy. That which is meant to be universal turns out in the end to be specific. Yet the specificity is not that of the real features of any actually existing capitalism.

The Limits of Contract and Exchange

Importantly, neoclassical economics addresses all social relations as if they were subject to contracts and exchange. Accordingly, neoclassical theorist Gary Becker (1976a) has developed a theoretical model of the family that treats the household as if it were itself a market and contract-based institution, essentially indistinguishable from a capitalist firm. Yet modern cultural norms make a very strong differentiation between, on the one hand, domestic and sexual activities obtained by money payment, and, on the other, those obtained by non-commercial means. Neoclassical theory is generally blind to these moral, cultural and institutional distinctions. There is no conceptual dividing line between the family and the marketplace. Accordingly, neoclassical economics is unable to conceptualize the specific institutional features of the household and the special human relations within that sphere.

This conceptual blindness is a serious handicap. Apart from failing to recognize the difference between commercial and non-commercial institutions and practices within capitalism, the question of the intrinsic limits to markets and contracts is thereby not addressed. This has devastating consequences both for the analysis of different types of capitalism and for the recognition of the limits to capitalism itself.

Notably, the modern family is still not completely invaded by commercial relations, and cultural norms are still sensitive to this fact. In fact, there are practical and more general limits to the extension of market and contractual relations within capitalism. Indeed, an over-extension of market and purely contractarian relations would threaten to break up cultural and other bonds that are necessary for the functioning of the system as a whole. As Joseph Schumpeter (1976, pp. 423–4) argues, 'no social system can work which is based exclusively upon a network of free contracts between (legally) equal contracting parties and in which everyone is supposed to be guided by nothing except his own (short-run) utilitarian ends'.

Consideration of the uncertainty governing the employee–employer relationship in the capitalist firm leads Alan Fox (1974) to argue convincingly that an element of supra-contractual trust is essential to industrial relations, and that a purely contractual system is not feasible.[5] The whole point about trust is that it is undermined by the cost calculus. As Arrow (1974, p. 23) candidly remarks: 'Trust is an important lubricant of the social system. ... If you have to buy it, you already have some doubts about what you've bought.' On reflection, trust is not best explained as a phenomenon resulting simply from the rational calculation of costs and benefits by given individuals: something else is involved. Accordingly, trust cannot be modelled with the universal contractarian framework of utility-maximization and exchange upon which neoclassical economics is based. Such an approach, which misses the specific cultural features and social relations involved in the generation and protection of trust, will be unable to understand some essential and specific features of any capitalist system.

In fact, the distinction between commercial and non-commercial relations within any capitalist society is both indelible and central to the nature of capitalism. Significantly, the precise boundaries of the demarcation profoundly affect the nature of the specific variety of capitalist system.

Actor and Structure

Neoclassical economics places great emphasis on individuality and choice. However, it is not only arguable that free choice is in fact denied, but also that neoclassical theory makes the individual a prisoner of his or her immanent and often invariable preferences and beliefs (Loasby, 1976, p. 5).

In modern neoclassical economics the individual, in all her richness and complexity, is simply reduced to a well-behaved preference function that obeys textbook axioms. The possible origins of this preference function in the human psyche or the social world are left unexplained. As argued at length elsewhere (Hodgson, 1988) this conception of the individual regards the person as detachable from the rich cultural world and the web of institutions upon which we depend. Instead, the individual is regarded as a self-contained contractarian atom. Institutions, in so far as they exist, are treated as the product of individual interactions and not as the moulders of individual purposes and preferences.

FRIEDRICH HAYEK AND THE INEVITABILITY OF MARKETS

With the Austrian School of economists an ahistorical conception of the individual with 'purposes and individual knowledge' is the point of departure.

There are obvious differences of policy outlook between Marx and Hayek. However, we are less concerned here about policy conclusions and more with Hayek's theoretical framework and his explicit or implicit conception of capitalism. On these points some remarkable convergences with Marx will later be noted.

In some passages Hayek (1982, vol. 3, p. 162) treats the market as the general context in which competition takes place: a forum in which individual property owners collide. Criticizing Hayek on this point, Viktor Vanberg (1986, p. 75) points out that the market 'is always a system of social interaction characterized by a specific *institutional framework*, that is, by a *set of rules* defining certain restrictions on the behavior of market participants'. Whether these rules are formal or informal the result is that there is no such thing as the 'true, unhampered market', operating in an institutional vacuum. 'This raises the issue of what rules can be considered "appropriate" in the sense of allowing for a beneficial working of the market mechanism' (*ibid.*, p. 97).

Notably, the market itself is a *social institution*, governed by sets of rules defining restrictions on some, and legitimating other, behaviours. Furthermore, the market is necessarily embedded in other social institutions such as the state, and is promoted or even in some cases created by conscious design.[6] Accordingly, it is reasonable to pay significant attention to the possibility of the emergence of different kinds of markets, with varied structures and constituent rules. Yet Jim Tomlinson (1990, p. 121) finds that Hayek, along with most other economists including neoclassicals and Marxists, treats the market as an abstract principle, independent of its institutional and cultural integument. In reality, however, markets are highly varied phenomena.

The Problem of Necessary Impurities

Clearly, higher levels of competitive selection must involve the selection of different types of institution, including varieties of both market and non-market forms. To work at such higher levels, institutional competition must involve different types of ownership structure and resource allocation mechanisms, all coexisting in a mixed economy. This is quite contrary to Hayek's preferred policy stance. Hayek follows the views of his teacher, von Mises (1949, p. 259) in proposing not only that a mixture of socialism with capitalism is impossible, but that capitalism prospered best in a 'pure' form. However, whilst Hayek and von Mises provided strong arguments why a socialist economic system planned entirely from the centre is not feasible (Hayek, 1935) they fail to demonstrate satisfactorily why a mixed economy is either unfeasible or severely disadvantageous.

Hayek and his co-thinkers have inspired policies to extend 'free markets' and 'roll back the state'. The view is that such policies are necessary both for economic efficiency and personal liberty. It is assumed that the extension of commercial contracts and individual property rights is both possible and desirable, and even necessary if civilization is to survive.

However, far from heralding an era of individual liberty, governments committed to these or similar ideas have often taken an authoritarian tone, such as that in Britain in the 1980s under the premiership of Margaret Thatcher. As Karl Polanyi (1944) argues in his classic study of the Industrial Revolution in Britain, the initial extension of the market was very much an act of the state. Subsequently there was strong pressure from all quarters to restrict the market through legislation to limit the working day, ensure public health, institute social insurance and regulate trade. Not only to provide social cohesion but also to ensure the smooth working of the market itself, the state had to protect, regulate, subsidize, standardize and intervene. Thus the extension of markets did not mean the diminution of the powers of the state, but instead led to increasing intrusion and regulation by central government. Accordingly, even in Victorian Britain, the introduction of free markets, far from doing away with the need for control, regulation and intervention, enormously increased their range. This was true *a fortiori* in France and Germany, where markets were typically more closely regulated.

Polanyi argues that the creation and maintenance of private property rights and functioning market institutions require the sustained intervention of the state to eject economic forms and institutions that are antagonistic to the private market system. Paradoxically, therefore, 'free market' policies can lead to a substantial centralization of economic and political power. Hayekian policies in practice actually threaten both economic and political pluralism and grant extended powers to the central state. Extreme individualism paradoxically takes on a totalitarian quality. Social forms and ideologies other than free-market individualism and private property are driven out.

It should again be emphasized that the unqualified goal of the 'free' market ignores the fact that trade and markets rely on other antiquated and often rigid institutions and other traditional features of social culture. As we shall see below, and despite their policy differences, both Marx and Hayek ignore the necessary 'impurities' in a market system.

There are many examples of essential but non-commercial spheres of activity within capitalism. One such example is the family, but this topic is awkwardly side-stepped in Hayek's writings. As Tomlinson (1990, p. 131) points out, families 'are extremely problematic in their implications for liberty in Hayek's sense'. Hayek ignores the question of what kind of liberty is provided for children within this institution, as well as the implications for liberalism of a lifelong marriage contract between partners. To address this issue, Hayekians may well have to abandon either extreme liberalism, or a conservative commitment to family values, or both.

Admittedly, the market continues to play an indispensable role in the modern era, but it is deceptive to suggest that it is the primary arena of social interaction for most agents. Even in contemporary economies much more daily activity is internal to organizations and outside the market (Simon, 1991).

Actor and Structure

Hayek does not believe in the inevitability of capitalism, socialism or any other type of economic system. In part this is because he emphasizes the essential creativity and potential novelty of human action. Yet in emphasizing the indeterminacy of human action the task of explaining what lies behind it is abandoned. Whilst Marx assumes that individuals are driven by their class position and interest, Hayek is reluctant to attempt to explain individual human actions. Both specific human motivations and systemic outcomes are indeterminate in his theory.

The polar opposite position would be to suggest that structures and institutions entirely determine human behaviour. Elsewhere it has been argued that some intermediate position is possible (Giddens, 1984; Hodgson, 1988). There are external influences moulding the purposes and actions of individuals, but action is not entirely determined by them. The environment is influential but it does not completely determine either what the individual aims to do or what he or she may achieve. The individual is ridden by habits of thought but not bereft of choice.

Both neoclassical and Austrian theorists start from universal assumptions about socio-economic systems and human behaviour. For Hayek the transhistorical elements of theoretical analysis are individuals and rules. There are markets but generally their specific nature is regarded as unproblematic and their prior existence is often assumed. Because of the extreme generality of his perspective, and despite the sophistication of his systemic view, he cannot enrich his theory with the specificities either of capitalism or of any particular type of capitalism. All Hayek can do is to recommend the best constitutional arrangement that is compatible with the bland generalities of markets, private property and individual liberty. On the abundant, actual or potential variety of forms of capitalism – and of human cultures and behaviours within capitalism – he has nothing of significance to say.

KARL MARX AND THE TRIUMPH OF CAPITALISM

Mainstream economists take the analytical starting point of the ahistorical, abstract individual. Marx's approach is different. As revealed in a letter to Pavel Annenkov, written in 1846, Marx expounds the methodological rule that '*economic categories* are but *abstractions* of ... real relations, that they are truths only in so far as those relations continue to exist'. This contrasts 'with bourgeois economists who regard those economic categories as eternal laws and not as historical laws which are laws only for a given historical development, a specific development of the productive forces' (Marx and Engels, 1982, p. 100).

In Marx's view, ahistorical categories such as 'utility', 'choice' and 'scarcity' cannot capture the essential features of a specific economic system. His recognition of the processes of historical development and revolutionary transformation of human society leads him to the choice of sets of specific concepts that capture the essences of particular, transient systems. Marx claims that the core categories in *Capital* are abstract expressions of real social relations found within the capitalist mode of production. Such categories are held to be operational as long as these social relations exist.

Marx's aim is to analyse the type of economy emerging in Britain and Europe in the nineteenth century. Thus in the Preface to the first edition of *Capital* he makes it clear that his objective is to examine not economies in general, nor even socialism, but 'the capitalist mode of production'. It is the 'ultimate aim' of that work 'to reveal the economic law of motion of modern society' (Marx, 1976, pp. 90, 92).

Marx does not start with a general and ahistorical 'economic problem'. Instead, Marx's economic analysis starts from what he regards as the essential social relations of the capitalist mode of production. This is clear from the key words in the titles of the opening chapters of *Capital*: commodities, exchange, money, capital, and labour power. Marx did not aim to write a text on economics that would be applicable to all economic systems. No such work, in his view, is possible. He argues that it is necessary to focus on a particular economic system and the particular relations and laws that governed its operation and evolution.

Contrary to empiricism, Marx accepts the need for a prior conceptual framework in order to understand the world. Generally, in their analysis of socio-economic systems social scientists are obliged to rely on 'ideal types'. Ideal types are abstract descriptions of phenomena that indicate the general features upon which a theorist will focus for purposes of explanation (Weber, 1968). A process of abstraction must occur where the essential structures and features of the system are identified. The crucial question, of course, is which ideal type is to be selected in the analysis of a given phenomenon.

Marx considers several possible types of socio-economic system, such as feudalism and classical antiquity in the past and the possibility of communism in the future. In specifying such different economic systems, Marx sees the need to develop specific analyses of the structure and dynamic of each one.

Clearly the definition of each type of economic system is crucial. The capitalist mode of production is regarded by Marx as a socio-economic system in which most production takes place in capitalist firms. Commodities are defined by Marx as goods or services that are typically exchanged on the market. The products of capitalist firms are commodities. Marx (1981, p. 1019) clearly identifies a 'characteristic trait' of the capitalist mode of production system as follows:

> It produces its products as commodities. The fact that it produces commodities does not in itself distinguish it from other modes of production; but that the dominant and determining character of its product is the commodity certainly does so. This means, first of all, that ... labour generally appears as wage-labour ... [and] the relationship of capital to wage-labour determines the whole character of the mode of production.

In short, for Marx, capitalism is generalized commodity production.[7] It is generalized in a double sense: first, because under capitalism most goods and services are produced for sale on the market, that is, they are commodities; second, because under capitalism one item is importantly a commodity: labour power. In other words, an important feature of capitalism is the existence of a labour market in which labour is hired by an employer.

The general relations that define the capitalist system are seen to validate the primary deployment of core concepts such as the commodity, exchange, money, capital, and labour power. For instance, the use of the concept of the commodity is validated by the generality of the commodity-form under capitalism itself. The upshot of this methodological procedure is that Marxian economics is distinguished radically from classical, neoclassical and Austrian economics.

The Hidden, Ahistorical Universals

However, there are major problems with this approach. First, whilst the historically specific analytical system seems to validate the key analytical concepts in the above manner, it does not validate its own meta-theoretical apparatus. Close examination of *Capital* indicates that at crucial stages in his argument Marx himself has to fall back on transcendental, ahistorical concepts. Most obviously, the concept of capitalism invokes the ahistorical concept of the mode of production. Further, in the very first chapter Marx invokes the ahistorical concept of use-value in his discussion of commodities and exchange. It is recognized that specific use-values may be socially and historically conditioned but the very concept of use-value, unlike the concept of a commodity, is not.

Similarly, the analysis of the production process in Chapter 7 of Volume 1 relies on a conceptual distinction between, on the one hand, labour in general – that is, the idea of labour as an activity that permeates all kinds of economic system – and, on the other, the organization and processes of production that are specific to capitalism. Likewise, the distinction between labour and labour power is conceptually quite general although the specific phenomenon of the hiring of labour power by an employer is far from universal. There are many other examples, including the twin concepts of forces and relations of production and Marx's general and quite universal theory that socio-economic change is promoted when the developing forces of production come up against and break down allegedly antiquated productive relations.

Indeed, the very generality and universality of the concept of labour in Marx's analysis helps him to sustain a supra-historical picture of labour as the life blood of all economic systems. This leads to the perceptive observation of Marco Lippi (1979) that despite the claimed historical specificity of Marx's analysis of 'value' in *Capital* it rests essentially on an ahistorical and 'naturalistic' concept of labour. Similarly, Elias Khalil (1990) shows that Marx's transhistorical concept of social labour amounts to asserting that the actions of agents can be *ex ante* calculated according to a global rationality. The assumption of global rationality is itself a reflection of the specific Western intellectual culture of the nineteenth century and ironically is prominent in neoclassical economic theory as well. This assumption links Marx's theoretical analysis of capitalism with his faith in the supposedly rational order of socialism.[8]

Marx is not being criticized here for appealing to universal and ahistorical categories. On reflection such an invocation is unavoidable. Any attempt to establish historically specific categories must itself rely on a transcendent imperative. There seems to be no way of avoiding this. However, Marx gives insufficient attention to this problem and provides only a limited discussion of the meta-theoretical issues involved. Furthermore, he falls back on a set of questionable categories and places unwarranted weight on his particular and rationalistic concept of social labour.

Again irony: but with double strength. Neoclassical economists attempt to construct a universal framework of socio-economic analysis but end up viewing the universe through the distorting lenses of a specific type of economic system. The universality of their allegedly universal principles is thus questioned. Marx, on the other hand, knowingly reacts from this kind of approach and attempts to site his analysis of specific systems on specific concepts appropriate to that system. Yet contrary to his own arguments he ends up relying on concepts and theories that are in fact universal. Neoclassical economics aspires to universality but ends up being specific; Marxism aspires to specificity but ends up relying on the general.

The Problem of Necessary Impurities

Further difficulties arise if the dominant system depends upon other subsystems or impurities. When analysing the capitalist system Marx assumes away all the non-capitalist elements in that system. This is not merely an initial, simplifying assumption. They are assumed away at the outset, never to be reincorporated at a later stage of the analysis. This is because he believes that commodity exchange and the hiring of labour power in a capitalist firm will become increasingly widespread, displacing all other forms of economic coordination and productive organization. Thus in the *Communist Manifesto*, Marx and Engels proclaim:

> The bourgeoisie ... has put an end to all feudal, patriarchal, idyllic relations ... and has left remaining no other nexus between man and man than naked self-interest, than callous 'cash payment'. ... The bourgeoisie has torn away from the family its sentimental veil, and has reduced the family relation to a mere money relation. (Marx, 1973, p. 70)

Certainty of the all-consuming power of capitalist markets is Marx's justification for ignoring impurities within the capitalist system. These are regarded as doomed and extraneous hangovers of the feudal past. Just as capitalism and commodity-exchange are assumed to become all-powerful, the theoretical system is built on these structures and relations alone.

Yet it has been noted above that some of the crucial subsystems within capitalism are unlikely ever to become organized on a strictly capitalist basis. Again consider the family. Contrary to Marx, there are practical and theoretical limitations to the operation of the market within that sphere. If the rearing of children was carried out on a capitalist basis then they would be strictly owned as property by the owners of the household 'firm' and eventually sold like slaves on the market. Yet anti-slavery laws within capitalism prevent the possession and sale of one person by another. Hence within capitalism the household can never typically be internally organized on the basis of markets, individual ownership and profit. Ironically, in both neoclassical and Marxian economics the characteristic features of the family disappear from view. Just as the neoclassical economists treat all human activities as if they took the form of contracted exchange, Marx wrongly assumes that the entire capitalist system can be understood solely on the basis of commodity exchange and the exploitation of hired labour power.[9]

As argued above, there are general limits to the extension of market and contractual relations within capitalism. The spread of market and contractarian relations can threaten to break up cultural and other bonds that are necessary for the functioning of the system as a whole. In particular, as Polanyi and Schumpeter have emphasized, the state is partly responsible for the bonding of society and the prevention of its dissolution into atomistic units by the corroding action of market relations.

The 'impurity principle' is proposed as a general idea applicable to all economic systems. The idea is that every socio-economic system must rely on at least one structurally dissimilar subsystem to function. There must always be a coexistent plurality of modes of production, so that the social formation as a whole has the requisite structural variety to cope with change. Thus if one type of structure is to prevail (for example, central planning), other structures (for example, markets, private firms) are necessary to enable the system as a whole to work effectively. As Michel Albert (1993, p. 101) writes succinctly: 'Just as there can be no socialist society in which all goods and services are free, so can there be no capitalist society in which all goods and services may be bought and sold.' In particular, neither planning nor markets can become all-embracing systems of socio-economic regulation. In general, it is not feasible for one mode of production to become so comprehensive that it drives out all the others. Every system relies on its 'impurities'.[10]

Although it cannot be formally proved, part of the justification for this principle can be derived from an analysis of past socio-economic formations in history. Capitalism today depends on the 'impurities' of the family, household production and the state. The slave mode of production of classical times depended on the military organization of the state as well as trade and an external market. Likewise, feudalism relied on both regulated markets and a powerful church. Finally, without extensive, legal or illegal markets the Soviet-type system of central planning would have ceased to function long before 1989. In each of the four major modes of production after Christ (slavery, feudalism, capitalism and Soviet-type societies) at least one 'impurity', that is, a non-dominant economic structure, has played a functional role in the reproduction of the system as a whole. What is involved is more than an empirical observation that different structures and systems have coexisted through history. What is involved is an assertion that some of these economic structures were *necessary* for the socio-economic system to function over time. As shown elsewhere (Hodgson, 1984, pp. 106–9; 1988, pp. 257, 303–4), additional and related arguments for the impurity principle can be derived from systems theory.

However, whilst the impurity principle contends that different kinds of subsystem are necessary for the system as a whole to function, it does not specify the particular kind of subsystem nor the precise boundaries between each subsystem and the system as a whole. Indeed, a variety of types of system and subsystem can feasibly be combined.[11] Furthermore, the boundaries between subsystem and dominant system are likely to be highly variable. Significantly, the nature of the combination and the precise boundaries of the demarcation profoundly affect the nature of the specific variety of capitalist system. A corollary of the impurity principle is the contention that an immense variety of forms of any given socio-economic system can exist.

Actor and Structure

Another acute problem in Marx's perspective is that human motivations are not explained in any detail: they are assumed to spring in broad and mysterious terms from the relations and forces of the system. As Marx (1981, pp. 1019–20) puts it: 'The principal agents of this mode of production itself, the capitalist and the wage-labourer, are as such *simply* embodiments and personifications of capital and wage-labour – specific social characters that the social production process stamps on individuals, products of these specific social relations of production' (emphasis added).

Accordingly, when discussing the mechanisms of change, Marx is extremely vague. There is reference to 'productive forces', as if technology itself is a driving force. True, it is assumed that workers will typically struggle for bigger wages and shorter hours, and capitalists for enhanced profits. But these are little else than the principles of maximization also common to neoclassical theory. What is missing is an explanation of the historical origin of such calculative behaviour and the mode of its cultural transmission. Marx assumes that values and motives are simply functional to the pursuit of class and economic interests.

Thus Marx believed that the class position of the workers as employed labourers, coupled with the tendency of capitalism itself to bring workers together in larger and larger firms and cities, would lead to the eventual combination and revolt of the working class against the capitalist system. Yet well over a hundred years after Marx's death there still has not been a single successful socialist revolution in any advanced capitalist country. Marx's faith that class positions and relations themselves are sufficient to impel action has to be questioned.

This issue is addressed by Michael Burawoy (1979). His detailed study of production workers in the United States shows that hierarchy and authority on the shop floor are themselves unlikely to lead to the production of socialist ideology or revolt. Shop floor culture and practices are not a likely transmission belt from wage labour to socialist revolution.

INSTITUTIONALISM AND VARIETIES OF CAPITALISM

We now turn to the alternative framework of the 'old' institutional economics. While it is argued that this intellectual tradition has the means to overcome some of the aforementioned problems, the institutionalist solution is underdeveloped.

Veblen's Critique of Marx

Veblen highlights the analytical gap in Marx's analysis between actor and structure. Although sympathetic to much of Marx's analysis of capitalism, he notes that it fails to connect the actor with the specific structure and to explain thereby human motivation and action. Forest Hill (1958, p. 139) elaborates Veblen's critique of Marx as follows:

In Veblen's opinion, Marx uncritically adopted natural rights and natural law preconceptions and a hedonistic psychology of rational self-interest. On these bases Marx elaborated his labor theory of value, with labor as the source and measure of value, and the corollary doctrines of labor's right to its full product, of surplus value, and exploitation of labor. He attributed rational self-interest not only to individuals but to entire classes, thereby explaining their asserted solidarity and motivation in class struggle. Veblen rejected the concept of rational class interest and the labor theory of value, along with its corollaries and natural rights basis.

Marx saw his scientific analysis of capitalism in *Capital* as a potentially revolutionary instrument in helping the working class both to analyse and end its own exploitation. However, Veblen rejected Marx's view that if working people reflected rationally upon their situation they would be impelled to criticize and revolt against the capitalist system. The questionable assumption of potential rational transparency is crucial here, and connects with Marx's teleology. As Stephen Edgell and Jules Townshend (1993, p. 728) elaborate:

Marx's portrayal of humankind as potentially rational also resolves the puzzle as to why Marx could simultaneously entertain the idea of an historical telos, with its deterministic implications, and uphold the voluntaristic and reflexive notions of praxis or practical activity. He assumes that workers – through rational thought, through reflecting on their experience of capitalism, and notably through their increasing immiseration and growing collective strength, will inevitably want and be able to overthrow it.

Essentially, the process of rational reflection is seen to drive the working class to the same 'inevitable' outcome. Even if we stress a more open-ended and less deterministic account of capitalist development than the one in the famous 'Preface' to the *Contribution to the Critique of Political Economy*, 'we are still left with a highly teleological theory of capitalism, with its downfall being the inevitable result of its inner contradictions' (Edgell and Townshend, 1993, p. 729).

Veblen rejected the continuously calculating, marginally adjusting agent of neoclassical theory to emphasize inertia and habit instead. Institutions are defined by Veblen (1919, p. 239) as 'settled habits of thought common to the generality of men'. They are seen as both outgrowths and reinforcers of the routinized thought processes that are shared by a number of persons in a given society. Institutions thereby help sustain habits of action and thought: 'The situation of today shapes the institutions of tomorrow through a selective, coercive process, by acting upon men's habitual view of things, and so altering or fortifying a point of view or a mental attitude handed down from the past' (Veblen, 1899, pp. 190–1). Importantly, Veblen also emphasizes the importance of novelty and human creativity and distances himself from cultural or institutional determinism. Furthermore, it is recognized that institutions are not simply constraints (Commons, 1934, p. 73).

The importance of institutions in shaping thought and action is implied in Veblen's attack on Marx's 'materialist conception of history'. This, according to Veblen (1919, p. 314), has very little to say regarding the efficient force, the channels, or the methods by which the economic situation is conceived to have its effect upon institutions. What answer the early Marxists gave to this question, of how the economic situation shapes institutions, was to the effect that causal connection lies through the selfish, calculating class interest. But, while class interest may count for much in the outcome, this answer is plainly not a competent one, since, for one thing, institutions by no means change with the alacrity which the sole efficiency of reasoned class interest would require.

Veblen suggests that the mere class position of an individual as a wage labourer or a capitalist tells us very little about the specific conceptions or habits of thought of the individuals involved. Even if the worker's interests would be served by joining a trade union, or voting for a political party that proclaims common ownership of the means of production, there is no necessary reason why the worker's position as an employee would necessarily impel him or her to necessarily take such actions. Individual interests, whatever they are, do not necessarily lead to accordant individual actions. Hence Veblen criticizes Marx's implicit rationalism in the following terms:

> it must be held that men's reasoning is largely controlled by other than logical, intellectual forces; that the conclusion reached by public or class opinion is as much, or more, a matter of sentiment than of logical inference; and that the sentiment which animates men, singly or collectively, is as much, or more, an outcome of habit and native propensity as of calculated material interest. There is, for instance, no warrant ... for asserting *a priori* that the class interest of the working class will bring them to· take a stand against the propertied class. (Veblen, 1919, p. 441)

In other words, the assumption of a class interest and rational calculation tells us nothing about the habits, concepts and frameworks of thought which are used to appraise reality, nor about the mode of calculation used to perceive a supposed optimum.

Contrary to Marx, human agents will not gravitate to a single view of the truth simply on the basis of empirical evidence and rational reflection. As Veblen (1919, p. 442) pointed out, the members of the working class could perceive their own salvation just as much in terms of patriotism or nationalism as in socialist revolution. The class position of an agent – exploiter or exploited – does not imply that that person will be impelled towards any particular view of reality or any particular pattern of action. Contrary to Marx, a given social structure or class system does not imply a tendency towards particular patterns of behaviour. This, as Abram Harris (1932, p. 743) has rightly noted, 'is the weakest link in his chain of reasoning'.

Such arguments have a wide relevance and apply to other calculative or rationalistic conceptions of action. Accordingly, there is also here an implicit attack on the optimizing rationality of neoclassical economics. The attack is especially apposite when upon a central idea of the 'rational expectations hypothesis', that through mere data-gathering, agents will become aware of the basic, underlying structure and mechanisms of the economy. This hypothesis likewise neglects the conceptual framing involved in the perception of data and the theory-bound character of all observation.

In general, even if objectives are given, neither class interest nor rational reflection upon circumstances will typically lead to a single outcome in terms of either perceptions or actions. For instance, although the capitalists' interests may be best served by striving for ever-greater profits, this tells us little about precise corporate strategy, the mode of management or the precise structure of the firm. In the case of the capitalist the Marxian response to this argument is familiar: capitalist competition will *force* capitalists to follow the more successful route to profit and the accumulation of capital. Lucky or shrewd capitalists will follow this imperative and the others will become marginalized or bankrupt. Thereby the strategy, structure and goals of the firm are uniquely determined by competition. Uncannily, a very similar argument is advanced by the far-from-Marxist Milton Friedman (1953) in a famous paper, where he argues that competitive 'natural selection' is bound to ensure that most if not all surviving firms are profit-maximizing.[12]

In response, Tomlinson (1982) points out that profit cannot act as a simple regulator of the growth or decline of firms. Even if firms are trying to maximize their profits this does not imply a single strategy as to how this maximization is to be achieved. 'Firms like generals have *strategies*, a term which itself implies room for manoeuvre, room for diverse calculations, diverse practices to be brought to bear on the objective' (p. 34). More concretely, case studies reveal a varied repertoire of strategic responses by firms. Note the study by Richard Whittington (1989) of the varied strategic behaviour of firms enduring a common recession, and the remarks about firm discretionary behaviour made by Richard Nelson (1991).

Veblen's theory of cumulative causation is both his answer to the Marxian argument that only strategic response is possible and his rebuff to the neoclassical concept of equilibrium. He sees both the circumstances and temperament of individuals as part of the cumulative processes of change: 'The economic life history of the individual is a cumulative process of adaptation of means to ends that cumulatively change as the process goes on, both the agent and his environment being at any point the outcome of the last process' (Veblen, 1919, pp. 74–5). Directly or indirectly influenced by Veblen, the notion of cumulative causation is developed by Allyn Young (1928), Gunnar Myrdal (1957), K. William Kapp (1976), Nicholas Kaldor (1985) and others. It relates to the modern idea that technologies and economic systems can get 'locked in' – and sometimes as a result of initial accidents – to relatively constrained paths of development (Arthur, 1989). Hence there is 'path dependency' rather than convergence to a given equilibrium. History matters.

Veblen's concept of cumulative causation is an antidote to both neoclassical and Marxian economic theory. Contrary to the equilibrium analysis of neoclassical economics, Veblen sees the economic system not as a 'self-balancing mechanism' but as a 'cumulatively unfolding process'. As Myrdal and Kaldor argue at length, the processes of cumulative causation suggest that regional and national development is generally divergent rather than convergent. This contradicts the typical emphasis within neoclassical economic theory on processes of compensating feedback and mutual adjustment via the price mechanism leading to greater uniformity and convergence.

Contrary to much Marxist and neoclassical thinking, Veblen argues that multiple futures are possible. Equilibriating forces do not always pull the economy back onto a single track. This exposes a severe weakness in Marx's conception of history. Veblen argues against the idea of finality or consummation in economic development. Variety and cumulative causation mean that history has 'no final term' (Veblen, 1919, p. 37). In Marxism the final term is communism or the classless society, but Veblen rejects the teleological concept of a final goal. This means a rejection of the ideas of the 'inevitability' of socialism and of a 'natural' outcome or end-point in capitalist evolution. There is no natural path, or law, governing economic development. Accordingly, and in rejecting any inevitability in capitalist development, Veblen accepts the possibility of varieties of capitalism and different paths of capitalist development.

Specificity and Universality

It has been noted that neoclassical and Marxian economics get trapped in obverse types of problem when it comes to assumptions about specificity or universality in economic analysis. Neoclassical economics is built on allegedly universal assumptions but these are not, in fact, universally applicable: they reflect the specific ideology of a particular moment of capitalist development. The analytical starting point of Marxian economics is the specific features and relations of the capitalist mode of production but the analysis ends up relying on concepts and theories that are in fact universal. Neoclassical economics aspires to universality but ends up being specific; Marxism aspires to specificity but ends up relying on concepts that are ubiquitous.

Two broad conclusions follow. The first is that the theoretical analysis of a specific economic system cannot rely entirely on concepts drawn exclusively from that system. This is because the very organization and extraction of these concepts must rely on other categories of wider applicability. To talk of capitalism we must refer to other economic systems; if we speak of economic systems we are using that transhistorical concept; and so on. Whilst historical and institutional specificity is important, we are obliged to rely to some degree on the universal.

The second conclusion is that the entire analysis of any given system cannot and should not be based on universal concepts alone. The first levels of abstraction must be quite general, but if those universalist layers are extended too far – as in the case of neoclassical theory – then the danger is that we end up with conceptions that are unable to come to grips with reality. The scope of analysis of the first levels of abstraction should be highly confined.

The above discussion suggests that universal concepts have to be grounded in some way. This is a problem which Marx ignored. A framework at a very high level of generality is provided by systems theory (Bertalanffy, 1971; Emery, 1981; Miller, 1978), particularly as developed and applied to economics by Janos Kornai (1971) and to sociology by Niklas Luhmann (1984). Notably, however, recent systems thinking has moved to encompass evolution as a unifying principle (Laszlo, 1987).

For Veblen the transhistorical analytical framework is evolution. The idea of evolution spans both the biotic and the socio-economic spheres and grounds social theory in some general metaphors and principles. This does not mean that biology has to be slavishly imitated in the social sciences (Hodgson, 1993b). Instead, an appeal to a variety of non-reductionist naturalism provides the transhistorical framework for social science.

In Veblen's (1899, 1919) writings the objects of evolutionary selection are institutions. The institution is a universal concept because institutions of various kinds are present in all human societies. However, specific institutions are historically grounded and are manifest in particular localities and periods of socio-economic development: they are delimited in time and space. The concept of the institution thus provides a link between the general and the specific. Institutions require theorization at both these levels.

The concept of evolution provides a ground plan for the general foundations. Inspired in particular by Darwin and Peirce, Veblen saw the importance and ontological priority of both variation and continuity (Hodgson, 1992b, 1993b). First, there must be sustained variation among institutions, and the sources and mechanisms of renewal of such variation must be considered, be they causal, random or purposive. Veblen considered such sources, including his principle of 'idle curiosity' (Dyer, 1986). Second, there must be some principle of continuity by which institutions endure and some principle of heredity by which succeeding institutions resemble their precedents or ancestors. The self-reinforcing and 'conservative' (Veblen, 1899, p. 191) features of habits and institutions are relevant here, as are the ideas of imitation and 'emulation' (*ibid.*, p. 23). Note that these two 'evolutionary' principles are very general and much broader than the specific mechanisms of evolution outlined by Darwin. The issues here are at root ontological, concerning the sources of novelty and the mechanisms of persistence, and do not themselves involve adherence to any specific evolutionary theory taken from biology or elsewhere.

Institutions as Units of Analysis

Abstraction involves identifying what is central and essential to an entity, and ignoring the superficial. More fundamentally, the identification of features, relations and structures depends upon acts of taxonomy and classification, involving the assignment of sameness and difference. Classification, by bringing together entities in discrete groups, must refer to common qualities. For classification to be enduring, it must be assumed that the common qualities themselves must be invariant. As Philip Mirowski (1989) points out, a kind of 'conservation principle' is required. However: 'No posited invariance holds without exceptions and qualifications. We live in a world of broken symmetries and partial invariances' (*ibid.*, p. 397).

The problem is to develop meaningful and operational principles of invariance on which analysis can be founded. As suggested above, the institutionalist tradition has a tentative answer to this problem, locating invariances in the (imperfect) self-reinforcing mechanisms of (partially) stable social institutions. Institutions have a stable and inert quality, and tend to sustain and thus 'pass on' their important characteristics through time. Institutions are both outgrowths and reinforcers of the routinized thought processes that are shared by a number of persons in a given society.

The power and durability of institutions and routines are manifest in a number of ways. In particular, with the benefit of modern developments in anthropology and psychology it can be seen that institutions play an essential role in providing a cognitive framework for interpreting sense-data and in providing intellectual habits or routines for transforming information into useful knowledge (Hodgson, 1988). The cultural and cognitive functions of institutions have been investigated by anthropologists such as Mary Douglas (1987). Reference to the cognitive functions of institutions and routines is important in understanding their relative stability and capacity to replicate. Indeed, the strong, mutually reinforcing interaction between social institutions and individual cognition provides some significant stability in socio-economic systems, partly by buffering and constraining the diverse and variable actions of many agents. Institutions become cumulatively 'locked in' to relatively stable and constrained paths of development.

Hence the institution is 'a socially constructed invariant' (Mirowski, 1987, p. 1034n.), and institutions can be taken as the units and entities of analysis. This contrasts with the idea of the individual as the irreducible unit of analysis in neoclassical economics, and applies to both microeconomics and macroeconomics. The approach based on institutional specifics rather than ahistorical universals is characteristic of institutional economics, and has parallels in some of the works of the Marxian and post-Keynesian schools.

Notably, institutions fill the key conceptual gap that we have identified in neoclassical, Austrian and Marxian theories. Institutions simultaneously constitute and are constituted by human action. Institutions are both 'subjective' ideas in the heads of agents and 'objective' structures faced by them. The concept of institutions connects the microeconomic world of individual action, of habit and choice, with the macroeconomic sphere of seemingly detached and impersonal structures. Actor and structure are thus connected in a circle of mutual interaction and interdependence.

These remarks are general and ahistorical. Taking an 'evolutionary' or naturalist grounding, the gap at this high level of generality can be filled by institutional economics. It is not suggested that this theoretical work is complete – indeed we have little more to work on than a number of key institutionalist passages – simply that institutionalism offers a most favourable basis for further theoretical development with its core concept of an institution and its deployment of the evolutionary metaphor.

Notably, the very concept of an institution points from the sphere of general principles to the study of the specific. Although some general principles regarding institutions can and have to be established, these tell us very little about the nature and dynamics of specific institutions. Institutional economists have thus rightly argued that it is essential to focus on specific institutions and to understand their nature and dynamics.

There are clearly two temptations to be avoided here. One is to erect an ahistorical theory: 'theory without data'. The other is to eschew theory and system-building for data-gathering: 'data without theory'. But it must be emphasized that this is not a matter of finding a golden mean between such extremes. They are both false navigational poles. It cannot be a question of the appropriate mixture of the two basic ingredients of theory and empirics because data cannot be considered or appraised independently of a theory. All attempts to gather data are informed unavoidably by a set of classificatory concepts and implicit or explicit theories. As well as the importance of concrete data, the primacy of theory has to be emphasized.

CONCLUSION

Clearly, institutional economics needs to be further developed to deal with the important issues raised here. This requires methodological work and conceptual analysis to supplement the foundational work of Veblen and other early institutionalists. An important supplementary idea discussed here is the impurity principle.

Variety and the Impurity Principle

It has been argued above that every socio-economic system must rely on at least one structurally dissimilar subsystem to function. As we have seen, neoclassical economists, Hayek and Marx all fail to recognize this point, although it is accepted by a number of other writers. Incorporating no conceptual distinction between commercial and non-commercial activity, neoclassical economics applies the same choice-theoretic framework to all kinds of social institution and is thus blind to the demarcation between contract-based and other social relations. Hayekian economics, by contrast, recognizes the significance of property and contract and is able to differentiate them from other social relations, but believes unrealistically – and with a strange silence on the question of the family – in the possibility and even necessity of a vast extension of commercial contracts and individual property rights. Finally, although Marx recognizes the coexistence of capitalist with non-capitalist social structures in any capitalist society, he shares with Hayek the view that commodity and market relations could grow to the eventual exclusion of all non-capitalist features.

Neither neoclassical, Hayekian nor Marxian economics recognize the functional *necessity* of non-capitalist structures and relations within capitalism. The critique implied in the impurity principle thus applies to Marx, Hayek and the neoclassical economists with substantial force. The impurity principle clearly dovetails with the ontological emphasis on variety in institutional economics. If every system relies on structurally dissimilar impurities then some degree of variety will always be with us.

It is necessary to adopt a system of analysis that recognizes both different modes of production and the fact that no single mode can triumph overall. All socio-economic systems are inevitably a combination of multiple types of subsystems or modes of production. Unlike neoclassical economics, the theoretical system of Marx is sufficiently sophisticated to recognize some key differences between one type of mode of production and another. However, the failure to recognize the functional necessity of a combination of different modes of production with a single socio-economic system has to be rectified.

The corollary of the impurity principle should be stressed here. By accepting the possible variety of combinations of subsystems with given systems, it is recognized that an immense variety of forms of any given socio-economic system can feasibly exist. The denial of the impurity principle would involve the denial of such a potential variety of combinations.

It is strange that two authors who have provided us with the deepest understanding of the workings of modern capitalism, Marx and Hayek, have little to say about specific economic policies. Marx advocates the broad but undetailed policy of central planning and public ownership. Hayek's policy stance is diametrically opposed to that of Marx but is hardly less bland: we are offered the generalities of more market competition and extended private ownership. Hayek, like Marx and his followers, has very little to say in detailed, policy terms. The common blindness to varieties of capitalism disables their theoretical systems in policy terms.

Varieties of Actually Existing Capitalism

No longer blind to the potential variety of systemic combinations, we may accept that an immense variety of forms of any given economic system can feasibly exist. Consideration of the contrast between Anglo-American and Japanese capitalism is fruitful, involving different boundaries between commercial and pecuniary relations on the one hand and relations of trust and loyalty on the other. The key to the difference lies in history. Capitalism in Britain and America emerged from a remote feudal past. In contrast, the inception of capitalism in Japan was recent, and quasi-feudal codes of loyalty and chivalry are still paramount.

In a classic and seminal study, Ronald Dore (1973) compares British and Japanese industrial relations. Chalmers Johnson (1982) examines the evolution of a distinctive type of industrial policy in Japan. Michio Morishima (1982) sees the origins of the Japanese economic 'miracle' in distinctive cultural traits formed through the interaction of religious, social and technological ideas and practices. Maureen McKelvey (1993) surveys the different kinds of Japanese institutions supporting technological innovation. Marco Orrù (1993) compares different forms of institutional cooperation in Japanese and German capitalism. Kyoko Sheridan (1993) argues that Japan is not on a convergence route to Western-type capitalism but is sustained on a different track by a distinctive type of politico-economic formation. Charles Hampden-Turner and Alfons Trompenaars (1993) survey the enormous diversity of cultures within modern capitalist countries. Richard Whitley (1994) provides a detailed examination of the distinctive forms of corporate structure and firm–market relations now found in East Asia. David Williams (1994) turns Fukuyama's view of an 'end of history' in the shape of American capitalism on its head: in his view Japan is not only a quite distinctive type of capitalist formation but also offers a far greater challenge to Western theories and values than the fallen systems of Eastern Europe have ever represented. Economic analysis cannot afford to remain blind to the immense and persistent variety of forms within modern capitalism.

Table 10.1 Varieties of analysis and varieties of capitalism

	Neoclassical Economics	Austrian Economics	Marxian Economics	Institutional Economics
General Unit of Analysis	given individuals	given individuals	socially formed and socially related individuals	institutions
Capital-Specific Unit of Analysis	—	—	maximizing individuals	institutions in capitalist systems
General Analytical Concepts	utility, scarcity, choice, equilibrium	individual purposeful behaviour, scarcity, choice	labour, labour process, forces of production, relations of production, mode of production	habit, emulation, labour, creativity, cumulative causation, economic relations and systems
Capital-Specific Concepts	—	—	commodities, exchange, money, capital	transactions, money, capital
General Micro-Motive Forces	utility or profit maximization	purposeful individuals	socially conditioned individuals	habit, emulation, curiosity
Capital-Specific Micro-Motive Forces	—	—	capital accumulation, profit maximization and worker resistance	specific cultural and institutional manifestations of capital accumulation, trade union activity, etc.
General Micro-Macro Link	—	—	—	institutions
General Macro-Motive Forces	—	—	forces of production	technological change, institutional inertia
Typical Analytical Outcome	unique general equilibrium, macroeconomic convergence	spontaneous order	typical or common path of historical and capitalist development, leading to communism	cumulatively divergent historical and capitalist developments with no asymptotic state

As suggested in Table 10.1, institutions fill the key conceptual gap that we have identified in neoclassical, Hayekian and Marxian theories. Institutions simultaneously constitute and are constituted by human action: actor and structure are thus connected. Institutional economics thus provides a fruitful approach to the formulation of relevant and operational economic policies. Much of this work may appear descriptive, but there is no reason why it should not be guided by the deepest theoretical and methodological insights. Instead of empty formalism there is the possibility that economics may thus be capable of providing inspiration and sagacious guidance for those in government, finance and business.

NOTES

Earlier versions of this chapter were first presented at the Universities of Cambridge, Manchester and Sheffield, at the 1994 EAEPE Conference in Copenhagen and at the DEMOS Institute in London. This version makes use of material first published in a much shorter article in the *Journal of Economic Issues* in June 1995. The author is grateful to the Association for Evolutionary Economics for permission to make use of this material and to Charles Hampden-Turner, Björn Johnson, Matthew Jones, Janet Knoedler, Klaus Nielsen, Ernesto Screpanti, Ian Steedman, Lazlo Vajda and others for critical and helpful comments.

1. Neoclassical economics may be conveniently defined as an approach which (1) assumes rational, maximizing behaviour by agents with given and stable preference functions, (2) focuses on attained, or movements towards, equilibrium states, and (3) excludes chronic information problems. Notably, some recent developments in modern mainstream economic theory come close to the boundaries of this definition.
2. Prominent 'economic imperialists' include Becker (1976b) and Hirshleifer (1977). See the critiques in Nicolaides (1988) and Udéhn (1992).
3. See, for example, Kropotkin (1902), Mead (1937), Reinheimer (1913).
4. For such statements see, for instance, Arrow (1986), Hahn (1988), and Machlup (1967).
5. This is denied by the transaction cost approach developed by Williamson (1975). For a critique of Williamson and evidence that trust is important see Berger *et al.* (1995).
6. See Commons (1934, p. 713) and Hodgson (1988, Chapter 8).
7. Note, however, that Marx does not explicitly use this three-word definition of capitalism and some Marxist and other economists have expressed a distaste for it. Yet these three words do connote the key issues of property rights, markets, employment relations and thereby class divisions within capitalism.
8. There is a clear link here between Marx's theoretical concept of social labour and his utopian vision of a planned economy. In the *Communist Manifesto* Marx and Engels foresee and welcome the time when of 'all production has been concentrated in the hands of a vast association of the whole nation' (Marx, 1973, p. 87). Accordingly, Marx misleadingly assumes that diversity and variety in the organizational and regulatory structures of production can be dispensed with in favour of a single, all-engrossing organization at the macroeconomic level.
9. With the rise of modern feminism in the 1970s, some Marxian theorists attempted to analyse the family as a distinctive entity. Yet the dominant theoretical approach was to subsume this institution within the parameters of the 'labour theory of value' and the guiding prerogatives of the capitalist order, just as neoclassical economists treat the family simply as another contract-based institution within capitalism.

10. The impurity principle is discussed extensively in Hodgson, 1984 (pp. 85–109, 220–8) and summarised in Hodgson, 1988 (pp. 167–71, 254–62).
11. For this reason the impurity principle is not subject to the charge of functionalism, as Dow (1991) has contended. Functionalism is typically defined as the notion that the contribution of an entity to the maintenance of a system is sufficient to explain the existence of that entity. However, the impurity principle does not purport to explain why any one given mode of production or subsystem exists.
12. Friedman's theoretical argument is criticized by Winter (1964) and Hodgson (1994).

REFERENCES

Albert, Michel (1993), *Capitalism Against Capitalism*, London: Whurr.

Arrow, Kenneth J. (1974), *The Limits of Organization*, New York: Norton.

Arrow, Kenneth J. (1986), 'Rationality of self and others in an economic system', *Journal of Business*, 59, October, pp. S385–99.

Arthur, W. Brian (1989), 'Competing technologies, increasing returns, and lock-in by historical events', *Economic Journal*, 99(1), March, pp. 116–31.

Becker, Gary S. (1976a), *The Economic Approach to Human Behavior*, Chicago: University of Chicago Press.

Becker, Gary S. (1976b), 'Altruism, egoism, and genetic fitness: economics and sociobiology', *Journal of Economic Literature*, 14(2), (December), pp. 817–26.

Berger, Hans, Niels G. Noorderhaven and Bart Nooteboom (1995), 'Determinants of supplier dependence: an empirical study', in John Groenewegen, Christos Pitelis and Sven-Erik Sjöstrand (eds), *On Economic Institutions: Theory and Applications*, Aldershot: Edward Elgar, pp. 195–212.

Bertalanffy, Ludwig von (1971), *General Systems Theory: Foundation Development Applications*, London: Allen Lane.

Burawoy, Michael (1979), *Manufacturing Consent*, Chicago: University of Chicago Press.

Commons, John R. (1934), *Institutional Economics – Its Place in Political Economy*, New York: Macmillan.

Dore, Ronald (1973), *British Factory, Japanese Factory: The Origins of National Diversity in Industrial Relations*, London: George Allen and Unwin.

Douglas, Mary (1987), *How Institutions Think*, London and Syracuse: Routledge and Kegan Paul and Syracuse University Press.

Dow, Gregory K. (1991), Review of G. Hodgson, *Economics and Institutions*, *Journal of Economic Behavior and Organization*, 15, pp. 159–69.

Dyer, Alan W. (1986), 'Veblen on scientific creativity', *Journal of Economic Issues*, 20(1) (March), pp. 21–41.

Edgell, Stephen and Jules Townshend (1993), 'Marx and Veblen on human nature, history, and capitalism: vive la différence!', *Journal of Economic Issues*, 27(3) (September), pp. 721–39.

Emery, Fred E. (ed.) (1981), *Systems Thinking*, 2 vols, Harmondsworth: Penguin.

Fox, Alan (1974), *Beyond Contract: Work, Power and Trust Relations*, London: Faber and Faber.

Friedman, Milton (1953), 'The methodology of positive economics', in M. Friedman, *Essays in Positive Economics*, Chicago: University of Chicago Press, pp. 3–43.

Fukuyama, Francis (1992), *The End of History and the Last Man*, New York: Free Press.

Giddens, Anthony (1984), *The Constitution of Society: Outline of the Theory of Structuration*, Cambridge: Polity Press.

Hahn, Frank H. (1988), 'On monetary theory', *Economic Journal*, 98(4), (December), pp. 957–73.

Hampden-Turner, Charles and Alfons Trompenaars (1993), *The Seven Cultures of Capitalism: Value Systems for Creating Wealth in the United States, Japan, Germany, France, Britain, Sweden, and the Netherlands*, New York: Currency Doubleday.

Harris, Abram L. (1932), 'Types of institutionalism', *Journal of Political Economy*, 40(4) (December), pp. 721–49.

Hayek, Friedrich A. (ed.) (1935), *Collectivist Economic Planning*, London: George Routledge. Reprinted 1975 by Augustus Kelley.

Hayek, Friedrich A. (1982), *Law, Legislation and Liberty*, 3-volume combined edn, London: Routledge and Kegan Paul.

Hill, Forest G. (1958), 'Veblen and Marx', in D.F. Dowd (ed.), *Thorstein Veblen: A Critical Appraisal*, Ithaca, N.Y.: Cornell University Press, pp. 129–49.

Hirschman, Albert O. (1985), 'Against parsimony: three ways of complicating some categories of economic discourse', *Economics and Philosophy*, 1(1), March, pp. 7–21.

Hirshleifer, Jack (1977), 'Economics from a biological viewpoint', *Journal of Law and Economics*, 20(1) (April), pp. 1–52.

Hodgson, Geoffrey M. (1984), *The Democratic Economy: A New Look at Planning, Markets and Power*, Harmondsworth: Penguin.

Hodgson, Geoffrey M. (1988), *Economics and Institutions: A Manifesto for a Modern Institutional Economics*, Cambridge and Philadelphia: Polity Press and University of Pennsylvania Press.

Hodgson, Geoffrey M. (1992a), 'The reconstruction of economics: is there still a place for neoclassical theory?', *Journal of Economic Issues*, 26(3) (September), pp. 749–67.

Hodgson, Geoffrey M. (1992b), 'Thorstein Veblen and post-Darwinian economics', *Cambridge Journal of Economics*, 16(3) (September), pp. 285–301.

Hodgson, Geoffrey M. (1993a), 'Institutional economics: surveying the "old" and the "new"', *Metroeconomica*, 44(1), pp. 1–28.

Hodgson, Geoffrey M. (1993b), *Economics and Evolution: Bringing Life Back Into Economics*, Cambridge and Ann Arbor: Polity Press and University of Michigan Press.

Hodgson, Geoffrey M. (1994), 'Optimisation and evolution: Winter's critique of Friedman revisited', *Cambridge Journal of Economics*, 18(4) (August), pp. 413–30.

Johnson, Chalmers (1982), *MITI and the Japanese Miracle: The Growth of Industrial Policy, 1925–1975*, Stanford: Stanford University Press.

Kaldor, Nicholas (1985), *Economics without Equilibrium*, Cardiff: University College Cardiff Press.

Kapp, K. William (1976), 'The nature and significance of institutional economics', *Kyklos*, 29, Fasc. 2, pp. 209–32.

Khalil, Elias L. (1990), 'Rationality and social labor in Marx', *Critical Review*, 4(1–2) (Winter–Spring), pp. 239–65.

Kornai, Janos (1971), *Anti-Equilibrium: On Economic Systems Theory and the Tasks of Research*, Amsterdam: North-Holland. Reprinted 1991, New York: Augustus Kelley.

Kropotkin, Petr A. (1972), *Mutual Aid: A Factor of Evolution*, 1st edn. published 1902, London: Allen Lane.

Laszlo, Ervin (1987), *Evolution: The Grand Synthesis*, Boston, Mass.: New Science Library/Shambhala.

Lippi, Marco (1979), *Value and Naturalism in Marx*, London: NLB.

Loasby, Brian J. (1976), *Choice, Complexity and Ignorance: An Enquiry into Economic Theory and the Practice of Decision Making*, Cambridge: Cambridge University Press.

Luhmann, Niklas (1984), *Soziale System: Grundriss einer allgemeinen Theorie*, Frankfurt am Main: Suhrkamp.

Machlup, Fritz (1967), 'Theories of the firm: marginalist, behavioral, managerial', *American Economic Review*, 57(1) (March), pp. 1–33.

Marx, Karl (1973), *The Revolutions of 1848: Political Writings – Volume 1*, edited and introduced by David Fernbach, Harmondsworth: Penguin.

Marx, Karl (1976), *Capital*, vol. 1, translated by B. Fowkes from the fourth German edition of 1890, Harmondsworth: Pelican.

Marx, Karl (1981), *Capital*, vol. 3, translated by David Fernbach from the German edition of 1894, Harmondsworth: Pelican.

Marx, Karl and Frederick Engels (1982), *Karl Marx and Frederick Engels, Collected Works, Vol. 38, Letters 1844–51*, London: Lawrence and Wishart.

McKelvey, Maureen (1993), 'Japanese institutions supporting innovation', in Sven-Erik Sjöstrand (ed.), *Institutional Change: Theory and Empirical Findings*, Armonk, N.Y.: Sharpe, pp. 199–225.

Mead, Margaret (1937), *Cooperation and Competition Among Primitive Peoples*, New York: McGraw-Hill.

Miller, James G. (1978), *Living Systems*, New York: McGraw-Hill.

Mirowski, Philip (1987), 'The philosophical bases of institutional economics', *Journal of Economic Issues*, 21(3) (September), pp. 1001–38.

Mirowski, Philip (1989), *More Heat Than Light: Economics as Social Physics, Physics as Nature's Economics*, Cambridge: Cambridge University Press.

Mises, Ludwig von (1949), *Human Action: A Treatise on Economics*, London: William Hodge.

Morishima, Michio (1982), *Why Has Japan 'Succeeded'?: Western Technology and the Japanese Ethos*, Cambridge: Cambridge University Press.

Myrdal, Gunnar (1957), *Economic Theory and Underdeveloped Regions*, London: Duckworth.

Nelson, Richard R. (1991), 'Why do firms differ, and how does it matter?', *Strategic Management Journal*, 12, Special Issue (Winter), pp. 61–74.

Nicolaides, Phedon (1988), 'Limits to the expansion of neoclassical economics', *Cambridge Journal of Economics*, 12(3) (September), pp. 313–28.

Orrù, Marco (1993), 'Institutional cooperation in Japanese and German capitalism', in Sven-Erik Sjöstrand (ed.), *Institutional Change: Theory and Empirical Findings*, Armonk, N.Y.: Sharpe, pp. 171–98.

Polanyi, Karl (1944), *The Great Transformation*, New York: Rinehart.

Reinheimer, Herman (1913), *Evolution by Co-operation: A Study in Bioeconomics*, London: Kegan, Paul, Trench, Trubner.

Robbins, Lionel (1932), *An Essay on the Nature and Significance of Economic Science*, 1st edn, London: Macmillan.

Sahlins, Marshall D. (1972), *Stone Age Economics*, London: Tavistock.

Schumpeter, Joseph A. (1976), *Capitalism, Socialism and Democracy*, 5th edn (1st edn 1942), London: George Allen and Unwin.

Sheridan, Kyoko (1993), *Governing the Japanese Economy*, Cambridge: Polity Press.

Simon, Herbert A. (1991), 'Organizations and markets', *Journal of Economic Perspectives*, 5(2) (Spring), pp. 25–44.

Sjöstrand, Sven-Erik (ed.) (1993), *Institutional Change: Theory and Empirical Findings*, Armonk, NY: Sharpe.

Tomlinson, James (1982), *The Unequal Struggle? British Socialism and the Capitalist Enterprise*, London: Methuen.

Tomlinson, James (1990), *Hayek and the Market*, London: Pluto Press.

Udéhn, Lars (1992), 'The limits of economic imperialism', in Ulf Himmelstrand (ed.), *Interfaces in Economic and Social Analysis*, London: Routledge, pp. 239–80.

Vanberg, Viktor J. (1986), 'Spontaneous market order and social rules: a critique of F.A. Hayek's theory of cultural evolution', *Economics and Philosophy*, 2 (June), pp. 75–100.

Veblen, Thorstein B. (1899), *The Theory of the Leisure Class: An Economic Study of Institutions*, New York: Macmillan.

Veblen, Thorstein B. (1919), *The Place of Science in Modern Civilisation and Other Essays*, New York: Huebsch.

Weber, Max (1968), *Economy and Society*, 2 vols, Berkeley: University of California Press.

Whitley, Richard (1994), 'Dominant forms of economic organization in market economies', *Organization Studies*, 15(2), pp. 153–82.

Whittington, Richard C. (1989), *Corporate Strategies in Recession and Recovery: Social Structure and Strategic Choice*, London: Unwin Hyman.

Williams, David (1994), *Japan: Beyond the End of History*, London: Routledge.

Williamson, Oliver E. (1975), *Markets and Hierarchies: Analysis and Anti-Trust Implications: A Study in the Economics of Internal Organization*, New York: Free Press.

Winter Jr, Sidney G. (1964), 'Economic "Natural selection" and the theory of the firm', *Yale Economic Essays*, 4(1), pp. 225–72.

Young, Allyn A. (1928), 'Increasing returns and economic progress', *Economic Journal*, 38(4) (December), pp. 527–42.

11. Financial markets and economic development: myth and institutional reality

Jan A. Kregel

It is a commonplace that economics is about markets. Amongst markets the stock exchange has a mythical role as representing the epitome of the operation of perfect competition. Recently, it has also taken on a mythical role as a necessary condition of economic development. Here I attempt to inject some realism into these myths by starting with the idea that Walras, normally vilified as having completely ignored institutions and the evolution of economic systems, should in fact be classified as an institutional economist.

The argument starts by challenging the idea that Walrasian general equilibrium theory is an abstract aberration of a mad French intellectual with no application to the real world. This is just not so, with respect to Walras's original theory, and also with respect to its extensions by Arrow and Debreu. Despite criticisms from post-Keynesians and institutional economists that the theory is devoid of real-world content, and the claims of applied general equilibrists that it can be applied independently of any real-world institutions, the theory of price formation of the *Elements* is a rather accurate rendition of operations of a particular institution, the Paris Bourse. If it can be criticized it is because it has little applicability outside of the historical context and particular conditions it describes. It is 'institution-bounded'.

But if the theory is institution-bounded this also calls into question the generally accepted proposition that competitive Walrasian markets allocate resources efficiently and thus promote growth by channelling resources to their most productive uses. Most economists when pressed for an example of efficient market allocation refer to the stock market. But the idea of efficient allocation, or a Pareto allocation, is just a description of the distribution of shares after the determination of the equilibrium prices on the Paris Bourse. If Walras's theory of price determination is institutionally bounded, then the concept of an optimal allocation is also bounded to the assets that can be traded in such markets.

What financial markets deal in are legal claims to the income deriving from the ownership of resources; they exist because of the requirement that in a capitalist economy everything must be owned by someone, but it need not be perpetual ownership. Stock markets thus provide for the distribution and redistribution of those claims. But it is not the resources that they distribute amongst users; rather, they distribute the losses and gains which arise from the failure of the market to efficiently distribute resources to the areas of highest productivity. They do this by adjusting the prices of claims so that their returns are equalized, taking into account realized rates of returns and expected future profits. The market allocates capital gains and losses which arise from investment errors, not the resources themselves. If there were no errors, then there would be no gains or losses or price adjustments, since all resources would be allocated so as to produce a uniform return. This is not an unimportant task, simply a rather different one than is usually claimed for financial markets.

Having challenged two of the myths surrounding the operation of stock markets, we can consider the myth that Walrasian financial markets are more efficient at channelling new resources to investment, and thus contribute positively to growth and development. This myth has gone so far as being used to justify the creation of securities markets in developing countries and the Central and Eastern European transforming economies, in order to increase their efficiency in the use of their scarce available resources. Even sub-Saharan Africa has become a target and countries such as Ghana, Nigeria and Botswana have recently created stock markets in the hopes of stimulating their development efforts.

The experience of the now developed countries suggests that it is not financial markets, but banks which determine the allocation of resources through the creation and allocation of credit. It is banks which not only provide the positive impetus to growth by overcoming liquidity constraints, but also are crucial to the creation of the financial markets in general and stock markets in particular.

In this context we can deal with an associated myth, that 'markets' might some day produce enough disintermediation to replace banks. Since most organized markets could not exist without bank credit (the Walrasian market providing an important exception to this rule), banks and markets should be considered as complements, not substitutes. Remember that J.P. Morgan managed to control US financial affairs without ever setting foot on the floor of the New York Stock Exchange, indeed some say he professed not to know where it was, despite his office being just across the street.

The rest of this chapter will start from the provocation that Walras should in fact be considered an honorary, if posthumous, member of EAEPE, and that the recognition of his contributions in this area may be used as a means of assessing the exaggerated claims for generality which have been made for the concept of the efficient allocation of resources via equity markets in the process of development.

WALRAS AND THE REAL WORLD OF FINANCIAL MARKETS – CIRCA 1860

The modern habit of referring to stock markets as examples of efficient markets is based on purely circular reasoning. It is but a reflection of Walras's clear intention to produce a theory which mirrors and reflects ... the operation of the stock market! Walras in the *Elements* declares that

> we must go to the market to study value in exchange. ... The markets which are best organized from the competitive standpoint are those in which purchases and sales are made by auction, through the instrumentality of stockbrokers ... This is the way business is done on the stock exchange ... Let us go into the stock exchange of a large investment centre ... Let us take for example trading in 3 per cent French Rentes on the Paris Stock Exchange (Walras, 1954, pp. 83–4)

Walras promises a theory which will render 'perfectly comprehensible' 'the confused uproar and chaotic movement', the 'clamour and bustle', that impresses any visitor to a stock exchange. In the type of market organization that prevailed on the Paris Bourse when Walras was writing, brokers met once a day at the same time in the same place to trade an officially approved list of stocks. Trading was organized by an employee of the exchange who started the trading session by quoting an opening price for the first stock on the list. Brokers signalled the size of the buy or sell orders given by their clients for that price; if the orders did not match, a new price was called, lower if offers predominated, and vice versa. This auction process of 'groping' or 'tâtonnement' only stopped when the market clearing price was discovered. This was the 'equilibrium' price, also known as the price 'fix'. All orders to buy or sell at this price are executed, as are orders that can be matched to buy at a higher price or sell at a lower price. There is a 'single price' for all bargains executed.

As Walras points out, what the *agent de change* carries with him in his little leather *carnet* of orders is the equivalent of his clients' demand and supply curves.[1] The process of tâtonnement carried out by the 'auctioneer' simply serves to make this information public and allows him to determine the equilibrium price as if it were the intersection of the market supply and demand functions which set the equilibrium price. Once the price of the last stock is fixed, the market is over, and no further trading takes place until the following day. It is thus a market which trades at 'discrete' intervals, with periodic trading 'suspensions' during which new orders are collected on the basis of new information which reaches clients. Price formation could thus be considered to take place in conditions of perfect information since all orders which exist at any price are presumed to be in the possession of the *agents de change* when they arrive at the market and they are made public during the auction. The trading suspensions mean that trade takes place on the basis of given and known quantity and allocation of stocks in individual portfolios.

Note that these are not *ad hoc* assumptions which Walrus imposes on his model in order to reach a particular desired result (as so often happens in current theorizing), they result from the official regulations governing the operation of the market. The French Commercial Code restricted trading to officially designated Bourses via a given number of officially appointed *agents de change* acting as officials of the Crown. In exchange for their monopoly on trading, the *agents* were forbidden from participating in the auction by entering their own orders, preventing them from intervening to influence market supply and demand.[2] At the close of each day's market session the auctioneer had thus produced a Pareto optimum allocation of stocks across individual portfolios, for if this were not the case individuals would have chosen to place their orders differently. Since all trades were voluntary, by definition any trade undertaken makes one side better off without making the other side worse off.

The idea that perfectly competitive markets produce an efficient allocation of resources is thus grounded in a particular institutional and regulatory framework, linked to a particular historical period. It is the market regulations which provide the conditions of perfect knowledge, the given quantities of stocks to be traded and the exogenous initial distribution of stocks required to specify the Pareto optimal allocation.

There is little difference between the Paris Bourse and the theory in Walras's *Elements*, except that in a real call market prices are fixed sequentially, while Walrus proposed a simultaneous system of price determination in which 'the whole world may be looked upon as a vast general market made up of diverse special markets' (Walras, 1954, p. 84); 'at the same time ... trading is going on in ... French Rentes, similar trading is taking place in ... English, Italian, Spanish, Turkish and Egyptian ... stocks and bonds; besides *cash* transactions there are *future* transactions, some *firm* and others *optional*' (Walras, 1954, p. 86).

If demand is also determined by the prices of other stocks, this may require reopening trading on stocks which had already been called earlier and had their prices fixed. There were provisions in markets to 'call-back' a stock (cf. Schwartz, 1991), and Edgeworth had suggested a similar process which he called 'recontracting'. Both are similar to Walras's account given above since they are types of contingency contract, similar to futures and options, which were already prevalent in Walras's day. Thus, although simultaneous determination of prices could not take place in a temporal sequential call, the use of 'call backs' and futures and options contracts could provide a close equivalent. All modern extensions of the theory from Debreu's *Theory of Value* onward simply provide proof that such close equivalents in the form of contingent contracting could indeed replicate the results of simultaneous trading.

The basic justification for the organization of economic activity by means of such Walrasian competitive markets is their contribution to the 'efficient' allocation of resources. The definition of 'efficient' is that no other allocation can be achieved which, starting from any given initial distribution of those resources, would improve the position of any individual without making another worse off. The elimination of Pareto improvements implies that all opportunities for profitable arbitrage have been exhausted. This is not to say that some other initial allocation could not produce greater overall well being, but that the operation of competition in the market is presumed to be independent of the initial allocation. Our discussion of Walras's modelling of the Paris Bourse shows that this description of allocative efficiency is simply another way of defining the competitive price fix.

Criticisms that tâtonnement and recontracting are unrealistic because they abolish time by ignoring the sequential order of actual trading appear to be misplaced. The more relevant criticism is that Walrasian general equilibrium theory is based on a peculiar set of regulations and institutions which produced perfect information, given initial allocations and price determination via an auction procedure. The theory thus has no claim to generality since it only has application to a particular market, the stock market. The results of the theory, and in particular the propositions of allocational efficiency or the ability to produce Pareto allocations, do not generalize either across markets or across institutions or across historical periods.

That allocative efficiency is just as 'institution bounded' as competitive equilibrium can be quite easily seen by reference to Walras's contemporary, Alfred Marshall, who also tried to emulate the stock market in his theory of price. But as geography and history would have it, his real world example was the older and differently evolved London Stock Exchange.

MARSHALL AND CONTINUOUS TRADING MARKETS

Marshall's point of reference, the London Stock Exchange, did not at all resemble the Paris Bourse. British clients were also represented by brokers who had exclusive access to the Stock Exchange, although not through government regulation, but as a member in what was essentially a private club. A client order received at any time during the trading day could be taken to the Exchange to seek out a counter party. This trading was usually done by consulting a number of brokers, known as 'jobbers', who bought and sold for their own investment purposes, in order to find the best available price. Other orders for the same stock might be negotiated at the same time by other brokers, or at other times during the day, and they could be executed at different prices, so that there was no guarantee of a 'single' price for all buyers and sellers, nor was there any possibility of complete knowledge of either the trades or prices occurring during the market day. Neither could the allocation of stock be taken as given and the quantities of stock outstanding brought to the market were a variable proportion of the total. There was no public information on transactions and reporting trades was voluntary.

In his presentation of price formation, rather than referring directly to the stock market, Marshall discusses 'the corn market in a country town' (Marshall, 1920a, p. 332). Actual prices vary over the day as individual buyers and sellers engage in a 'continuous' open outcry auction market in which repeated bilateral bargaining takes place throughout the day. The same calling out of prices takes place, but it is now the buyers and sellers themselves who do the calling, there is no auctioneer. In the London Stock Exchange this same process takes place, but it is the individual brokers, as agents for their clients (or the broker and the jobbers), who bargain until a price is agreed at which a specific exchange can take place.

In such markets there is a series of exchanges occurring throughout the day. Each is the result of an individual auction process and each one may be concluded at a different price. The evolution of the prices of these individual bargains occurring during the day will be determined by the arrival times of buyers and sellers in the marketplace, the size of their bargains, and their astuteness and ability to drive a hard bargain. In such conditions it is impossible to define a single 'equilibrium' price 'fix' since each price is an equilibrium for a specific and unique bilateral auction process.

But such a result contradicts Marshall's idea of competition which requires that a homogenous commodity such as corn, traded in a competitive public marketplace, should have a uniform price. Marshall thus asserts that the average of the prices at which corn has traded during the market day will be the same as the price which would have been determined by the demand and supplies of all traders taken together had they all traded simultaneously, that is, as if there had been a Walrasian auction to 'fix' a uniform equilibrium price. Indeed, Marshall presents aggregate market supply and demand functions based on all traders and calculates the equilibrium (and average) price of corn directly from them (Marshall, 1920a, p. 333).

This procedure requires precisely the same information that the auctioneer discovers by means of the process of *tâtonnement*, but it is the organization of the discrete call market which requires all existing orders to be presented at the same time that produces perfect information concerning the market supply and demand curves and allows the auctioneer to calculate the equilibrium price. There seems to be no reason why the prices concluded in a continuous trading market should produce an average price which is identical to the equilibrium price 'fix' of a discrete call market.

To support his assertion Marshall introduces 'dealers' (who much resemble London Stock Exchange 'jobbers') who possess 'perfect knowledge of the conditions of the market'. This produces what has some claim to be called the true equilibrium price: because if it were fixed at the beginning, and adhered to throughout, it would exactly equate demand and supply ...; and because every dealer who has perfect knowledge of the circumstances of the market expects that price to be established. If he sees the price differing much from [the equilibrium price] he expects that a change will come before long, and by anticipating it he helps it to come quickly. (Marshall, 19209a, pp. 333–4)

The continuous trading auction market thus reproduces the call 'equilibrium' price, but it is the arbitrage activity of the perfectly 'well-informed dealer' who replaces the process by which the auctioneer produces perfect information by revealing the market supply and demand curves.

Independently of how the dealer might 'discover' the equilibrium price, Marshall's description of how average prices converge to equilibrium creates another type of problem. While neither the auctioneer nor the *agents de change* are allowed to trade for themselves in Walras's tâtonnement, the income of Marshall's dealers depends on their trading activities and on how they influence total supply and demand. If a dealer buys at a low price in the morning in the expectation of selling at a better price in the afternoon he has to pay for and hold corn during the day. He may have to hold corn from day to day, or week to week. If he sells at a high price in the morning in the expectation of buying at a lower price in the afternoon, he must have carried over these stocks from a prior market. Yet, Marshall's assumption that the average of prices over the day converges to the equilibrium 'fix' precludes dealers from being net buyers or sellers. If a dealer carries stocks over time then the quantities which farmers bring to the market will no longer determine available supply which can no longer be considered as fixed for the market day. If quantity available, or quantity demanded, may be influenced by dealer positions, then the equilibrium price may be influenced by the existence of dealers' trading and depart from equivalence with the equilibrium price 'fix'.

Although Marshall denies that dealers require perfect knowledge for average prices to equal equilibrium prices, in its absence it is virtually certain that dealers will have to hold stocks over time. Marshall precludes the possibility that non-equilibrium prices produced by dealers imperfect knowledge might produce income effects which would change individuals' demand functions by means of a 'latent' assumption: the constancy of the marginal utility of money. This rules out 'income effects' arising from the temporal path of prices. According to Marshall

This assumption is justifiable with regard to most of the market dealings with which we are practically concerned. When a person buys anything for his own consumption, he generally spends on it a small part of his total resources; while when he buys it for purposes of trade, he looks to re-selling it, and therefore his potential resources are not diminished. In either case there is no appreciable change in his willingness to part with money. There may indeed be individuals of whom this is not true; but there are sure to be present some dealers with large stocks of money at their command; and their influence steadies the market. (Marshall, 1920a, p. 335)

Now, if a professional dealer 'can therefore make considerable purchases without depleting his stock of money or greatly altering its marginal value' (Marshall, 1920a p. 336), there is another latent assumption required: that the arbitrage activities of the dealer are costless. This means either that there is no risk involved in such activity, or that there is no cost in carrying stocks, so that the purchases and sales required to assure that the average of the day's prices converges on equilibrium are without either risk, or cost (just as the services of the auctioneer in Walras) to the dealer. But, this also requires that each dealer finishes each market day without open positions and without loss. which can only be the case if dealers expectations are always fulfilled.[3]

What is then the basic difference between Marshall and Walras?[4] First, note that it is Marshall who has to impose perfect knowledge, in the form of perfectly well-informed dealers, to produce equilibrium price in the case of continuous trading, while for Walras this is a result of the official regulations organizing market trading. But more importantly, Marshall recognized that this theory was not general, but only applied to particular types of commodities in certain well-specified conditions. Indeed, Marshall classifies markets in which quantities are fixed and stocks predominate through to special order production markets, noting that 'between these extremes lie the great majority of markets which the economist and the businessman have to study' (Marshall, 1920a, p. 329). This is presumably one of the reasons why he distinguished between different market periods. Stock exchange prices were clearly limited to the 'market day', where supplies could be considered as given and there was no possibility for substitution on the demand side.[5] There was no reason for this explanation of equilibrium prices to apply to markets in which production could influence available supplies, or in which the means of production could be adjusted, i.e. in what he called the short and the long period.

From this standpoint Marshall could argue that the returns defined on the basis of market prices would be different from those defined on the basis of either short or long period prices. Market prices thus need never reflect the real productivity of the allocation of resources to any particular investment. They thus cannot provide the basis for the optimal allocation of resources. If the Walrasian price-fixing mechanism cannot be extended beyond the determination of stock prices on the Paris Bourse, it cannot provide the basis for allocative efficiency outside that particular institutional framework and historical period. Short of imposing perfect knowledge, or creating it by regulation, there is no method for Walrasian or any other type of market organization to produce allocative efficiency.

In the absence of perfect knowledge, Marshall's analysis suggests that dealers will be required to carry positions over time, just as specialists on the New York Stock Exchange and jobbers in London before the Big Bang did. Traditionally their trading positions have been financed by credit. Now there are a number of ways in which this credit can be provided, either endogenously to the market or exogenously. No matter how it occurs, the fact that the dealers take positions will destroy the theoretical groundwork upon which equilibrium prices based on given and known quantities and allocations rests. With it falls the presumption for the efficient allocation of resources.

Thus the presumption of the efficient allocation of resources via the 'operation of the market' loses its foundation once we move outside the strict institutional assumptions of Walrasian theory or if we relax the presumption of perfectly informed dealers in Marshall's approach. Neither can it be rescued by the more recent elaborations of the theory. This is not to deny that stock markets allocate the ownership rights to already committed resources, just to say that they can tell us very little about the allocation of new resources in the process of development.

THE STOCK MARKET, BANKS AND DEVELOPMENT[6]

Given the way in which Walrasian general equilibrium theory emulated institutions it is thus not surprising that it has very little to say about the creation of resources in the growth and development process as opposed to their allocation or distribution. It is in this context that Schumpeter's Theory of Economic Development should be judged. Of course, Schumpeter reflects the German tradition of the *Grossbanken*, which were directly involved in the financing of enterprises and which operated directly in the stock market for this purpose. Although the original Kreditbanks were pure Banques des Affaires on the lines of the French model, only investing their own capital to provide equity for enterprise, they soon expanded into deposit-taking as a source of funding for their purchase of industrial participations. Deutsche Bank was the innovator in this respect. But the banks did not retain ownership of firms for either control or long-term investment purposes. Generally they retained ownership and control only long enough to get the companies into shape to be sold to the general public on the stock market.

From a post-Keynesian or Schumpeterian point of view, it is thus the credit creation process, inherent to banks, which provides for the initial allocation of purchasing power which allows entrepreneurs to appropriate resources for investment purposes. It is only once bank credit has been obtained that investment decisions become effective. At this point, either the firms, or in the case of the Kreditbanks, the banks themselves, turn to the financial markets for long-term funding. The role of the financial markets is to provide long-term financing to make the bank lending or direct investment in firms liquid. To the extent that households provide the demand for long-term securities, despite their preference for liquid assets, they do so only because the secondary market for equity provides sufficient liquidity to allow them to sell without substantial impact on market price. It is the liquidity provided by the financial institutions operating in the secondary market, not the intermediary function of financial institutions, which provides the maturity transformation by which the public's demand for relatively short-term liquid assets is matched to the firms' requirement for permanent sources of finance for long-term investment:

> So long as it is open to the individual to employ his wealth in hoarding or lending *money*, the alternative of purchasing actual capital assets cannot be rendered sufficiently attractive (especially to the man who does not manage the capital assets and knows very little about them), except by organizing markets wherein these assets can be easily realized for money. (Keynes, 1936, pp. 160–61)

The essential contribution of financial markets to the process of development is then to render long-term financing commitments sufficiently liquid to validate the commitment of resources to long-term uses without requiring individual investors to make long-term financing commitments. This also is what makes it possible for the Kreditbanks to borrow short and lend long or to finance ownership of industry with public deposits.

Looking at financial markets in this way emphasizes the basic distinction between banks as *creators* of liquidity and financial markets as *users* of liquidity. Since financial markets can only operate efficiently if they are sufficiently liquid, the evolution of most financial systems has relied on interaction between both bank and non-bank financial intermediation, just as it has required the intervention of government to control and regulate the operation of both banks and free markets. The choice is not between the two extremes of bank- or market-based systems, but in the way the two elements are combined.

THE HISTORICAL EXPERIENCE OF BANKS AND MARKETS IN THE US

The US market provides a good example of the way in which bank credit and stock markets interact, and allows us to challenge the third myth of the stock market as the most efficient organizer and allocator of scarce 'resources'. The securities markets which emerged in the late eighteenth century provided a purely speculative market in the original thirteen colonies' debt, and then in the new federal government's securities. The first securities other than government debt to be traded on US stock markets were not issued to raise funds to finance investment by manufacturing companies, they were shares issued to found joint-stock banks, including the Bank of the United States, and insurance companies. Indeed, without the flotation of bank shares an organized stock market would not have survived. Trading in bank stocks was also largely speculative, with shares pledged as collateral for the loans used to finance them. The New York market grew to dominate other regional stock markets in the US (Philadelphia and Boston were founded earlier) because the New York joint-stock banks, formed by the sale of their shares on the market, willingly lent money at call to speculators to finance their purchases of bank shares.[7] Since it was not considered appropriate, even in the 1800s, for a bank to lend to its owners, the existence of the stock market provided an intermediation mechanism which allowed the banks to use their ability to create credit to finance the purchase of their capital stock, as banks lent at call to finance the purchase of the stock of the other banks.[8] Very little in terms of scarce resources was involved in the formation of the joint-stock banks and the market cannot be said to have attracted, or allocated, real resources to new productive investment.

The same was true of insurance companies which after banks were the most common stocks on the exchange. Morgan's grandfather made the family fortune by buying up the stock of the Aetna insurance company after the New York fire. The stockholders, just like those in the other major insurance companies, had subscribed the stock but had never been called to pay, so that the company had no equity with which to meet the fire claims! The elder Morgan organized a syndicate which bought the stock for a song, paid all claims in full, and then put up the premiums to the grateful customers as well as for all others who quickly switched their policies to a company with an unblemished record of paying claims. He then sold the company at a handsome profit for the syndicate.

Nor did the major New York joint-stock banks or insurance companies do a great deal of lending to finance manufacturing business, either short-term or long. The big, powerful New York banks, such as the National City Bank and the First National Bank of New York, did not look anything like what we would now call a commercial bank, lending to finance industry's need for short-term funds.[9] They kept large company deposits and private accounts for wealthy individuals, usually paid no interest, lent call money to broker-dealers and speculators in the stock market and themselves invested in government stocks. They were also centres of correspondent networks which made them the equivalent of small central banks.[10] Their basic role was to provide security to depositors, not financing to business. Their direct contribution to the real sector was in financing the reorganization of industry at the turn of the century, when together with J.P. Morgan's more famous private banking firm, banks made equity investments in railroads and manufacturing. But, such activity was more akin to the merger and acquisition activity of the banks in the 1980s than to the allocation of real resources.

Although the large New York banks in the nineteenth century seldom financed long-term investment directly, they did do so indirectly by means of providing call loans to allow stock market intermediaries to carry the stocks of railroads and then other manufacturing companies which provided depth and liquidity to the securities market, and were crucial in the development of market liquidity through the provision of funding to 'financial firms' who organized the market. They also held small amounts of stock themselves. It was primarily the country banks which specialized in short-term commercial and agricultural lending.

The division of labour between commercial banks providing short-term finance and the financial markets providing funding for long-term capital investments was, however, imposed by law in the 1933 Banking Act. But this did little to change the fact that most financing of investment by US companies has been done from retained earnings held in the banks,[11] and the stock market has generally been used as a source of replenishing company liquidity only after the investments have already been undertaken and the real resources committed, or when market conditions were propitious for raising funds. Given the securities legislation regulating markets since 1933–34, it is virtually impossible for a new company to be launched by the issue of shares in the market prior to its commencing operations, while existing quoted companies rarely if ever go to the market for the funding of particular investment projects. The 1980s represented the extreme case of companies reducing their outstanding equity financing, as banks financed upwards of 60 per cent of the 'privatization' via leverage buyouts. Indeed, looking at the more recent period, during the 1980s most major markets provided a negative contribution of resources as companies retired more outstanding stock issues than the funds raised by initial public offerings of newly listed companies.

Thus, the US experience would suggest that financial markets are auxiliary to the creation of joint-stock banks which are more efficient than private banks in promoting industrial development. The same pattern may be seen in Germany. In the US case it was only the lending of the banks themselves which allowed the issue and sale of their equity in the market and provided the first shares traded in the market. Thus, no real resources were generated or allocated by the stock market. From a Keynes–Schumpeter point of view this proposition is general in the sense that bank credit allows the initial creation of income by entrepreneurs which produces real assets which are then financed in the stock market. Stock markets may make this process more efficient; they cannot initiate it. This would suggest that the initiative in the development process should be in developing the banking system. The creation of stock markets, without a supporting credit system, or already existing assets to be traded, can neither increase the total of resources available, nor increase growth by providing for a more efficient allocation. In particular, they cannot have the liquidity which is necessary to make equity investments attractive to households.

CONCLUSIONS

Thus, accepting the shocking proposition that Walras should be taken into the core of institutional economics and challenging the myth of an institution-free general approach to economics provide the insights to challenge two additional myths concerning the operation of markets in general and stock markets in particular. Markets cannot provide a basis for the evaluation of alternative allocations of resources, although they may provide a mechanism of valuing those resources once they have been committed. Neither can they aid in the process of economic development by directing resources to the most advantageous uses – the market knows no better than Marshall's dealers what those uses are, or what returns they can produce without assuming perfect knowledge. Much more important is Schumpeter's point that banks, by providing claims on resources, allow entrepreneurs to attempt to discover which types of innovations will be the most profitable. All that markets do efficiently is to confirm whether or not their expectations were correct. It thus seems inappropriate to recommend to developing countries that the creation of a stock market provides the key to economic development.

NOTES

This chapter draws together a series of papers that I have published since 1990 dealing with the relationship between economic theory and institutional organization of financial markets. Most have been developed within the context of a MURST (40%) research group dealing with the relation between market forms and economic dynamics directed by Alessandro Roncaglia and Mario Tonveronachi.

1. 'But if he were prevented from going to the market himself, or if, for one reason or another, he had to ... give his orders to a broker, he would have to anticipate all possible values of pa [the price of stock a] from zero to infinity and determine accordingly all the corresponding values of da [the demand for stock a]' (Walras, 1954, p. 93).
2. This is what I have called, following Braudel, a 'public market' since all information is exposed simultaneously to all participants (see Kregel,1990a). It is interesting to note that the discussion of Article 71 in the *Esprit du Code de Commerce*, pp. 310–11, lists four advantages of concentrating exchange in a regulated market. The first is facilitating the search of buyers and sellers, the second is to facilitate government surveillance to insure operation in the public interest and the last two to facilitate dissemination of information regarding prices and the financial positions of traders to the general public.
3. This costless carry would be the case in conditions of delayed settlement or dealing for the 'account' period.

4. There are other differences, for example, Marshall rejected the idea that the 'method of curves' could be applied to the case of temporary equilibrium which is under discussion. Cf. Kregel, 1992c for a more complete discussion of price formation in Marshall's other 'periods'.

5. Indeed, Marshall recognized the case in which the whole of the supply is in the market and the case in which supplies may be withdrawn or destroyed by suppliers rather than sold in order to limit prices. In *Industry and Trade* (3rd edn) there is a note which refers to the concept of 'elasticity of supply' in a dealer's market which recognizes the possibility that 'a given rise in price will cause an increase in the offers which sellers accept according ... as they have formed high or low estimates of the level of prices at the next market' (Marshall, 1920b, pp. 187–8).

6. This is not intended as an exhaustive analysis of the problem. Readers looking for one are referred to Singh, 1993 for an excellent review of the issue.

7. Indeed, because of the dominance of speculation the market, which was originally organized as an outdoor auction open to the general public, was banned by the New York State legislature and forced to trade in private through intermediaries.

8. Thus also explains a basic difference between the New York and London money markets. Since the British joint-stock banks grew up in a system which was already populated by merchant banks, their primary liquid short-term asset was a discounted bill, while in New York it was the loan of call money on the Stock Exchange.

9. See the descriptions given by Grant.

10. Indeed, most of their discounted bills came from correspondents and thus already had two or more names on them. A substantial amount of the funds lent at call were also correspondent funds.

11. To gain perspective, in the post-war period from 1946 to 1981 retained earnings accounted for an average of 65 per cent of the sources of funds available to non-financial corporate business in the US. Common equity contributed 4 per cent, preferred equity 1.5 per cent and bonds and notes 20 per cent.

REFERENCES

Grant, James (1992), *Money of the Mind*, New York: Farrar Straus Giroux.

Kregel, J.A. (1990a), 'Market design and competition as constraint to self-interested behaviour', in K. Groenveld, J.A.H. Maks and J. Muysken (eds), *Economic Policy of the Market Process: Austrian and Mainstream Economics*, Amsterdam: North Holland, pp. 45–57.

Kregel, J.A. (1990b), 'Mutamenti nella Struttura delle Negoziazioni e "Block Trading" nei Principali Mercati Azionari', IRS Rapporto sul Mercato Azionario 1990, Milan: Il Sole 24 Ore, pp. 110–29.

Kregel, J.A. (1992a), 'Some considerations on the causes of structural change in financial markets', *Journal of Economic Issues*, vol. 26, pp. 733–47.

Kregel, J.A. (1992b), 'Aspetti della Concorrenza Internazionale e Organizzativa nei Mercati Mobiliare: L'impatto dei sistemi di Contrattazione Elettronica Privati del Terzo e Quarto Mercato', Rapporto IRS sul Mercato Azionario 1992, Milan: Il Sole-24 Ore, pp. 213–33.

Kregel, J.A. (1992c), 'Walras' auctioneer and Marshall's well-informed dealers: time, market prices and normal supply prices', *Quaderni di storia dell'economia politica*, vol. 10, pp. 531–51.

Kregel, J.A. (1993), *Instability of the Economy and Fragility of the Financial Structure*, University of Bologna Working Paper no. 158, February.

Locré, J.G. (1807), *Esprit du Code de Commerce*, Paris: L'Imprimerie Imperiale.

Marshall, Alfred (1920a), *Principles of Economics*, 8th edn, London: Macmillan.

Marshall, Alfred (1920b), *Industry and Trade*, 3rd edn London: Macmillan.

Marshall, Alfred (1924), *Money, Credit and Commerce*, London: Macmillan.
Schwartz, Robert A. (1991), *Reshaping the Equity Markets*, New York: Harper Business.
Singh, Ajit (1993), 'The stock-market and economic development: should developing countries encourage stock markets?', *UNCTAD Review*, no. 4, pp. 1–28.
Walras, Léon (1954), *Elements of Pure Economics*, trans. W. Jaffe, London: Allen and Unwin.
Werner, Walter and Steven T. Smith (1991), *Wall Street*, New York: Columbia University Press.

12. Moral standards and transaction costs: long-term effects

Michael Yaffey

INTRODUCTION

In this chapter I discuss the economic importance, and to a lesser extent the social importance, of moral norms or shared values. There is of course no universally accepted morality, nor any single dimension on which different moral codes can be measured together for intercultural comparisons. However, the role of moral norms in reducing opportunism in market transactions and elsewhere provides a possible conceptual basis for defining a universally valuable type of morality. Despite some unresolved difficulties, it is suggested that the existence of counter-opportunistic moral standards and norms constitutes an important though intangible social asset, which requires and justifies maintenance expenditure. The problematical role of institutions in forming this social asset is also discussed. In order to look into the genesis of institutions and moral norms which reduce opportunism, it is necessary to consider opportunism and honesty in psychological terms.

THE ROLE OF MORAL NORMS IN THE NIE PARADIGM

Economics traditionally abhors value-judgments, but in recent years some discussion of the formation and role of subjective values insofar as they affect economic behaviour has entered economic literature as an element of the New Institutional Economics. It is therefore convenient to begin by considering the treatment of moral standards and norms within the NIE paradigm first.

This paradigm is generally considered to have begun with the work of Ronald Coase. The pioneering work of Coase ([1937] 1988) emphasizing the complexity and cost of business transactions, and the remarkable unreality which would characterize a world of zero transaction cost, ushered in the NIE without explicit discussion of business ethics.

Coase with his background in commercial law assumes without discussion that contract negotiations are adversarial and driven by self-interest. He points out the high cost, notably legal expenses, involved in negotiating long contracts containing clauses attempting to cover every contingency in full detail. The inevitable result, incomplete contracts, is assumed to lead to exploitation of the contingent situations. Every negotiator therefore faces a tradeoff between legal expense and risk.

Coase is concerned with showing that what is sold in a market is not simply a commodity measurable by the single dimension of quantity, but a complex bundle of legal rights, which despite rational behaviour will not be completely specified. He is not concerned with the ethical or anthropological aspects, and does not say or indicate that the adversarial behaviour found in the lawyer's office is characteristic of economic activity in general, nor of non-economic life. On these aspects Coase is silent.

He goes on to describe an imaginary world of cost-free information, in which market operators know everything, not only the facts which others might wish to deny them, but with all uncertainties removed including the outcome of research exercises to be undertaken in the future. The time dimension collapses and all possibilities become simultaneous. However, the main thrust of Coase's work is concerned with adversarial uncertainty and deceit.

The NIE progressed towards a characterization of the adversarial behaviour in the work of later writers, who described more clearly the defensive counter-measures, the cost of which is defined as transaction cost. One might say that first the shields and then the swords appear on the stage, before finally we glimpse the scabbards.

According to Coase (1988, p. 6) it was Dahlman who 'crystallized the concept of transaction costs by describing them as "search and information costs, bargaining and decision costs, policing and enforcement costs" '. The reference to policing and enforcement suggests that the detection and prevention of contract-breaking is needed, because an adversary may sign contractual undertakings yet decide not to honour them. Searching, bargaining and decision-making, on the other hand, could be necessary even if the other transactors were to adopt a wholly honest and even non-adversarial procedure.

Oliver E. Williamson (1975, 1985) refers to transaction cost as a defence against opportunism, which he defines very briefly as self-interest with guile. Guile means being cunning, the use of intelligence in an attempt to deceive or mislead. This follows Dahlman in treating the problem as essentially the cost of contract-making and post-contract administration. Opportunism is one of Williamson's troika of transactor motivations, along with asset specificity and bounded rationality.

Further clarification comes from the historical work of Wallis and North (1986), perhaps the single most important empirical research finding of the NIE paradigm. They estimated total transaction cost in the USA economy between 1870 and 1970. They included the costs of the activities of the 'transaction industries', namely, finance, insurance, real estate, wholesale and retail trade; the work of, for example, accountants, lawyers, judges, and notaries, and 'protective services' namely police, guards, sheriffs and the like; government; and certain occupations within the productive sectors, namely purchasing and sales staff, owners, managers, proprietors, foremen and inspectors. Wallis and North leave it unsettled whether or not military costs should be included.

From these activities we can see what opportunism consists of. It is evident, though not made totally explicit (pp. 102–5), that transaction cost pays for counter-measures not only to ensure that the buyer receives the goods or services and the seller receives the consideration as per contract but also to ensure continued 'peaceful possession'[1] of these, against theft and/or violence by third parties (with whom there is no transaction as such) as well as by the deceitful transactor. Such counter-measures represent a substantial overhead cost for the market economy; Wallis and North's team found that transaction cost rose from a quarter of GNP in 1870 to a half in 1970, approximately, with an increase in every decade in between.

Douglass C. North in his recent work (1990, 1994) builds on Williamson's concept of opportunism. Opportunistic behaviour is reduced by institutions, which have formal rules, conventions, or informal codes of behaviour: 'Institutions define and limit the set of choices of individuals' (North, 1990, p. 4). The presence of these rules, and the penalties for breaking them, constrain the behaviour of market transactors, and thus reduce opportunistic actions. This means that expenditure by individual transactors, to defend against opportunistic actions (transaction cost) can be reduced, in relation to production costs. Efficient institutions make for efficient economies. Progress in this area is according to North the key to economic and political development.

North shares with Williamson the concept of wholly self-interested transactors who calculate whether they can break the institutional rules with impunity, taking into account whether the institutions will publicize their transgressions to other market operators with whom further business might otherwise be hoped for. They share with others the concept that an operator might have built up a valuable reputation for good conduct, so valuable that no single temptation to opportunistic infringement at the cost of destroying that reputation might be attractive. Such an operator is locked in to conformist behaviour. Add to this another of Williamson's concepts, bounded rationality, and it pays to adopt the unthinking habit of good behaviour rather than reiterate the calculus every time an opportunity for infringement presents itself. The result is a type of impersonal moral behaviour which is generalized, though not altruistic. However, North does not develop this theme; he seldom refers to operators who internalize the rules, and usually speaks of a calculated self-interest which determines whether a rule is obeyed or disobeyed.

Thus, acceptable behaviour is said to originate in self-interested calcᵤlation, in the presence of efficient institutions. This will be particularly effective in a mature society where people belong to a large number of efficient institutions forming a dense network with mutually consistent rules: 'The increasing returns characteristic of an institutional matrix that produces lock-in come from the dependence of the resultant organization on that institutional framework and the consequent network externalities that arise' (North, 1990, pp. 7–8). Even in such a network, a calculating self-interest remains the driving force for North, though the calculation becomes more complicated and difficult: 'There is nothing the matter with the rational actor paradigm that could not be cured by a healthy awareness of the complexity of human motivation and the problems that arise from information processing' (North, 1990, p. 111).

Jean-Philippe Platteau (1994) extends the work of Williamson and North but with new ideas on moral norms. His recent paper (1994, pp. 533–77 and 753–817) is a major contribution both to Development Studies (with special reference to sub-Saharan Africa) and to institutional economics on the wider stage. Although this writing approaches the topic from a different ethical starting point, Platteau does not express specific disagreement with North or Williamson, and builds upon their concept of transaction cost. To that extent it seems reasonable to regard Platteau's work as an extension of the NIE paradigm, though we shall see later that it also embodies a major new departure.

The gist of Platteau's paper is that market mechanisms require most or all transactors to observe norms of veracity, which he calls honesty, a form of moral behaviour which has its psychological origins in socialization processes.

While the earlier-mentioned NIE writers have courageously conjoined economics, law, and history, Platteau adds a wealth of material from two additional areas: psychology, which has a bearing on human motivation and therefore on behaviour (such as greed, dishonesty, and group favouritism, which influence the working of markets), and sociology, in which the study of institutions had traditionally been centred before it entered the realm of economics.

Platteau argues that transaction cost can be kept down if operators are self-policing, that is, if they (or at least a high proportion of them) choose not to deceive, under the influence of a conscience or moral code which is internalized within their own minds. The basis of this, he says, is regard for others, a form of altruism. This is formed in infancy, normally by parents ('primary socialisation') developed further in childhood, normally by schooling ('secondary socialisation'), and reinforced in adult life by institutions, such as religious rituals. This socialization is governed by the socio-cultural matrix in which the market economy is embedded. Moral development leads to 'norms of generalised morality', to which market operators conform and trust one another to conform. However, the circle of 'trusted others' may be confined to specific known persons, for example, a kin-group or village. Such a narrow limitation is not conducive to modern markets, especially in international trade. The norm of more extensive mutual trust, which accepts unknown (indeed even anonymous) strangers into the trusted circle, is characteristic only of the 'western world' which Platteau suggests 'has a somewhat unique history rooted in a culture of individualism pervaded by norms of generalised morality' (p. 770). It follows that the Western type of economy cannot be transplanted into other cultures such as those of sub-Saharan Africa or Eastern Europe in the hope that it will immediately function there with the same degree of success. Indeed, certain aspects of market behaviour may tend to alter the socio-cultural matrix in such a way as to undermine those very norms on which the market depends, and Platteau suggests that this process is at work in Western societies. This may impede 'further expansion of the market system and perhaps even give rise to a major crisis' (p. 794).

SOME WEAKNESSES IN THE NIE PARADIGM

The New Institutional Economics has drawn attention to the importance of costs other than production (transformation) costs. This is undeniably enriching and insightful, especially perhaps for economists who had been accustomed to working within the neoclassical assumptions of perfect markets. However, if we consider what light it throws on the dynamic effects of moral standards and norms (not its major objective) it is less compelling, and in some respects unsatisfactory. Even its treatment of transaction cost can be questioned. Six particular weaknesses appear, which we shall consider in turn.

First, the definition of opportunism is fuzzy. Its extent is not clear. From the examples given by North and Williamson it appears to mean fraud and misrepresentation of various kinds associated with incomplete contracts: sub-standard merchandise, late deliveries, shirking labour, wound-back odometers, disappointing responses to unforeseen circumstances and the like, all related to transactions and imposing pre-transaction and post-transaction costs on the parties. For Wallis and North and for Platteau it includes these but also simple theft or burglary, robbery with violence, murder, even armed invasion; these are not transaction-related, but they are dangers, against which production activities need to be protected by expenditures which cannot be classed as production costs.

The NIE paradigm continues to use Williamson's term, opportunism, rather than the wider concept of Wallis and North. 'Self-interest with guile' could possibly mean either of these. Here we shall speak of commercial opportunism and general opportunism. Similarly the term transaction cost is in use for the cost of counter-measures whether in the narrow or the wider sense; here we shall speak of transaction cost and non-production cost respectively.

Second, there is no agreed explanation of the major empirical finding by Wallis and North, cited above. Why did USA non-production costs rise from a quarter to half the national income? Is it because technical progress in the non-production activities made them relatively more attractive than production activities? Or is it because the development of long-distance transportation (especially railways and telephones) made possible larger business organizations, demanding larger and more anonymous markets which gave greater scope for commercial opportunism and so raised transaction costs? A more general version of this explanation can be discerned in North (1990, p. 35): 'The returns on opportunism, cheating and shirking rise in complex societies'. Or could it be that more complex productive processes (not more complex societies) require more transactions per unit of output? Or is it because the rise of per capita wealth over time provides a stronger inducement to general opportunism, regardless of complexity and company size? Or could there be an increase in opportunist behaviour caused by a strengthening of self-interest as a motivator (increased covetousness), regardless of inducement? Was there a fortuitous political change in the USA between 1870 and 1970 whereby the functions of the state became larger and more detailed, requiring more staff and more expense? And perhaps in the non-state sector a large part of the explanation of the Wallis-North finding is an artifact of measurement, whereby transaction and governance activity previously performed by owners gradually came to be done by specialists and so fell into the measurable sector? Three of these suggestions were made by Wallis and North themselves (1986, p. 123) but inconclusively. Finally, leaving aside the USA, what happened in other countries? Without answers to these questions the whole NIE edifice stands on flimsy foundations of evidence.

Third, NIE does not make clear what is the nature and genesis of opportunism (commercial or general). Williamson proposes it as part of a troika of assumptions, counterposed to the neoclassical assumptions. Opportunism is therefore presented as a thought-exercise rather than an empirical observation of human nature. It is not clear whether it is a psychological motivation or a form of behaviour which may be forced on market operators by competitive pressure regardless of their desires. If it is a psychological motivation it is presumably also in operation in non-market economies and in non-economic life activities. Is it universal, widespread, or merely sufficiently common to make defensive non-production costs necessary? In fact the NIE paradigm prior to Platteau adopts a minimalist approach to these questions, neither measuring nor explaining opportunism. If opportunist behaviour is sufficiently common it is apparently not necessary to know how widespread it is. Given this behaviour it is not necessary to know what are the underlying psychological drives (a position which is characteristic of the behaviourist school of psychology). If it generates transaction or non-production costs sufficiently to affect the efficiency of markets, it is not necessary to know what happens in other aspects of life. Platteau introduces elements of non-behaviourist psychology whereupon these three dark areas can no longer be overlooked.

Fourth, the measurement of transaction cost (or more generally non-production cost) requires the definition of a counter-factual situation, which has not been elicited and examined. Wallis and North sought to capture the difference between actual (paid) non-production costs, and counter-factual (perfect-market) transaction costs, the latter being zero. The non-production costs are seen as the costs of countering opportunism. But this requires further examination.

As noted above, Coase sought to include all those costs which would not arise in his imaginary world of perfect information: costs of countering human opportunism, costs of countering natural uncertainties including the outcome of future research exercises, and costs of communication. To this list we might add the costs incurred by the opportunists themselves; given the Marshallian basis of the Coasean starting point, non-production cost ought to capture the jemmy and the skeleton key as well as the burglar alarm.

This extended list of items falls into two groups: costs which are the result of a specific and modifiable type of human behaviour, and costs which are by nature irreducible. It seems reasonable to postulate a counter-factual case without the first group, which isolates the cost of opportunism, as Wallis and North appear to have done to the extent that data was available, rather than without both groups, which would compare the USA economy against an extremely unnatural Coasean world, so strange that the only outcome of the test is to serve the limited Coasean purpose of emphasizing the need to bring information cost into the teaching of economics.

This has implications for the interpretation of the Wallis-North findings about the USA economy. Non-production costs may be relatively high in the USA because North America has a highly developed advertising trade, compared to other continents. Selling and promotional expense, including sales commissions, are a form of transaction cost which receives relatively little attention in the literature. I suggest that the cost of promotional communicating, persuading and deceiving is as much a transaction cost as is the cost of scientific inspection, verification, and protection against deceit. Lawyers' fees on both sides of a dispute (or criminal litigation) must be included, as indeed they are included in the Wallis-North data.

Thus non-production costs are partly adversarial; yet not entirely so, since innocent mistakes, oversimplification and ignorance also generate some commercial transaction cost (Simon, 1957; North, 1994) which cannot be excluded from the Wallis-North figures owing to lack of data. Adversarial costs are mutually offsetting, and do not generate a net gain in the real economy, even though they present themselves as efficient expenditures to the individual actor who decides to undertake them. The net impact on market efficiency is not necessarily beneficial, as Wallis and North argued it was. There is, therefore, no obvious reason to assume that successful economies have high non-production costs, and that in developing country economies these costs will form a lower proportion of total costs than in the USA.

A corollary of this is that moral norms which reduce opportunist behaviour and so reduce the non-production cost of defence against it are doubly effective: they reduce expenditure on both attack and defence. This makes Platteau's stress on the cost-effectiveness of moral norms even more important.

Fifth, the concept of institutions which lies at the heart of NIE is fuzzy. In Coase, Williamson and North, the discussion of the mechanism by which efficient institutions reduce opportunism is in terms of repeated transactions: any opportunist breach of rule by a transactor in a market will be made known to other members of the market and will make further business less likely. On reading this discourse one thinks of a professional association blacklisting an errant member, or a regulatory body withdrawing an operating licence. These are essentially related to specific markets, with known sets of transactors; the mechanism works at the micro level. Yet if, like Platteau,[2] one considers the creation of moral standards by social processes, and the creation of moral norms by religious bodies, it is clear that institutions must be conceptualized much more widely, to include the social processes and religions. But these do not work via transactions in markets. North's definition of institutions is certainly wide (he defines institutions as constraints) and his reference to dense networks of institutions with economies of scale is a pointer to mutually reinforcing social pressures, so one might at a stretch consider North compatible with Platteau here, but the move from transaction-related micro-level commercial probity to socio-cultural belief systems all sharing the same mechanism of constraint and all addressing a common purpose (commercial and general opportunism) would seem to involve some sleight of hand.

Just as NIE fails to distinguish commercial from general opportunism, and transaction from non-production cost, so it fails to distinguish between business institutions and social institutions, and between commercial honesty and the full spectrum of current moral virtues. In each case, commercial behaviour is seen as general behaviour.

From this, the sixth point follows. The benefit of moral norms is seen to lie in the reduction of transaction cost. Again, life is reduced to a market. Their non-economic benefits, their benign impact on human relations, their presence as possible values within a social objective function, is overlooked. Consider for example the promulgation of the Ten Commandments by the prophet Moses as an exercise in reducing transaction cost, and the reductionism becomes implausible. Certainly the Commandments may have had a beneficial effect on long-term economic development and so indirectly on the quality of life, but their direct effect on the quality of life must not be excluded.

THE PSYCHOLOGICAL CORRELATIVE OF COMMERCIAL OPPORTUNISM

The present writer can recall working as a development economist in the 1960s when specific national characteristics (such as the dominance of certain activities by particular groups of people) were characterized as 'institutional factors'. This meant a 'black box' which economists were allowed to omit from their scrutiny and which was excluded from the permissible range of policy recommendations by academic economists. Since then, economists have advanced rapidly into the institutional domain. In the spirit of Schumpeter, Tsuru, Galbraith and others, history in particular has been adjoined. North is a professor of both economics and history; his recent book (1990) on institutions has especially helped to free economists from the monodisciplinary straitjacket. As already noted, Platteau (1994) adds a wealth of material from psychology and sociology. All these extensions are enormously encouraging and creditable, and it would be idle to criticize a single-authored paper on the ground that it would have been more realistic if a fifth discipline had been added, or even more, such as jurisprudence, anthropology, political science, or moral philosophy. Obviously the claims of these schools to be directly relevant to the subject matter are undeniable, and any such omission is a likely cause of error, but, as Platteau says, the difficulty faced by an academic venturing into a new field is severe, and the present writer finds that same difficulty.

The addition of psychology to history and economics is a dramatic change which leads Platteau outside the NIE paradigm. Its importance stems from the fact that all three disciplines have sought to explain the negation of opportunism but with completely different explanations resting on different types of evidence. It will be argued below that the psychological explanation is more persuasive than the other two traditions, but before making this overview, let us examine the psychological offering.

In the New Institutional Economics, transactions are conducted by persons who may be referred to as market operators, principals and agents, or simply as transactors. They are not identified as persons; no attempt is made to describe their characteristics and proclivities empirically. Naturally there is no description of their psychological profiles. It is assumed, however, that a significant number of transactors are to a significant extent self-interested, deceitful and cunning when the opportunity arises. This is referred to as opportunism. When the opportunity is temporarily absent, the tendency or proclivity is still there.

Opportunism is therefore not only a behaviour but a proclivity among transactors. This proclivity is a given; it is exogenous. Like original sin, there are no reported cases of it changing over time. It is not directly discussed in NIE, except in terms of ways of constraining it. Behaviour, on the other hand, can and does change; when it pays more to be honest, honesty increases, and when it pays more to be opportunistic, opportunism increases.

In the paradigm of Coase, Williamson and North (but not Platteau), the underlying mentality is treated as a black box, as is customary in the behaviourist school of psychology when dealing with adults. Educational psychology, on the other hand, which deals with the formation of moral standards and behaviour in children, does furnish us with an observed set of moral norms or standards, which though founded in childhood development emerges as the basis of morality in the adult. From this observed set of developed adult norms and behaviours we can identify those which implicitly are assumed by the NIE paradigm. This is the psychological correlative, the missing psychological profile, of the opportunism which under NIE the market operators are assumed to display. We can then proceed to consider what would be the social effects if people actually did behave in this way.

Before examining the concepts of morality used or implied in NIE it may be helpful to set out the prevalent conceptual frameworks in psychology today. There is no single dominant paradigm, but six approaches will be mentioned here. Only the briefest of summaries can be offered here, with no pretension to do justice to them. For a more extensive description of those which are currently leading in English-language discourse, see Kurtines and Gewirtz (1991); for an excellent comparative study of ten modern paradigms, see Krebs and Van Hesteren (1994).

1. Freudian (psychoanalysis) paradigm: the mind is divided into three regions,[3] consisting of the id (containing primary instinctive drives), the ego (containing perception and reasoning power, used to think how the demands of the id can most effectively be satisfied), and the superego (conscience) which reflects the demands of parents (or other authority figures), originally external but now internalized. In this view, deficient moral development is a failure in the formation of the superego, or the formation of a weak superego which struggles sporadically and ineffectively against the id. The content of the formed superego is an undefined set of moral principles. Truthfulness may be one of these, but obedience to authority (possibly subsuming truthfulness) is more common. Exclusive self-interest is considered to be rare (except in very young children), a clinical aberration ('narcissism').

2. Piaget paradigm:[4] children as they get older progress through recognizable stages of moral development, just as by a connected process they pass through stages of cognitive development. The transition from (moral) stage

to stage is driven by changes in social relationships (from parents to peer-groups etc.) and enabled by changes in cognitive ability. Some reach the highest stage (passing from a concept of equality to a concept of equity), others never do.

3.   Kohlberg paradigm:[5] children mature in their ability to think about moral problems. They are induced to do so by their own experiences (direct and indirect). The individual's own enquiring mind drives the process forward. Kohlberg distinguishes more stages than Piaget (see Appendix); again, a person may not reach the highest stage. In the fifth stage (at which Kohlberg rates the US Constitution – Power, 1991, p. 30), there is a sense of obligation to law, commitment to contract, objective impartiality and due process. At the highest stage, individuals are committed to self-chosen ethical principles, superior to specific legal and social arrangements (Kohlberg, 1976).[6]

4.   Hoffman paradigm:[7] moral motives are driven by empathy, which is biologically built-in, though its mechanisms are stronger in young children than in adults. Empathy is defined as the feeling of emotions appropriate to the situation in which someone else is perceived to be (almost the same as sympathy, the feeling of emotions which someone else is perceived to feel). Among the empathetic emotions are grief and anger, which can be reinforced by mobilizing the grief or anger which are residues of one's own past experiences. Empathy for pain drives the moral behaviour caring; empathy for deprival motivates the moral principle of justice. Such motivations are biased in favour of persons similar to the empathetic individual, because of the mechanisms of empathy, which are stronger in such cases. Out-groups may therefore be disfavoured by this bias, so that moral principle does not necessarily result. However, some writers suggest that actions guided by empathetic emotions are valid moral actions – see Blum (1980) on moral obligations to friends, and Kurtines and Gewirtz (1991, pp. 232–3) for a gendered analysis of family duties.

5.   Badcock paradigm:[8] from a biological point of view, success is measured by numbers of offspring, and altruism is a deviant phenomenon requiring biological explanation. For the normal self-serving individual, hypocrisy and deceit are primary purposes of communication, and there is no preference for veracity. Reciprocal altruism (rational co-operation) can be a successful strategy for both individual and species. True altruism, however, in the sense of beneficent action with no likelihood of reward, is dysfunctional. Badcock argues (quoting Nietzsche) that those who press for it in others are serving themselves thereby. Kantian and other universal ethical principles are rejected.

6.   SCS paradigm (summarized in Kurtines *et al.*, 1991, especially pp. 316–19): the socio-moral competence scale locates an individual subject in each of five dimensions. These are: absolute versus relative principles; moral

motives versus moral outcomes; individual versus social obligation; religious versus secular morality; and intuitive versus rational (cognitive) morality.

Piaget, Kohlberg and Hoffman form a cluster of paradigms sufficiently close to be, arguably, integrated into one (therefore dominant) paradigm (Gibbs, 1991; Krebs and Van Hesteren, 1994). All three contend that individuals proceed through distinguishable stages of moral development. Each stage builds upon, and transforms, the previous stages. Such a process is essentially irreversible; there is no theory of moral decline.

Because of the similarities found between the major paradigms, I have referred in this paper to levels of moral behaviour on the Kohlberg scale implying the appropriate cross-references on other scales which use isomorphic structures.

The agreement between the paradigms is strongest on the lower levels. Habermas (1990, pp. ix, 35–6) argues that Kohlberg's 'post-conventional' stages (five and above) represent contentious moral values, contrary to Rawls's correct intuition that universal moral standards must command universal assent. Habermas attempts to ground the post-conventional stages upon his own theory of communicative action, while accepting that the lower levels are based on empirical research.

Some dissenting investigators deny that the highest stages exist in reality, or affirm that they are very rare, as Badcock's paradigm would indeed lead us to expect. Other critics suggest that the definition of the higher stages is weak, that self-chosen ethical principles are a reflection of Kohlberg's male liberalism, that Maslow's self-actualization provides a better model, that universal altruism at the highest level is a purely religious phenomenon, that the developmental process through the higher levels (especially in adults) is obscure, or that the vast majority of human behaviour falls into Stages 2 and 3 only. Others argue that higher levels, because they occur later in the personal development process, are not necessarily better in any absolute sense (Krebs and Van Hesteren, 1994). From any of these arguments one could proceed to the proposition that, if market forces (or other forces) destroy the higher levels or reduce their incidence as Platteau warns they may, society may not lose thereby – provided only that the levels do not fall below what is necessary for the efficient operation of the markets themselves. One would contend that the higher levels never really existed, or were a religious delusion, or that they were not beneficial in any absolute sense, or that moral reprobates were just as entitled to their preferences as saints. However, most of the literature – and all of the paradigms except Badcock and possibly Freud – would concur that such a destruction of highly-evolved moral behaviour would indeed be a social loss and ought to be resisted. I shall follow this approach in regarding the higher moral levels as a form of public good, or social capital, which (like the natural environment) has direct beneficial effects on individuals quite outside the North-type effects on the honesty of operators in market transactions. As in questions of the destruction of the natural environment, the onus of proof rests with those who argue that the loss is negligible.

THE PARADIGMS OF ALTRUISM

There is of course a considerable literature on altruism in economics with a number of interesting models. Rather than address them all here it will be convenient to distinguish some different meanings of the term altruism so as to permit some further analysis in the terms of the preceding discussion:

- Altruism as an individual driving force, an inherent motivation: this would be so rare as to be aberrant. In the language of cybernetics, altruism is not hard-wired.
- Altruism as a moral standard acquired by an individual, in an otherwise self-interested society: this would be costly for the individual and might have no net benefit for society (though there could be a net benefit by the elimination of adversarial costs). In the absence of a social norm, in which altruism appears as a value shared with other people, the standard may be expected to decay. This type of altruism is therefore transient.
- Altruism as a moral standard acquired by an individual, in conformity with a moral norm widely shared in society: here the individual has the benefit of being among like-minded persons, which gives a sense of security, mutual esteem, and self-esteem. This however implies a finite group of persons; the mutual esteem and sense of security may not extend among out-groups. The honour of cosa nostra is often cited as such a case. This type of altruism may be long-lasting, if the in-group is large and stable. Kin-altruism may be unselfish and empathetic or it may be based on a selfish calculation of reciprocal assistance. In an individual whose contacts are confined to the kin-group it may be indistinguishable from generalized altruism. As empathy it may be hard-wired, but it may also be learned, or at a higher level of personal sophistication it may be chosen. For these reasons it may be mapped to more than one level on the Kohlberg Scale.
- Altruism as an observed outward behaviour in the sense that an individual abstains from opportunistic violations of property rights: this is merely the converse of opportunism, and may be selfish or unselfish in its motivation. Its incidence will the outcome of various social processes, including:
- Altruism as a social norm, statistically found to exist within a society, perhaps by measurement of its proxy in the Kohlberg Scale: this is a characteristic of the society, not of the individual (because of individual

variability). This is what is postulated here to be a hidden capital asset, when taken together with its network of contributing institutions as a system.

Badcock in common with many other writers does not distinguish these five. In conflating them, because the first is aberrant and the second rare, the Badcock paradigm rejects the other three, regarding kin-altruism as disguised reciprocal self-interest, personal altruism as insincere, and altruism in society as dysfunctional. This dismissal seems to go too far, even though there are problems with the multidimensional measurement of altruism, of norms, and of institutions. Hidden among all these could be an essential asset which ought to be preserved, and as Platteau has warned us its absence in certain circumstances might provoke a major crisis.

For North too, altruism is an aberration, induced by ideologies which mislead the rational ego:

> How do we account for altruistic behaviour (the anonymous free donation of blood, for example); for the willingness of people to engage in immense sacrifice with no evident possible gain ... ? Certainly an individualistic calculus of costs and benefits would suggest that cheating, shirking, stealing, assault and murder should everywhere be evident ... Indeed, a neoclassical world would be a jungle and no society would be viable ... Individuals may ignore such a calculus ... because of deep-seated ideological convictions ... Change and stability in history require a theory of ideology to account for these deviations from the individualistic rational calculus of neoclassical theory. (1981, pp. 11–12)

WHAT DEGREE OF HONESTY DOES MODERN BUSINESS NEED?

It will be noticed that honesty per se does not figure prominently in any of the psychological paradigms described above ('truthfulness' does appear in a less favoured paradigm, not discussed here, but among the higher and rarer moral levels – see Gilligan, 1977). Nevertheless, the calculated honesty in which a transactor conforms to a social norm and expects to benefit by others doing likewise, as described by North and as tested in game-theoretic simulations, can be seen to fit within the 'reciprocal altruism' of Badcock. If this kind of behaviour is internalized and conscience-driven, it corresponds also to a stage of individual development in the Piaget-Kohlberg-Hoffman paradigm, in fact one of the lower levels to which mature adults might be expected to graduate; from the Appendix the reader may recognize this calculated honesty as Kohlberg Stage 2. If, however, the individual is committed to honesty as a generalized principle even in situations where it is contrary to self-interest, it corresponds to Stage 3 or higher stages, possibly even the highest.

This is the nub of the difference between North and Platteau. North goes for the wholly selfish solution: a calculus of payoffs, with only a hint of 'self-imposed codes of behaviour' (1990, p. 43). Idealistic attitudes operating against self-interest are, for North, delusions created by the acceptance of ideologies (North, 1981, pp. 15–16). Platteau argues that self-imposed regulation is cheaper, because the policeman inside the head is more cost-effective than the policeman in the regulatory office. He argues further, that honesty which is learned and inculcated by a desire for repeat business in a market will not appear in modern markets which are increasingly global and anonymous; what is needed is honest behaviour in one-off transactions.

Platteau refers variously to (verbatim): ethical elements, moral norms as a substitute for external rules, generalized morality, conscience, fair play, non-opportunism, other-regarding norms, self-policing, superego, identification in the maturation process, emotions capable of leading people to avoid short-term self-interest, loyalty towards a large reference-group, civic humanism, and probity. These terms belong to a number of different paradigms, but almost all of them refer to the higher stages of morality.

North offers plain self-interest, which has as its psychological correlative Kohlberg Stage 2, as the source of honesty, internalized (or partly internalized) by peer pressure, by repeated exhortation, or by the inertia of habit. In short, the moral level required by the market economy to minimize its transaction costs is well below the higher levels to which Platteau's terminology alludes; but North does require relational transactions, or at least an expectation of repeat business within a known group of transactors. As Platteau warns, this cannot work in a fully anonymous, global market. Platteau appears to suggest therefore that the latter requires a purposive effort to coordinate the sources of morality and strengthen the moral norms, implying a correlative target of Stage 3 or higher. It is not clear who or what would lead such an effort. One might draw the tentative conclusion that a fully anonymous, global market would require a virtuous world government.

OPPORTUNISM AND ALTRUISM IN THE LIGHT OF CONFLICTING DISCIPLINES

This compels us to reconsider the sources of morality and their mechanisms. As previously noted, we have economic, historical and psychological explanations on offer. Well before Platteau's intervention the economic and historical explanations were the subject of a survey by Albert O. Hirschman (1977,

1982). Hirschman recalls the 'gentle commerce' thesis of the late eighteenth century, exemplified by Samuel Ricard (1781, p. 463):

> Through commerce the moral and physical passions are superseded by [self-]interest ... Commerce has a special character which distinguishes it from all other professions ... Through commerce, man learns to deliberate, to be honest ... Sensing the necessity to be wise and honest in order to succeed, he flees vice ... he would not dare make a spectacle of himself for fear of damaging his credit standing .... (quoted in Hirschman 1982, p. 1465)

Hirschman identifies the same thesis in Montesquieu, Sir James Steuart, William Robertson, Condorcet, and even Thomas Paine. He calls it the 'doux commerce' thesis, from the French origins. Later, Friedrich List attributed the same benefits to the combination of commerce and manufacturing in a well-balanced economy:

> Drawn towards one another by their business, manufacturers live only in society ... The prosperity and existence of the manufacturer mainly depend on his commercial intercourse ... Everywhere he has to deal with men, with changing circumstances, with laws and regulations; he has a hundred times more opportunity for developing his mind than the agriculturist ... Manufactures are at once the offspring, and at the same time the supporters and the nurses, of science and the arts. (1841, pp. 197–201)

Writers in this tradition ascribe the development of other-regarding behaviour to the nature of occupations in the emerging new sectors of the modern market economy – occupations in which it pays to listen and to communicate, to establish enduring business relationships, and it pays to be trustworthy because it pays to be trusted. As Hirschman comments (1982, p. 1467), this view proceeds from a 'realistic-pessimistic appraisal of human nature' and expects moral values to be generated by the practices and incentives of commerce. This is precisely the position adopted by the NIE paradigm. NIE can therefore be characterized as an extension of the 'doux-commerce' thesis.

The writers of this tradition, from Montesquieu to North, cannot be described as narrow economists, but they give an economic explanation for the emergence of moral behaviour, at least up to Kohlberg Stage 2, countering and softening self-interest and reducing opportunism.

Hirschman contrasts this with the historical approach, exemplified by Fred Hirsch (1976). In this tradition, the moral norms which are needed for the efficient working of markets are a residue of an earlier pre-capitalist society. Belief in communal goals and such public (common) goods as monarchy, justice and the church have given way to what Marx famously called the 'cash nexus': 'The social morality that has served as an understructure for economic individualism has been a legacy of the precapitalist and preindustrial past. This legacy has diminished with time' (Hirsch, 1976, p. 117).

Against the background of the economic approach, by which morality is claimed to be generated by market transactions, and the historical approach, by which morality is provided by an earlier epoch, the addition of the psychological approach saying that morality is developed in childhood, regardless of market activities, in all forms of society, is a major development.

It is also a development which has a strong body of evidence in its favour, stronger (I would argue) than that for the other two approaches. The economic approach, as has been noted, does not explicitly discuss human nature, presents no research evidence on the matter, and is possibly open to the Marxist critique that it is merely a bourgeois glorification of bourgeois values generated by bourgeois activities to the exclusion of all others. Moreover the claim that morality is generated by market transactions is not borne out by the Wallis and North finding of rising transaction costs. The historical approach is open to the complaint that it is non-historical, that is, fails to identify any previous epoch as a golden age in which morality was at high levels, and in any case fails to explain clearly the mechanisms by which morality was generated in the golden age. And, as Hirschman notes, the alleged positive features of earlier epochs, stressed by this group of writers, can be matched by negative features alleged by other writers who decry the harmful after-effects of feudalism. The psychological approach, by contrast, can point to empirical evidence in the work of Jean Piaget and his collaborators, confirmed and extended in recent years by Kohlberg and others.

If indeed moral development up to a fixed stage occurs in childhood, before an individual embarks upon market activities, what role is left for markets in the formation of moral behaviour?

First, if an individual has reached Stage 2, which is a calculating kind of self-interest willing to entertain the idea of reciprocity, a market may teach the lesson that certain forms of pro-social behaviour are expected, such as honesty in the description of merchandise. The rational ego may be taught the specifics of what behaviour pays and what does not. This may be positive in relational markets, where repeat business is expected. Equally, markets in non-repeat anonymous transactions may teach the lesson that probity does not pay. Different markets may produce different types of behaviour.

Second, if the individual behaviour does not correspond to what pays, the individual may fail in business. That is, the market may provide a test rather than a training in moral behaviour. Such a procedure must have a hidden cost.

In this scenario markets do not determine the levels or stages of moral behaviour either individually or in the mass. It may be noted in passing that, if one accepts the view that markets generate morality in individuals, each individual will be brought up to the level required by the markets in which he or she operates, and therefore the social aggregate or mean level of morality on the Kohlberg scale will be just what market efficiency requires. This helpful result of the invisible guiding hand is not available with the psychological approach, however, because the levels are fixed in childhood. It follows that the aggregate or mean level may be higher or lower than what market efficiency requires, and may be rising or falling, perhaps without any equilibrating mechanism. If there is any equilibrating mechanism, for example a ruler who will strengthen the church or the police whenever morality is perceived to be decaying, it may tend towards a level which is not that of maximum market efficiency, and may be higher or lower.

We cannot suppose, of course, that mechanisms of moral development operate in such a way that all children emerge as adults with the same level. There must be some spread, some distribution of attainment. Platteau is therefore correct in dealing with a suspected deficiency of moral development in terms of a modal value or skewness for the distribution as a whole.

In other words, to raise the behaviour of most market operators up to a level at which the market is efficient (Kohlberg Stage 2 for relational markets, or Stage 3 for anonymous markets), the non-market mechanisms which do this must, because of human variability, achieve a mean value higher than this desirable minimum. More than half the individuals must be raised to higher levels than the guiding hand of market-generated morality would achieve for them. This in turn suggests that the social values which drive the mechanisms aim at levels which are higher, rather than lower, than those of market operators.

MORAL DEVELOPMENT AS A PROCESS WITH COSTS AND BENEFITS

From the point of view of minimizing transaction costs[9] in the market, this unnecessary attainment is an undesirable waste, unless the mechanisms which produce it are assumed to operate at zero cost. This assumption seems unrealistic: here I take issue with Platteau, who writes (p. 771):

> The Church ... played a central role in the process of moral norm generation and maintenance throughout modern western history. Its impact was all the more significant as (1) it promised a considerable reward ... for ... behaving in other-regarding ways; and (2) monitoring costs could be brought to a minimum insofar as God was thought to act as an impartial and free monitoring agent. (emphasis added)

But the work of the church has substantial real and financial inputs, subsidized by the taxpayer in some countries. The same holds good for the work of other religious and humanist groups,[10] school teachers, reformatory workers, and foster parents. As for natural parents, who (at least for pre-school children) play a major role in moral development, their labour input is free of charge, and in real terms the valuation of the labour input is problematical, as is the case with other forms of family nurture. In short, moral development is not without economic cost, even though no monetary charge may be made by some of its creators. Therefore, the economic optimum is not one of maximum moral development. Nor is it necessarily that which any sections of society, or society as an integral whole, would prefer.

Of course, the concept of a set of moral values endorsed by society as an integral whole is very problematical. Some individuals, such as Kohlberg himself, desire to find ways of raising the levels, of getting more individuals through to the highest possible stages, of promoting socio-moral development. In this respect Kohlberg may have been representative of many individuals who have a personal preference for living in a society of ethically-guided persons quite beyond the Stage 2 or 3 requirements of the market economy. But his position does not necessarily represent the typical preference of everyone in society.[11] Others who operate on the lower levels may have a preference to live among persons like themselves. Others again may prefer diversity. It is far from clear how an aggregate objective function can be derived from this. Clearly a simple unweighted addition of individual preferences, like individual demand curves, cannot be justified. Even if there were a consensus, it would be difficult to articulate; a clear unimodal peak in moral behaviour does not translate into a consensus as to what is perceived as the most satisfactory pattern of moral behaviour, still less into what would be a social optimum in some long-run dynamic sense.

In view of these weaknesses in the concept of the social optimum, we cannot be certain that it will necessarily always exceed that optimum which minimizes costs for the market economy.

Indeed, market activities and non-market activities may be performed by the same individuals, only at different times of the day.[12] As Platteau puts it, quoting Bromley (Platteau, 1994, p. 795), 'the market is embedded in society rather than conversely'; but we might go further and say that the economy, whether market-based or not, is only part of society, its agents are only part of the population, and we spend only part of our life in it; moral values are important in our non-economic life too. However, expectations (perceived norms) governing business deals have been found to elicit Stage 2 moral judgments among adults who in a non-business context were ranked in Stages 3 to 4 (Carpendale and Krebs, 1992).

North is not concerned with the non-business benefits of morality. Platteau does not discuss it, nor even say that for the sake of the market economy the moral level ought to be raised; he merely warns that in some countries it is at present low in relation to the efficiency needs of the envisioned market economy.

The neglect, by both North and Platteau, of the non-business benefits of moral development seems to be unfortunate.

DOES THE COMPETITIVE MARKET WORK AGAINST MORAL MOTIVATOR MECHANISMS?

Platteau, following Hirsch (*op. cit.*) reminds us that the activities of a market, in which competition is essentially opposed to other-regarding morality, can paradoxically undermine the morality-building mechanisms which serve the market's needs for self-policing.[13] By what process can self-interest damage a norm of so-called reciprocal altruism, which is essentially driven by Stage 2 self-interest? Platteau does not go into this, but some mechanisms can be distinguished, linked with different paradigms:

1. Internalized, habituated honesty is not completely self-serving; it contains an 'irrational', other-regarding element, which is weakened by repeated observation (and imitation) of competitive (other-disregarding) behaviour (Badcock paradigm).
2. The pursuit of victory in competitive conflicts trains people to disregard their empathetic emotions. This weakens the motivating force of moral behaviour generally, according to the Hoffman paradigm.
3. The constellation of moral values of Stage 2 competitiveness conflicts in detail with the constellation of values of which honesty is one. In this SCS paradigm the entire concept of a 'level of morality' in society as a whole is set aside. Even if the best schema were found, individuals located on it by research, and the modal level taken to represent the social average, it would still be a unidimensional measure. The SCS approach measures not one dimension but five. The possibility exists, therefore, that the economic and non-economic optima differ, not in their levels on a common unitary scale, but in detail. Whilst agreeing in general about the self–other balance, or the kin–alien boundary, transactors in a competitive market might have distinct specific values. For example, the needs of the market might value punctuality as a virtue (for manufacturing labourers especially),[14] whereas the needs of the non-economy might value craftsmanship (with its connotations of pleasant labour and job enrichment). Both of these are partly self-regarding. Neither can be held morally superior to the other on a unidimensional scale. Yet they can conflict.
4. The morality required in markets is generated during childhood by a socio-cultural matrix made up of institutions operated by adults. These adults are parents and other mentors who provide their services wholly or largely free of charge; to do so is encouraged by a moral code which is to a sufficient extent held in common. This code can be challenged and disrupted if there are many free-riders, or worse still, adults who not only fail to make a comparable contribution but actually maximize what they take for

themselves. In this connection one must remember the pressure of competition upon those who must maximize their profits because in imperfect financial markets accumulated profits are a future source of competitive strength.

5. If one accepts the surplus-value paradigm the problem is particularly severe, because there is no moral meum and tuum, but only amoral maximization of the meum. If this becomes and is accepted as the dominant form of social organization, and measure of social success, it is clearly difficult to maintain, and probably impossible to maintain indefinitely, a socio-cultural matrix which acts altruistically.

Thus according to all these different paradigms competition is damaging to altruism and to the internalized moral code. This will operate by damaging the morality-forming institutions, especially those which rely on a common social code. The education of children up to Stage 2 is likely to be less damaged, since Stage 2 is not really altruism at all. It is the higher stages and particularly the post-conventional stages which are more directly at risk. But the individuals who are discouraged or demotivated by destruction of their higher levels are likely to include some who are working with younger children making the transition to Stage 2; for instance, school-teachers and parents bringing up infants. Thus even Stage 2 attainment scores will be reduced if the entire socio-cultural matrix is damaged.

This supports and amplifies the Hirsch-Platteau proposition, that the market may damage itself, particularly if Platteau is right in supposing that the markets of the future will require levels higher than Stage 2. If he is wrong, and North is right about Stage 2, the market may largely escape the 'grave crisis' of which Platteau speaks, while the remainder of society suffers from it.[15]

MORALITY AS SOCIAL CAPITAL

Whether moral norms are learned from repeated encounters in markets, or from social processes, time is required for their construction. Each individual spends time growing through the childhood stages of personal moral development. In adult life, endless time is spent in collective effort developing and perpetually modifying the institutions and practices (especially schools) which guide future cohorts of the young. Likewise the reinforcement of moral norms among adults, through organizations (especially religious movements, and in North's view also ideologies), requires continued input of effort by volunteers and employees.

The benefit arising from this cost may be found in modification of an individual's behaviour over a period of years. Since reinforcement of moral standards is achieved in part by reiteration and by habituation, the behaviour modification may be assumed to be strengthened progressively during exposure to the formative social processes, but thereafter weakened progressively if exposure ceases, or if for some reason the social processes are weakened or damaged in any way.

The time aspect here is analogous to that of sales promotion by advertising. An advertising campaign is cumulative, in that its effects can be strengthened by spending more, but if the advertising ceases, sales will progressively fall. A company which has recently conducted an advertising campaign therefore has an intangible asset. Such an asset can be expected to provide a stream of benefits to the company over a period of years. This is also the case with productive fixed assets. These require continued maintenance expenditure, and the provision of replacement funds for indefinite enjoyment of operating revenues. If these expenditures cease, productive capacity will drop and operating receipts will gradually fall. In the event of cash flow problems, advertising or maintenance may be cut without short-term impact on revenues, but there is a loss of value which will have a deferred impact. Accounting principles seek to include in each year's income statements any such loss of value in capital assets, but this is not always possible, especially with intangibles. The interpretation of accounting statements therefore requires an awareness of the presence of hidden yet important (even essential) capital assets which may be rising or falling in value uncaptured in the accounts. This holds for social as well as company accounts. In recent years the depletion of natural capital has come to be recognized by environmentalists as such a case; moral norms may be another. The enumeration and valuation of intangible environmental assets is intractable and was therefore long resisted, but is now gaining acceptance; that of moral assets may perhaps achieve a similar status.

These two types of asset, the environmental and the moral, share another characteristic: they are public goods, and their preservation under weak individual incentives evokes the well-known problem of the commons. The dynamics are different, however, in the moral case. The destruction of environmental capital does not cause more of the same; indeed, by price effects, it may be self-inhibiting. The destruction of moral capital, however, aggravates the problem of the commons and thus may be expected to reduce the efforts which altruistic individuals devote to institutions by which moral capital is maintained.

An analogy in the domain of private fixed assets may make this point more forcibly. If a chemical process plant is not maintained it may corrode, but the damage does not extend to other companies' plants. However, if one can imagine a form of corrosion which gives off fumes affecting the health and productivity of the maintenance workers, so that by a vicious circle the damage is self-sustaining over time: these fumes spread geographically, so all plants are affected.

Here a key question is: what exactly is the hidden asset here? Is it the institutions, some selected institutions, the collection of moral norms, or the modal level of adult society on the Kohlberg Scale? Any of these might be regarded as intangible long-term assets requiring and (up to an optimal level) justifying continuous maintenance expenditure by society.

Because it is intangible it is problematical. A collection of moral norms will be disparate, perhaps largely mutually consistent but not entirely so, shared by many but not all of the adult population. These norms may be capable perhaps of being represented in the five coordinates of the SCS paradigm but not all mapping to the selfish-unselfish coordinate which is the strongest candidate for a unified scale of morality in the Piaget-Kohlberg-Hoffman cluster, nor the honesty-dishonesty coordinate which may be useful in constraining commercial opportunism.

What of the institutions themselves? Some would argue strongly that not all institutions are beneficial, citing the Gestapo as an example. It would clearly be absurd to propose subsidizing all institutions. A way round this might be to adopt North's definition of institutions as constraints, not to be confused with organizations. But are all constraints beneficial? The Gestapo also imposed constraints. We therefore have to separate good institutions from bad ones. Here we may again follow North with his concept of efficient institutions, in the sense of those which effectively and cheaply distinguish rule-following from rule-breaking behaviour and so modify behaviour efficiently. Unfortunately the Gestapo did this too. We may therefore look for institutions which efficiently create moral norms with certain characteristics, including the norms which combat general opportunism; this would exclude instruments of power such as the Gestapo which themselves display general opportunism. However, this discussion makes it clear that it is the norms, or the institutions together with the norms, which are the intangible social asset, not the institutions alone.

THE MEASUREMENT OF MORAL CAPITAL

The cost of maintaining this intangible social asset might be expressed in money terms, though this cost is so widely dispersed that it would be difficult to measure. The benefits, whether to the market economy or to social life generally, are likewise expressible in value though problematical to measure. But if we are to measure any erosion of the asset, analogous to a fall in productive capacity due to poor maintenance of a fixed asset, this must be in terms of volume rather than value. In what dimension(s) does the asset exist? In what units can its effects be measured? We are immediately confronted by the five dimensions of the SCS paradigm, and by the very wide range of items considered good or bad in different human societies. To put it crudely, if we cannot agree on what is good, how can we determine that there is less good in the world? A narrower concept is required, not universalist but well-defined and capable of operational use, offering a single-dimensional measure.

The obvious candidate for numéraire is the degree of altruism, carefully redefined for this purpose. Altruism is in broad terms a consideration for the wishes of others, sometimes including anonymous members of out-groups. Any norm (shared moral standard) which combats general opportunism (which we have defined to include commercial opportunism) might therefore be held to promote altruism in individuals.

Altruism is central to the paradigms of Piaget, Kohlberg, and Hoffman. We may therefore expect that such norms will be mutually reinforcing, and contrary or irrelevant norms will be ephemeral, or weak and peripheral; the institutions which create these norms will be mutually reinforcing, and contrary institutions will be ephemeral, or weak and peripheral. This creates a cluster of norms and institutions forming a dynamic self-sustaining system. The moral norms of such a system would be centred upon a particular level or stage of morality (in the Kohlberg or Piagetian sense), high or low. This central level is the suggested key variable; in the case of a unimodal distribution, having a single cluster of institutions, the modal value would be appropriate. The hidden asset is the entire system. Even if the level is historically low, the asset is non-negative.

The average value (mean and modal values have commonly been adopted) of adults on the Kohlberg Scale, found by various researchers, based on their behaviour or on their attitudes, is no more than a proxy indicator of the productive capacity of the hidden social asset thus modelled.

Perhaps the strongest opposition to such a concept lies in the Badcock paradigm, rooted in biology, according to which altruism is dysfunctional. Yet what is dysfunctional and therefore in economic terms a cost for the individual can be a social asset. The need to distinguish carefully between different concepts of altruism has already been referred to.

STAGE 2 AND BELOW: WHAT IT WOULD MEAN

Two contending views appear to describe the actual levels of moral capital in Western societies. In both views, it is the behaviour of individuals, though characterized above as a proxy or indicator for the hidden social asset, which is the primary focus.

What may be called the educational psychology view offers a distribution of moral behaviours in adults with a significant number achieving Stages 4 and 5 in the Kohlberg Scale, and a few rare adults confined in Stage 1. Because of skewness, this is consistent with mean scores between 2 and 3, as found by research studies.

What may be called the game-theory view is that to all intents and purposes the spectrum of behaviours ranges from Stage 1 to Stage 2. Discussion of behaviours by North and Williamson is in these terms. North refers to various game-theoretic studies in which the moral behaviour of an individual is determined by a self-interested calculation; given certain expectations and certain payoffs this can lead to the selection of honesty, or cooperation, as the best policy. Apparently altruistic behaviour can be grown on the soil of self-interest. However, as reference to the Kohlberg schema (see Appendix) will show, this is a development from Stage 1 to Stage 2. There is nothing in game theory and nothing in the calculus of repeated exchange which would produce a Stage 3 or higher outcome. This does not mean that game theories could not be constructed with expectations and payoffs which would produce a higher-stage outcome in terms of observed behaviour; but where the whole basis of the individual decision is self-interest rooted in Stage 1, a player cannot progress beyond Stage 2, unless by passing through not one game but a series of games with different rules, as does a child in personal development. Games based on the outcome of opportunism versus honesty in market transactions have essentially fixed and simple rules.

The implication of North's work is that Stage 2 provides sufficient honesty for efficient commerce. Since opportunism is understood as merely commercial opportunism and transaction costs are merely costs imposed on market transactions, higher stages are superfluous. However, if the educational psychology view is correct, and if our model of social capital is correct, the achievement of Stage 2 by the great majority of individuals depends on the presence of a system of institutions and norms centred significantly higher. The Stage 2 achievement is merely the lower tail of the distribution.

We have already noted Platteau's argument that the market economy with its stress on self-interest and competitive disregard of others can erode the moral norms clustered around a higher central level. It follows that the mechanisms lauded by North may actually be damaging. Even if, contrary to the psychological approach, market transactions raise some few adult individuals from Stage 1 to Stage 2, the benefit of so doing may be more than offset by the effect of undermining the cluster of norms at the higher stages which will later be responsible for pulling most individuals now still in their childhood up to Stage 2. In that event, not only may the competitive market reduce the quality of social life which many people outside their market activities may prefer, but even the market itself may be adversely affected, with higher transaction costs.

An assessment of this proposition must depend on the question of fact, whether most individuals are within the range of Stages 1 to 2, or above that. The higher the modal value achieved by socio-cultural institutions above Stage 2, the more vulnerable is the hidden social asset to damage by competitive behaviour in adult life.

It seems highly unlikely that anything less than Stage 2 is common in adults. Let us, after all, consider what pure self-interest (Kohlberg Stage 1) really means. It may mean that we walk off, if we can, without paying our taxi, as Basu suggests in the title of an article (1983), or that we do not bother to walk to the polling station and vote when the local outcome is predictable. These may be good examples of free-riding for the purpose of obtaining empirical data. But these are very innocuous cases. With fully narcissistic self-interest, we may murder the taxi-driver, steal his taxi, eat his body and use the polling station as a lavatory. Why not? This is Nietzschean rationality. Who is to stop us, if the police and the politicians are self-serving too?

The innocuous cases are set in a scenario of a single self-server, or, like the prisoners in the famous dilemma, two such persons operating within a framework of law. Solitary self-servers may be termed sociopaths, or psychopaths, terms which denote rarities. An entire society of such creatures would be unconstrained by law. It would be the Hieronymus Bosch scenario. No such human society does or could exist. It might be rational for the psychopathic individual, or for a species versus other species, but it would be dysfunctional for human society on a large scale. As North said, it would be a jungle.

This is not intended to argue that Stage 1 individuals are so very rare that they cannot disrupt the functioning of markets. Even a small percentage below Stage 2, quite possibly less than 5 per cent, may be sufficient to transform transactor expectations (downward) and generate a significant increase in transaction cost. Unfortunately, though, that same lowering of expectations caused by a small minority may be disruptive of the entire moral system outside the markets, with negative effects on the behaviour levels of both contemporary and future adults, bringing larger numbers into the lower tail of the frequency distribution in due course. Such an effect would be dynamically self-sustaining, essentially because of the time taken to form individual moral codes.

There is no correcting mechanism, because the damage is not clearly visible, and because it is damage to a public asset for the conservation of which individuals have only a weak incentive. At any given moment during such a decline, the asset can be perceived as a legacy of earlier years, though not necessarily of an earlier epoch, one which has recently suffered from insufficient maintenance.

CONCLUSION

We have observed that human behaviour driven by simple self-interest, far from producing the beneficent results expected in neoclassical theory, would be intolerable both for the economy and for society. The psychological correlative of this neoclassical assumption is Kohlberg Stage 1. This is not observed to prevail in the real world, but opinions differ as to whether the higher moral development occurs in childhood and adolescence (as all psychological paradigms agree) or in adult life where behaviour is modified by ideologies (North's supposition) or by economic incentives arising in commercial relationships (Williamson's NIE paradigm, supported by various game theories). We have argued that the psychological approach has the strongest empirical foundation, the NIE paradigm is open to certain objections, and the game theories focus on the behaviour of individuals who are confined to Stage 2 or below. This disconnects the generation of moral behaviour patterns from market experiences.

While accepting the Coasean proposition that markets work more efficiently when transactors are honest, we have remarked that both inside and outside the world of commerce society benefits from an absence of theft, violence and deceit; accordingly we have looked outside the concept of transaction cost into non-production cost, and outside commercial opportunism into general opportunism. We have viewed general opportunism as the natural behaviour of the youngest infants, but in adults we see a range of behaviours as the outcomes of a process of moral development carried out by a matrix of institutions, linked and interlocked by widely accepted moral standards, values, and norms. Market operations benefit from this, but do not themselves undertake it, and indeed competitive self-interest militates against those standards which represent Kohlberg's higher stages.

We have argued that the process of personal development takes many years, and the institutions in the socio-cultural matrix are (being institutions, and because they are interlocked and hierarchical) slow to change. For these reasons the aggregate (mean or modal) score of a village or a nation on the Kohlberg scale will not change perceptibly in the short term. The whole constitutes an intangible social asset, important and arguably vital for survival. It is impossible to measure, for reasons we have seen, except through proxy indicators. A vital asset which is difficult to measure and which can decay imperceptibly presents a threat. In some parts of the world, as Platteau has said, it is already an existing desideratum.

The preservation and increase of this social asset might be regarded as a major economic objective, to be classed perhaps with health and education as a form of desirable social infrastructure, were it not confidently left to market forces under the neoclassical and NIE paradigms. The new multidisciplinary approach shatters this confidence, and places morality on the agenda of economists.

APPENDIX

Table 12.1 Kohlberg's six stages of moral development

Level and stage	What is right	Moral outlook
LEVEL I – PRECONVENTIONAL		
Stage 1 – Heteronomous morality	To avoid physical damage to persons and property; to be obedient. To avoid punishment.	No recognition or consideration of the interest of others. Actions considered physically, not in psychological terms. Morality is entirely external in its origin (heteronomous).
Stage 2 – Individualism, Instrumental Purpose, and Exchange	To follow rules only when it is to someone's immediate advantage. To act in one's own interests and to let others do likewise. To resolve conflict in a fair manner, based on equality or equal exchange, or an agreed deal.	Concrete individualistic perspective; self-serving, but aware that others have their own interests and rights. Aware that these may conflict.
LEVEL II CONVENTIONAL		
Stage 3 – Mutual Interpersonal Expectations, Relations, and Interpersonal Conformity	To live up to what people expect of you in your role as son, sister, friend, etc. To show concern about others. To maintain relationships, such as trust and loyalty.	The individual is seen in relationships with others. Aware of shared feelings, agreements, and expectations which override individual interests. Conflicting interests or views are related through application of a single rule: seeing the other person's position. No perception of a generalised system of morality, however.

Table 12.1   continued

Level and stage	What is right	Moral outlook
Stage 4 – Social System and Conscience	To do what you have agreed to do. To uphold laws unless they conflict with other fixed duties. To contribute to the group or society.	Sees societal as well as interpersonal interests. Sees relationships in societal framework. Concern to avoid societal breakdown by individual rule-breaking in pursuit of self-interest.
LEVEL III POSTCONVENTIONAL, OR PRINCIPLED		
Stage 5 – Social Contract or Utility and Individual Right	To respect a variety of value-based rules, perceiving their importance in relation to your group. To accept these relative rules as a social contract. Usually to obey them as such. To apply them impartially. To uphold also some universal values regardless of prevailing opinions.	A prior-to-society perspective, perceiving a rational individual aware of values and expectations before entering into social contracts with family, friends, and society generally. A sense of duty to a framework of rules and work obligations because of social contracts freely made. Desire that the rules should serve social utility, and should be made by rational negotiation, while recognizing that in practice conflicts are hard to resolve.
Stage 6 – Universal Ethical Principles	To develop and apply your own ethical principles. To consider particular laws or social agreements on the basis of such principles. To obey principle rather than law.	Belief in the validity of universal moral principles. Sense of personal commitment to these. An individual must use reason and knowledge to apply these to concrete situations. Desire to develop social arrangements in conformity with moral principles.

Sources: Kohlberg (1983) and Colby (1987).

ACKNOWLEDGEMENTS

Thanks are due to the Editors and to anonymous referees, and to Prof. J.-P. Platteau for helpful comments; also to members of EAEPE at the conference in Copenhagen in October 1994 and to colleagues at Bradford, for seminar discussions which have identified defects in earlier drafts of this work. Remaining errors are the responsibility of the author.

NOTES

1. Peaceful possession is a legal term, used here for convenience, but not found in the NIE literature.
2. Platteau himself does not make this point, however.
3. This may be considered pre-Freudian. For a much earlier view of internal conflict see Cooper, 1977, esp. sections 180–196, pp. 68–76. However, the behaviourist school of psychology now tends to ignore the regions of the mind 'discovered' by Freud.
4. Piaget (1977). The passage 'Towards [age] 11–12 we see a new attitude emerge, which may be said to be characterised by the feeling of equity, and which is nothing but a development of equalitarianism in the direction of relativity ... the child no longer thinks of the equal rights of the individuals except in relation to the particular situation of each' (p. 305) may be compared with Kohlberg's post-conventional stage of moral development (see Appendix). See also Piaget (1960) and Krebs and Van Hesteren (1994, p. 130). In connection with the distinction between moral motivation and moral outcomes, see the exploration of benevolence, making use of its proxy charitableness, in Ribar, 1992.
5. Kohlberg (1971, 1976). See Appendix.
6. Although Kohlberg's paradigm has been one of the leading contenders, and most researched, it has been criticized on the grounds that the concepts of the highest levels are Western-liberal concepts and thus culture-bound. John Snarey ('The Cross-Cultural Diversity of Socio-Moral Development', *Psychological Bulletin*, 97, pp. 202–32) found Kohlberg's Stages 1–4 in a wide range of cultural groups, but concluded that Stages 5–6 were culture-bound in that they postulated individualistic rather than collectivistic norms. It has also been suggested that Kohlberg's concepts are male-dominated in that they do not recognize empathy and caring in the higher stages. This does not mean, however, that Stages 5–6 should be removed from the schema without replacement. Kohlberg himself was not dogmatic about them.
7. Hoffman, 1978, pp. 169–218; 1981, pp. 121–37; 1984, pp. 283–302; 1991, pp. 275–301. On the limitations of empathy as an effective motivator of advanced altruism, Wilfred C. Trotter (the proponent of 'herd instinct' in humans) is not far removed from Hoffman: 'Altruism does not at present ... pay the individual in anything but feeling ... Man is altruistic because he must be, not because reason recommends it, for herd suggestion opposes any advance in altruism, and when it can the herd executes the altruist, not of course as such but as an innovator' (Trotter, 1942, p. 46).
8. Badcock, 1986. Besides Freud and Darwin, Hayek and Nietzsche are approvingly cited.
9. And indeed non-production costs generally.
10. It may be that atheists are among the most vociferous on the specific principle of veracity.
11. Some may actively dislike those who operate from higher levels.
12. Just as lower and higher attainments are created as joint products, we also benefit from them both in our market-economy activities and in our other activities. There can be no question, therefore, of hypothesizing that each activity should pay for its separate share of the cost of moral development in order to examine which level each would then choose for itself.
13. An interesting parallel to Platteau's warning on the effects of the market economy on moral standards can be found in a sermon in 1922 by the then Archbishop of York, quoted by the Webbs (1923, p. 171): 'The vast system of beliefs and practices ... which we roughly call western

civilisation ... was admirably contrived for the production of wealth and power ... But its motives, governing individuals and classes and states, were non-Christian self-interest, competition, the struggle of rival forces. Now these motives have overreached themselves. They are breaking the fabric which they built ... The fabric itself cannot be overthrown without a disaster. But if it is to be a blessing, not a blight, to mankind, its motives must be transformed.' I would add, either transformed or subdued. That is essentially Platteau's thesis as I understand it.

14. Flinn (1967, pp. 14–149) contains an interesting historical description of Sunday School morality, and of the Wesleyan standpoint.

15. Gough (1994) analyses institutions in relation to their ability to meet 'human needs' (not the needs of the market) and concludes that probably neoliberal capitalism would be no more conducive than minimally regulated capitalism; corporate capitalism (associated with Western European social democracy) would be the best of the actually existing systems (pp. 55–7).

REFERENCES

Badcock, C.R. (1986), *The Problem of Altruism: Freudian-Darwinian Solutions*, Oxford: Basil Blackwell.

Basu, K. (1983), 'On why we do not try to walk off without paying after a taxi-ride', *Economic and Political Weekly*, vol. 18, no. 48.

Blum, Lawrence A. (1980), *Friendship, Altruism and Morality*, London: Routledge and Kegan Paul.

Bromley, D. (1989), *Economic Interests and Institutions*, Oxford: Basil Blackwell.

Carpendale, J. and D.L. Krebs (1992), 'Situational variation in moral judgement: In a stage or on a stage?', *Journal of Youth and Adolescence*, 21(2) April, 203–24.

Coase, R.H. ([1937] 1988), *The Firm, the Market and the Law*, Chicago: University of Chicago Press.

Colby, A., L. Kohlberg *et al.* (1987), *The Measurement of Moral Judgment*, Cambridge, New York: Cambridge University Press.

Cooper, A.A. (Earl of Shaftesbury) (1699/1711/1977), *An Enquiry Concerning Virtue, or Merit*, edited by D. Walford, Manchester: Manchester University Press.

Dahlman, C.J. (1979), 'The Problem of Externality', *Journal of Law and Economics*, vol. 22, no.1 (April).

Flinn, M.W. (1967), 'Social theory and the Industrial Revolution', in M. Argyle *et al.*, *Social Theory and Economic Change*, London: Tavistock Publications.

Gibbs, John C. (1991), 'Towards an integration of Kohlberg's and Hoffman's theories of morality', in Kurtines and Gewirtz (1991), vol.1, pp. 183–222.

Gilligan, C. (1977), 'In a different voice: women's conceptions of self and of morality', *Harvard Educational Review*, vol. 47, pp. 481–517.

Gough, Ian (1994), 'Economic institutions and the satisfaction of human needs', *Journal of Economic Issues*, vol. XXVIII, no. 1, (March), pp. 25–66.

Habermas, J. (1983/1990), *Moral Consciousness and Communicative Action*, trans. C. Lenhardt and S. Weber Nicholsen, intro. by T. McCarthy, Cambridge: Polity Press, and Oxford: Basil Blackwell, 1990; originally *Moralbewusstsein und kommunikatives Handel*, Frankfurt: Suhrkamp, 1983.

Hirsch, F. (1976), *Social Limits to Growth*, Cambridge, Mass., and London: Harvard University Press, 1976.

Hirschman, A.O. (1977), *The Passions and the Interests: Political Arguments for Capitalism before Its Triumph*, Princeton, N.J.: Princeton University Press.

Hirschman, A.O. (1982), 'Rival interpretations of market society: civilizing, destructive, or feeble?', *Journal of Economic Literature*, vol. XX (December), pp. 1463–84.

Hoffman, Martin L. (1978), 'Empathy, its Development and Prosocial Implications', in C.B. Keasey (ed.), *Nebraska Symposium on Motivation*, Lincoln: University of Nebraska Press, vol. 25, pp. 169–218.

Hoffman, Martin L. (1981), 'Is altruism part of human nature?', *Journal of Personality and Social Psychology*, 40, pp. 121–37.

Hoffman, Martin L. (1984), 'Empathy, its limitations and its role in a comprehensive moral theory', in J.L. Gewirtz and W.M. Kurtines (eds), *Morality, Moral Development and Moral Behaviour*, New York: Wiley, pp. 283–302.

Hoffman, Martin L. (1991), 'Empathy, social cognition and moral action', in Kurtines and Gewirtz (1991), vol. 1, pp. 275–301.

Kohlberg, Lawrence (1971), 'Stages of moral development as a basis for moral education', in C.M. Beck *et al.*, *Moral Education: Interdisciplinary Approaches*, Toronto: University of Toronto Press.

Kohlberg, Lawrence (1976), 'Moral stages and moralization', in T. Lickona (ed.), *Moral Development and Behaviour*, New York: Holt, Rinehart, Winston.

Kohlberg, L., C. Levine and A. Hewer (1983), 'Moral stages: a current formulation and a response to critics', Bowel, New York: Karger.

Krebs, Dennis L. and Frank Van Hesteren (1994), 'The development of altruism: towards an integrative model', *Developmental Review* (Academic Press, Orlando, Florida), vol. 14, no. 2, pp. 103–58.

Kurtines, W.M. and J.L. Gewirtz (eds) (1991), *Handbook of Moral Behaviour and Development*, 3 vols, Hillsdale, N.J.: Lawrence Erlbaum Associates.

Kurtines, W.M., E. Maycock, S.R. Pollard, T. Lanza and G. Carlo (1991), 'Social and moral development from the perspective of psychosocial theory', in Kurtines and Gewirtz (1991), vol. 1.

List, F. ([1841] 1966), *The National System of Political Economy*, trans. S.S. Lloyd ed. J.S. Nicholson, London: Longmans, Green & Co., 1885. Reprinted New York: Augustus M. Kelley.

North, Douglass C. (1981), *Structure and Change in Economic History*, New York and London: W.W. Norton.

North, Douglass C. (1990), *Institutions, Institutional Change and Economic Performance*, Cambridge and New York: Cambridge University Press.

North, Douglass C. (1994), 'Economic performance through time', *American Economic Review*, vol. 84, no. 3 (June), pp. 359–68.

North, D.C. and R.P. Thomas (1973) *The Rise of the Western World: A New Economic History*, Cambridge: Cambridge University Press.

Piaget, Jean (and seven collaborators) (1977), *The Moral Judgement of the Child* (originally *Le Jugement Moral chez l'Enfant*, 1932), Harmondsworth: Penguin Education Books, 1977.

Piaget, Jean (1960), 'The general problem of the psycho-biological development of the child', in J.M. Tanner and B. Inhelder (eds.), *Discussions on child development*, New York: International Universities Press, vol. 4, pp. 3–27.

Platteau, Jean-Philippe (1994), 'Behind the market stage where real societies exist', *Journal of Development Studies*, vol. 30, no. 3 (April) and no. 4 (June).

Power, C. (1991), 'Lawrence Kohlberg: the vocation of a moral psychologist and educator', in Kurtines and Gewirtz (1991), vol. 1.

Ribar, D.C. and D. Wilhelm (1992), 'Welfare generosity', Working Paper, Department of Economics, Pennsylvania State University.

Ricard, S. (1781), *Traité général du commerce*, Amsterdam: van Harrevelt.

Simon, H.A. (1957), *Models of Man*, London: Wiley.

Snarey, John (1985), 'The cross-cultural diversity of socio-moral development', *Psychological Bulletin*, 97, pp. 202–32.

Trotter, Wilfred C. (1942; 1st edn 1916), *Instincts of the Herd in Peace and War*, London: Scientific Book Club, 2nd edn 1942.

Wallis, J.J. and D.C. North (1986), 'Measuring the transaction sector in the American economy 1870–1970', in S.L. Engerman, and R.E. Gallman (eds), *Long-Term Factors in American Economic Growth*, Chicago: University of Chicago Press.

Webb, Sidney and Beatrice Webb (1923), *The Decay of Capitalist Civilisation*, London: George Allen and Unwin (and the Fabian Society).

Williamson, O.E. (1975), *Markets and Hierarchies: Analysis and Anti-Trust Implications: A Study in the Economics of Internal Organisation*, New York: Free Press.

Williamson, O.E. (1985), *The Economic Institutions of Capitalism: Firms, Markets, Relational Contracting*, London: Macmillan.

Index

Abernathy, W.J. 63–4
Abramowitz, M. 39, 40
accelerator effect 11, 14
accumulation regimes 10, 12
actor, structure and 218, 221, 226–7
Aetna insurance company 253
agency/agents 3, 4, 6–7, 18–20
agents de change 245–6, 249
Aglietta, M. 9, 10, 13–14
ahistoric universals (capitalism) 223–4
Ahmad, S. 111
Albert, Michel 226
Ali, A.I. 116
Allen, P.M. 59
altruism 261, 268–75, 277, 281–2
Amable, B. 11, 16
Amendola, G.G. 14, 62
Amesse, F. 103
André, C. 10
Annenkov, Pavel 221
Aoki, Masahiko 207
Archibugi, D. 85, 86
'area of acceptance' 158
Arjona, Luis 73–4, 75
Arrow, Kenneth 33, 35, 47, 160, 162,
    165, 218, 243
Arthur, W. B. 5, 231
artifacts 60, 62
assets 178, 259, 279–81, 284
auction process/auctioneer 245–6, 248–9
Austrian economics 218–21, 234, 237–8
Auty, R.M. 77
Axelrod, R. 189

Baba, Y. 99
Bacdayan, P. 24
Badcock, C.R. (Badcock paradigm) 268,
    269, 271, 277, 281
Bancal, J. 96
bank–industry networks 200–210
bank convention 201, 205, 207–10
Bank of the United States 253

banker–entrepreneur interaction 200–210
Banking Act (USA, 1933) 254
banks, economic development and 251–5
Banques des Affaires 251
Basalla, G. 5, 142
Basu, K. 283
Becker, Gary S. 206, 217
behaviour 58–9, 221, 263–4
Bell, G. 99
Bellini, N. 96
Bellon, B. 102
Beralanffy, Ludwig von 232
best-practice technologies 109–10,
    112–13
Bianchi, P. 96
Billandot 11
black box (theory of firm) 153–66
Blau, P.M. 47
Blum, Lawrence A. 268
BMFT project 86
Boden, M. 60, 61–2
bond convention 201, 205, 207–8, 209
bottom-up approach 16, 18, 23, 97
bounded rationality 4, 5–6, 7, 20, 111,
    164, 172, 174, 202, 209, 259, 260
Boyer, R. 9–10, 11, 16–17, 19
Bresson, C. de 103
Bretton Woods regime 14
Bromley, D. 276
Bruno, S. 62
Burawoy, Michael 227
Burns, Arthur F. 75

calculativeness 154, 164–5
Callon, M. 99
Canon 69, 71
Cantwell, J. 88, 140
capitalism 101
    actually existing (varieties of) 236–8
    triumph of (Marx) 221–7
    varieties of 215–38
Caroli, E. 11

Carpendale, J. 276
Carter, A. P. 37, 42
Casson, M. 88
cephalization 155, 156, 162
Chandler, Alfred 9
change
    acceleration of 41–2, 44
    rate of (learning) 37–8
    slowing down 46–7
Chapman, Keith 76, 77
Charnes, A. 114
Chesnais, F. 88
Chiaromonte, F. 5, 9, 17
Clark, K.B. 63, 64
classical theory 10, 132
Coase, Ronald 154–5, 157–8, 161, 172,
    258–9, 264–5, 267
Coase theorem 207
codified knowledge 33, 42–3
cognitive competencies 173
Cohen, M. 24
Colby, A. 286
collective action (bank–industry
    network) 201, 206–9, 210
commercial opportunism, 266–70
commodity production/exchange 222–3,
    225
Commons, John R. 6, 173, 229
communism 222, 231
competence 34–5, 173
competition 10, 42, 135, 138, 219, 248
competitive advantage 100, 186
competitive market 277–8
COMTAP database 142
Conlisk, J. 5
consumption (norms of) 10
continuous trading markets 247–51
contracts 259
    limits of 217–18
    scope of 153–66
'control loop' 179, 180
Cooper, W.W. 114
cooperation 188, 189, 193
    sources 174–7
Coordination game 202
Coriat, B. 9, 11, 20, 21
Cosgel, M. 162
costs
    switching 172, 177–9, 182–3, 185,
        187–90, 193–5, 197
    transaction *see* transaction costs

credit 244, 251–4
    banker–entrepreneur interaction
        200–210
cross-border networks (in IT) 99–100
cumulative causation 230–31
Cyert, R. 164

Dahlman, C. J. 259
Dalton, D. 90
Dalum, B. 101, 142
Darwin, Charles 232, 233
Data Envelopment Analysis (DEA) 109,
    113–16, 117, 119, 126–7
David, Paul 5, 7, 42, 122
Day, R. 5
de-societalization (of innovation process)
    84
Debreu, Gerard 162, 243, 246
Delapierre, M. 95
Delorme, R. 10
depreciation (Swedish crown) 141–2
deregulation 48, 141
design configurations 62, 68–9, 70
Deutsche Bank 251
devaluations (in Sweden) 141
development, economic (role of financial
    markets) 243–55
Dietrich, M. 172, 173
diffusion of innovation 5, 62–77, 78, 85
DiMaggio, P.J. 7
division of labour 13, 36, 156, 157, 163,
    166
dominant design hypothesis 63–4, 190
Dore, Ronald 236
Dosi, G. 4, 5, 7, 9, 14, 15, 20, 21, 24, 61,
    133
Douglas, Mary 233
'doux-commerce' thesis 273
Dunning, J.H. 88
Durand, T. 63
Dyer, Alan W. 232

EAEPE 244
Easton, G. 173
economic change (institutional/
    evolutionary theories) 3–24
economic development, financial
    markets and 243–55
economic imperialism 216

economic routines 8–9, 17, 20–21, 35, 58–61
economic theory
   challenges to (learning economy) 33–51
   varieties of capitalism and 215–38
economies of scale 13, 14, 173
Edgell, Stephen 228
Edgeworth 246
Edquist, Charles 131–2, 138
efficiency 7, 173
   analysis (DEA method) 109, 113–16, 117, 119, 126–7
   relative 119, 122–6
   technical (German electronics industry) 109, 117–26
Egidi, M. 24
EIRMA 41
'elastic barriers' 122
Eliasson, G. 5
Elster, Jon 201
Emery, Fred E. 232
employer–employee relationship 155, 158–9, 165, 218
employment contract 158–9, 166
Engels, Friedrich 222, 225
entrepreneur 156, 158, 161, 165
   –banker interaction 200–210
equilibrium price 245, 248–51
Ergas, H. 95
ESPRIT programme 85–6
ethical dimension (in learning economy) 47–8
Etzioni, Amitai 200
EUREKA programme 85–6
Europe 44–5
European Patent Office 117
evolutionary approach
   co-evolutionary processes 21–3
   definitions 4–6
   future (interaction/integration) 21–4
   institutional specification 17–18
   research programmes (appraisal) 3–24
   spontaneous (bank–industry networks) 200–210
   technological change 57–79
evolutionary stable strategy 201–2, 204, 208–9
exchange, limits of (in neoclassical economics) 217–18

exit and voice 180
export growth (Sweden) 142–3

factor prices 111–12
Fagerberg, J. 14, 95
Fama, Eugene 200
family 220, 225
Farrell, M. J. 115
farsight/farseeing 154, 155, 164–6
Feldman, M.P. 98
Fellner, W. 111
feudalism 222, 225, 226, 236, 274
financial markets 10, 48
   economic development and 243–55
firm-specific techniques 112
firm, theory of
   governance of transactions 172–97
   scope of contracts 153–66
firms
   behaviour 40
   relations between (life cycle) 188–90
   size 193, 197
First National Bank of New York 253
flexibilization strategy 50, 51
flexible specialization 41
Foray, D. 103
Fordist phase, 3, 10, 11, 12–14
foresight/foreseeing 154, 155, 163–4
Foss, N.J. 173
Fox, Alan 218
Frank, Robert H. 206
Freeman, C. 5, 9, 33, 62, 70, 91, 92
French Commercial Code 246
Freudian paradigm 267, 269
Friedman, Daniel 203–4
Friedman, Milton 230
frontier production functions 109, 113, 115
Fuji-Xerox 67
Fukuyama, Francis 215, 236
functionalism 18–19

Gambetta, D. 174
game theory 172, 181, 185, 189, 282
game tree 185–7
Ganther, P.A. 90
GDP (Swedish paradox) 131–2, 139, 141
general equilibrium theory 110, 162, 243, 247, 251
Georghiou, Luke 62, 63

Germany (electronics industry) 109–27
Gewirtz, J.L. 267, 268
Ghazanfar, Agha 70
Gibbs, John C. 269
Giddens, Anthony 221
Gilligan, C. 271
global exploitation of technology 85,
    87–8
global generation of technology 86–8
global technological collaboration 85–6,
    87
globalization 40, 48
    of technology 84–104
glocalization of technology 84–104
Goto, A. 70
governance 20, 163
    general model 177–80
    strategies of 180–83
    of transactions (strategic process
        model) 165, 172–97
Granovetter, M. 6
Granstrand, O. 5, 90
Grendstad, G. 7
grey box (scope of contracts) 153–66
Grossbanken 251
growth process/patterns (interpretations)
    12–14
Grübler, A. 5
Guelle, F. 90
Guerrieri, P. 100

Habermas, J. 269
Hagerdoorn, John 61, 62, 86
Hagg, I. 173
Håkanson, L. 90, 140
Hakansson, H. 173
Hampden-Turner, Charles 236
Harris, Abram 230
Häusler, J. 86
Hayek, Friedrich 215, 218–21, 235–6
Hedlund, G. 87
Héraud, J.A. 103
Hicks, John 11
high density polyethylene (HDPE) 72,
    73, 75
Hill, Forest G. 227
Hirsch, Fred 273, 277–8
Hirschman, A.O. 176, 180, 216, 272–3,
    274
Hitachi 90

Hodgson, Geoffrey M. 4, 58, 59, 172–3,
    200, 217, 218, 221, 226, 232–3
Hodson, C. 88
Hoechst 71
Hoffman paradigm 268, 269, 271, 277,
    280–81
Holvad, T. 123
honesty 258, 261, 271–2
horizontal technological variety 112–13
Hougaard, J.L. 123
Howell, D. R. 40
Howells, J. 87, 102
Hufbauer, G. C. 77
human capital 38–9
Humbert, M. 85, 88, 99, 101
hyper-acceleration 46–7

IBM 69
'ideal types' 222
ideological specifics (neoclassical
    economics) 216–17
Imai, K. 99
impurity principle (capitalism) 219–21,
    224–6, 235–6
income growth 15
income multipliers 18
indirect electrostatic photocopying (IEP)
    66–72
individual/individualism 215, 218, 220,
    221
industrial networks 33–4
industrialization, skills and 38
industry
    definition of 60–62
    development of (technological
        change) 62–4
Industry Canada 39
information
    economics of (learning economy)
        33–51
    infrastructures 34, 46, 51
    society 34
    systems 197
    technology 33, 34, 40–43, 46–7,
        99–100, 102
innovation
    banker–entrepreneur interaction
        200–210
    diffusion 5, 62–77, 78
    industrial development and 62–4

localized societal process 84–104
national systems 5, 9, 44, 49–51,
    91–4, 96–7, 99–104
R&D intensity (Sweden) 131–46
INPADOC database 125
institutional theory 237–8
    banker–entrepreneur interaction
        200–210
    future (interaction/integration) 21–4
    regulation approach 3, 9–16, 18–21
    research programmes (appraisal) 3–24
    units of analysis 233–4
    varieties of capitalism and 227–34
    weak/strong institutionalism 7–8
instrumental rationality 47–8
intellectual property rights 85
interaction, strategic 172, 174, 184–8,
    191
interactive learning 47–8, 49
International Marketing and Purchasing
    Group (IMP) 173–4, 182
international system of exchanges 10
international trade, diffusion of
    innovation and 65–77
internationalization 49
invariance principles 233–4
investment
    relation-specific 172, 178, 181, 188–9,
        193–4
    transaction-specific 190
ISIC system 135, 137, 138, 139, 144–6
Iwai, K. 63

Jacobsson, S. 131
Japan 44, 45, 49, 50, 89–91
Jessop, B. 9, 91, 101, 103
Jobs Study (OECD) 39, 44
Johanson, J. 173
Johnson, B. 35, 101, 102
Johnson, Chalmers 236
judgement 154, 156, 161–2, 165
Juillard, M. 11, 16
'just in time' production 41

Kahneman, Daniel 207
Kaldor, Nicholas 231
Kalle 71
Kanai, Tsutomu 90
Kandori, M. 5
Kaniovski, Y. 5

Kapp, K. William 231
Katz, L. F. 40
Kendrick-Ott productivity index 114
Keynes, J. M. 252
Keynesianism 14, 18
Khalil, Elias 224
Kin-altruism 270, 271
Klepper, S. 5
Knetch, Jack 207
Knight, F.H. 154, 155–7, 161, 162–3,
    165
know-how 23, 36, 37–8, 48, 111, 112,
    113, 191, 195
know-what 23, 35
know-who 23, 36, 37
know-why 23, 36
knowledge 60–61, 133, 173
    -based economy 35
    codified 33, 42–3
    different kinds 35–7
    gap 155, 161–3, 164, 165
    learning economy 33–51
    stock of 35
    tacit 33, 37, 42–3, 48, 111, 134
Kodak 69
Kogut, B. 95
Kohlberg paradigm 268–76 *passim*,
    280–86
Kornai, Janos 232
Krebs, Dennis L. 267, 269, 276
Kreditbanks 251–2
Krueger, R. B. 40
Kurtines, W. M. 267, 268
Kuznets, Simon 75

labour 10, 38, 223–4, 225, 228
    employer–employee relationship 155,
        158–9, 165, 218
    employment contract 158–9, 166
    unemployment 44, 46, 51, 141
    wages 16, 39, 40
Lall, S. 102
Landes, David 15
Langlois, R. 162
Laszlo, Ervin 232
Lauritzen, F. 40
lean production strategies 41
learning 5
    acceleration of 41–2
    by-doing 35, 37, 38, 216

by-financing 200, 201–2, 206, 207–9
by-using 35
different kinds 35–6
interactive 47–8, 49
to master knowledge 37
processes 23–4
rate of change and 37–8
learning economy 33–51
Leong, L.M. 103
Leontief-type production function 110, 112
Lerme, C.S. 116
Leroy, C. 16
Lesourne, J. 5
Lesser, M. 59
Levinthal, D. 5
life cycle
patterns of evolution 15
of products 46–7, 62–3, 65, 69–70, 77
of relationships 188–90
Lindgren, R. 5
linear low density polyethylene (LLDPE) 66, 72–7, 78
linear programming approach (DEA) 109, 113–16, 117, 119, 126–7
Lippi, Marco 224
liquidity 252, 254–5
constraints 244
preference 166
of resources 154, 159–61, 165–6
List, Friedrich 273
Loasby, Brian J. 218
London Stock Exchange 247–8, 251
Lordon, F. 11
low density polyethylene (LDPE) 66, 72–7, 78
Luhmann, Niklas 232
Lundvall, B.Å 9, 35, 44, 91, 93–7, 101, 132, 200

Machlup, Fritz 153
McKelvey, Maureen 95, 97, 138, 236
Madeuf, B. 84
Malerba, F. 5, 17
Manhattan project 42
Mansfield, E. 84
March, James 7, 18, 164
Marengo, L. 5, 24
marginal productivities 116
Mariti, P. 86

markets
efficiency 274–5
failure 51, 109, 111
historical experience (in USA) 252–5
inevitability of (Hayek) 218–21
mechanisms 261
Marshall, Alfred 247–51, 255
Marx, Karl 215, 219–26, 232, 235–6, 273
Veblen's critique 227–31
Marxian economics 10, 224, 225, 230–31, 234, 237–8
Maslow, Abraham 269
Mattson, L.G. 173
MERIT-CATI database 86
meso-systems 15, 99, 100
Metcalf, J.S. 60, 61–2
Metcalf, S. 5
methodological individualism 18–20, 21, 173
Michalet, C.A. 95
Michie, J. 85, 86
microeconomic analysis (of technological change) 57–79
microfoundations 11, 15, 18–20, 23
Miller, James G. 232
Miller, R. 89
Mirowski, Philip 233
Mises, Ludwig von 219
Mistral, J. 9, 10
MITI (Japan) 67, 90, 92
Mokyr, J. 5
monocultural technologies 85
monopoly rents 133, 135
moral capital (measurement) 280–83
moral development 275–6, 285–6
moral hazard 160
moral norms, role (in NIE paradigm) 258–62
moral standards, transaction costs and (long term effects) 258–86
Morgan, J.P. 244, 253
Morishima, Michio 236
Mowery, D.C. 86, 90, 102, 103
multinational enterprises 84, 87–8, 89–90, 102–3
Murphy, K.M. 40
mutual adjustment 181
mutual trust 200, 202
Myrdal, Gunnar 231

Mytelka, L. 86

Nakicenovic, N. 5
Nash equilibrium 181
Nashua 71
nation states (changing role) 49
National City Bank 253
national systems of innovation 5, 9, 44,
    49–51, 91–4, 96–7, 99–104, 133
nations as societal systems 95–7
Nelson, R.R. 4, 5, 9, 13, 15, 17, 23, 61,
    62, 91–4, 98, 230
neo-institutionalism 6, 21, 173, 175
neoclassical economics 7, 109, 110–11,
    132, 173, 225, 237–8
    universality of 215–18, 224, 231–2
networks
    access 33–4, 45–6, 49
    bank–industry 200–210
    commitment 206–7, 210
    position 191, 193
New Deal (need for) 43–9
New Institutional Economics 201,
    258–67, 273, 284
New Institutionalist (TCE) 172, 175
New York Stock Exchange 251, 253
nexus of contracts 154–61, 165
NIE paradigm 258–67, 273, 284
Nielsen, K. 91
Niosi, J. 102
Nobel, R. 140
non-contractible outcomes
    (cephalization) 155, 156, 162
non-production costs 262–5, 284
Nonaka, K. 43
Nooteboom, Bart 173, 174–5, 180, 188,
    193–4, 197
North, Douglass C. 6, 160, 259–67,
    271–2, 274, 276, 278, 282–4
North American Free Trade Agreement
    40
novelty (role) 4, 6, 58
NUTEK 139

Odagiri, H. 70
OECD 13, 34, 38–9, 41, 44–5, 50, 84,
    131–2, 134–9, 141–6
OLS method 122–3
Olsen, J. P. 7
Olson, Mancur 201, 206

opportunism 47–8, 49
    altruism and 272–5, 281, 282
    commercial 266–70
    moral standards and 258–60, 262–7,
        272–5, 280–82, 284
    strategic process model 172–86, 193,
        195, 197
Orrù, Marco 236
Orsenigo, L. 5, 17
Ouchi, W. 96
ownership 236, 243–4, 251

Palmer, R.G. 5
Papanastassiou, M. 89
Pareto–Koopmanns criterion 115
Pareto allocation 243, 246–7
Paris Bourse 243, 245–6, 247, 250
Patel, P. 13, 90, 91, 94, 96, 138
patents/patenting 69, 85, 87–90, 110
    relative efficiency and 117, 125–6
path dependence 4, 5, 7, 231
Pavitt, K. 5, 13, 37, 90–91, 94, 96, 125,
    133, 136, 138
Pearce, R. 89
Pederson, O.K. 91
performances, technological
    German electronics industry 109–27
    international differences 94–5
Peters, L.S. 88
Petrella, R. 84
Piaget, Jean 274
Piaget paradigm 267–8, 269, 271,
    280–81
Pitelis, C. 172
Platteau, Jean-Philippe 261–6, 269,
    271–2, 275–7, 278, 284
Polanyi, Karl 220, 225
Polanyi, M. 36, 37
polyethylene technologies 66, 72–7, 78
Porter, M. 95, 132, 142
Posner, M. V. 65, 77, 78
Post-Keynesians 234, 243, 251
post-war growth process 12–14
Powell, W.W. 7
preference function 19–20, 218
price mechanism 157, 161, 231
prices
    equilibrium 245, 248–51
    factor 111–12
    formation 245–6, 247–8

principal–agent theory 155, 164
Prisoners' Dilemma 202, 207
private sheltered sector 45
product life cycle 46–7, 62–3, 65, 69–70,
  77
production functions 109–10, 112–16
productivity 15, 16, 125, 134, 138
  total factor 114, 116
product, R&D intensive (Sweden)
  131–46
profit maximization 230
property rights 47, 85, 207, 220, 235
psychological correlative of commercial
  opportunism 266–70

Rank-Xerox 67
Rawls 269
rational self-interest 7, 8, 228, 259,
  260–61
rationality 47–8, 163, 164, 228–30
  see also bounded rationality
reciprocal altruism 268, 270, 271, 277
Reddy, P. 102
regulation approach 3, 9–16, 18–21
relation-specific investments 172, 178,
  181, 188–9, 193–4
relative efficiency 119
  German electronics industry 122–6
representative agents 18–20
research and development
  abroad 8–9, 84–91, 102–3
  expenditures (German electronics
    industry) 122–5
  inter-firm agreements 85–6
  Sweden's high intensity 131–46
resources
  allocation 243–4, 246–7, 250–55
  liquidity of 154, 159–61, 165–6
Ricard, Samuel 273
Ricoh 71–2
risk 174, 186
Rivaud-Danset, Dorothée 200
Robbins, Lionel 216
Ronstadt, R.C. 84
Rosenberg, N. 5, 35, 92–3, 94, 98
routines 8–9, 17, 20–21, 35, 58–61
rules (market mechanism) 219
rules of the game 6, 86

Sahal, D. 63

Sahlins, Marshall 216
Saillard, Y. 9, 10, 11, 16, 19
Salais, Robert 200
Salter, W. 111
Sandler, Todd 201, 206–7
Savin 71
Saviotti, P.P. 60
scarcity 216, 222
Schakenraad, J. 86
Schumpeter, Joseph A. 200, 217, 225,
  251, 255
Schwartz, M. 7, 246
SCS paradigm 268–9, 277, 280
selected technologies 60–61
selection mechanism 58, 59, 61
self-actualization 269
self-interest 266–7, 270, 272, 274, 277,
  282–3
  rational 7, 8, 228, 259–61
'self-organization' models 5, 7
Selle, P. 7
shared values (moral standards) 258–86
Sharpe, Steven A. 200
sheltered sector, private 45
Sheridan, Kyoko 236
Sigurdson, J. 90, 102
Silverberg, G. 4, 5, 15
Simon, Herbert A. 154, 155, 158–9, 164,
  165, 221, 264
SIND 132, 138
Sjölander, S. 90
skills 34, 36, 37, 38–9, 40, 45–6
Smiley, R. H. 86
Smith, Adam 159, 163
social capital, morality as 269–70,
  278–80, 282
social class 227, 228, 229
social policy 45–6
socialism 215, 219, 221, 222, 224, 227,
  231
socio-economic systems 16–17, 23, 216,
  221–6, 235
Soete, L. 5, 133
specialization 10, 41, 44, 132–4, 136–7,
  139–43, 163–4, 173
specificity, universality and 231–3
spontaneous order conjecture 201–5
Stag Hunt game 201–6, 207, 208
STAN database 136, 142–6
standardization 14, 43, 63

state intervention 10
Stifterverband 117
Stobaugh, R.B. 77
stock exchange 243, 244–5, 247–8, 250–51
stock market 243–8, 250–52, 255
Strange, S. 95
strategic interaction 172, 174, 184–8, 191
strategic process model 172–97
structural change (employment) 41
structure 3
    actor and 218, 221, 226–7
Suárez, F.F. 5, 64
subcontracting 177, 180, 191, 196, 197
Sugden, Robert 200, 201, 202, 206
Sweden (research and development expenditure) 131–46
Swedish Industrial Board 132, 138
switching costs 172, 177–9, 182–3, 185, 187–90, 193–5, 197
systems theory 232

tacit knowledge 33, 37, 42–3, 48, 111, 134
tâtonnement process 245, 247, 248, 249
technical dominance 112
technical efficiency
    DEA 109, 113–16, 117, 119, 126–7
    German electronics industry 109, 117–26
technico-economic network 99
techno-globalism 84, 85–8, 99
technological capability 191
technological change 40
    evolutionary approach 57–79
technological performance 94–5
    German electronics industry 109–27
technological trajectories, nations as societal systems and 95–7
technological variety (German electronics industry) 109–27
technology
    definition of industry and 60–62
    diffusion 5, 62–77, 78, 85
    gap 65, 69, 77, 95
    globalization/glocalization 84–104
    growth patterns and 13–14
    Sweden (expenditure/products) 131–46
    transfer 85, 101–2, 103–4

Teece, D.J. 86, 90, 140
temporary general equilibrium 19
Thaler, Richard 207
Thatcher government 50, 220
Thompson, M. 7
Tomlinson, James 219, 220, 230
top-down approach 16, 18, 23
Tordjman, H. 5, 24
total factor productivity 114, 116
Townshend, Jules 228
trade flows, innovation and 65–77
trading markets, continuous 247–51
transaction-specific assets 178
transaction-specific investments 190
transaction costs 34, 47–9
    contract theory 153, 157–9, 163–5
    governance (strategic process model) 172–97
    moral standards and 258–86
Trompenaars, Alfons 236
trust 47–9, 174–7, 189, 200, 202, 218, 236, 262
Turvani, M. 154
Tylecote, A. 100
Tyson, L.A. 134

Ullmann-Margalit, Edna 202
UN Yearbook of International Trade Statistics 68, 74
uncertainty 200, 202, 209, 218
    contract theory 154–8, 160–65
UNCTAD 103
unemployment 44, 46, 51, 141
Union Carbide 72–3, 75
universality, specificity and 231–3
USA 44–5
    banks and markets (historical experience) 252–5
    patents to overseas firms 85, 89
    research and development abroad 85, 89–90
use-value 223
user–producer relationship 97, 99
utility maximization 18, 216, 218
Utterback, J.M. 5, 64

value (governance strategies) 182–3
Vanberg, Viktor 219
Van Hesteren, Frank 267, 269
Vázquez-Barquero, A. 102–3

Veblen, T. 6, 8, 58, 173, 232, 235
    critique of Marx 215, 227–31
Verdoorn–Kaldor law 11, 15
Vernon, R. 65, 69–70, 77, 78
Verspagen, B. 4, 5, 14
Vincenti, W. 5
VLSI project 85
voice and exit 180
von Hippel, E. 38

wage-labour 10, 223
wages 16, 39, 40
Wallis, J.J. 259–60, 262–3, 264–5, 274
Walras, Léon 243, 244, 245–7, 249, 250,
    255
Warglien, M. 5
Warrant, F. 89
Weber, Max 222

welfare state 50
Whitley, Richard 236
Whittington, Richard 230
Williams, B. 174
Williams, David 236
Williamson, O.E. 6, 154, 159, 164–5,
    173, 259–63, 265, 267, 282, 284
Winter, Sidney 4, 5, 15, 17, 61
Witt, Ulrich 201
Wolfman, Lydia 67
working class 227, 228, 229
Wright, G. 13

X-inefficiency 109
Xerox 66–9

Young, Allyn 231
Young, P. 5